Caesarism and Bonapartism in Gramsci

Historical Materialism Book Series

The Historical Materialism Book Series is a major publishing initiative of the radical left. The capitalist crisis of the twenty-first century has been met by a resurgence of interest in critical Marxist theory. At the same time, the publishing institutions committed to Marxism have contracted markedly since the high point of the 1970s. The Historical Materialism Book Series is dedicated to addressing this situation by making available important works of Marxist theory. The aim of the series is to publish important theoretical contributions as the basis for vigorous intellectual debate and exchange on the left.

The peer-reviewed series publishes original monographs, translated texts, and reprints of classics across the bounds of academic disciplinary agendas and across the divisions of the left. The series is particularly concerned to encourage the internationalization of Marxist debate and aims to translate significant studies from beyond the English-speaking world.

For a full list of titles in the Historical Materialism Book Series available in paperback from Haymarket Books, visit:
https://www.haymarketbooks.org/series_collections/1-historical-materialism

Caesarism and Bonapartism in Gramsci

Hegemony and the Crisis of Modernity

Francesca Antonini

Haymarket Books
Chicago, IL

First published in 2021 by Brill Academic Publishers, The Netherlands
© 2021 Koninklijke Brill NV, Leiden, The Netherlands

Published in paperback in 2021 by
Haymarket Books
P.O. Box 180165
Chicago, IL 60618
773-583-7884
www.haymarketbooks.org

ISBN: 978-1-64259-595-6

Distributed to the trade in the US through Consortium Book Sales and Distribution (www.cbsd.com) and internationally through Ingram Publisher Services International (www.ingramcontent.com).

This book was published with the generous support of Lannan Foundation and Wallace Action Fund.

Special discounts are available for bulk purchases by organizations and institutions. Please call 773-583-7884 or email info@haymarketbooks.org for more information.

Cover art and design by David Mabb. Cover art is a detail of *Long Live the New! no. 43*, Kazimir Malevich drawing on Morris & Co. design, paint and wallpaper on canvas (2016)..

Printed in the United States.

10 9 8 7 6 5 4 3 2 1

Library of Congress Cataloging-in-Publication data is available.

Contents

Preface: Gramsci on Caesarism and Bonapartism IX
Acknowledgements XV
Abbreviations XVII
Note on the Text XIX

1 **The Concepts of Bonapartism and Caesarism from Marx to Gramsci** 1
   1 The Genesis of the Category between Historiography and Political Polemics 1
   2 Marx: From *The Eighteenth Brumaire* to *The Civil War in France* 3
   3 Across the Nineteenth and Twentieth Centuries 7

2 **The Pre-prison Writings** 10
   1 Two (Almost) Neglected Categories 10
   2 Marx, Gramsci and the Marxian Sources 11

3 **Socialism and Romanticism** 15
   1 Against Maximalism and Reformism: Reckoning with Italian Socialism 15
      1.1 *Cadorna and Bonapartism* 15
      1.2 *Trade Unionism and Bonapartism* 19
      1.3 *Parliamentary Cretinism and Socialist Reformism* 21
      1.4 *In Memory of Serrati* 25
   2 The 'Romanticism' of the Italian Bourgeoisie 28
      2.1 *Marx, Gramsci and the* feuilleton 28
      2.2 Gioda o del romanticismo *and* Parabola discendente 29
      2.3 *Italy's Tragic Farce* 33

4 **Crisis and Balance: Between Revolution and Restoration** 36
   1 Gramsci's Political Theory: Crisis and Balance 36
   2 The Catastrophic Crisis of Capitalism 37
      2.1 *Gramsci and the Third International* 37
      2.2 *A Decay and a Genesis* 39
      2.3 *Revolution and Crisis of the Bourgeois-Capitalist World* 41
      2.4 *The Elections of November 1919* 43
      2.5 *A Short Revival* 48

3   The Balance Metaphor: The Origins of the 'Relations of Force'   51
   3.1   *A 'Catastrophic' Balance*   51
   3.2   *Dictatorship of the Bourgeoisie or Dictatorship of the Proletariat?*   53
   3.3   *An Illiberal Order*   57

5   **Bonapartism, Caesarism and Fascism in Gramsci's Journalistic Works**   61
   1   The Crisis of the Liberal Order and the Rise of Fascism   61
   2   A (Critical) Theory of State and Politics   62
   3   Marx's *Eighteenth Brumaire*: Analogies and Analyses   66
   4   On the Gramsci-Marx Relationship in the Pre-prison Writings   69

6   **Towards the *Prison Notebooks*   73**
   1   Continuity and Novelty   73
   2   The Editions of Marx's Texts   75
   3   Overview of the Occurrences   76

7   **The Meanings of 'Bonapartism'**   78
   1   Bonapartism in the *Prison Notebooks*   78
   2   Militarism and War of Movement   79
      2.1   *Cadornism and Bonapartism*   79
      2.2   *Trotsky and the War of Movement*   81
   3   Gramsci and the So-called 'Dictatorships of Depretis, Crispi and Giolitti'   85
   4   Bonapartism and Bureaucracy   89
      4.1   *At the Origin of the Relationship*   89
      4.2   *Between Marx and the Southern Question*   93

8   **Between Bonapartism and Caesarism**   97
   1   Anachronistic Revival or Useful Analytical Tool?   97
   2   Q 13, §§ 23 and 27 and Their First Drafts   99
   3   Further Occurrences   102

9   **Gramsci and the Theory of Caesarism**   105
   1   Michels and 'Charismatic Leadership'   105
      1.1   *Q 2, § 75*   105
      1.2   *A 'Programmatic' Ambivalence*   108

	2	'The Old Is Dying and the New Cannot Be Born' 110
		2.1 *The Balance Formula in the* Prison Notebooks 110
		2.2 *Balance and Catastrophe* 112
	3	The Dreyfus Affair and the 'Tendential' Character of the Catastrophic Crisis 115
	4	The 'Taxonomy' of Caesarism 118
		4.1 *Great Personalities and Historical Analogies* 118
		4.2 *The Articulation of the Category* 120
		4.3 *An 'Incomplete' Scheme* 124
10	**Caesarism and Historical Analysis** 126	
	1	Gramscian 'Concerns' 126
		1.1 *Practical Criteria of Interpretation* 126
		1.2 *Julius Caesar and Caesarism* 129
	2	The Historico-political Framework of the *Prison Notebooks* 130
		2.1 *Gramsci's 'Plural Temporalities' and the Case of France* 130
		2.2 *The 'Waves' of History* 133
		2.3 *Napoleon III as Archetype of Caesarism* 135
	3	Caesarism and Passive Revolution 138
		3.1 *The Meanings of a Category* 138
		3.2 *Marx's 'Canons' and the Issue of the Marginal Forces* 140
		3.3 *'Effectual Reality' and New Instruments of Analysis* 144
11	**Hegemony and Modernity** 147	
	1	Twentieth-Century Caesarism 147
		1.1 *MacDonald, the Labour Party and the Coalition Governments* 147
		1.2 *Italy in the 1920s* 150
		1.3 *Fascism and Caesarism: A Controversial Match* 151
	2	Crisis of Authority and Caesarist-Bonapartist Solutions 155
		2.1 *The Organic Crisis* 155
		2.2 *The 'Massive Structure of the Modern Democracies'* 158
	3	A New Form of Hegemony 160
		3.1 *A Post-Jacobin Framework* 160
		3.2 *The Issue of the 'Dark Powers'* 161
		3.3 *Bureaucracy, Military Associations, Police* 163
		3.4 *Bonapartism, Caesarism and Fascism* 165

12   Contemporary Caesarism(s)   167
1   Totalitarian Trends   167
1.1   *War of Position, Siege, and Concentration*   167
1.2   *A 'Totalitarian' Conception of the World*   170
1.3   *The Role of the Party*   172
2   Between Moscow and Rome   176
2.1   *Progressive or Regressive Authoritarianism?*   176
2.2   *Fascist Corporatism*   177
2.3   *'Statolatry' and the 'Return' of the Economic-Corporative Phase*   179
2.4   *Trotsky, Bonapartism and Napoleonism*   183
3   'Alternative Modernities'   187
3.1   *Black Parliamentarism, Critique and Self-critique*   187
3.2   *The Legal-Real Opposition and the Image of the Barometer*   190
4   'Caesarism without a Caesar' and the Issue of the Modern Prince   193
4.1   *Individual Action and Collective Will*   193
4.2   *Caesarism and the Modern Prince*   195
4.3   *The 'Party-Caesar' and the Role of Charismatic Figures*   199

13   Caesarism, Bonapartism and the 'Return to Marx' in the Prison Writings   201
1   Gramsci and the Marxian Legacy   201
2   Caesarism and Bonapartism in the *Prison Notebooks*   202

Bibliography   207
Name Index   223
Subject Index   228

Preface: Gramsci on Caesarism and Bonapartism

This book analyses Antonio Gramsci's usage of the concepts of Bonapartism and Caesarism, both in his pre-prison writings and in the *Prison Notebooks*. My work aims to fill a gap in the scholarship on Gramsci, by investigating a hitherto neglected aspect of his thought. However, this investigation also represents a contribution to the history of political thought and to intellectual history more broadly, notably to the history of the concepts of Caesarism and Bonapartism.

While many scholars have referred to these categories in their interpretations of Gramsci's work, they have not always engaged in serious analysis of their meanings.[1] An analysis of them can be valuable not only in grasping specific aspects of his thought, but also in better understanding the wider sense of his intellectual commitment.

In the pre-prison articles, the deployment of the categories of Caesarism and Bonapartism is linked predominantly to episodes of early twentieth-century Italian or European history and to Gramsci's own political activity. Nevertheless, these references are also relevant on a more general level, since they contribute to the evolution of his understanding, for example, of the role and the nature of political parties, of power relations among different social groups, and of the transformation of the state with the advent of authoritarian regimes.

In the *Prison Notebooks*, Gramsci's investigation of the categories of Caesarism and Bonapartism is more organic and articulated. On the one hand, the Caesarist-Bonapartist pattern is closely connected to the historical dimension of Gramsci's thought in prison. This is the case both with situations from the past (such as, for instance, the Second French Empire or the Italian *Risorgimento*) and, especially, with cases from recent times ('modern' ones, as he says). This model is essential to Gramsci's understanding of the interwar period and of the 'totalitarian' systems that characterise it. However, Bonapartism and Caesarism are also valuable on account of their location 'at the crossroads' of different lines of research in the notebooks. These concepts are intertwined with key categories such as 'war of position', 'organic crisis', 'passive revolution' and 'modern prince'. More generally, the Caesarist-Bonapartist model relates crucially to Gramsci's reflections on 'hegemony' and on its transformations in the passage from a nineteenth-century political scenario to a twentieth-century one.

---

1   For a critical discussion of the secondary literature on these categories in Gramsci's thought before and after his imprisonment, see, respectively, Chapter 2 (section 1) and Chapter 6 (section 1).

Approaching Gramsci's writings from the point of view of Caesarism and Bonapartism also helps to illuminate his attitude towards Marxism and the Marxian legacy. This approach allows us not only to contextualise Gramsci's account within the intellectual and political panorama of his time, but also to highlight the specificity of his 'philosophy of praxis' and the role of his reassessment of Marx in this framework. Furthermore, it stresses the continuity between the pre-prison texts and the *Notebooks*.

With regard to Gramsci's role within the history of Bonapartism and Caesarism, his account represents an unavoidable (but often underestimated) point of reference for the study of the complicated development of these concepts in the nineteenth and early twentieth centuries.[2] These concepts (whose 'life' has been relatively short in comparison to other political categories, spanning roughly the period between the mid-nineteenth century and the mid-twentieth century)[3] have had a limited success among intellectual historians and historians of political thought, especially in recent times. If some interest in the topic was registered in the 1970s and in the 1980s, in the subsequent decades only a few (albeit important) contributions on the theme were published.[4] Furthermore, the attention dedicated to the history of Caesarism and Bonapartism has been very uneven in terms of their 'focalisation'. Not only is a comprehensive history of the categories still lacking, but scholars have mostly focused on specific linguistic areas and on specific readings of the concepts.[5]

---

2 Scarce attention has been paid to Gramsci in the secondary literature on Caesarism and Bonapartism; the few exceptions are the contributions of Luisa Mangoni (1976 and 1979) and Benedetto Fontana's chapter in Baehr and Richter 2004. See also my contributions on the topic in Antonini 2013a, 2016 and 2019b, which anticipate the research contained in this book.

3 On this point, however, see Richter 2005, which stresses the fact that Caesarism and Bonapartism are part of a broader conceptual family, which includes categories such as tyranny, despotism and dictatorship.

4 The very first contributions are by Gollwitzer 1952 and Momigliano 1956. As regards the bibliography between the 1970s and the 1980s, it includes Griepenburg and Tjaden 1966, Abendroth 1967, Groh 1972, Kitchen 1973, Hanisch 1974, Botz 1976, Mangoni 1976 and 1979, Wistrich 1976, Hammer and Hartmann 1977, Rapone 1978, Bluche 1980, Wippermann 1981 and 1983 (a more theoretical approach is the one adopted in Poulantzas 1970). More recent publications include: Mackenbach 1994, Cervelli 1996, Baehr 1998, Cassina 2001, Ceretta 2003, Baehr and Richter 2004, Richter 2005, Riosa 2007, McDaniel 2016 and 2018. See now also Prutsch 2019.

5 One of the most interesting features of these concepts is the fact that they have been adopted by intellectuals from diverse backgrounds and, due to their intrinsic complexity, have been employed to analyse a range of backgrounds. Scholars have seldom acknowledged this 'trans-ideological' character (as well as their 'transnational' use, i.e. their application in a variety of national contexts).

In this context, an analysis of Gramsci's understanding is a desideratum from many points of view. In the first place, the investigation of his reading of Caesarism and Bonapartism could contribute to the revival of interest in these categories, and especially in their (complex and sometimes contradictory, but always fascinating) usage in the twentieth century, by promoting a balanced and contextualised (non-ideological) reading of their significance.[6] In particular, it could shed meaningful light on the role of the Caesarist-Bonapartist model within a Marxist framework, which follows a quite independent and consistent line of development. Last but not least, Gramsci's reflection on Caesarism and Bonapartism could represent the starting point for a (critical) reassessment of other related concepts, such as the categories of 'totalitarianism' or, more recently, 'populism'. As the latter is one of the most disputed political concepts of our times,[7] analysing it from the perspective of its 'forerunners' (as are, I argue, Caesarism and Bonapartism) may offer a new and unexpected insight into the (historical and conceptual) presuppositions and potential consequences of populism.

This work reconstructs the evolution of Gramsci's thought on Bonapartism and Caesarism in a diachronic way, from the early newspaper articles to the late prison notes. Methodologically speaking, it relies on the achievements of the Gramsci scholarship, notably Italian, of the last two decades, which has inspired a growing number of publications, as well as a new critical ('national') edition of Gramsci's works, in the course of publication.[8]

The book is structured in thirteen chapters. The first chapter (*The Concepts of Bonapartism and Caesarism from Marx to Gramsci*), which has a preliminary character, provides a brief sketch of the history of the categories of Bonapartism and Caesarism from their origins to Gramsci. In particular, I focus on

---

[6] This is a major flaw within many of the contributions from the 1970s and the 1980s, especially those devoted to the interpretation of the categories of Caesarism and Bonapartism in the Marxist framework (see, in particular, the works by Wippermann).

[7] Significantly, it was made the Cambridge Dictionary 'Word of the Year' in 2017.

[8] As regards the new critical ('national') edition and its articulation, see the specific section on the website of the Fondazione Istituto Gramsci. See also the bibliographical indications contained in the 'Note on the text' and the 'List of abbreviations'. On the recent developments of Gramsci scholarship, both with regard to the editions of the texts and to the secondary literature, see the articles contained in three special journal issues: *Studi Storici* 2011, 52, no. 4 ('L'edizione nazionale e gli studi gramsciani'), *Laboratoire italien. Politique et société* 2016, 18 ('Gramsci d'un siècle à l'autre'), *International Gramsci Journal* 2018, 2, no. 4 ('Readings and Applications of Gramsci / The National Edition of Gramsci's Writings'). See also Vacca 2011. Notable examples of single-authored contributions include Thomas 2009, Frosini 2010b, Carlucci 2013a, Liguori 2015 and Cospito 2016 (the last two are translations of previous Italian publications, respectively Liguori 2006 and Cospito 2011c).

the role of Marx in elaborating these concepts and on the interpretation of the Caesarist-Bonapartist model within Marxist thought across the nineteenth and the twentieth centuries.

Chapters 2–5 are devoted to Gramsci's pre-prison writings. In Chapter 2 (*The Pre-Prison Writings*), I offer an overview of the (small number of) interpretations of the Caesarist-Bonapartist model in the pre-prison texts. I then examine Gramsci's early readings of Marx, which are fundamental for understanding why and how he develops his conception of Caesarism and Bonapartism. Subsequently, in Chapter 3 (*Socialism and Romanticism*), I analyse the usages of these categories in Gramsci's journalistic articles from the post-war period. I show that the category of Bonapartism is primarily used for the sake of his controversy with his fellow members of the PSI (and, after the formation of the PCd'I in 1921, with former comrades), with a clear strategic perspective. On the other hand, Caesarism is employed in a comparative fashion, in order to highlight the weakness of the 'Caesarist' solution proposed by Mussolini, through historical and literary comparisons. Chapter 4 (*Crisis and Balance: Between Revolution and Restoration*) studies the issue of the 'catastrophic crisis of capitalism' promoted by the Comintern since 1919 and Gramsci's progressive detachment from this doctrine. Ultimately, he instead adopts the formula of a 'balance of class forces', which is strictly connected to the Marxist reading of Bonapartism. In the following chapter (*Bonapartism, Caesarism and Fascism in Gramsci's Journalistic Works*), the Gramscian interpretation of Fascism in 1924–26 is at stake; moreover, by summarising his use of the Caesarist-Bonapartist model in the pre-prison writings, I also concentrate on Gramsci's debt to Hegel's *Philosophy of Right* and to Marx's *Eighteenth Brumaire*.

Chapter 6 (*Towards the Prison Notebooks*) turns to the presence of Caesarism and Bonapartism in the *Prison Notebooks*, which constitute the object of analysis of the remainder of the chapters. I provide, in this initial chapter, an overview of the occurrences of these concepts in Gramsci's prison writings and an account of the texts by Marx to which he had access in prison. The concept of Bonapartism constitutes the focus of Chapter 7 (*The Meanings of 'Bonapartism'*). Here I develop two lines of investigation. On the one hand, I show that in the *Prison Notebooks* we can detect a polemical meaning of the category comparable to that found in the pre-carceral writings, linked to the concept of Cadornism. On the other hand, Bonapartism is also connected to Gramsci's reflections on the civil and military bureaucracy and on its political role, from the *Risorgimento* onwards.

The following chapter (*Between Bonapartism and Caesarism*) introduces the key notes on Caesarism contained in notebook 13, the 'special' notebook in which the reflection on the Caesarist-Bonapartist model is most fully presented. On the basis of a close comparison to the first drafts of these notes, I try to demonstrate the originality and the richness of Gramsci's developing understanding of their significance. In Chapter 9 (*Gramsci and the Theory of Caesarism*), I concentrate on Gramsci's 'theory' of Caesarism. I deal first with Gramsci's critique of Weber's formula of the 'charismatic leader', taken up and expanded by Robert Michels. Subsequently, I stress the relevance of the formula of the 'balance of forces' for the definition of the concept of Caesarism in a non-deterministic perspective. I then reconstruct Gramsci's taxonomy of Caesarism such as it emerges from Q 13, § 27. While highlighting the role of analogies in this argument, I formulate some observations regarding the structure of this taxonomy.

In the following chapter (*Caesarism and Historical Analysis*), Gramsci's conception of historical development is analysed (as well as his 'worries'). Against the background of a reconstruction of the *Prison Notebooks*' 'plural temporalities', Louis Napoleon's Second French Empire is conceived as the archetype of Caesarism: rather than Julius Caesar's or Napoleon Bonaparte's regimes, this is the real point of reference for Gramsci's evaluation of contemporary Caesarist phenomena. I show also how this interpretation of Caesarism is closely connected to another pivotal Gramscian category, that of 'passive revolution'. Chapter 11 (*Hegemony and Modernity*) is devoted to the reconstruction of Gramsci's conception of early twentieth-century politics and of its peculiar dynamics. More specifically, I address the question of the analysis of Fascism from a Caesarist perspective. I then consider the characterisation of the 'organic crisis' and the new, 'post-Jacobin' form of hegemony after 1870, of which the Caesarist-Bonapartist model is an important element. Contemporary Caesarisms – that is, those forms of Caesarism that Gramsci saw at work in his own historical context – are thoroughly investigated in Chapter 12 (*Contemporary Caesarism(s)*). In the first place, I reflect on the 'totalitarian' conceptions of the world, by explaining the meaning of the term 'totalitarian' in Gramsci's language. The main concrete historical references are represented by the two opposite one-party systems, fascist Italy and the USSR. In this perspective, the complexity of Gramsci's reading stands out. He develops a multilayered analysis, according to which Fascism and Communism represent two forms of 'alternative modernities', which try to address (in profoundly different ways!) the radical transformations going on at the economic, social and political levels. A crucial element in this regard is represented by the analysis of so-called 'black parliamentarism'. Furthermore, in the last part of this chapter, I propose a comparison between Caesarism and the issue of the modern prince, which highlights how Gramsci understood the distinctive features of politics in the 1930s. The final chapter (*Caesarism, Bonapartism and the 'Return to Marx' in the Prison Writings*) returns to Gramsci's relationship to Marx, by reassessing previously existing narratives of a 'return to Marx' in the *Prison Notebooks*; it concludes by providing an overall assessment of the usage of the categories of Bonapartism and Caesarism in Gramsci's carceral writings.

To conclude, the research developed in this book firstly aims to provide the reader with a (still missing) thorough investigation, beginning from Gramsci's early writings, of a circumscribed but remarkable aspect of his reflection, notably his interpretation of Caesarism and Bonapartism. Yet it also aspires to put forward a more general reading of the author's thought, focused on the issue of 'modernity', conceived both theoretically and historically, as the cornerstone of his understanding of past and present political, economic and social dynamics, as well as of the elaboration of his own revolutionary project. In a broader perspective, this analysis is also a contribution towards a wider (and, in part, yet to be written) history of the categories of Bonapartism and Caesarism.

Finally, yet importantly, this work is of some importance also for contemporary political and intellectual debates. Indeed, there are, regrettably, numerous analogies between Gramsci's age and our situation in the early twenty-first century. Consequently, I believe that an historical analysis, such as the one proposed here, provides us with stronger conceptual means to face the substantial challenges of our own time.

Acknowledgements

My book could only have been conceived in the 'laboratory' where the most recent Gramsci scholarship has been born, meaning the University of Pavia (Italy), where I landed as an undergraduate student. In more recent years, Pavia is also where I developed the PhD thesis of which this work is a further re-elaboration.

In Pavia, Gianni Francioni and Giuseppe Cospito introduced me to Gramscian studies. They provided me with a rigorous philological training, a valuable intellectual *habitus*. I was fortunate enough to develop my research on Gramsci in the lively atmosphere of the Italian Gramscian community, during a moment of *renaissance* of studies on the author. At the same time, I have tried always to combine this 'Italian' approach with an openness towards the international debate on Gramsci, and towards the most recent achievements in the fields of intellectual history and of the history of political thought. In this respect, I have benefited greatly from intellectual exchanges with many scholars from different countries and from different disciplines.

I would like to express my deepest gratitude, first of all, to Giuseppe Cospito, Gianni Francioni and Fabio Frosini (the latter, even if not based physically in Pavia, is perfectly in line with the 'spirit' of the research developed there; he was also my mentor on the same level), for their steady support alongside the writing and the development of this work (and beyond).

I am extremely grateful also to Peter D. Thomas, who encouraged me to translate my research into English to make it accessible to a broader audience. As a Gramscian scholar, he has provided me with valuable suggestions on how to improve the work and as a co-editor of the Historical Materialism Book Series he has made this publication possible.

Thank you also to Danny Hayward and to the staff of the Social Science section of Brill, who never complained about my delays and were very supportive in every phase of the publication.

I am indebted to the Fondazione Gramsci in Rome and in particular to Giuseppe Vacca and Francesco Giasi, who represent a point of reference for any research on Gramsci I have carried out so far.

I also wish to thank Hagen Schulz-Forberg, who generously hosted me in Aarhus (Denmark) in 2014 and encouraged me to become acquainted with the methods and themes of intellectual history.

A special thanks to Robert P. Jackson, colleague and friend, with whom I have shared many convivial moments (as well as many Gramscian discussions), and who greatly helped me with the linguistic revision of this work.

I would like to acknowledge the support of the institutions at which I have been based, and the people with whom I have been working while completing my book, for their patience and understanding. Giuseppe Ricuperati and Francesco Tuccari at the Fondazione Luigi Einaudi in Turin, where I was the recipient of the 'Manon Michels Einaudi' Research Fellowship; Romain Descendre and Jean-Claude Zancarini at the ENS Lyon, where I held a research position in the framework of the LabEx COMOD/UMR 5206 Triangle.

Several scholars have provided me with feedback during conferences, seminars and private talks at different stages of my research: I am grateful to all of them and their interest reassured me that I was on the right path. In particular, Vittorio Morfino, Leonardo Paggi, Pasquale Voza and André Tosel read a first version of this work and gave me useful comments and criticisms that I took into account while revising the text. Thanks to David Broder and Mark McNally, who read the final version of the book. I am also most indebted to Federico Santangelo for his numerous and punctual comments on my manuscript, as well as for his genuine interest in my research on Gramsci. Finally, I owe a major debt of gratitude to Derek Boothman, a reader of rare generosity and sensitivity, from whose deep knowledge of Gramsci's language and thought I greatly benefited.

I dedicate this book to my loving husband Stefano: without him it simply would not exist.

Abbreviations

Gramsci's Letters – Italian Edition

LL   Gramsci, Antonio 1996, *Lettere dal carcere*, edited by Antonio A. Santucci, 2 vols., Palermo: Sellerio.

Gramsci's Pre-prison Writings – Italian Editions

CF   Gramsci, Antonio 1982, *La città futura. 1917–1918*, edited by Sergio Caprioglio, Turin: Einaudi.
CPC   Gramsci, Antonio 1971, *La costruzione del partito comunista. 1923–1926*, edited by Elsa Fubini, Turin: Einaudi.
CT   Gramsci, Antonio 1980, *Cronache torinesi. 1913–1917*, edited by Sergio Caprioglio, Turin: Einaudi.
NM   Gramsci, Antonio 1984, *Il nostro Marx. 1918–1919*, edited by Sergio Caprioglio, Turin: Einaudi.
ON   Gramsci, Antonio 1987, *L'Ordine Nuovo. 1919–1920*, edited by Sergio Caprioglio and Antonio A. Santucci, Turin: Einaudi.
PV   Gramsci, Antonio 1974, *Per la verità. Scritti 1913–1926*, edited by Renzo Martinelli, Rome: Editori Riuniti.
SF   Gramsci, Antonio 1971, *Socialismo e fascismo. L'Ordine Nuovo. 1921–1922*, Turin: Einaudi.
SNaz   Gramsci, Antonio 2015–, *Scritti. 1910–1926*, Rome: Istituto della Enciclopedia Italiana (published so far: 2. *1917*, edited by Leonardo Rapone, with the collaboration of Maria Luisa Righi and the contribute of Benedetta Garzarelli, Rome: Istituto della Enciclopedia Italiana 2015).

Gramsci's Pre-prison Writings – English Editions

HPC   Gramsci, Antonio 1975, *History, Philosophy and Culture in the Young Gramsci*, edited and translated by Pedro Cavalcanti and Paul Piccone, St. Louis: Telos Press.
PPW   Gramsci, Antonio 1994, *Pre-Prison Writings*, edited by Richard Bellamy, translated by Virginia Cox, Cambridge: Cambridge University Press.
SPW-1   Gramsci, Antonio 1977, *Selections from Political Writings, 1910–1920*, edited and translated by Quintin Hoare and John Mathews, London/Minneapolis: Lawrence and Wishart/University of Minnesota Press.

SPW-2   Gramsci, Antonio 1978, *Selections from Political Writings, 1921–1926*, edited and translated by Quintin Hoare, London/Minneapolis: Lawrence and Wishart/University of Minnesota Press.

Gramsci's *Prison Notebooks* – Italian Editions

Q1975   Gramsci, Antonio 1975, *Quaderni del carcere*, edited by Valentino Gerratana, 4 vols., Turin: Einaudi.

QAnast Gramsci, Antonio 2009, *Quaderni del carcere. Edizione anastatica dei manoscritti*, edited by Gianni Francioni, 18 vols., Rome-Cagliari: Istituto della Enciclopedia Italiana-L'Unione Sarda.

QNaz   Gramsci, Antonio 2007–, *Quaderni del carcere*, Rome: Istituto della Enciclopedia Italiana (published so far: *1. Quaderni di traduzioni (1929–1932)*, edited by Giuseppe Cospito and Gianni Francioni, 2 vols., Rome: Istituto della Enciclopedia Italiana 2007; *2. Quaderni miscellanei (1929–1935)*, edited by Giuseppe Cospito, Gianni Francioni and Fabio Frosini, vol. 1, Rome: Istituto della Enciclopedia Italiana 2017).

Gramsci's *Prison Notebooks* – English Editions

FSPN   Gramsci, Antonio 1995, *Further Selections from the Prison Notebooks*, edited and translated by Derek Boothman, Minneapolis: University of Minnesota Press.

PN   Gramsci, Antonio 1992–, *Prison Notebooks*, edited by Joseph A. Buttigieg, translated by Joseph A. Buttigieg and Antonio Callari, New York: Columbia University Press.

SPN   Gramsci, Antonio 1971, *Selections from the Prison Notebooks*, edited and translated by Quintin Hoare and Geoffrey Nowell-Smith, New York: International Publishers.

Works by Marx and Engels – English Edition

MECW   Marx, Karl and Engels, Friedrich 1975–2004, *Collected Works*, 50 vols., London: Lawrence and Wishart.

Note on the Text

This research emerges from an analysis of the texts of Antonio Gramsci in their original Italian versions. Waiting for the completion of the publication of the new, complete critical edition of Gramsci's *oeuvre* (*Edizione nazionale degli scritti di Antonio Gramsci* – SNaz; QNaz), I refer primarily, for the sake of consistency, to the previous Italian editions, both of the pre-prison articles (CT, CF, NM, ON, SF, CPC, PV) and of the *Prison Notebooks* (Q1975). As regards the chronology of the *Notebooks*, however, I rely on the chronological appendix in Cospito 2011a, which illustrates the chronology adopted in the new edition.

While revising my work, I have greatly benefited from existing English translations of Gramsci's works (SPW-1, SPW-2, PPW, HPC, PN, SPN, FSPN) and I always refer to them when possible (the reference to the English edition follows the one to the Italian edition). However, when the English version is not available, I have provided my own translation.

As regards the prison writings, I follow the established quotation standards in Gramscian scholarship. I refer to the note of the *Prison Notebooks* by indicating it with the number of the notebook (Q), that of the paragraph (§) and, if necessary, page numbers.

Moreover, following the criteria established by Francioni (2009 and 2016), I adopt the terms 'first draft', 'second draft' and 'single draft' to classify the different typology of the notes. This terminology supersedes the classification of individual notes adopted in Gerratana's critical edition ('A texts', 'B texts', 'C texts'; cf. Q1975, p. xxxvi). When appropriate, I have also translated excerpts from secondary literature in languages other than English.

CHAPTER 1

The Concepts of Bonapartism and Caesarism from Marx to Gramsci

1   The Genesis of the Category between Historiography and Political Polemics

Both Bonapartism and Caesarism are neologisms that are closely connected to the French political situation of the mid-nineteenth century. As Cristina Cassina writes,

> the neologism Bonapartism appears immediately after the fall of Napoleon I. The *Treasure of the French Language* [*Trésor de la langue française*] (1975) dates the first use of the term to 1816, quoting from a pamphlet by Paul-Louis Courier entitled *Petition to both Houses* [*Pétition aux deux Chambres*] … The word Bonapartism, in this first use, therefore served to indicate the group of those who had joined, and benefited from, the regime of Napoleon Bonaparte.[1]

This first usage also contributed to laying the foundations of the so-called 'Napoleonic legend'. In the case of the term 'Caesarism', the first occurrence is in a text by Auguste Romieu (1800–55) entitled *The Age of Caesars* [*L'ère des césars*], written in 1850.[2] With this term Romieu indicated the 'domain of the sabre' which he hoped would be realised shortly thereafter in France; he described a form of power based on the support of military force which 'takes over the hereditary monarchy in particular situations of crisis', but which, unlike this, is not hereditary.[3]

Originally, Romieu's classicising neologism was distinguished from the Bonapartist phenomenon, whose main features (the *coup d'État* and political legitimation through a plebiscite) have little to do with Romieu's reference to the monarchical principle, and to the conquest of political power through the

---

1   Cassina 2001, p. 19.
2   Romieu is also the author of another famous anti-socialist pamphlet, *The Red Spectre of 1852* [*Le spectre rouge de 1852*], which is cited by Marx in *The Eighteenth Brumaire*.
3   Cervelli 1996, pp. 102 and 109.

exercise of force embedded in the concept of Caesarism.[4] Very soon, however, these concepts were brought into proximity with each other. Their original meaning was quickly set aside to make room for a different and, so to speak, more general conception, which is the result of a 'mixture' of elements of both categories.

From the early 1840s onwards, the category of Bonapartism was increasingly conceived of as a 'third way', i.e. as a form of strong but democratically legitimised government, as it emerges clearly in the works by Louis Napoleon Bonaparte (1808–73), in particular in *On the Opinions and Policy of Napoleon* [*Des ideés napoleoniennes*] (1839) and *The Extinction of Pauperism* [*Extinction du pauperisme*] (1844).[5] In fact, if Napoleon I was the one from whom Bonapartism took its name, his nephew was its true theoretician. Napoleon III's works greatly contributed to defining the Bonapartist political project, by drawing skilfully on both the conservative and the revolutionary tradition. He also based his politics on this Bonapartist theory. His political action began precisely in those years and became fundamental in the post-1848 phase.[6]

The concept of Caesarism also underwent a rapid evolution. Shortly after its appearance in Romieu's text, the expression was picked up by other thinkers and used in a different sense, which was more or less politically oriented. On the one hand, for example, Jacob Burckhardt (1818–97) makes it an almost technical term, while, on the other, Pierre-Joseph Proudhon (1809–65) broadens its meaning several times.[7] If the Swiss historian uses it in his discussion of the imperial military designations of the Constantinian age, the French socialist turns Caesarism into one of the two poles of his teleological and 'dilemmatic' conception of history. Proudhon interprets Caesarism as the only alternative to non-government and anarchy, as well as the only possibility of producing a revolutionary situation. It is noteworthy that Proudhon also significantly transforms the content of the concept: in fact, he attributes to Caesarism a 'democratic' character, thus bringing it closer still to Bonapartism, also defined in democratic terms, although in a very peculiar way. On the other hand, through his works *The General Idea of the Revolution in the Nineteenth Century* [*Idée générale de la révolution au XIXe siècle*] and *The Social Revolution Demonstrated by*

---

4 See Cervelli 1996, pp. 102–11.
5 In this context, a role was played also by the strengthening of the Napoleonic legend, following the return of Napoleon I's ashes to his homeland.
6 On Napoleon III and on the Second Empire, see, among others, Price 1997 and Milza 2006.
7 On Burckhardt's *The Age of Constantine the Great* [*Die Zeit Constantins des Grossen*] (published in late 1852), see Cervelli 1996, pp. 111 ff. On Proudhon and his enlargement of the concept, harshly criticised by Marx, see Cervelli 1996, pp. 145 ff.

the *Coup d'Etat of December 2, 1851* [*Révolution sociale démontrée par le coup d'État*], Proudhon was one of the most significant figures in the spread and success of the category in this extended and non-technical meaning.

Historical events did the rest. *The Age of Caesars* was printed at the same time that Louis Napoleon conceived his *putsch*. The outcome of this process is therefore the transformation of Bonapartism from an autonomous category linked to a specific historical moment and with specific features into a 'translation of the Caesarist model in the contemporary French situation'.[8] The margins between these two concepts become increasingly blurred, and the terms appear to be substantially interchangeable. The consequence of the disappearance of the original conceptual gap between the two categories is an interpenetration of the different perspectives embedded in Caesarism and Bonapartism (the technical and the non-technical level, the political and historiographical reading, the contextualising and actualising interpretation).[9]

2   Marx: From *The Eighteenth Brumaire* to *The Civil War in France*

Karl Marx (1818–83) produced one of the most significant readings of the categories of Caesarism and Bonapartism in the second half of the nineteenth century. This is offered in his historical works, *The Class Struggles in France 1848–1850* [*Die Klassenkämpfe in Frankreich 1848 bis 1850*], *The Civil War in France* and, above all, *The Eighteenth Brumaire of Louis Bonaparte* [*Der achtzehnte Brumaire des Louis Bonaparte*], concerning the *coup d'État* of Louis Napoleon.[10] The relevance of this reading is due not only to the exceptional fortunes of these works

---

8   Cassina 2001, p. 19.
9   In the following pages, I will concentrate on the application of the concepts within the Marxist framework, in order to provide the reader with a reconstruction of the debate on the Caesarist-Bonapartist model that is directly related to Gramsci's interpretation. It does not imply, however, that this is the only possible history of Caesarism and Bonapartism. On the contrary, there is a variety of interpretations, which connect these categories to different ideological situations and different conceptions of politics.
10   On Marx on Bonapartism, see also, in addition to the classic discussion of Rubel 1960, Wippermann 1983, Bongiovanni 2003 and Bravo 2003. On *The Eighteenth Brumaire*, see, in particular, Carver 2004 and Antonini 2013b. Here, I will always refer to Marx's historical masterpiece as *The Eighteenth Brumaire of Louis Bonaparte*, according to the title adopted in the second edition of the work (1869). The title of the first edition of the book (1852) is slightly different (*The Eighteenth Brumaire of Louis Napoleon*) and was chosen by the editor, Joseph Weydemeyer, despite Marx's opposition. Similarly, in the following chapters I may sometimes refer to Louis Napoleon simply as Louis Bonaparte.

within the Marxist tradition, but also to the specific features of Marx's interpretation, which represents a turning point in the history of Caesarism and Bonapartism.

His judgement on Caesarism contained in the preface to the second edition (1869) of the *Eighteenth Brumaire* is well known. Marx here affirms that combining the concepts of Caesarism and Bonapartism is misleading and that such an interpretation is caused by an oversight.

> I hope that my work will contribute towards eliminating the school-taught phrase now current, particularly in Germany, of so-called Caesarism. In this superficial historical analogy the main point is forgotten, namely, that in ancient Rome the class struggle took place only within a privileged minority, between the free rich and the free poor, while the great productive mass of the population, the slaves, formed the purely passive pedestal for these combatants. People forget Sismondi's significant saying: The Roman proletariat lived at the expense of society, while modern society lives at the expense of the proletariat. With so complete a difference between the material, economic conditions of the ancient and the modern class struggles, the political figures produced by them can likewise have no more in common with one another than the Archbishop of Canterbury has with the High Priest Samuel.[11]

By blaming those who linger on unfounded historical parallels, Marx rejects Caesarism as an 'extrinsic or improper classificatory form', reducing it to a 'descriptively political category'.[12] Consequently, he admits only an analysis of the *putsch* of Louis Napoleon that is based on a 'scientific' investigation of the real socio-economic structures, in line with his conception of historical materialism. Thus, while Marx does not reject Caesarism in its entirety, he insists on referring it back to its historical dimension, that is, to classical antiquity. However, he also strongly contextualises the category of Bonapartism: Marx rigorously focuses on the historical phase in which this concept is developed, namely French political history between the July Revolution (1830) and the birth of the Second Empire of Napoleon III (1852).[13] Despite Marx's efforts to avoid any confusion between Caesarism and Bonapartism, however, the majority of the contemporary and later writers did not adopt his position – by the

---

11   MECW, vol. 21, pp. 57–8.
12   Cervelli 1996, p. 82.
13   It should also be noted that Marx does not use the term 'Bonapartism' explicitly, either in *The Eighteenth Brumaire* or in the other historical works, in order to avoid the risk of typification that accompanies the use of neologisms.

middle of the nineteenth century, the two concepts were already considered synonymous, and Marx's arguments could not do much to prevent the confusion between them.[14]

Moreover, by evoking the 'school-taught phrase now current ... of so-called Caesarism',[15] Marx is clearly alluding to the debate waged in the nineteenth century on these categories. In particular, he polemicises directly against Proudhon and Victor Hugo (1802–85), two French intellectuals who greatly contributed to the spread of the Caesarist-Bonapartist paradigm. I have already mentioned the work of Proudhon. Hugo, one of the greatest writers of the nineteenth century, was the author of *Napoleon the Little* [*Napoléon le petit*], a very popular pamphlet on Louis Napoleon.[16] In his preface, Marx establishes a double comparison that disassembles the two positions simply by contrasting one against the other. While Proudhon is deterministic, Hugo is fatalistic. If Proudhon calls into question a teleological interpretation, Hugo cannot move beyond the contingency of the situation, taken by surprise at the accomplished fact ('the event itself appears in his work like a bolt from the blue. He sees in it only the violent act of a single individual').[17] By distancing himself from both attitudes, Marx strongly reaffirms his interpretation based on the recognition of the specificity of the events of 1848–51 and their insertion within a precise historico-political framework. Only such a perspective, Marx argues, enables the explanation of the specific nature of the Bonapartist phenomenon ('I demonstrate how the class struggle in France created circumstances and relations that made it possible for a grotesque mediocrity to play a hero's part').[18]

With regard to the *pars construens* of Marx's analysis in the *Eighteenth Brumaire*, he concentrates first on the political strategy of the future Napoleon III. Second, he examines the ways in which Napoleon III seeks the support of the various social classes. Finally, and above all, he explores Louis Napoleon's role within the French institutions, within the state and the parastatal apparatuses. In short, Marx reveals how Bonaparte acts as a 'representative' of different social classes, towards which he adopts different strategies at different moments (albeit from the same perspective of seeking consent). At the same

---

14 In spite of the rejection by Marx, Engels also used the Caesarist-Bonapartist model to describe the nature of Bismarck's political power. The reference is, specifically, to the text *Violence and Economics in the Formation of the New German Empire* [*Gewalt und Ökonomie bei der Herstellung des neuen Deutschen Reiches*] (1896).
15 MECW, vol. 21, p. 57.
16 On Hugo, see, for instance, Giocanti 2009.
17 MECW, vol. 21, pp. 56–7.
18 MECW, vol. 21, p. 57.

time, Napoleon III ensures that he maintains his independence at the political level. From the theoretical point of view, Bonapartism is thus an unprecedented form of 'relative independence' of the executive power, highlighting the importance of the political-ideological dimension.[19]

If the *Eighteenth Brumaire* is undoubtedly Marx's most important historical work, it should be noted that the success of his conception of Bonapartism is linked mainly to his later writings, and notably to *The Civil War in France* (1871). This short pamphlet, connected to the new insurrectionary experience that had shaken France in the spring of that year (the Paris *Commune*), represents a revival of and, to a certain extent, a 'vulgarisation' of the 1852 essay.

With regard to the historical framework sketched here, Marx partly takes up (sometimes even literally) what was said in the *Eighteenth Brumaire*. But there is a substantial difference between the two analyses, which originates in their different political contexts. On the one hand, the 1852 text begins with an analysis of the defeat of the 1848 revolution and the subsequent need to rethink the political strategy of the proletariat. *The Civil War in France*, on the other hand, conveys a message of revolutionary optimism (even if only in the sense of the long-term world-historical possibilities that the *Commune* has placed on the agenda). In this later work, he proposes a reading of recent French history in terms of the birth and decline of bourgeois domination. One element of this historical and political reconstruction, in particular, had a great success. In this passage, Marx affirms that the Second Empire is 'the only form of government possible at a time when the bourgeoisie had already lost, and the working class had not yet acquired, the faculty of ruling the nation'.[20] It is from this phrase that successive interpreters have drawn inspiration to coin the formula of the 'balance of class forces'.[21]

---

19 Thus, the issue of Bonapartism is related to the autonomy or heteronomy of the state, according to Marx. This theme has been debated at length in the scholarship (see Antonini 2014a).

20 MECW, vol. 22, p. 330.

21 Marx, while referring to the studies of French historians Thierry and Guizot, already in 1847 had spoken of the independent character of the French absolute monarchy as the product of the rivalry between nobles and the third state at a time when the ancient aristocracy and its feudal privileges were in decline. At the same time, the bourgeois class was not yet sufficiently prepared to make its revolution. Starting from this 'formulation of the thesis of the class balance as the condition of the possibility of absolutism' (Winkler 1978, p. 37), Marx elaborates, a few decades later, a similar thesis to interpret the Bonapartist phenomenon. However, it is necessary to recognise Engels's double 'primacy'. In fact, he was the first to adopt the term 'balance' (in German: '*Gleichgewicht*') to describe the absolute monarchy (see *The Peasant War in Germany* [*Der deutsche Bauernkrieg*] of 1850). Furthermore, Engels talks about 'balance of class forces' with regard to the regime

The consequence of this new reading is, in a certain sense, a 'simplification' of Marx's earlier account of Bonapartism. In short, the balance formula did not only imply a redefinition of the role of the Bonapartist figure and his relationship with social classes (in *The Civil War in France*, Napoleon III is described as a mere spokesman for the bourgeoisie). More generally, the concept of Bonapartism was identified, from that point on, with the struggle between two opposing socio-political blocs, and with top-down intervention conceived of as an instrument of momentary neutralisation of this conflict, and also as a tool to preserve the existing order.

3   Across the Nineteenth and Twentieth Centuries

Despite this 'new' approach (or, perhaps, precisely because of it), the Bonapartist model was very successful, and became a *Leitmotiv* of Marxist historico-political interpretations. In the late nineteenth and early twentieth century, the Caesarist-Bonapartist model spread widely among Marxist intellectuals, who adopted it as a means of political polemic in the day-to-day debate but also as a tool for historical interpretation.[22] These usages became particularly frequent and significant in the aftermath of the First World War, because of the emergence, on the European stage, of new, authoritarian political forms. As Luisa Mangoni writes,

> the turning point between the Twenties and Thirties, with the advent of Nazism in Germany and the clear affirmation of Fascism as a European phenomenon ... contributed to making 'obligatory' ... the idea of Bonapartism, to mean, by affinity or by contrast, the substance of Fascism.[23]

A leading role was played by socialist and communist theorists, who, from the early 1920s onwards, reassessed, in more or less 'faithful' ways, the Marxian heritage. In particular, in this framework, Gramsci's 'recovery' of the categories of Caesarism and Bonapartism stands out for its richness and originality.

---

of Louis Bonaparte already in February–March 1852. In an article entitled *The Real Causes of the Relative Inactivity of the French Proletarians last December* [*Die wirklichen Ursachen der verhältnismäßigen Inaktivität der französischen Proletarier im vergangenen Dezember*], Engels states that Louis Napoleon created a balance between French social classes by making them fight each other.

22   On the evolution of the reflections on Caesarism and Bonapartism between the nineteenth and twentieth centuries, see in particular Groh 1972 and Mangoni 1976.

23   Mangoni 1976, p. 49.

In his pre-prison writings but especially in the *Prison Notebooks*, he does not limit himself to a superficial reference to the Caesarist-Bonapartist model, but instead re-elaborates it thoroughly. This does not mean that Gramsci is completely cut off from contemporary discussions. Even if, for various reasons (primarily his imprisonment), he was probably not aware of the most recent national and international developments in this debate, he was certainly aware of the current meaning of Bonapartism and Caesarism and he consciously elaborated his own conception in opposition (but also in relation) to it. Two elements testify to this: on the one hand, the predominant use of the concept of Caesarism (in a programmatic combination with that of Bonapartism) and, on the other, his reference to the formula of the balance of class forces.

Alongside Gramsci, during the same years, other Marxist intellectuals also adopted the Caesarist-Bonapartist model to interpret contemporary phenomena. These figures included the Austro-Marxist Otto Bauer (1881–1938), August Thalheimer (1884–1948), Leon Trotsky (1879–1940), but also other minor figures, such as some German and Italian socialists (respectively, Arkadij Gurland (1904–79), Franz Borkenau (1900–57) and Alexander Schifrin (1901–51); Pietro Nenni (1891–1980)).[24] They elaborated important analyses of the genesis and nature of autocratic phenomena in the post-war world. Thanks to the adoption of the categories of Caesarism and Bonapartism, they effectively described the radical transformations going on within European society, by recognising the novelty of the political dynamics that had been identified.

However, these analyses remain exceptions within the more general reflection of the European left. We can say that the major communist and socialist organisations were initially 'lukewarm' in their opposition to the fascist phenomenon, underestimating the danger deriving from the affirmation of the new regime. Later, they adopted rather dogmatic positions and were unable to explain the real nature of these authoritarian tendencies (and, as a consequence, they were not able to elaborate a fruitful political strategy to oppose them).[25] The significance of this revival of the Caesarist-Bonapartist model is therefore twofold. If, on the one hand, it represents a form of explicit theoretical 'heterodoxy' (a conscious 'return to Marx' in opposition to the Marxist

---

24 On Bauer, see in particular Botz 1976 and Marramao 1977. On Thalheimer, see Griepenburg and Tjaden 1966 and Kitchen 1973. On Trotsky, see Wistrich 1976 and Rapone 1978. As regards the usage of the categories in German and Italian socialism in the 1920s and 1930s, this is still largely insufficiently investigated (especially with regard to the Italian context).

25 On the strategies adopted by communist and socialist parties against Fascism, see, for starters, Hájek 1985, Natoli 2000, Agosti 2009.

vulgata), on the other, it raises a series of difficult questions concerning the status of historical materialism itself, as well as its role and political effectiveness.

Furthermore, it is worthwhile to recall the negative judgement of the categories of Caesarism and Bonapartism expressed by Palmiro Togliatti (1893–1964) in his *Lectures on Fascism* [*Lezioni sul fascismo*] (1935). He affirms that 'Marx and Engels' analyses, valid at the time for that era of capitalism's development, become incorrect when mechanically applied today, in the age of imperialism'.[26] Togliatti's rejection should not discourage us from investigating Gramsci's reading of the categories of Caesarism and Bonapartism. It should rather be taken, I argue, as an invitation to stress the way in which a nineteenth-century political category was adapted to the social, political and economic context of the twentieth century and how, in this new context, it proved to be fruitful.

On the basis of this brief history of Bonapartism and Caesarism with a particular emphasis on the Marxist tradition, we can now move on to a closer investigation of Gramsci's account. The following analysis will have a 'monographic' character, by focusing solely on Gramsci's texts, but, as this reconstruction has shown, it cannot be conceived in isolation from the background of the socialist and communist debates of that time, and of the previous Marxian model.

---

26   Togliatti 1976, p. 3. On Togliatti's reading, see the introduction by Giuseppe Vacca in Togliatti 2004.

CHAPTER 2

The Pre-prison Writings

1   Two (Almost) Neglected Categories

The categories of Bonapartism and Caesarism play an important role in the pre-prison works of Antonio Gramsci. If a certain amount of attention has been paid to their use in his *Prison Notebooks*, interest in Gramsci's use of them in his newspaper articles has been limited, with the exception of books by Leonardo Paggi and Christine Buci-Glucksmann, which deal with these categories, albeit in a rather cursory way.[1]

There are various reasons for this neglect. First, we should mention the preference historically granted to his prison notes. In fact, scholars (used to) read the pre-prison writings as a mere 'preparatory phase' for Gramsci's *magnum opus*.[2] Another reason lies in the nature itself of the primary sources. As has been demonstrated, the history of studies of his pre-prison writings is particularly tortuous due to the troubled editorial process and problems in establishing the authorship of these articles.[3] However, great efforts have been recently undertaken towards a complete critical edition of these texts, within the framework of the *Edizione nazionale degli scritti di Antonio Gramsci*.[4]

In my analysis, I will capitalise on this new interest in Gramsci's pre-prison writings in two different but complementary directions. First, I want to propose a philologically-oriented investigation of the few explicit occurrences of the concepts of Caesarism and Bonapartism, some of which have never been analysed, and all of them more or less underestimated. Second, my aim is to offer a broader understanding of Gramsci's political reasoning, as it develops on the basis of these (and cognate) categories.

---

1   Paggi 1970 and 1984; Buci-Glucksmann 1980. For a critical overview of the Gramscian bibliography since 1922, see Liguori 2012.
2   This approach 'affected' Gramscian scholarship especially in the 1960s and 1970s. A change took place from the 1990s onwards, when, taking its cue from Francioni's pioneering work (Francioni 1984), a new philological approach to Gramsci's writings, including the pre-prison writings, was developed. As for Gramsci's journalistic articles, in particular, Leonardo Rapone has amply demonstrated that they have an autonomous status and deserve to be studied in their own right (see in particular Rapone 2011a).
3   On the difficulties in the attribution of the articles and on the general problems related to the editing of these texts, see Giasi 2011a.
4   On current Gramscian scholarship, see my 'Preface' above.

These two levels of analysis will be developed in chapters 3, 4 and 5 of this book. In the next chapter, in particular, after some necessary preliminaries on the categories of Caesarism and Bonapartism as well as on Gramsci's Marxian sources, I will focus on the occurrences of the term 'Bonapartism', which Gramsci evokes twice: on the one hand, in connection with the figure of the Italian army general Luigi Cadorna; on the other, in the context of his struggle against the political currents of maximalism and reformism in Italian socialism, first from inside and then from outside the Italian Socialist Party (*Partito Socialista Italiano* – henceforth abbreviated: PSI). As for the category of Caesarism, I will analyse the only explicit reference that we find in the pre-prison writings by contextualising it within Gramsci's reflections on the French serial novel. Here the category of Caesarism is conceived of in terms of a comparison with the Italian post-war political situation.

2 Marx, Gramsci and the Marxian Sources

The originality of Gramsci's account derives in part from his direct reading of Marx's historical works, and especially of the *Eighteenth Brumaire*. This is true of the *Prison Notebooks*, but it is also true of the pre-prison writings. In this sense, investigating Gramsci's use of the categories of Caesarism and Bonapartism prior to his imprisonment means also investigating the way in which he approaches Marxist thought.[5]

But *which* Marx did Gramsci read? When? And how? This knowledge was primarily made possible by a number of editions of Marx's and Engels's works available in Italian at the beginning of twentieth century.[6] When Gramsci arrived in Turin, 'the first initiative of the systematic translation into Italian of Marx's and Engels's writings was concluded'.[7] From 1899 the socialist publisher Luigi Mongini printed the texts by Marx, Engels and Lassalle in fortnightly instalments under the editorship of the socialist historian and politician Ettore Ciccotti (1863–1939). A few years after the death of Mongini (in 1909) the pro-

---

5 Despite the importance of this topic, rigorous studies focused on Gramsci's early approach towards historical materialism have been published only in recent years (Cospito 2008 and 2011b, Giasi 2011b, Izzo 2009 and 2011; see also, more recently, Vacca 2017). The most important work is without doubt the one by Francesca Izzo (2009). I will discuss her account in more detail later.
6 For a detailed account of the socialist publications at the beginning of the twentieth century, see Bravo 1992, Gianni 2001 and 2004.
7 Giasi 2011b, p. 55.

ject was interrupted and in 1914 the *Società editrice Avanti!*, owned by the Italian Socialist Party, resumed the publication of these writings. In this second phase the booklets were collected in eight volumes, edited by Ciccotti. The first, second and seventh volumes were devoted to Marx; the third, fourth and a part of the eighth volumes to Engels; the fifth and sixth volumes to Lassalle; *History of German Social Democracy* [*Geschichte der deutschen Sozialdemokratie*] by Mehring was split between the end of the sixth volume and the beginning of the eighth. A first edition of the *Works of Marx, Engels and Lassalle* [*Opere di Marx, Engels e Lassalle*] was published between 1914 and 1916, and a second edition (falsely labelled 'revised') between 1921 and 1922. From 1917 onwards, the works contained in the eight volumes were published separately in the series entitled *Writings of Marx, Engels and Lassalle* [*Scritti di Marx, Engels e Lassalle*].

By consulting the collection of Gramsci's books kept at the Gramsci Institute in Rome, we can find six out of the eight volumes of the *Works* in the 1921–22 edition (vols. II, III, IV, V, VI and VIII) and one of the volumes of the 1914–16 edition (vol. VII – *Capital* by Marx). Only volume I is missing, which contains Marx's writings up to 1852. Nevertheless, we can argue that Gramsci had at his disposal the entire 1921–22 edition. In all likelihood two of those volumes got lost and at least one of them has been replaced by a copy from the first edition of the *Works*. In this sense it is noteworthy that both the missing volume and the replaced one are devoted to those of Marx's works that Gramsci probably read the most (which might explain why they were lost).[8] In addition to these volumes, Gramsci owned many single editions from the series of the *Writings of Marx, Engels and Lassalle* with the publication date of 1925. Moreover, other books were also bought before 1926.[9]

Even if we suppose that Gramsci's knowledge of Marx's texts dates back to the Turin years (as we could do according, for instance, to the testimony of Togliatti[10]), on the basis of his buying and collecting the volumes available, we could reasonably affirm that his reading of Marx became more careful and systematic in the 1920s.[11]

---

8   The catalogue is available here: http://www.fondazionegramsci.org/categoria/agmono/?ap=a. As Giasi (2011b, p. 55) notes, 'the volumes without prison marks that date to the years before imprisonment' are not many; however, a good number of them are Marxian texts. As a general rule it should be noted that Gramsci did not underline sentences or take notes directly on books – his books are usually 'clean', even if he read them many times.
9   Some of these volumes have multiple frontispieces, with different publication dates (for an example, 1925, 1922 and 1902). These are reprints of the Mongini–*Avanti!* editions; however, they were printed in 1925.
10 See Togliatti 1958.
11 It should be noted that in this period Gramsci also engaged in a close reading of Labriola's

In any case, Gramsci's stay in Moscow as a representative of the Italian Communist Party (*Partito Comunista d'Italia* – henceforth abbreviated: PCd'I) at the Executive Committee of the Comintern and then in Vienna was without doubt a watershed in this respect.¹² The experiences he had in 1922–24 deeply influenced his relationship with the founding texts of Marxism and made him aware of the necessity of a historically contextualised and philologically rigorous reading of these texts. In Russia, in particular, he knew the 'editorial work, interpretation and use of Marx that took place in those years under the auspices of the Comintern, through its cultural institutions, journals and Russian publishers'.¹³ The achievements of this intellectual journey became clear when he moved to Vienna, where he was placed in charge of the new series of *L'Ordine Nuovo*. Here he also developed the new editorial line of the Italian Communist Party, by identifying a number of works to be translated into Italian, with the aim of 'popularising' Marx's thought – in spite of the failure of many of his projects this remains a crucial point.¹⁴

In this context, Marx's historical works stand out. Their importance emerges clearly not only from their presence in the list of Marxian works owned by Gramsci, to which we should add the ones that he probably owned and were lost, as well as the ones he very likely read between the 1910s and the 1920s.¹⁵ It is

---

Essays on the Materialistic Conception of History [*Saggi intorno alla concezione materialistica della storia*], which could have played a role in stimulating Gramsci's interest in Marx's texts. On Gramsci and Antonio Labriola (1843–1904), see Burgio 2014, pp. 414–47 and, more recently, Olsaretti 2016.

12 On Gramsci's stay in Moscow, see Carlucci and Balistreri 2011 and Righi 2011. On the Vienna period, see in particular Somai 1979 and Giasi 2009.

13 Giasi 2009, p. 57. For a succinct description of these experiences, see also Antonini 2018.

14 See again Giasi 2009 for a detailed account of Gramsci's projects – among these, of particular interest is the plan to translate (jointly with his wife Julia) David Ryazanov's notes on the *Communist Manifesto*. On Gramsci's 1924 project of the translation of a Russian anthology on historical materialism, very much in line with his anti-determinist account, see again Antonini 2018.

15 *The Eighteenth Brumaire of Louis Bonaparte* and *The Class Struggles in France 1848 to 1850* were contained in the first (lost) volume of the *Works of Marx, Engels and Lassalle*, whereas *The Civil War in France* and the letters on *The Eastern Question* are in the second; Gramsci also had a single edition of *The Civil War in France* and *The Eighteenth Brumaire* (while the latter is indicated as the translation of 1852, in reality it is the text of 1869; in the online catalogue it is suggested incorrectly that the volume could have lost a few pages); the Russian anthology mentioned previously contains extracts from all of these works as well as from Engels's 1885 *Preface* to *The Eighteenth Brumaire*, his 1891 *Preface* to *The Civil War in France* and his 1895 *Preface* to *The Class Struggles in France*. Marx's 1869 *Preface* to *The Eighteenth Brumaire* is not contained in any of these texts, but it was famous and it is very likely that Gramsci knew of it.

also the case in terms of content: Marxian historical analyses seem to be more present in Gramsci's early writings than Marx's economic thought.

The antideterminist and antidogmatic approach towards historical materialism that informs the *Prison Notebooks* strongly capitalises on a close reading of Marx's historical works, especially the book on Louis Bonaparte's *coup d'État*. These texts, combined with an extremely innovative interpretation of the 1859 *Preface* to *A Contribution to a Critique of Political Economy* [*Zur Kritik der politischen Ökonomie*] and other Marxian works (above all the *Theses on Feuerbach* [*Thesen über Feuerbach*]), provided Gramsci with the conceptual tools to elaborate his original philosophy of praxis while in prison.[16] The first elements of this reading, however, can be traced back to his pre-prison writings, as I will demonstrate in the following chapters.

---

16   On this point, see Bernstein 2016.

CHAPTER 3

Socialism and Romanticism

1   Against Maximalism and Reformism: Reckoning with Italian Socialism

1.1   *Cadorna and Bonapartism*
The first occurrence of the term 'Bonapartism' in Gramsci's writings is contained in an article published in *L'Ordine Nuovo* in March 1921. The piece, entitled *The Grave-diggers of the Italian Bourgeoisie* [*I becchini della borghesia italiana*] is a strong condemnation of Giovanni Giolitti's attitude in the months before the Italian parliamentary elections of May 1921.[1] Gramsci is attacking the petty bourgeoisie as well, insofar as Giolitti is their political representative: he affirms that the petty bourgeoisie is acting irrationally in this delicate political phase and therefore it is putting at risk the bourgeois political system. The entire scene is pessimistically described by Gramsci (with the exception of recalling the 'saving' communist ideal at the end), and the picture of the old politician he sketches offers an excellent synthesis of the 'mood' he is trying to express:

> Giolitti is an old man who was afraid during the war. After decades and decades of undisputed power, in May 1915 he suffered the worst insults and humiliations that an old man accustomed to power may suffer. He is an old man without a future, with no vision for the future. He was bloodthirstily defamed, he was afraid to end up on the scaffold (if in 1917 Cadorna had realised his dictatorship, Giolitti would have received the worst blows of the Bonapartist and militarist reaction). He has only one wish, cruel revenge, to be the grave-digger of a class that he must intimately despise. The Right Honourable Giolitti, after the armistice, was the true representative of the middle classes. They had also been afraid, because they did not have a line of action, since they were not anchored

---

1 Giovanni Giolitti (1842–1928) was one of the most influential political figures in liberal Italy and he was head of the government five times from the 1890s onwards. During the elections of May 1921, fascist representatives gained their first access to parliament (35 fascist deputies were elected thanks to a coalition – the *blocchi nazionali* – with the liberals). As a consequence of that, fascist violence escalated and the political struggle became more and more violent.

to the modes of existence that are rigidly tied to the workers' wages or to the capitalists' profit. They are unable to make predictions for the future, they also want to vent their unslaked thirst for vengeance ... The middle class is today ruling Italy, and is represented by a man who synthesises all of its psychology and disorientation. Sceptical, without aspirations, with no predictions for the future, no longer tied by any bond to the population he despises because he has always known its worst and most ineffective part, Giolitti, who has lived all the satisfactions and all the torments that a man can live, wants to be the grave-digger of the bourgeoisie.[2]

Gramsci's early 'anti-Giolittism' is well known and recent studies have dealt with it in detail.[3] The parenthesis in which Gramsci establishes a parallel between the attempted *coup d'État* of the general Luigi Cadorna in 1917 and the *putsch* of Louis Bonaparte described by Marx is revealing. This parallel is evoked by the expression 'Bonapartist and militarist reaction'.[4]

The adjective 'Bonapartist' has here a quite generic meaning, without any specific reference either to the French context or to the Marxian analysis. The formula chosen by Gramsci is a piece of evidence in this sense, i.e. the couple of adjectives 'Bonapartist and militarist'. Due to its link with the attribute 'militarist', the concept of Bonapartism tends to be read on the basis of this category. They are connected, since the military element plays a crucial role in shaping the original concept of Bonapartism. Gramsci chooses the word 'Bonapartist' because of its provocative and evocative character rather than for the sake of a concrete historico-political analysis.

The ambiguity of the expression is played down by Gramsci's reference to the figure of Cadorna, to whom Gramsci dedicates great attention in his pre-

---

2 'The Grave-diggers of the Italian Bourgeoisie', *L'Ordine Nuovo*, 7 March 1921 (SF, pp. 97–8).
3 See Rapone 2011b and 2008.
4 Luigi Cadorna (1850–1929) was an Italian general and politician. He was the commander-in-chief of the Italian army during the First World War and he was responsible for the defeat of Caporetto, one of the most ruinous of the entire conflict. On Cadorna's alleged desire to instal a military dictatorship and on the political situation in Italy at that time, see Kramer 2007. As regards the *coup d'État*, this is a significant theme in Gramsci's thought already in the *biennio rosso* (1919–20), and it is connected to his analysis of the political strategy of the newly-born fascist movement. The first references to a possible fascist takeover appear in texts that date to the occupation of the factories (September 1920). After that, on Gramsci's explicit request, this possibility is mentioned also in the Rome theses (*Tesi di Roma*), the party manifesto published in *L'Ordine Nuovo* in preparation for the second congress of the PCd'I (March 1922) – this episode is evoked in the *Prison Notebooks* by Gramsci (see Q 14, § 25). Therefore, I would argue that Gramsci's observations on Cadorna's *coup d'État* might also help to illuminate his reflections on post-war politics, and notably those on Fascism.

prison writings.⁵ He talks specifically about Cadorna's (alleged) missed seizure of power in an article of 1920. Analysing the events that occurred after August 1917 he hints at the 'dark forces' that organised the *coup d'État*:

> If the higher ranks of the army and the careerist military hierarchy generally, on which the industrial plutocracy operates, would give the order to march against the working people, would the majority of the armed forces obey, [would the majority of the armed forces accept] ... the discipline of the army only because it has the conviction to perform a duty for the nation? It is certain that the industrialists show so much confidence in their strength and are persuaded to slap the working class and the government, which remains neutral because they have had pledges from the higher echelons of the military. The same dark forces that after the events of August 1917 had organised the *coup d'État* to give all power to Cadorna, the same forces that had then prepared the blacklists and condemned Giolitti to the firing squad along with the major figures of the working class, the same forces that in 1917, precisely because they were dealing with internal politics more than their military skills and obtaining the victory for their faction, led the army into the trap of Caporetto, the same forces today are plotting and preparing for the 'big day'.⁶

Gramsci is more explicit in another piece written a few years later, where he establishes a comparison between the military *coup* and the fascist one,⁷ by showing the nature of those 'dark powers' and making more concrete the reaction, of which the *'generalissimo'* (as Cadorna was named) should have been the spokesperson.⁸

In this context, the elliptic parenthesis of 1921 gains importance and weight. The reference to the seizure of power seems to suggest (albeit roughly and implicitly) that a specific reading of the category of Bonapartism already existed in Gramsci's thought in the 1920s. This reading goes alongside his interpretation of the figure of Cadorna and it represents the starting point for a more in-depth reflection on Bonapartism.

---

5 Despite the importance of the topic in Gramsci's view, the way in which he deals with the figure of Cadorna has not been investigated (cursory hints are contained in Paggi 1984, p. 139, Fresu 2005, D'Orsi 2008, p. 145 and D'Alessandro 2011).
6 'Chiaroscuro' ['Chiaro-scuri'], *Avanti!*, 8 September 1920 (ON, pp. 676–7).
7 'Elections' ['Le elezioni'], *L'Ordine Nuovo*, March 1924 (SF, pp. 162–5).
8 On Cadorna's epithet, see 'Caporetto and Vittorio Veneto' ['Caporetto e Vittorio Veneto'], *L'Ordine Nuovo*, 28 January 1921 (SF, p. 51).

There are quite a number of texts dating from 1920 and 1921 that show a meaningful connection between maximalism, Bonapartism and Cadornism (to adopt a relevant expression from the *Notebooks*).[9] Gramsci recalls not only Cadorna's failed *putsch*, but especially his tactical irresponsibility, which finally led to the defeat of the Italian army and to the death of thousands of soldiers.

Cadorna is depicted by Gramsci as a 'Napoleonic mind', leading a 'passive mass of manoeuvre' completely devoted and faithful; with the bourgeoisie's blessing, he would have established his dictatorship, if the historical circumstances had not swiftly changed.[10] Cadorna is deployed as the main representative (within the military field) of a 'bureaucratic and authoritarian [relationship] between leaders and led', whose political counterpart is represented by maximalism, within mainstream socialist ideology.[11]

It is clear that the importance of Caporetto and Cadorna's military choices does not depend exclusively on their own importance as particular historical/military events. Equally fundamental, in Gramsci's view, is the opportunity to turn the war-time strategy into a political metaphor, by capitalising on it to criticise the leadership of the PSI. It is not by chance that the articles in which Gramsci criticised the attitude of the maximalist leaders through a comparison with Cadorna are concentrated in the period in which he actively works for a (communist) split from the Socialist Party.[12] This is evident from the following quotations from the articles *Caporetto and Vittorio Veneto* and *Culprits (I colpevoli)*:

---

9   See, in particular, 'A President' ['Un presidente'], *Avanti!*, 28 June 1920 (ON, pp. 565–6); 'The Struggle in Turin' ['La lotta di Torino'], *Avanti!*, 2 November 1920 (ON, pp. 752–4); 'Caporetto and Vittorio Veneto', cit.; 'Culprits', *L'Ordine Nuovo*, 12 August 1921 (SF, pp. 279–82). On Cadornism in the *Prison Notebooks*, see Chapter 7 (section 2.1).

10 See, respectively, 'Caporetto and Vittorio Veneto', cit. (SF, pp. 50–2) and 'A President', cit. (ON, pp. 752–4). Significantly, Cadorna was against parliamentarism. His willingness to break with the 'legal country' not only explains Gramsci's 1921 parenthesis, but also justifies Giolitti's concern for his safety.

11 Paggi 1984, p. 139. In addition to the already mentioned articles, see also 'War is War' ['La guerra è la guerra'], *L'Ordine Nuovo*, 31 January 1921 (SF, pp. 55–9). On the maximalist faction, see Eley 2002, pp. 165 ff. More generally, on early twentieth-century Italian socialism, see De Grand 1989, Favilli 1996, Elazar 2001 and Smith 2012. Useful indications can also be found in the works on Gramsci by Cammett 1967, Roberts 1979, Adamson 1980 and Martin 2002. As regards the Italian bibliography, the monumental work by Paolo Spriano (1967–75) is still a valid reference (but see also De Felice 1971).

12 On the tension within the PSI in the period immediately before the Livorno congress (6 January 1921) and on the necessity, for the newly-born Italian Communist Party, to demonstrate the inevitability of the break, see again Eley 2002, *passim*.

Maximalism, which is today in full flight, indeed completely decomposing, applied in the civil war the same tactics which General Cadorna applied in the national war. It wasted the proletarian forces in a multiplicity of disorganized and chaotic actions; wore the masses out; deluded them about the ease and speed with which victory would be achieved. Italian maximalism and General Cadorna had forerunners: the Chinese Boxers, who thought they could dislodge the English and Germans from their forts by advancing against the machine-guns in a turbulent mob, preceded by paper banners on which horrible, frightening monsters were painted.[13]

All the generals of Serrati's maximalism raised to the dignity of leaders when they could not even distinguish between their incompetence and the tangle of forces deployed in battle, saw their guilt in outside forces. The defeats were not their work, no. The Cadornas of Serrati's maximalism had to cover their responsibilities by throwing mud on the face of the fighting masses.[14]

1.2 Trade Unionism and Bonapartism

Gramsci's polemics in the early 1920s against the 'Bonapartistic tradition of the PSI' are clearer within the context of this reading of the 'Cadornas of Serrati's maximalism'.[15] An article written in October 1921 and entitled *Trade Unionism and Bonapartism* [*Bonapartismo sindacale*] is of particular interest. Here Gramsci attacks harshly the behaviour of the maximalists towards the General Confederation of Labour [CGdL – *Confederazione Generale del Lavoro*].[16] He claims that they come to terms with the capitalists and with the government, and that under maximalist leadership, 'the vital interests of the Italian working class become a play-thing for the personal fortunes of any Serrati'.[17] Gramsci says that the PSI and its most radical part, the maximalists and their

---

13 'Caporetto and Vittorio Veneto', cit. (SF, p. 51; SPW-2, p. 3; translation modified).
14 'Culprits', cit. (SF, p. 280).
15 Paggi 1970, p. xxxv (but see also pp. xxxiv–vi); 'Culprits', cit. (SF, p. 280).
16 The split of the PCd'I from the socialists did not affect the trade unions, whose leadership was shared by the two parties (on this point, see Giasi 2008b). The General Confederation of Labour, founded in 1906, was a major Italian trade union, linked both to the Socialist and to the Communist Party. It is not to be confused with the Italian General Confederation of Labour (*Confederazione Generale Italiana del Lavoro* – CGIL), CGdL's descendant after the Second World War.
17 'Trade Unionism and Bonapartism', *L'Ordine Nuovo*, 18 October 1921 (PV, p. 222).

leader Giacinto Menotti Serrati (1872–1926), sacrifice the masses' claims for the achievement of personal benefits. In other words, he accuses the leadership of the party of 'personalism', that is, careerism.

Beyond Gramsci's personal antipathy towards Serrati, his analysis of the Italian workers' movement is meaningful. Although pitiless, the picture Gramsci sketches is realistic. When he talks of an 'any Serrati [*qualsiasi Serrati*]', he is criticising all of these people who conceived the socialist ideal only as a 'foot-bridge' to reaching a position of prestige and influence, and, having achieved that, rapidly drew away from this ideal.[18] From this perspective, the trade union was the very point of conflict. After the breakdown of the Livorno Congress, the trade union (which was not affected formally from the split) became the battlefield between the Communist and the Socialist Parties. Gramsci accused the leaders of the PSI of trying to manoeuvre the proletariat at will, depriving it of any real capacity of action. He was particularly eager to combat the continuing domination of the socialists (and especially of Filippo Turati and other reformist leaders) over the CGdL. This emerges from Gramsci's distraught appeal to his party colleagues to work from within to restore the union, in order to avoid the failure of the labour movement.[19] Far from being an impromptu debate, Gramsci's accusations are connected strongly to his reflections on the nature and the organisation of the party (and of the union).[20]

By condemning the 'Bonapartistic tradition of the PSI', he asserts his belief that the party should take charge of the political and cultural education of the masses, in order to reduce the distance between leaders and led, and, thus, to make the political action of the proletariat genuinely effective. According

---

18   Paggi 1970, p. 133. Serrati himself had already attacked careerist attitudes within the workers' movement – see 'Against Personalism' ['Contro il personalismo'], *Il Secolo nuovo*, XIII, 34, 23 August 1913 (Paggi 1970, p. xxxvi). On Gramsci's relationship with Italian socialism, see Rapone 2011b, pp. 259 ff. and a number of essays on the topic in Giasi 2008a (Natoli 2008, Panaccione 2008, Lucarini 2008, Giasi 2008b).

19   Although Gramsci accuses Serrati of manoeuvring the union at will, direction is firmly in the hands of the reformists. Gramsci's misleading affirmation, however, is justified by the strongly controversial nature of the text, which, for political reasons, aims to discredit the action of the socialists as a whole.

20   On Gramsci's reflections on the structure of the party, see De Felice 1971, Paggi 1970, pp. 304 ff., Paggi 1984, pp. 306 ff., Buci-Glucksmann 1980, pp. 158 ff. The renewal and strengthening of the trade union structure is an important topic for Gramsci, as numerous articles show (see for example the piece entitled 'Syndicalism and Councils' ['Sindacalismo e Consigli'], *L'Ordine Nuovo*, 11 October 1919, ON, pp. 297–301; here the term 'syndicalism' clearly expresses the tendency to ossify and create the 'corporate interest' that Gramsci condemns). On this issue, see also Rapone 2011b.

to Gramsci, the reform of the party, the reform of the trade union, and the intellectual formation of the base and of the leadership, are all interconnected elements.[21]

It is not by chance that here Gramsci sarcastically calls the Italian socialist leaders '*stenterelli della politica sindacale*'.[22] This extremely caricatured expression (Stenterello is a traditional character of the Italian *commedia dell'arte*) represents a meaningful example of Gramsci's verbal inventiveness.[23] The polemical expressionism of his style is also notable in the second occurrence of the term 'Bonapartism' in this article. At the end of the text, pointing out the difference between the attitude of the socialists and of the newly-born Communist Party towards the working class, Gramsci states:

> Communists need to intensify their propaganda and organisation in the leagues and the chambers of work to emancipate the working class from this regime of Bonapartism and intrigue, which threatens to lead us to the most shameful defeat that the proletariat ever experienced.[24]

Once again Gramsci has chosen to use a couple of adjectives (that is, 'Bonapartism and intrigue'). As we saw above, this rhetorical tool, on the one hand, contributes to flattening the meaning of the expression and, on the other, it emphasises its polemical nature. The term 'Bonapartism' exemplifies here the climate of mystery and intrigue that characterises the leadership of the workers' union.

1.3   *Parliamentary Cretinism and Socialist Reformism*

As we saw when discussing Gramsci's position on the trade unions, he also strongly criticises the reformist faction of the PSI between 1920 and 1921, by adopting the formula of 'parliamentary cretinism'. This formula recalls a famous expression from Marx's *Eighteenth Brumaire*, which was common within the socialist milieu.[25] Thanks to this definition, Gramsci criticises the reform-

---

21 Paggi 1970, p. xxxv (for Gramsci's criticism of maximalist careerism, see also pp. xxxiv–vi). On the importance of the cultural dimension in Gramsci's political reflection (with particular reference to the proposal of the creation of a cultural association), see Rapone 2011b, pp. 293 ff.
22 'Trade Unionism and Bonapartism', cit. (PV, p. 222).
23 Regarding Gramsci's use of the expression '*stenterello*', see Rapone 2011b, pp. 130–40.
24 'Trade Unionism and Bonapartism', cit. (PV, p. 222).
25 In an 1852 article published in the *New York Daily Tribune*, Engels defines 'parliamentary cretinism' as the 'disorder which penetrates its unfortunate victims with the solemn conviction that the whole world, its history and future, are governed and determined by a

ists' conviction that the Italian political crisis can be resolved on the parliamentary level. This is evidenced by the fact that, in two cases, this is paired with the synonymic expression of 'reformist and opportunist illusion' ('the remains of parliamentary cretinism, the reformist and opportunistic illusions must be destroyed implacably'; 'they have seen in them only parliamentary "cretinism", reformist and opportunist illusions, and counter-revolution').[26]

The articles in which 'parliamentary cretinism' is deployed are concentrated in two specific phases of Gramsci's pre-prison production, between 1919 and 1921, and 1925 and 1926, with a climax in 1921.[27] Despite the similarities in content, there is an essential difference between the two groups of occurrences, as can be seen from the chronology. Before January 1921, when Gramsci refers to parliamentary cretinism he is responding to a controversy inside his own party (split into different currents). After the birth of the PCd'I (but also, in some ways, in the weeks immediately before the Livorno Congress) his polemics become a critique from the outside. It is no coincidence that the most important occurrences are precisely those of 1921, when Gramsci's effort for the creation of a new Communist Party was greater.

---

majority of votes in that particular representative body which has the honor to count them among its members, and that all and everything going on outside the walls of their house ... is nothing compared with the incommensurable events hinging upon the important question, whatever it may be, just at that moment occupying the attention of their honorable house' (MECW, vol. 11, p. 79).

26 See the entire quotations: 'We need to tie tighter and stronger the masses to the Party. The revolutionary conviction that the proletarians themselves may and must be the creators of their emancipation must increasingly be spread. The remains of parliamentary cretinism, the reformist and opportunistic illusions must be destroyed implacably' ('The Results we are Waiting for' ['I risultati che attendiamo'], *Avanti!*, 17 November 1919; ON, p. 322). 'Revolutionary workers and peasants and conscious socialists have not seen any reflection of their interests or aspirations in these parliamentary initiatives to do with control over industry and "uncultivated or poorly cultivated lands". They have seen in them only parliamentary "cretinism", reformist and opportunist illusions, and counter-revolution ... These parliamentary moves could have served some purpose. They could have served to inform the workers and all the peasants of the precise terms of the industrial and agricultural problem, and of the necessary and sufficient requirements to resolve it' ('Workers and Peasants' ['Operai e contadini'], under the column 'The Week in Politics' ['La settimana politica'] [XV], *L'Ordine Nuovo*, 3 January 1920; ON, pp. 376–7; SPW-1, p. 148).

27 Cf. 'The Results we are Waiting for', cit.; 'Workers and Peasants' [1920], cit.; 'The Monkey People' ['Il popolo delle scimmie'], *L'Ordine Nuovo*, 2 January 1921 (SF, pp. 9–12; SPW-1, pp. 372–4); 'The Situation' ['La situazione'], *L'Ordine Nuovo*, 21 February 1922 (PV, pp. 252–3); 'Honourable Treves and Georgia' ['L'onorevole Treves e la Georgia'] [I], *L'Unità*, 22 July 1925 (CPC, pp. 379–81); 'Disorder and Intellectual Dishonesty' ['Disordine e disonestà intellettuale'], *L'Unità*, 28 July 1926 (CPC, pp. 430–3).

The most meaningful example is probably the article entitled *The Monkey People* (2 January 1921), which recalls explicitly Rudyard Kipling's *The Jungle Book*, one of Gramsci's favourite texts.[28] This famous article is important for two reasons. On the one hand, it is central to understanding Gramsci's interpretation of Fascism in its early stages.[29] On the other hand, it suggests an unprecedented reading of the formula of parliamentary cretinism. Here, he says:

> The ruination of the petty bourgeoisie began in the final decade of the last century. With the rise of large-scale industry and finance capital, the petty bourgeoisie lost all importance and was removed from all its vital posts in the field of production: it became a purely political class and specialised in 'parliamentary cretinism'. This phenomenon, which plays an important role in contemporary Italian history, has been called by various names in its various stages. It was originally called 'the coming to power of the left', then it became Giolittianism, then the struggle against the Kaiserist aspirations of Umberto I, and finally it broadened into socialist reformism. The petty bourgeoisie encrusts itself to the institution of Parliament. Parliament has evolved from a controlling organ of the capitalist bourgeoisie over the Crown and Civil Service, to a talk-shop for gossip and scandal, a means of parasitism. Corrupt to the very marrow, enslaved completely to the governing power, Parliament has lost all prestige in the eyes of the mass of the people.[30]

The context is that of the polemic against rising Fascism in the aftermath of Fiume's 'eviction' by the Giolitti government (December 1920).[31] The tone of the piece reflects Gramsci's hope for an imminent uprising of the masses against the ruling powers, who unsuccessfully try to 'hide' themselves behind

---

28 See Zunino 1988b, pp. 314–22, Pissarello 2008, and especially Carlucci 2013b.
29 On this point, see Gagliardi 2016, but also Zunino 1988a and 1988b. It has to be noted, however, that Zunino unduly extends Gramsci's early 'dismissing' of Fascism to the entire pre-prison writings (such a reading is highly dubious and problematic).
30 See 'The Monkey People', cit. (SF, p. 9; SPW-1, p. 372, translation slightly modified).
31 The Adriatic city was occupied between 1919 and 1920 by a various group of Italian 'legionnaires' and nationalists led by Gabriele D'Annunzio (1863–1938) during the so-called *impresa di Fiume*. The self-proclaimed 'Italian Regency of Carnaro' [*Reggenza Italiana del Carnaro*] was established in the city, seeking unification with Italy. In December 1920, the Italian government, led at that time by Giolitti, sent its troops against the city and defeated D'Annunzio's forces, making the town free – these facts are known as 'bloody Christmas' [*Natale di sangue*].

the rising fascist movement. This is depicted by Gramsci as the latest incarnation of the petty bourgeoisie, i.e. the middle class, according to his Marxist terminology.

To justify his thesis and to give depth to his interpretation of Fascism, Gramsci opens up a historical digression in which he traces a connection between the fascist movement and the liberal state, where the *Leitmotiv* is represented by the destructive action of the Italian petty bourgeoisie. Before the war, this group, tricking the bourgeoisie with the promise to defend its interests, 'corrupted and ruined the institution of Parliament' and now it breaks the whole State from its foundations upwards.[32] The petty bourgeoisie, as with Kipling's Bandar-log,[33] has an essentially destructive nature and is unable to create a new order; as a consequence, Fascism will also inevitably fail in this effort.

In this framework, 'parliamentary cretinism' is the very clearest manifestation of this inefficiency. Furthermore, Gramsci's variation on the theme is here particularly remarkable. By reassessing Marx's formula, he draws a 'history of parliamentary cretinism': he shows how the middle class gradually takes control of the legislative power and adopts transformational new faces, one of them represented by socialist reformism.[34] In addition to this, the proximity with the fascist movement (the petty bourgeoisie's final incarnation) is also very provocative.

Therefore, by applying to his (not yet former) comrades the formula of 'parliamentary cretinism', Gramsci is expressing an extremely harsh judgement against reformism, condemning the distance between its political representatives and the proletarian masses.

This judgement finds its pair with the (equally severe) one expressed about the maximalist current within the PSI. The category of Bonapartism (applied to the maximalists) and that of parliamentary cretinism (applied to the reformists) here show similar features, insofar as they describe two aspects of the same political 'solipsism' that undermines the capacity for action of the work-

---

[32] 'On an ever-increasing scale, it is replacing the "authority" of the law by private violence. It practises this violence in a chaotic and brutal fashion (and cannot help but do so), and in the process it is causing ever broader sections of the population to revolt against the State and against capitalism' ('The Monkey People', cit.; SF, p. 12; SPW-1, p. 373).

[33] 'Bandar-Log' is the name of the monkey of the Seeonee jungle in Kipling's *The Jungle Book*.

[34] For a use of this expression, see 'The Situation', cit. (PV, p. 253): 'It would be really interesting in the history of parliamentary cretinism that the game succeeds: maybe in 1920–1921 the Socialists did not allow it to their own damage?' On Gramsci's criticism of 'transformism' (strictly connected to the one of parliamentary cretinism), see Paggi 1984, pp. 267 ff. and Rapone 2011b, pp. 170–80.

ing class. On a more general level, this unfolds in the context of a critical view on the workers' movement as a whole, and justifies Gramsci's close attention to issues relating to the structure and the functioning of the party.[35]

1.4 In Memory of Serrati

It is clear that, in Gramsci's pre-prison writings, the concept of parliamentary cretinism is closely connected to that of Bonapartism. Even if the two expressions never appear in the same article, this is not due to a substantial difference in meaning, but rather to the fact that each of them addresses a specific polemical target. That also emerges from later occurrences, which come after Gramsci's closer engagement with Marx's thought.[36]

This affinity sheds a meaningful light on the last article containing the term 'Bonapartism'. This text, due to its peculiar nature of eulogy, represents, as Paggi writes, a 'general recapitulation of the different opinions expressed by Gramsci on Italian socialism'.[37] The article, entitled simply 'Giacinto Menotti Serrati', was published a few days after the death of Serrati (10 May 1926). It is a reconstruction, with moving and vibrant tones, of Serrati's political action within the Socialist Party, then of his role in the foundation of the Third Internationalist faction of the movement; eventually, it deals with his subsequent joining of the Communist Party.[38] The complete reversal of Gramsci's attitude towards Serrati, who only a few years before was presented as the cause of all the ills of the Italian proletariat, might be quite astonishing.[39]

---

35 On a more general level, these observations are also important in defining Gramsci's concept of 'democracy', where this concept has to be conceived of more broadly, as 'democratic strategy', to use the language of Mark McNally (2017). On this complex issue, see Burgio 2014, pp. 60–79 and Rapone 2011b, pp. 352–63 *et passim*.

36 See 'Honourable Treves and Georgia' (I), cit.; 'Disorder and Intellectual Dishonesty', cit. These articles also contain a criticism of socialist reformism, and especially of Claudio Treves (1869–1933), one of the major leaders of the reformist faction within the Socialist Party (for a comparison of Gramsci's and Treves' accounts, see McNally 2017). On Gramsci's derision of the figure of Treves, see Rapone 2011b, pp. 16–18 *et passim*.

37 See Paggi 1970, p. 133.

38 'Giacinto Menotti Serrati', *L'Unità*, 14 May 1926 (CPC, pp. 109–13). On the figure of Serrati and the events relating to the fusion between the so-called Third Internationalist faction of Italian socialism and the Communist Party, see, in addition to the bibliography mentioned above, Detti 1972.

39 As he says, 'all the weaknesses that were inherent in the old structure of the Italian socialist movement were revealed violently in the post-war period ... The younger generations did not give all the importance to the drama then experienced by the older generations. So we have perhaps over-measured the extent of the aggression on what seemed useless sentimentalism and sterile love for old formulas and old symbols'. 'Giacinto Menotti Serrati', cit. (CPC, p. 112).

However, despite this reassessment of Serrati's action, Gramsci's judgement on the Socialist Party leadership remains strongly negative; he attacks as 'Bonapartists' those who, having seen in the adherence to the socialist ideal a 'bridge' to reach a position of prestige, quickly abandoned the party.[40] In fact, Gramsci states:

> The fundamental weaknesses of the traditional Italian revolutionary movement are known. The greatest weakness, at least determined in the decisive moments, can be characterised thus: there was always lacking a strong group of revolutionary leaders in Italy that had close contact with the proletarian core of the Socialist Party ... It is also evident that in such a situation, where the actual organisation was in inverse relationship with the size of the party, the duty of the head of the party was enormous and the responsibility that was burdened upon the person that was leading the party was overwhelming. This situation justified the fact that the revolutionary tendency of the Italian socialist movement, unlike what happened to the reformist trend, saw a revolving door in its leadership, while the reformists were strongly clustered around Turati. Not only that, but this situation also explains the sad fact that all, or almost all the leaders of the revolutionary faction, after a moment of great splendor, have degenerated, have renounced their previous positions or even crossed to the other side of the barricade. This is certainly one of the reasons for the persistence of a certain fortune of reformism among the Italian working masses: that in it the tradition of the tendency is closely related to the same person, to the same group of people.[41]

Gramsci sketches a very brief history of the first decades of Italian revolutionary socialism, by highlighting the absence of a coherent and sustained political leadership, able to give continuity to the political faction. He writes: 'to express it with an approximate political term, it can be said that in the Italian revolutionary socialist movement there has always been a situation of Bonapartism, where it was possible for more or less sincere, more or less convinced men, to

---

40 See Paggi 1970, p. 133, but also pp. 128 ff. Gramsci quotes as an example of this transformational attitude Enrico Ferri (1856–1929), head of the *intransigente* faction and director of *Avanti!* in the early years of the century, who later joined the fascist movement. However, I think that this passage can also be read as an allusion to Benito Mussolini (1883–1945), certainly the most famous of those who passed over to the opposite political field.

41 'Giacinto Menotti Serrati', cit. (CPC, p. 110).

acquire the place of the highest leadership'.[42] There then follows a long eulogy of the greatness of comrade Serrati, albeit within the limits dictated by his vision of politics:

> Giacinto Menotti Serrati broke this tradition [of Bonapartism] insofar as he came to the leadership of the party as a man whose main qualities were undoubtedly his strength of character and self-denial. He could not break [this tradition] completely, because he did not succeed, and did not even aim to succeed, at forming a new party, at giving the party a new structure that made it more capable of action and initiative.[43]

The framework outlined by Gramsci is particularly meaningful, since it draws a close connection between the unity of the workers' movement, the moral rectitude of its leadership and the party's strong support base. In short, it recalls some of the salient aspects of the conception of the party Gramsci had been developing since 1921.

It may be said that, although Gramsci defines Bonapartism as an 'approximate political term', this is not completely true. Bonapartism, in Marx's usage, but also in the above-mentioned uses by Gramsci, is a well-defined concept, circumscribed in its content and used with a specific purpose.[44] On the one hand, Gramsci endorses the polemical aspect entailed in the concept of Bonapartism as well as in the cognate formula of parliamentary cretinism. On the other hand, he grasps the heuristic value of this Marxian formula, by using it in a profitable way to stigmatise the distance between leaders and led, as far as it concerns the working class.

By imparting to the concept of Bonapartism a specific theoretical interpretation, a Gramscian 'mark' of this category became increasingly clear, starting from Gramsci's attempts to conceptualise the category in the early 1920s, to the framing of Bonapartism as a generic form of authoritarianism, passing through its combination with external categories that 'filled' and concretised it.

---

42 'Giacinto Menotti Serrati', cit. (CPC, p. 110).
43 'Giacinto Menotti Serrati', cit. (CPC, pp. 112 and 110).
44 In my opinion, this definition ('approximate political term') should be read as a 'confession' of a debt towards the socialist tradition. While in Marx the concept had a well-defined meaning, in the following Marxist tradition Bonapartism became a generic form of authoritarianism.

2   The 'Romanticism' of the Italian Bourgeoisie

2.1   *Marx, Gramsci and the* feuilleton

Following Gramsci's stay in Moscow and Vienna in 1922–24, the first two occurrences of Caesarism and Bonapartism that we encounter in his writings share a common reference to the French serial novel and have a clear Marxian flavour.[45] Gramsci is fascinated from an early stage by Marx's reading of the serial novel. Many of Gramsci's pre-prison articles mention his condemnation in *The Holy Family* [*Die heilige Familie, oder Kritik der kritischen Kritik*] of the 'novel's socialism'.[46]

Gramsci read Marx's work by January 1918 and the effects of this reading are visible in his articles.[47] However, already in Gramsci's articles from 1916 and 1917, there are references to Hugo's and Sue's novels. This seems to suggest that a reference to Marx's polemics in *The Holy Family* was common in the Italian socialist environment (and beyond) through the late nineteenth and early twentieth centuries – Marx's rebuttal of the moralism of Sue's *The Mysteries of Paris* [*Les Mystères de Paris*] is indeed one of the most popular sections of *The Holy Family*.[48] From 1918 onwards, Gramsci describes many people, socialists and others, as being imbued with a romantic conception of the people and political action, by referring explicitly to the 'bad models' of Sue's and Hugo's novels.[49]

These books, however, do not only represent negative paradigms. Indeed, they act as a stimulus for reflection on a well-known theme in Gramsci's *Prison Notebooks*, but whose roots can be found in his pre-prison writings:

---

[45] See 'Gioda or about Romanticism' ['Gioda o del Romanticismo'], under the column 'Italian Characters' ['Caratteri italiani'], *L'Unità*, 28 February 1924 (CPC, pp. 367–9); 'Descending parabola' ['Parabola discendente'], *L'Unità*, 19 July 1924 – this text is not included in the editions of Gramsci's pre-prison writings, but it is certainly Gramscian, as demonstrated by Paggi 1984, p. 278. There is no bibliography on literary issues in Gramsci's pre-prison writings (with the exception of the theatre reviews). However, some useful hints can be found in Gervasoni 1998, pp. 107–8 and pp. 118–25, Durante 2004, Paladini Musitelli 2004 and 2008. See also the related entries in the *Dizionario gramsciano* (Liguori and Voza 2009).

[46] On Marx's criticism of Sue, see Mehring's Introduction to *The Holy Family* (1902), and Prawer 1976, pp. 86–102.

[47] On Gramsci's reading of *The Holy Family*, see Izzo 2009.

[48] See 'The Court of Miracles' ['La corte dei miracoli'], under the column 'Under the Mole' ['Sotto la Mole'], *Avanti!*, 20 March 1916 (CT, pp. 205–6) and 'Offenders' ['Pregiudicati'], under the column 'Under the Mole', *Avanti!*, 2 August 1916 (CT, pp. 464–5).

[49] See 'The Serial Novels', *Il Grido del Popolo*, 25 May 1918 (NM, pp. 60–1); 'Literary News' ['Notizie letterarie'], *Avanti!*, 1 November 1918 (NM, pp. 385–6), '"La Volata" by D. Niccodemi' ['"La volata" di D. Niccodemi'], *Avanti!*, 24 April 1919 (NM, pp. 690–1). See also, the already mentioned 'Gioda or about Romanticism' and 'Descending Parabola'.

the 'national-popular' character of the literary phenomenon. In a piece from May 1918, entitled *The Serial Novels* [*I romanzi d'appendice*], Gramsci sketches a short but significant history of the literary genre of the French *feuilleton*, by establishing a clear distinction between its 'romantic ancestors' and degenerate contemporary productions. While the romantic origins of the novel provided 'an invaluable service to the popular mentality', giving voice to the needs and aspirations of the lower classes, with the works of the epigones 'literature is declining' and the link between the intellectuals and the people that represented the strength of the French cultural scene was lost.[50] Moreover, the issue (closely related to that of the popular dimension of the serial novel) of the differences between French and Italian culture is already outlined here.[51]

Nonetheless, this positive interpretation of the *feuilleton* does not reappear in the pre-prison writings, where the influence of Marx's criticism of the French serial novels prevails.[52] Moreover, after 1924 there is an evolution in the use of such a model: alongside the criticism of 'romantic socialism' taken from *The Holy Family*, Gramsci makes a further step, by combining it with an innovative interpretation of the historical works of Marx, and in particular of the *Eighteenth Brumaire*. The result is an original *pastiche*, which allows Gramsci to cast events and attitudes in a grotesque light.

2.2 Gioda o del romanticismo *and* Parabola discendente

In 1924, Gramsci twice takes up Marx's paradigm to speak of the fascist phenomenon. The first article, written in February, is entitled *Gioda or about Romanticism* and its core is represented by a harsh criticism of Mario Gioda (1883–1924), one of the leaders of the fascist movement in Turin and a former anarchist.[53] Even more than his polemic against Gioda as an individual figure, what emerges here is the parallel between the sentimentality of serial novels and that of 'left-wing Fascism', embodied by Gioda.[54]

---

50 'The Serial Novels', cit. (NM, pp. 60–1).
51 See Gervasoni 1998, pp. 97 ff. and the entries *Cultura francese, cultura italiana* and *Romanticismo italiano* in Liguori and Voza 2009, respectively, pp. 194–6 and pp. 732–4.
52 See, for instance 'A Lesson to the Workers' ['Una lezione agli operai'], *Avanti!*, 8 December 1919 (ON, pp. 358–60); 'The Factory Workers' ['L'operaio di fabbrica'], *L'Ordine Nuovo*, 21 February 1920 (ON, pp. 324–7) and 'Freedom for All, if you like that at least' ['Libertà per tutti, se così almeno vi pare!'], *L'Ordine Nuovo*, 24 November 1921 (SF, pp. 407–12). However, this 1918 article is Gramsci's only positive reference to the serial novel before his imprisonment; in the rest of the pre-prison writings he sticks to Marx's polemical use of the category.
53 See 'Gioda or about Romanticism', cit. (CPC, pp. 367–9 – regarding Mario Gioda's letter, to which Gramsci refers, see CPC, p. 367, n. 1).
54 On Gramsci's early distinction between the various souls of Fascism, see 'Gioda or about

Taking his cue from Gioda's loose sentimental language, Gramsci establishes a point of correlation between fascist ideology and romanticism that sheds a meaningful light on Fascism itself. Fascism, according to Gramsci's description of it as a 'deep synthetic vision', is a movement steeped in a romantic ideology, if not the very embodiment of 'Italian romanticism' itself. Referring to the cultural formation of the 'fascists of the first hour' (recalling an expression of Filippo Tommaso Marinetti (1876–1944)), Gramsci says:

> The environment in which the individual fascists have formed, the ideology through which they have been abundantly nourished, can be called romanticism ... Massimo Rocca was employed by Casa Sonzogno, where he translated, and collaborated in the dissemination of thousands and tens of thousands of specimens of novels by Ponson du Terrail, by Hector Malot, by Henry [sic: Émile] Richebourg, by Eugène Sue. Mario Gioda was the 'friend of Vautrin' of Paolo Valera's *La Folla*, he was the most genial and promising disciple of Paolo Valera, must still have in the drawer a big novel on Turin's slums, a novel like *The Mysteries of Paris* by E. Sue, a novel in which, with the extensive method of Carolina Invernizio, a peaceful provincial town of honest workers, of peaceful petty bourgeois pensioners, becomes a den of every vice, an aquarium of sea-snakes, a court of miracles of every social monster. Here is the romanticism, here is the romantic setting in which the fascist soul was formed.[55]

He also further specifies the type of romanticism of which Fascism is the representative, namely that of the serial novel:

Romanticism', cit.; CPC, p. 368: 'I speak of the fascists like Mario Gioda, not as Cesare Maria De Vecchi, as Massimo Rocca, not as Cesare Forni, fascists of old Mussolinism, fascists who were anarchists, trade unionists, revolutionary socialists until August 1914 and then became interventionists for the revolutionary war, fascists of the first hour, and so on, not of fascists of rural origin, who then conquered Fascism and do not want to release it'. I agree with Paggi when he affirms that the 'characterisation of left-wing Fascism' elaborated by Gramsci in this article is based on the 'analogy with a generic and confusing populism typical of the characters of French novels, according to Marx's polemic characterisation' (Paggi 1970, p. 278). However, I would argue that this definition is not just a contingent criticism (as Paggi seems to suggest), but a true 'aetiological' research into Fascism, a judgement on its historical development.

[55] 'Gioda or about Romanticism', cit. (CPC, p. 368). Massimo Rocca (1884–1973) was, like Mario Gioda, a socialist who became an interventionist in 1914 and then joined Fascism.

The *feuilleton*, the ideology for which the *feuilleton* is well known and has had great luck, is romanticism. Victor Hugo was a great romantic and the greatest writer of *feuilletons*: Scampolo is the sister of Gavroche; Mario Gioda, Massimo Rocca have become anarchists by reading the fights of Jean Valjean against Javert, they have been touched by Marius' idyll, by Fantine's maternal heroism, by the capitulation of the nobility in front of the people's rights, [people who are] generous despite their degradation and their crimes. Mario Gioda and Massimo Rocca have strengthened their conception in Eugène Sue's novels, have become anticlericals by reading *The Wandering Jew* [*Le Juif errant*], have absorbed the theory of delinquency of Eugène Sue, the most complete representative and grandly imbecile of all this romantic movement, yes sirs!, romantic and profoundly romantic and extensively romantic and socially romantic.[56]

The Gramscian discourse is complex and synthesises many elements scattered across previous articles. Beyond literary considerations (on the relationship between French and Italian literature, on the differences between Hugo and Sue),[57] what emerges is primarily Gramsci's negative judgement of the fascist movement. In other words, the complaint of its deliquescence, inspired by Marx. Just as Marx criticised the socialist sentimentality of *The Mysteries of Paris* in *The Holy Family*, so Gramsci now condemns the anarchists who became fascists due to their proximity to 'mummified' forms of romanticism (exemplified precisely with a reference to the novels of Sue).[58] Although limited to a part of the movement, Gramsci's political judgement highlights a 'romantic side' of Fascism as a whole, by defining it as 'an unbalanced fantasy, a shiver of heroic fury, a psychological restlessness that has no other ideal content than the widespread feelings in the serial novels of the French romanticism of '48'.[59]

---

56 'Gioda or about Romanticism', cit. (CPC, pp. 368–9).
57 These findings also have a political meaning beyond their literary value. The issue of the relationship between the French and Italian serial novels evokes the issue of the historical and cultural relations between the two nations. Furthermore, the distinction between Hugo's novels and those of Sue is similar to that between the 'good' and the 'bad' serial novel illustrated in the 1918 article on the topic. The 'good' *feuilleton* represents a positive form of dissemination of the socialist doctrines that could emancipate the lower layers of the population; the 'bad' *feuilleton* is a negative popularisation that favoured the rise of Fascism. The reversal of the judgement on Sue, highly praised in 'The Serial Novels', is not surprising here: in the article analysed above, Gramsci was mostly following Marx's praise for Sue expressed in *The Holy Family*.
58 On the concept of 'mummification' in Gramsci, see Jackson 2016.
59 'Gioda or about Romanticism', cit. (CPC, p. 369).

As in *The Monkey People*, Gramsci stresses the ideological weaknesses of Fascism. Between the monkey metaphor and that of the serial novel there is an affinity that deserves to be underlined. In both cases, the petty bourgeoisie is accused of representing the social basis of Fascism and of having adopted its own ideology (see the 'strange ideological mish-mash of nationalist imperialism, "true revolutionism", and "national syndicalism"' of the monkey people-petty bourgeoisie).[60] Furthermore, Gramsci's monkeys, rather than the petty bourgeoisie led by Ledru-Rollin, resemble the *Lumpenproletariat* described by Marx in the *Eighteenth Brumaire* as the embodiment of the worst type of Romanticism.[61]

The historical context is, however, much changed, and what in 1921 may have looked like a surmountable political phenomenon now appears as an essential socio-economic feature of the country. The inconsistency of the ideology of the fascist intellectuals is added to the observation that Fascism is 'a social movement, that is, a politico-economic [movement]', which became popular especially among the bourgeoisie, and 'that in Italy has occurred and was able to triumph because of an exceptional historical moment'. The fact that the advent of Fascism is the result of a peculiar 'historical conjuncture', as Gramsci repeats twice in the text, does not mean that it is not deeply rooted in civil society.

But how can he combine Fascism's rootedness in civil society with its ideological weakness? The conclusion of the article explains this apparent contradiction, through a(n implicit) parallel between France in 1848 and 1920s Italy:

> French romanticism of '48 also launched a part of the petty bourgeoisie onto the barricades, alongside the working class. But the working class was still weak, unable to take power; Power was taken by Louis Bonaparte, the petty bourgeoisie became caesarean ... Anarchists conceived of the revolution as a chapter of *Les Misérables* with its Grantaire, the Aigle de Meaux and C., with in addition Gavroche and Jean Valjean; fascists want to be the 'prince Rudolphs' of the good Italian people. The historic conjunction made possible for this romanticism to become a 'ruling class' and turned Italy as a whole into a serial novel ...[62]

---

60   'The Monkey People', cit. (SF, p. 11; SPW-1, p. 373).
61   Alexandre Auguste Ledru-Rollin (1807–74) was a left-wing liberal French politician; after the 1848 Revolution he attempted to became President of the Republic but he was not elected. On Marx and Engels on France, see e.g. Hamilton 1991.
62   'Gioda or about Romanticism', cit. (CPC, p. 369).

During the Revolution of February 1848 in France, which destroyed the old ruling bloc of the July Monarchy, the petty bourgeoisie was in disarray, and its serial novel 'rages' were intercepted by the pseudo-popular ideology of Louis Napoleon. In Italy in 1921, the middle class, weakened and impoverished by the war, was captured by the 'populism' of Mussolini, enabling his political conquest. 'The petty bourgeoisie became Caesarean', meaning that the middle class has taken up the Bonapartist and fascist ideals, fascinated by the charm of the strong man, of the charismatic leader. This is in fact the only occurrence of the term 'Caesarism' or similar terms in Gramsci's political writings before prison.

There is an element that confirms that the fascist movement is overshadowed in the reference to the post-1848 French events. Gramsci claims that serial novels played a significant role in moving individuals such as 'the Balzachian Mario Gioda' first towards anarchism and then towards Fascism.[63]

From the standpoint of its historical reality, however, fascist ideology does not appear only 'romantically' confused and therefore ridiculous. This picture is also somehow tragic, insofar as it draws attention to the shortcomings of Fascism and its inability to run the country. This dramatic element is taken by Gramsci from Marx's interpretation of the farce. In the element of parody, beyond the surface of the ridiculous, there is a tragic element consisting in the revelation of the inadequacy of words to reality, of ideologies to the facts.[64]

2.3 Italy's Tragic Farce

In *Gioda or about Romanticism* Gramsci goes beyond the scope of Marx's 'critical criticism', by analysing Fascism in terms of its moral decadence.[65] At the end of the piece the register of the serial novel overlaps with that of caricature. Gramsci's statement that 'the historic conjunction made possible for this romanticism [i.e. fascism] to become a "ruling class" and turned Italy as a whole into a serial novel' clearly displays the influence of Marx's historical work, even more than the analysis of popular literature in *The Holy Family*. It seems to me that his description of fascist romanticism contained in this article exhibits an atmosphere reminiscent of *The Eighteenth Brumaire*. On the other hand, Gramsci's reappraisal of Marx's book-related metaphor reinforces this belief.

---

63 'A Wood' ['Un bosco'], *Avanti!*, 8 February 1918 (CF, p. 638).
64 On parody in Marx and especially in *The Eighteenth Brumaire*, see Prawer 1976, pp. 166–96 *et passim*, and Tomba 2013; see also Antonini 2013a.
65 The expression 'critical criticism' evokes the subtitle of *The Holy Family* (*Critique of Critical Critique*).

This parallel recalls the one established by Marx in *The Eighteenth Brumaire* between Second Empire France and the 'tragic comedy', whose 'author' is Louis Bonaparte.[66]

This variation in a farcical sense is even more remarkable in a piece written in August 1924. It consists in a smug prediction of the impending collapse of the fascist regime, which, after the murder of the socialist deputy Giacomo Matteotti (1885–1924), 'is now going along a downward spiral', as the title of the article says.[67] Beside the (over-)confident tone of the article, we should note that, to emphasise his 'faith' in the decline of Fascism, Gramsci revives a famous definition by Hugo (made even more famous by Marx). Speaking about Mussolini, Gramsci says: 'He is reduced to the "rôle" of modest demagogue. A right-wing oriented demagogue today as yesterday a left-wing oriented demagogue. No longer Napoleon the Great, but, in this case, Napoleon the Little. Small, small, small, as Hugo wrote in *History of a Crime*'.[68]

If in the previous article Mussolini was compared to Prince Rudolph (one of the main characters in Sue's *Mysteries of Paris*) for his ambition to become a 'friend of the people', now Gramsci compares the leader of the fascist movement directly to Louis Napoleon, whose figure and actions had been ridiculed not only by Marx, but also by Hugo in his pamphlet entitled *Napoleon the Little*,[69] quoted in Marx's 1869 introduction to the second edition of *The Eighteenth Brumaire*. That Gramsci was influenced primarily by his reading of Marx's preface rather than by Hugo's texts seem to me a strong likelihood.[70]

---

66 On editorial metaphors in *The Eighteenth Brumaire*, see again Prawer 1976. Equally important, however, are the other applications of this 'bookish' key of interpretation, in particular the parallel between Mussolini and Prince Rudolph, which appears in the following article.

67 'Descending Parabola', cit. On the conviction (supported by Gramsci in the second half of 1924) that the crisis of government which opened with Matteotti's murder would have resulted in the end of the fascist regime, see Paggi 1984, pp. 215–22.

68 'Descending Parabola', cit.

69 By establishing such a parallel, Gramsci does not rely directly on Victor Hugo's political pamphlet (to which he likely had no access). He mentions the fictionalised version of the events published by Hugo in 1877 and best-known also in Italy (*Histoire d'un crime. Déposition d'un témoin*). The pamphlet written by Hugo in 1852 did not experience the great fortune and the editorial diffusion of the book he published more than twenty years later. On this point, see e.g. Giocanti 2009.

70 Gramsci had already read *The Eighteenth Brumaire* at that stage and without doubt he knew Marx's 1869 introduction. In this text Marx, albeit implicitly, introduces the small/great opposition of which Gramsci also speaks ('[Hugo] does not notice that he makes this individual great instead of little by ascribing to him a personal power of initiative such as would be without parallel in world history' – MECW, vol. 21, p. 57).

In general, it is noteworthy that Gramsci compares Mussolini directly to Louis Napoleon, showing an additional element of closeness to *The Eighteenth Brumaire*. The fusion of two different Marx-inspired characterisations of the figure of Mussolini, in his incisive brevity, says quite a lot about Gramsci's analysis of Fascism in his pre-prison writings and also about the growing importance of 'ideologies' for his thought.

CHAPTER 4

Crisis and Balance: Between Revolution and Restoration

1 Gramsci's Political Theory: Crisis and Balance

In the previous chapter I analysed the occurrences of the terms Bonapartism and Caesarism that can be found in Gramsci's pre-prison writings. It would be a mistake, however, to limit the influence of these categories to their explicit and often polemical references. Gramsci's reappraisal of the Caesarist-Bonapartist model is in a significant part mediated by the adoption of formulas and reasonings that belong only indirectly to *The Eighteenth Brumaire*. These formulas are the result of the reception and of the (mis)interpretation of the Marxian historical works as a whole, already in Marx's and Engels's time, but especially in later Marxism. There is in fact no doubt that the most successful development of Marx's thought on Caesarism and Bonapartism is represented by the 'balance of class forces' (or, in German, *Gleichgewicht der Klassenkräfte*). As previously noted, this formula was first suggested by Engels in the 1850s and was very popular among intellectuals in the nineteenth and the early twentieth centuries. It was used to describe situations of social and political uncertainty, when the hegemony of one group is thrown into crisis but a new leadership is not yet established. In this interregnum, an intervention from above can act as a means of momentary neutralisation of the contrast between the two opposing blocs, as well as a temporary solution to preserve the existing order.[1]

Gramsci also adopts the balance model in his pre-prison writings to draw attention to the complex social dynamics embedded in structural political changes. The formula evolves along with Gramsci's thought, becoming increasingly sophisticated and original, and providing a fruitful key to the interpretation of the rise of Fascism in Italy, as well as the failure of the socialist movement, in the 1920s.

If we consider Gramsci's journalistic output, however, it is evident that this application is the result of the reinterpretation of a previous interpretative cat-

---

[1] For more discussion on the categories of balance and equilibrium, also in relation to Gramsci's thought, see McNally 2008.

egory, that of the 'catastrophic crisis of capitalism', clearly related to Gramsci's adhesion to the doctrine of the Communist International. Independently of its connection with the theory of balance of class forces, however, the model of the catastrophic crisis plays a significant (and still neglected) role in Gramsci's thought, and deserves to be investigated in greater detail.

Thus, in the following pages I will concentrate first on the formula of the crisis of the capitalist system, focusing on its rise and fall (as well as on its 'legacy') in the pre-prison writings. Then, I will dwell on Gramsci's use of the balance model, by showing the different stages of its development and its role within his analysis, in particular with regard to his interpretation of the fascist movement. Finally, I will deal with Gramsci's political thought: I will highlight his debt to Hegel's *Philosophy of Right* [*Grundlinien der Philosophie des Rechts*] and Marx's historical works, especially *The Eighteenth Brumaire*. On this basis, I will take stock of his use of the categories of Caesarism and Bonapartism and put forward some ideas about the relation between Gramsci and historical materialism.

2 The Catastrophic Crisis of Capitalism

2.1 *Gramsci and the Third International*

The theme of the catastrophic crisis of the capitalist system recurs in Gramsci's writings from 1919 onwards. Indeed, Gramsci's adoption of this formula is related closely to his increasing interest in Russian affairs and to his approach to the positions of the Third International, which had been founded in March that year.[2]

Prior to 1919 Gramsci makes a generic use of the terms 'catastrophe' and 'catastrophic', applying them mostly to the Great War.[3] As regards his political

---

2 On the Russian Revolution and the Third International, see, among others, Rees and Thorpe 1998, LaPorte, Morgan and Worley 2008, Agosti 2009, Pons 2014; see also Pons 2017. On the connection between the catastrophic crisis of capitalism and the socialist revolution, see e.g. Telò 1978.

3 Notable exceptions are two articles, written in 1917 and 1918, respectively. The first is the famous piece entitled 'The Revolution Against "Capital"' ['La Rivoluzione contro il *Capitale*'] (*Avanti!*, 24 December 1917; CF, pp. 513–17; SPW-1, pp. 34–7), while the latter is 'Wilson and the Socialists' ['Wilson e i socialisti'] (*La voce del popolo*, 31 October 1918; NM, pp. 313–17) – on these articles, see Rapone 2011b, pp. 270–2 and 247–57. However, with regard to their content, both texts represent exceptions in a certain sense within Gramsci's early output. Despite that, the formula of the capitalist crisis is used here in a somewhat vague sense. While in the 1917 article he speaks in a generic way of the 'catastrophe of the capitalist world' (SPW-1, p. 36),

vision, up to the end of 1918 Gramsci is concerned mostly with the bourgeois parliamentary system and its ever-increasing difficulties, while the proletariat occupies a relatively marginal position in his thought (he deals especially with the political and cultural preparation of socialism).[4] As Rapone has pointed out, it is only from the beginning of the following year that the category of revolution becomes an issue of great topical interest for Gramsci.[5]

If 1919 in Italy there begin the so-called 'Two Red Years', the creation of the Comintern and the revolutionary experiences in Hungary and Bavaria also play a fundamental role in establishing the formula of the catastrophe of the capitalist system.[6] From this moment on, the formula of the capitalist crisis will be pivotal in Gramsci's thinking.[7]

The first recorded occurrence in this sense is a long piece written in February 1919 and published in Piero Gobetti's journal *Energie Nove* under the title *State and Sovereignty* [*Stato e sovranità*]. The piece was written before the formal opening of the first congress of the Third International (Moscow, 2–6 March 1919). However, this is not surprising. Already in Russia on 24 January, a message was being spread that announced the foundation of the Communist International, and in which the thesis of the imminent collapse of capitalism was to be summarised. The text of the message (an invitation for political movements to join this new political platform) was immediately broadcast by radio in a number of European countries. It is therefore very likely that it could have been heard by Gramsci.[8]

Here Gramsci writes:

> The concrete problem today, after that war (destroying and sterilising the sources of wealth) has made men frenzied at the prospect of half humanity being condemned to die of exhaustion, because of the physiological impossibility that the individualistic free-trade regime would restore

---

in 1918 he hints at the 'dialectical and historical catastrophe of the regime' (NM, p. 317). In both cases he applies 'unusual' adjectives to the catastrophe, as compared with the predominantly economistic interpretation of the term of the 1920s.

4 See Rapone 2011b, pp. 387 and 391.
5 Rapone 2011b, pp. 393–4.
6 For a survey of the transformation going on in Europe after the Russian Revolution, see Newman 2017.
7 Gramsci's 'youth orthodoxy' was only partially recognised by critics, who (with few exceptions: Buci-Glucksmann 1980, pp. 137 ff.; Rapone 2011b, p. 392) did not highlight the connection between the affirmation of the capitalist crisis and that of the actuality of the revolution that characterises Gramsci's early writings. Along these lines, see for instance Michelini 2011.
8 On this point, see also Rapone 2011b, p. 392.

rubble and give new opportunities of life – the concrete problem today, in a full social disaster, when everything has been dissolved and every authoritarian hierarchy is irretrievably discarded – is to help the working class to seize political power, is to study and look for the right means to make the translation of the power of the state possible with minimal blood flow, to realise widely the new communist state after a short period of revolutionary terror.[9]

2.2   *A Decay and a Genesis*

In a highly significant article, published a few weeks later, in the first issue of *L'Ordine Nuovo*, Gramsci refers to that 'dark and catastrophic phase to which all capitalist aggregates are heading'.[10] The piece, which begins the column *International political life* [*Vita politica internazionale*], has an explicit programmatic character, that stands out from its two-part structure. While in the first part Gramsci outlines the general coordinates of his reflections, in the second he starts his concrete historico-political investigation, taking his cue from an 'exemplary country' such as (in his opinion) Spain.

The initial section of the article entitled *A Decay and a Genesis* [*Uno sfacelo ed una genesi*] is then of particular significance. Here Gramsci investigates the crisis of the contemporary capitalist system, expressing economic considerations with a strong 'moral' slant.[11] His thesis is clear and can be summarised as follows. The capitalist economy, at its imperialist stage, is succumbing to its weaknesses and structural contradictions, while the bourgeois society formed

---

9   'State and Sovereignty', *Energie Nove*, 1–28 February 1919 (NM, p. 522). The call of the Third International is here understood by Gramsci as the condemnation of a bad form of socialism. This emerges from the polemical nature of the article, whose primary purpose is to fight against the theses of Balbino Giuliano (1879–1958, nationalist and former socialist) expounded in the essay 'Why I am a man of order' ['Perché sono uomo d'ordine']; this essay was published in *Energie Nove* between the end of 1918 and the beginning of 1919. On this piece, see also Paggi 1970, p. 232.

10   'A Decay and a Genesis', *L'Ordine Nuovo*, 1 May 1919 (ON, p. 7). The second part of the article, on Spain ('An Exemplary Country: Spain' ['Un paese esemplare: la Spagna']), was heavily censored in *L'Ordine Nuovo* and then republished in the socialist newspaper *Avanti!* under the title 'Spain' ['Spagna'] (on the troubled publication history of this piece, see ON, p. 10, n. 1).

11   In my opinion, the moral crisis depicted here anticipates meaningfully the account of the atmosphere of 'romanticism' that characterises Italian Fascism, as shown previously (see Chapter 3, section 2). As for the importance of the moral dimension for Gramsci, we should recall the interpretation of Socialism as 'intellectual and moral reform' put forward by Gramsci, as well as his concrete initiatives in this sense (see Paggi 1970, pp. 86–95 and 104–10; Rapone 2011b, pp. 110–29; on Gramsci's 'club of moral life', see also Rapone 2011b, pp. 79–80).

with it has exhausted all its 'historical possibilities' and it is progressively disintegrating, overwhelmed by 'disorder' and 'moral barbarism'. The only alternative to the catastrophe of the capitalist world is represented by the 'international class of workers and peasants' who will create a 'new international order' from the ruins of the old world, i.e. a renewed society and economy, inspired by the principles of communism.[12] In conclusion, he states:

> We will record and study in this chronicle the revealing phenomena of the double historical process through which society decomposes and renews itself, dies and rises from its unhonoured ashes: the decomposition of the liberal states, which, to defend themselves, commit suicide by denying the principle of liberty from which they were born and for which they had developed and the slow and tenacious effort that the most conscious and historically efficient nuclei of the world's proletariat perform to give themselves order (within the Moscow Communist International), to recreate the fabric of society, to stimulate a wider and more comprehensive moral unity in the world, to realise the Marxist theses of communism through the establishment of a federal republic (of the workers' and peasants' councils of the five continents).[13]

From a theoretical point of view, this article is particularly important for three aspects: the connection between the catastrophic crisis of capitalism and the advent of socialism (the 'double historical process'); the link between the theme of the socialist revolution and that of the council strategy; the reference to the doctrine of the Third International.

---

12 'A Decay and a Genesis', cit. (ON, pp. 3–6). The imagery used by Gramsci to express the necessity of the decay of the capitalistic-bourgeois world (and, on the other side, the new scenario of the proletarian revolution) is meaningful. See for instance: 'this phenomenon [the emergence of the contradictions of capitalism] is paramount in the process of historical development of civilisation; it marks the pillars of Hercules of the historical possibilities of the capitalist class, which has exhausted its task (and must disappear)'; 'the picture of international life, as it has been defined in recent months, gives the impression of a scary storm in a ruinous landscape'; 'metropolitan liberal states disintegrate from inside, at the same time that the system of colonies and spheres of influence crumble; this process of decomposition follows the rhythm of a lightning speed, which threatens human companionship in its deepest vital roots: hunger and epidemics have spread a burial on the lineage of men'; 'History is perpetual; evil cannot prevail, disorder and barbarism cannot prevail, abyss will not swallow men'; 'a society, the capitalist one, disintegrates, a revolution, the communist one, arrives at forced marches. The dead seek to infect the living, but the triumph of life is now safe and certain as destiny' (ON, pp. 3–6 *et passim*).

13 'A Decay and a Genesis', cit. (ON, p. 6).

The historical dialectic of crisis and rebirth is significant in the approach adopted by Gramsci (it also anticipates in some ways the relationship between the 'old' and the 'new' analysed in the *Notebooks*, on the basis of Marx's famous 1859 *Preface*). Furthermore, far from asserting dogmatically and deterministically the coming of socialism, he is rather looking for elements that will make the socialist strategy successful.

From this moment on, the Third International will indeed be a regular reference point in Gramsci's writings. He sees in the organisation of Communist parties on an international level an essential element of the rising movement of the world revolution – the call for a 'federal Republic' is eloquent from this point of view. Nevertheless, despite his full and genuine agreement with the doctrinal platform of the Third International, Gramsci's reflection maintains its specificity. This emerges, in particular, from the repeated emphasis on the importance of the alliance between workers and peasants and on the centrality of the council strategy he had elaborated in previous months.[14]

2.3 Revolution and Crisis of the Bourgeois-Capitalist World

The same strategic proposals also return in Gramsci's articles from the second half of 1919. These represent the most important evidence of Gramsci's proximity to the theses of the Communist International. These articles can be divided into two groups, one comprising the pieces written from August to October 1919, the other including the texts from November.

In the first group we can count four articles: *Workers and Peasants* [*Operai e contadini*], *Centrist Tendency* [*La tendenza centrista*], *Chronicles of L'Ordine Nuovo* [*Cronache dell'Ordine Nuovo*] [IX] and *The Development of the Revolution* [*Lo sviluppo della rivoluzione*].[15] In these texts, with the exception of the

---

14 On Gramsci's council theory, see in particular Spriano 1971 and 1975, Williams 1975 and Schecter 1991.

15 'Workers and Peasants', *Avanti!*, 2 August 1919 (ON, pp. 156–61; SPW-1, pp. 83–7); 'Centrist tendency', under the column 'The Week in Politics' [V], *L'Ordine Nuovo*, 2 August 1919 (ON, pp. 162–5); 'Chronicles of *L'Ordine Nuovo*' [IX], cit. (ON, pp. 166–7; this text does not have a specific title, but only the title of the column); 'The Development of the Revolution', *L'Ordine Nuovo*, 13 September 1919 (ON, pp. 203–7; SPW-1, pp. 89–93). The first two articles were published on the very same day (2 August 1919). This did not happen by chance. At the end of July (between 20 and 21 July), a general strike took place (the so-called *scioperissimo*). This strike (which was a significant success) was read by Gramsci as the beginning of a 'period of profound changes in the current economic structure', or as the beginning of the 'post-war crisis'. See '20–21 July' ['20–21 Luglio'], under the column 'The Week in Politics' [IV], *L'Ordine Nuovo*, 19 July 1919; ON, p. 147: 'The general strike of 20–21 will be eminently revolutionary. Not because it will be able to overthrow the capitalist state (we have shown that the conquest of the state by the proletarians will only happen when workers

third article, which contains a peculiar 'moral' occurrence of the catastrophe formula,[16] Gramsci reaffirms his communist doctrine. This means intertwining his affirmation of the need for an alliance between peasants and workers with arguments for the intransigent position within the Italian Socialist Party and with arguments against the opportunism of the reformists. Gramsci's attention in this period is in fact focused on the Party congress that was held in October in Bologna, which saw the revolutionary faction prevailing and the Italian party becoming a member of the Comintern.[17]

> Historical conditions in Italy were not and are not very different from those in Russia. The problem of the class unification of the workers and peasants is expressed in identical terms: it will be achieved through the practice of the socialist State and will be based on the new psychology created by communal life in the trenches ... Factory workers and poor peasants are the two driving forces of the proletarian revolution ... Any revolutionary work has a chance of succeeding only to the degree that it is based on the necessities of their life and on the needs of their culture. It is essential that the 'leaders' of the socialist and proletarian move-

---

and peasants have established a system of state institutions capable of replacing the institutions of the democratic parliamentary state), but because it will begin a period of profound changes in the current economic structure. The post-war crisis will begin in 20–21'.

16   See 'Chronicles of *L'Ordine Nuovo*' [IX], cit. (ON, p. 167): 'One is detached from the past, does not adhere to the present, there is no vital momentum for the future. It is an episode of the moral catastrophe coordinated to the economic catastrophe of the capitalist system. But even of it, like the economic catastrophe, communism can be the only solution'.

17   See 'The Development of the Revolution', cit. (SPW-1, pp. 89–90): 'The basic theses of the Communist International can be summarized as follows. 1. The 1914–18 World War represents the coming to pass on a tremendous scale of that moment in the process of development of modern history which Marx summed up in the expression: the catastrophe of the capitalist world ... what adhering to the Communist International means in practical terms this: it means being convinced of the urgent need to organize the dictatorship of the proletariat, i.e. to equip the proletarian movement with the appropriate structures and procedures for the proletarian political system to become a normal and necessary phase of the class struggle waged by the worker and peasant masses ... These fundamental innovations need to be inserted into the 1892 Programme [of the PSI adopted in Genoa] as a result of the concrete experiences of the workers of Russia, Hungary, Austria and Germany in their revolutionary activities. They may be assumed to be a necessary, intrinsic aspect of the industrial development of world capitalist production, for they have been carried out by English and American workers, quite independently from the consequences of general political circumstances (military defeat, etc.), as a normal reflection of the class struggle in the most intensely capitalist countries'. On Gramsci's 'propaganda' for joining the Third International, see in particular 'For the Communist International' ['Per l'Internazionale Comunista'], *L'Ordine Nuovo*, 26 July 1919 (ON, pp. 150–3; SPW-1, pp. 79–82).

ment understand this. And it is essential that they see the urgency of the problem of giving this irrepressible revolutionary force the structure best adapted to its diffuse mentality. In the backward conditions of the pre-war capitalist economy, there was no scope for the emergence and development of mass peasant organizations on a wide scale, in which the agricultural workers could acquire an organic conception of class struggle as well as the discipline needed to reconstruct the state after the capitalist catastrophe.[18]

To this bourgeois propaganda in the vein of social democracy and to the tools of the bourgeoisie, the communists must oppose their own thesis: the catastrophic crisis in which European civilisation was struggling can only be stopped by the radical replacement of the democratic-parliamentary state by a system of councils of workers and peasants; by the dictatorship of the proletariat that gives to the producers the power of the factories and the fields to make the most of with communist methods. Only in this way can work discipline be restored, and the disintegrating process of civilisation towards the most horrendous forms of moral barbarism be stopped. Capitalism cannot but obey the immanent laws in its methods of production and trade: freedom of trade, competition between capitalists in the national and international spheres will lead to new destruction, new unemployment, new corruption, new economic and moral disorder, famine and massacres. Collaboration on the social-democratic or state-socialist basis is not different from the forms of the most vulgar reformist collaboration: the class is reduced to a mere political party, and the class struggle to a form of competition between parliamentary leaders.[19]

2.4 The Elections of November 1919

Gramsci's renewed interest in the Third International and in the connection between capitalist crisis and socialist revolution dates back to autumn 1919, before and after the political elections of 16 November, in which the socialists gained a significant victory.[20] Most of the occurrences deal indeed with this

---

18 'Workers and Peasants' [1919], cit. (SPW-1, pp. 85–6, translation slightly modified).
19 'Centrist Tendency', cit. (ON, pp. 163–4).
20 See the articles 'Italy and the United States' ['Italia e Stati Uniti'] under the column 'The Week in Politics' [XI], *L'Ordine Nuovo*, 8 November 1919 (ON, pp. 302–5); 'The Bourgeois Defeat' ['La disfatta borghese'], *Avanti!*, 19 November 1919 (ON, pp. 323–4); 'Out of the Dilemma' ['Fuori dal dilemma'], *Avanti!*, 29 November 1919 (ON, pp. 335–7; PPW, pp. 132–

particular political juncture.[21] Gramsci's attention is still devoted to the catastrophe of the world capitalist system but, at the same time, is now turned especially to the analysis of the revolution that will have to follow this crisis. Gramsci is dealing with the issue of the realisation of the socialist revolution, i.e. the 'power issue' (the titles of articles of this period are indeed extremely eloquent).[22]

The articles of November 1919 contain a recognition of the symptoms of the global economic catastrophe. This recognition takes its cue from a careful analysis of the Italian economic situation, in which the role played by the events of the war is highlighted as a catalyst.[23] This is connected with the reflection on how, given the positive electoral outcome, the Socialist Party can and must achieve its purpose concretely. In other words, Gramsci is investigating how the economic, political and social system can be reorganised in such a way as to put peasants and workers at its centre, according to an ideal structure that has its

---

5), 'The Problem of Power' ['Il problema del potere'], *L'Ordine Nuovo*, 29 November 1919 (ON, pp. 338–43; SPW-1, pp. 130–4).

[21] The only exception is 'Italy and the United States', cit., where Gramsci writes: 'Taken in the grip of the capitalist world system, American owners are also sliding into the abyss, American productivity is already heading towards catastrophe: the capitalist production and distribution order has become incapable of meeting the corporate needs of the mass of the workers and these masses rise up, these masses stop the production process, that is, they make it impossible for the American economy to help the European economy, make it unable to avoid the failure of the European economy and, thus, they accelerate the fall of American productivity, accelerate the fall of the American capitalist economy towards the abyss, towards catastrophe' ('Italy and the United States', cit.; ON, p. 303).

[22] See 'The Problem of Power', cit., 'The Results we are Waiting for', cit., 'The Bourgeois Defeat', cit., etc. It should be noted, however, that there is a shift between Gramsci's statements and the attitude of the Comintern in that historical context. After the failure of the European experiences of council democracy, 'among a section of the leaders of the Third International (and especially Lenin and Trotsky) an awareness began to take shape more or less clearly that the revolutionary process in Europe would develop more slowly and less directly than they had hoped for' (Agosti 2009, p. 56). At the same time, Gramsci seemed very optimistic about a revolutionary outcome in Italy. See 'The Bourgeois Defeat', cit. (ON, p. 324): 'The Italy of Revolution was born. The ranking of the parties demonstrated by the ballot boxes marks the different phases of the revolutionary maturity of the Italian people ... The revolutionary process is the process of the cleansing and purifying of the great masses of the people who are increasingly convinced that the salvation of human life and dignity, the restoration of order, the energetic halt of dissolution and economic and moral disaster can only be achieved through a stringent discipline imposed on the parasitic and politicised classes by workers and peasants organised in their state, in the state where those who do not work do not eat'.

[23] See in particular on this point 'The Problem of Power', cit. On the role of war, cf. Natoli 2008, pp. 51–76, Rapone 2011b, pp. 189 ff. and Thomas 2015c.

basis in the councils and its head in the Party ('revolution' is therefore synonymous with the 'establishment of the council democracy').[24] See for example, the following passage, taken from the article published on 29 November in *L'Ordine Nuovo*:

> To advance along the road of revolution to the point of expropriation of the expropriators and the foundation of a communist State is in the immediate interests of the two most numerous orders of the class of Italian producers ... The vanguard workers and peasants have realised that all these things are necessities inherent in the current economic situation, the catastrophic tension between the forces and organisms of production. And they have done all that they could do in a democratic society, a society that is politically defined: they have pointed to the Socialist Party, which represents the ideas and programmes to be accomplished, as their natural political leader; and they have pointed out to the Party the road to power, the road to government – based constitutionally not on a Parliament elected by a universal suffrage encompassing both exploited and exploiters, but on a system of workers' and peasants' Councils embodying the rule of industrial as well as of political power: bodies which, in other words, are instruments for the expulsion of the capitalists from the process of production, and instruments for the suppression of the bourgeoisie, as dominant class, from all the nation's institutions of control and economic centralisation. Thus the immediate, concrete problem confronting the Socialist Party is the problem of power; the problem of how to organise the whole mass of Italian workers into a hierarchy that reaches its apex in the Party; the problem of constructing a state apparatus which internally will function democratically, i.e. will guarantee freedom to all anti-capitalist tendencies and offer them the possibility of forming a proletarian government, and externally will operate as an implacable machine crushing the organs of capitalist industrial and political power.[25]

From Gramsci's perspective, the alternative is not between parliamentarism and revolution (an alternative that he rejects as a false 'dilemma'), but between the 'life' and the 'death' of the Italian people, which fully justifies his 'catastrophic attitude'.[26]

---

24   See Paggi 1970, pp. 281–3.
25   'The Problem of Power', cit. (ON, pp. 341–2; SPW-1, pp. 132–3).
26   'Out of the Dilemma', cit. (ON, p. 337; PPW, p. 134, translation slightly modified).

> The reality of Italy today consists of a movement of subterranean, uncontrollable forces, which have not yet begun to figure – and, at this point, never will – within the traditional political parties' picture of the situation. To reduce the problem of Italian life to the powerplay of party politics, to believe, or pretend to believe, that the Italian people can escape from the terrible vice-like grip of history with some act of parliamentary politics, is already, at the present moment, mere charlatanism and tomorrow it could become a tragic farce – the Italian people's last, definitive collapse into economic catastrophe, with a foreign heel grinding into the neck of Italian workers and peasants, who will be dropping dead at the machine or the furrow, after 12–14 hours of hard labour, all for a crust of bread thrown at them by a Senegalese or Papuan master.[27]

It is interesting to note that, arguing against the 'Marxist philologist' of *La Stampa*, Gramsci operates a peculiar combination of economic analysis and anti-determinism, demonstrating that his prediction of the crisis of capitalism does not imply at all a 'fatalistic' attitude. Socialist revolution has been always conceived by Gramsci as the result of a process of organisation both of the proletarian masses and of the party that leads them. Discipline is a key concept in this sense.[28] See the following quotation in this regard:

> The Italian state no longer functions as a political entity, because the apparatus of industrial and agricultural production which is the substance of the political state no longer functions … The Italian economic apparatus has become a purely fiscal phenomenon, which is to say that it has reached that phase of decomposition and collapse which could have been predicted as the dialectical phase that was to follow – logically and chronologically – the phase of maximum industrial development. The pedantic Marxist kicks out against this fearsome reality. It strikes him as … anti-historical; he feels that before reaching the proletarian revolution it

---

[27] 'Out of the Dilemma', cit. (ON, p. 337; PPW, p. 132). In this text we can also detect a hint towards Gramsci's category of parliamentary cretinism, embedded in the controversy against 'charlatanism' and 'tragic farce' (it is no accident that the formula occurs for the first time in an article by Gramsci published on the same day and in the same newspaper). I would argue that besides a sincere ideological conviction, Gramsci was also prompted by tactical considerations to reject parliamentarism so clearly. In particular, echoes of Amadeo Bordiga's thought can be traced here; as a matter of fact, the very same formula of the catastrophe of the capitalist system is clearly derived from Bordiga. On this issue, see also Paggi 1970, pp. 335 and 416 ff.

[28] On this point, see McNally 2008.

is necessary for the course of historical development to solder the earlier links in the chain of progress ... But real history has no use for intellectual schemes or hypotheses about how events are going to unfold, other than as hypotheses, indications which may serve to steer our practical action in what may prove the right direction. And revolutionaries adhere to real history, not the play of party politics: to the dialectic of real economic forces, not to the pious hopes and trepidations of self-important asses.[29]

After the elections, however, Gramsci soon became aware of the inability of the socialists to capitalise on the recent success and to put forward a solution to the economic and moral crisis of the bourgeois world. Between the end of 1919 and the beginning of 1920, he remained faithful to the interpretative model based on the dual concept of crisis and revolution; nevertheless, he harshly condemned the tactical errors of the PSI and denounced the extrinsic and formal character of its participation in the Communist International.

At this stage he wrote two articles in which there is a reference to the catastrophic crisis of capitalism: *The Skilled Revolutionary* [*Il rivoluzionario qualificato*] (20 December 1919) and *Power in Italy* [*Il potere in Italia*] (11 February 1920). In the first article he refers to a letter sent by Lenin (1870–1924) to Serrati at the end of October and published in *Avanti!* in early December 1919. Relying on that, Gramsci attacks the maximalist faction of the Socialist Party, accused of opposing to the catastrophe 'another worse catastrophe'.[30] In the second piece, by taking up his previous historical-economic analysis, he describes Italy's industrial and financial crisis, and urges the proletariat to take control of the situation, although in quite generic terms.[31]

---

29 'Out of the Dilemma', cit. (ON, p. 337; PPW, pp. 132–3).
30 See 'The Skilled Revolutionary', *L'Ordine Nuovo*, 20 December 1919 (ON, pp. 363–4). On Lenin's letter, see ON, p. 364, n. 1. Lenin also coined the expression that Gramsci uses as the title for his article. See the following quotation: 'Italian Communists have worked little to become "skilled revolutionaries". They move among the gigantic gears of history as a country-person who visits a large workshop and that ventures – arrogant and with trepidation – into the uproar and movement of large machines. Lenin's letter demonstrates a situation of little joy and reassurance: we were shaky between the catastrophe and ... the Constituent, that means, between a catastrophe and another worse catastrophe, since one cannot imagine in Italy the necessary resistance to enter an indefinite and dark period of crisis and despair' (ON, p. 364).
31 See 'Power in Italy', *Avanti!*, 11 February 1920 (ON, p. 412): 'Capitalists are powerless to stem the corrosive action of poisons developed within the social body; destructions follow each other, ruins accumulate on ruins, civilisation's values threaten to be irremediably over-

After the article of 20 February 1920, Gramsci will not use the formula of the catastrophe of the capitalist system for over a year. He would describe the present situation rather as the 'imperialist phase of world capitalism' – this expression is in fact more 'nuanced' and does not unavoidably imply an impending overthrowing of capitalism.[32] Very likely, this is connected also to the fact that the workers' movement, after the repression of factory occupations in September 1920, had lost most of its strength.[33]

2.5   A Short Revival

A temporary but important reappraisal of the category of 'catastrophe' occurs only in the first half of 1921, when, after the foundation of the PCd'I, Gramsci returns to a more 'optimistic' position. Nonetheless, that optimism does not imply a blind faith in the necessary advent of socialism. It never did: and the association with Romain Rolland's motto adopted by Gramsci ('pessimism of the intellect, optimism of the will') is clear in this sense.[34] The reasons that urged his reappraisal of this formula are connected to the necessities of the newly founded Italian Communist Party, i.e. the necessity, for communists, to distinguish themselves unambiguously from socialists and to make clear their revolutionary programme.

Between May and June 1921, Gramsci uses the term 'catastrophe' twice. The first occurrence is contained in an article that comments on the results of the recent elections (15 May). Here Gramsci, arguing against the attitude held in this context by the socialists and by the journalists of the socialist newspaper *Avanti!*, writes:

---

whelmed. Only the working class, taking state power in its hands, can renew it ... The working class, which abhors patriotic phraseology, which abhors the phraseology of the rescuers of industry and production, is in fact the only one that tends to "save the country" and to avoid industrial catastrophe'.

32   On capitalism and imperialism, with specific reference to Lenin's model, see McDonough 1995.

33   The occupation of the factories was one of the main features of the period of intense social and political conflict called 'Red Biennium'. The strikes started in Turin, in the FIAT factories and became more and more frequent from March onwards; they reached their peak during the late summer of 1920, when the workers occupied the factories as a form of protest against the union of industrialists. In September, however, the Giolitti government resolved the crisis peacefully and the parliamentary elections of May 1921 were a clear demonstration of the defeat of the workers' movement (just as the elections of the November 1919 had hinted in the opposite direction).

34   'Speech to the Anarchists' ['Discorso agli anarchici'], *L'Ordine Nuovo*, 3–10 April 1920 (ON, pp. 396–401; SPW-1, pp. 185–9).

> Elections have revealed ... that a part of Italy's workers and peasants is 'tired of the political struggle'. This is true especially for that part who, for months and months, indeed for years, fought as the vanguard of the revolutionary army of Italy, a phalanx that had chosen for itself the hardest task, to put into effect the first daring experiences, to make the first assaults, to undergo the first and most raging counteroffensive of the enemy. Today, these workers are tired. But what are they tired of? Is their tiredness an element that can bring them back to the party ranks [of the Socialist Party] that they have left with open eyes, full of awareness, not beguiled with any vain catastrophic preaching, or with any sentence that does not respond to the thought of the person who said it, but with the only purpose of forming a disciplined, orderly minority, conscious of the needs of its class, of the means to satisfy them, of the way to follow in order to keep its ideals intact and to prepare for their realisation?[35]

The second occurrence is more explicit. In a piece published at the end of June 1921, Gramsci establishes a distinction between 'crisis' and 'catastrophe', in order to make clear his distance from socialist reformists. Moreover, he also reaffirms his reliance on the revolutionary predictions of the Comintern, by showing how even liberal economics confirm them.[36]

> Communists believe that the current crisis is a catastrophe rather than a crisis. Communists are confirmed in their opinion not only by the criticism of the capitalist economy made by the Communist International but also by the opinion of liberal economists. Liberals have always denied the possibility of an economic crisis that hit all industries and countries at the same time: this crisis has in fact happened, it is underway; it can no longer be defined as a phenomenon limited in time and space, which could be expected according to the normal calculations; we can only speak of a catastrophe, of an exceptional phenomenon, solvable only by exceptional means, [we can only speak] of a phenomenon of complete disintegration of the bourgeois economic system, which can be circumscribed and overcome only through the conquest of the state, with the imposition of the proletarian dictatorship.[37]

---

35 '"Come with me"' ['"Vieni meco"'], *L'Ordine Nuovo*, 21 May 1921 (PV, pp. 151–2).
36 On the link established by Gramsci between liberal doctrine and socialism, see Rapone 2011b, pp. 156–70, 236–57 and 314 ff., Michelini 2011 and Losurdo 1997.
37 'A line of action ...' ['Una linea d'azione ...'], *L'Ordine Nuovo*, 30 June 1921 (SF, p. 216). On the distinction between crisis and catastrophe, see also 'Opportunism of the Trade Union

Gramsci saw in the emergence of various forms of reaction (from the burning of the head office of *Avanti!* in Milan in 1919 to the increasing violence of the *squadristi*), the last, desperate attempt of the bourgeoisie to maintain its power and he interpreted it as the moment for proletarian forces to intervene.[38] These two occurrences of the double concept of capitalist crisis and proletarian revolution were nevertheless the last. In the following years there is no longer such a usage of the term 'catastrophe' in Gramsci's works.[39]

The new political context undoubtedly played a role in this 'retirement' of the model of the catastrophic crisis of capitalism, and in particular the Comintern's radical change of strategy. As is well known, in March 1921 the thesis of the imminence of the revolution was replaced by the theory of the united front, which implies a reconsideration both of the economic analysis of the current situation and of the strategy of the workers' movement.[40]

This change of paradigm emerges clearly from one of Gramsci's articles published in 1925. In this text he analyses the behaviour of the maximalist faction in the political context following the assassination of Matteotti (June 1924). Here he writes:

Confederation' ['L'opportunismo confederale'], *L'Ordine Nuovo*, 10 July 1921 (SF, pp. 232–4): 'Will the current "crisis" end up in the death or renewal of capitalism? Is it a crisis or a catastrophe for the bourgeois system?'

38 'Squadrismo' is the organisation of violent activities aimed at repressing and intimidating political opponents undertaken by small groups of non-regular armies (squads). In particular, it describes the social-political phenomenon that took place in Italy since 1919 and that is strictly connected to the rising Fascism. On this topic, see Payne 1995 and Elazar 2001.

39 In this context the focus is rather on the transformation of the capitalist system. On this point, see 'Petty bourgeois Maximalism' ['Massimalismo piccolo-borghese'], *L'Unità*, 17 June 1925 (CPC, p. 374): 'Poor us! Why! Since last century bourgeois economists have reported, studied and investigated the economic-political features of imperialism; in 1910 the Austrian Marxist Rudolph Hilferding published a *Theoretical Study on the Most Recent Evolution of Capitalism* [sic]; the Basel Congress of 1912 of the Second International dealt with the topic; all the international literature confirms the "new phase" into which capitalism entered some time ago; Jack London, in the novel *The Iron Heel*, offers a fascinating aesthetic incarnation of the theme; in 1917 Lenin published his invaluable and definitive little volume, *Imperialism, the Highest Stage of Capitalism*, and Massimo Fovel ignores all this and dreams of returning to individualism and calls for the end of monopolies and industrial trusts'.

40 On the theory of the united front, see especially Del Roio 2015 and McNally 2015. The reason why Gramsci still uses the formula of the catastrophic crisis in May and June – after the Comintern's decision of March 1921 – can be explained, in my opinion, on the basis of the specific Italian context (as is known, the PCd'I was founded in January).

> *Avanti!* does not want to understand that the relationship of forces was disastrous because the so-called workers' parties, reformist and maximalist, had subordinated the majority of the proletariat to the bourgeois programme of constitutional opposition. If a man has his hands tied, his forces are in an unfavourable relationship with those of any brigand who wants to rob him; but would not it be the ultimate in criminal recklessness if the one who observes the 'relationship of catastrophic forces' has his hands tied up and keeps them tied together?[41]

In this framework, the adjective 'catastrophic' no longer describes the crisis of the capitalist system. It refers instead to the relationship between classes (relying on the Caesarist-Bonapartist paradigm). Furthermore, it has an explicitly polemical meaning, as becomes clear from the reference to the hands of socialists being tied while waiting for the advent of the proletarian revolution: the 'catastrophic' feature belongs to an excessively rigid model of interpretation, and therefore reveals a failing political strategy.

3   The Balance Metaphor: The Origins of the 'Relations of Force'

3.1   A 'Catastrophic' Balance

As emerged from the previous analysis, the double concept of catastrophic crisis and revolution has a short life within Gramsci's thought. The occurrences are mostly concentrated in 1919 (especially in the Autumn). In the second half of 1921 this interpretative model is already superseded. If this timeframe reflects clearly the evolution of the international workers' movement (from the declaration of the timeliness of the revolution to the strategy of the united front), the use of these formulas is always connected to specific events in Italian politics: the general strike of July 1919; the elections of November; the foundation of the PCd'I at the beginning of 1921. Furthermore, Gramsci never applies this interpretative model in a dogmatic way, not even under the influence of Amadeo Bordiga (1889–1970). According to him, revolution can be only the result of the efforts of the party in bringing socialist ideals to the popular masses and in creating a valid political and social alternative to the bourgeois system.

It is not surprising, therefore, that when Gramsci dismisses the formula of the catastrophic crisis of capitalism he moves towards a more in-depth invest-

---

41   'The Maximalists and the Situation' ['I massimalisti e la situazione'], *L'Unità*, 30 August 1925 (CPC, p. 278).

igation of Italian society and politics, both conceived of as the combination of different instances and forces. In this respect, the reference to 'class balance' is essential. But where does this model come from?

The formula of the balance of class forces can be traced in Gramsci's writings back to 1917. The first explicit occurrence is contained in an article published on 28 July in *Il grido del popolo*. Here Gramsci analyses the relations between the various political groups in the aftermath of Russia's February Revolution. He states that 'Kerensky, Tsereteli, Chernov – these men are the present expression of the revolution, they have brought about an initial social balance, a resultant of forces in which the moderates still have an important part to play'.[42]

A similar perspective can be found in another piece written a few weeks later, even if in much more general terms:

> In normal times there is an equilibrium of forces whose instability only shows up in very small oscillations. The more these oscillations become irregular and capricious, the more people say times are disastrous. When equilibrium tends to shift itself irresistibly, people admit that they have entered a period of new life.[43]

This sort of historical law is of great importance, since it puts in a nutshell the essence of the formula of the balance of class forces, which Gramsci will rework and enrich over the following years. More than a conscious recovery of Marx's model, however, this text (as well as the previous one) reflects the cultural and political background from which Gramsci's thought emerges – the formula of the balance of class forces appears here as a common expression taken over from the political language of the socialist milieu.

So far Gramsci's interest is indeed in the 'liberal' balance and in the way in which the bourgeois-capitalist forces maintain it. Even at the beginning of 1919, Gramsci speaks of a 'balance of forces' in reference to the coexistence between classes within the different national states.[44]

---

42 'Russian Maximalists' ['I massimalisti russi'], *Il grido del popolo*, 28 July 1917 (CF, p. 265; SPW-1, p. 31). Kerensky and Chernov were Social Democrats, whilst Tsereteli was a Menshevik. It should be remembered, however, that at this stage Gramsci had a very limited knowledge of the events taking place in Russia.

43 'The Watchmaker' ['L'orologiaio'], *Il grido del popolo*, 18 August 1917 (CF, p. 281; HPC, pp. 36–7, translation slightly modified).

44 See 'Russia and the World' ['La Russia e il mondo'], *Avanti!*, 27 January 1919 (NM, p. 511). See also 'Italian State' ['Lo Stato italiano'], *L'Ordine Nuovo*, 7 February 1920 (ON, p. 406; PPW, p. 144): 'The Tsarist State was a State of landowners. That explains the boorishness of the ministers of the Tsar: country people call a spade a spade and beat down their enemies

It is only during this year, after the adoption of the thesis of the catastrophic crisis of capitalism, that Gramsci's focus shifts decisively to the moment of imbalance. A clear sign in this regard is his use of the expression 'catastrophic balance of forces', contained in an article analysed above, 'The Problem of Power' (November 1919).[45]

If Gramsci previously saw the imbalance as one of the moments of a 'normal' political dialectic, in the light of post-war Italian politics and of the Third Internationalist theory of the crisis of capitalism, he depicts the imbalance as a struggle to the death between two opposing and antithetical forces, the capitalist bourgeoisie and the proletariat. In other words, in this exceptional historical junction, the ability of the bourgeoisie to absorb other forces into its hegemonic project is over; compromise and confrontation are no longer viable options and one of the forces must necessarily win over the other.

Thus, the economism embedded in the adjective 'catastrophic' has given to the original sociological model of the balance an extremely original nuance, one that fits very well with the Italian political context of the early 1920s – both interpretative models (that of the capitalist crisis and that of the balance) are thus strengthened.[46]

If the economic dimension of Gramsci's affirmations is still predominant in this text, as well as in the general framework of his analysis, the affinity between revolutionary crisis and 'organic crisis' (or 'crisis of hegemony') here posited is very significant in the future development of his thought.[47]

3.2 Dictatorship of the Bourgeoisie or Dictatorship of the Proletariat?

Given this catastrophic scenario, however, which force will be successful? Between 1919 and 1920 Gramsci had no doubts: the losing part is identified with the bourgeoisie.[48]

---

with clubs. The revolution of March 1917 was an attempt to introduce a balance between industrialists and landowners into the State. The liberal State is born out of the balance between these two forces of private property'.

45 'The vanguard workers and peasants have realized that all these things are necessities inherent in the current economic situation, the catastrophic tension between the forces and organs of production' ('The Problem of Power', cit., ON, p. 341; SPW-1, p. 131).

46 It is no surprise that Gramsci merges here different interpretative models. Alongside the fact that we are dealing with journalistic pieces, that, written day by day, record all the slight variations of Gramsci's thought, this way of reasoning is very typical of Gramsci. As will emerge more clearly from the *Prison Notebooks*, he studies analytically every concept in all its possibilities and he keeps those elements that can be fruitfully reassessed in other interpretative contexts.

47 On this point, see Buci-Glucksmann 1980, p. 145.

48 See for instance the following occurrences: 'The defeat of Ludendorff is not simply the

It is noteworthy that two opposite alternatives are already sketched by Gramsci in a programmatic text written in May 1920, *Towards a Renewal of the Socialist Party* [*Per un rinnovamento del partito socialista*]. Here Gramsci writes that

> the present phase of the class struggle in Italy is the phase that precedes: either the conquest of political power on the part of the revolutionary proletariat and the transition to new modes of production and distribution that will set the stage for a recovery in productivity – or a tremendous reaction on the part of the propertied classes and governing caste.[49]

As Christine Buci-Glucksmann says, already in 1919–20 it is clear 'that the crisis of the state can give way to a different type of power, and finally to a strengthening of the state'. However, by now, these analyses are 'entirely subordinate to the priority of a situation of revolutionary crisis'.[50]

In 1921, Gramsci's priorities changed. The model of the crisis of the capitalist system was set aside (or was about to be set aside), and Gramsci's attention was now entirely directed towards Italy, to the problems of its political system and to the transformations within its society. In the framework of the irretrievable collapse of the liberal parliamentary State, both options are on the table: that of the dictatorship of the bourgeoisie as well as that of the dictatorship of the proletariat.

The most important manifestation of this change of perspective is represented by the inauguration of a new column in *L'Ordine Nuovo* in Spring 1921, *The Death of the Liberal State* [*La morte dello Stato liberale*]. The task of this new section is to 'follow day by day the chronicles of the attacks launched by

---

defeat of the German military caste: it is one of the most important stages in the development of the German revolution, because it indicates the prevalence of proletarian power over the power of the bourgeois state, because it indicates that in Germany the balance of forces has shifted to the benefit of the working class' ('German Revolution' ['La rivoluzione tedesca'], under the column 'The Week in Politics' [XX], *L'Ordine Nuovo*, 20 March 1920, ON, p. 469). 'The trade union … consists in an office staffed by functionaries, organizational technicians (when they can be called technicians), specialists (when they can be called specialists) in the art of concentrating and guiding the workers' forces in such a way as to establish a favourable balance between the working class and the power of capital' ('Trade Unions and Councils' ['Sindacati e consigli'], *L'Ordine Nuovo*, 12 June 1920; ON, p. 547; SPW-1, p. 265).

49 'Towards a Renewal of the Socialist Party', *L'Ordine Nuovo*, 8 May 1920 (ON, p. 511; SPW-1, p. 191).
50 Buci-Glucksmann 1980, p. 145.

squadrismo against the socialist political and social movement in all the most important regions of the country'.[51]

From the beginning of that year the fascist movement had been getting stronger and stronger and was preparing the creation of the Fascist Party (September 1921). The frequency of violent actions made clear that a change was happening in Italian politics and that the anti-socialist offensive was gathering increasing support from the bourgeoisie (the agrarian squads and the *blocchi nazionali* are the most patent manifestation of this). In this context, the foundation of the PCd'I did not reflect an increasing force of the workers' movement, which, on the contrary, was losing its strength. Generally speaking, the crisis of the parliamentary system was evident and intensified the clash between the bourgeoisie and the proletariat.[52]

That the collapse of the post-unification liberal state represents a fundamental turning point for Gramsci, which opens a new and threatening phase in Italian political history, is evident from the emphasis he places on the demise of constitutional legality. In this sense, an article published in August 1921 is extremely meaningful. The title of the piece is *Legality* [*Legalità*]:

> In capitalist society, legality is represented by the interests of the bourgeois class. When an action in any way affects private property and the profits that derive from it, then that action immediately comes to be considered illegal ... The working class, by exercising its right to vote, had won control over a great number of communes and provinces. The organisations that represented it had achieved an impressive growth in membership and had succeeded in forcing through agreements that were advantageous for workers. But as soon as the vote and the right to organize became means of attacks against the boss class, this latter dropped any pretence of formal legality and started obeying nothing but its true law – the law of its own interest, the law of its conservation. The communes were violently stripped away from the working class; working-class organizations were dissolved by the use of armed force; the industrial working class and the peasantry were ousted from their positions, having become

---

51 Paggi 1970, p. 371.
52 On this point, see 'Continue in the Fight' ['Proseguire nella lotta'], *L'Ordine Nuovo*, 24 August 1921 (SF, p. 294): 'Workers and peasants must now fight for their release. The crisis that has thrown them into the arms of hunger is not like the usual ones that occur periodically in the world of capitalist production. The extent of the crisis is such that there are only two ways to get out of it: either with the general crushing of the working class or with the complete death of capitalism. But with this difference: only the working class is capable of restoring the balance in the world of production that the war has destroyed'.

> too much of a threat to the existence of private property. And thus we saw the birth of Fascism, which grew and established itself as a movement by making illegality into the only thing that was legal. No organizations, except the fascist organization; no right to vote, except the right to vote for the agrarian and industrial representatives of Fascism. This is the kind of legality that the bourgeoisie is prepared to recognize when it is constrained to renounce the other, formal kind ... There comes a point in history when the bourgeoisie is constrained to repudiate what it has itself created. This point has arrived in Italy.[53]

Incidentally, it should be remembered that 1921 was also the moment of Gramsci's sharp polemic against parliamentary cretinism and his rejection of the false alternative between parliamentarism and revolution (see *Out of the Dilemma*).

Despite the pessimistic affirmations of the article 'Legality', it is hard for Gramsci to say what part will be successful in establishing its rule. The following article illustrates well this situation of uncertainty:

> Has there ever been a better demonstration of the impossibility in which the forces of today's society are to return into unity, that is to say in balance, without the creation of a bourgeois class dictatorship or a proletarian dictatorship? Not only that, but where can one find a better demonstration of another of the fundamental theses of communism than in the current events in Italy: that only the proletarian dictatorship can, through the discipline of hard work and production, rebuild order, civilization, and recreate a state, while the bourgeois dictatorship is unnecessary ferocity, barbarity without purpose, systematic dissolution and a regression process that you cannot see how it can be arrested?[54]

As emerges clearly from this text, however, at that stage this 'new' dilemma (dictatorship of the bourgeoisie or dictatorship of the proletariat?) cannot be resolved, for obvious reasons related to the recent foundation of the PCd'I and to Gramsci's major role within the party. Thus, if, on the one hand, Gramsci recognises theoretically the possibility of a conservative alternative to the realisation of socialism, on the other hand he seems to deny the likelihood of its concrete achievement.

---

53 'Legality', *L'Ordine Nuovo*, 28 August 1921 (SF, pp. 305–6; PPW, pp. 230–2).
54 'Journalistic Fascism' ['Fascismo giornalistico'], *L'Ordine Nuovo*, 13 May 1921 (SF, pp. 157–8).

3.3 An Illiberal Order

A partial solution to this quandary occurs after 1924. Back in Italy after his stays in Moscow and Vienna, Gramsci is facing a complex situation: Mussolini is ruling Italy and the struggle between Fascism and its opponents has reached its climax with the murder of the deputy Giacomo Matteotti. In this context, Gramsci returns to the model of the balance of class forces in order to explain the current circumstances, even if on the basis of a deeper political reasoning, developed during his time in Russia in close contact with the Bolshevik leading group.[55]

The application of the balance formula has a different meaning both in terms of political strategy and of historical analysis in 1924. On the one hand, the restoration of the bourgeois order by the fascists should urge the workers' movement to fight more effectively against Fascism. On the other hand, at the centre of this reading there are now the two years 1920–21, conceived by Gramsci as the real turning point in recent Italian history (much more than the '*biennio rosso*' 1919–20). Some weeks after the disappearance of the Socialist parliamentarian, he asks:

> What is Fascism? It is the most energetic and active part of the Italian petty bourgeoisie that wanted to resolve, for capitalism's benefit and for its own benefit, the situation of the balance of forces that existed in 1920 and 1921 between capitalism and proletariat.[56]

Thus, as Gramsci writes, the fascist regime no longer appears as a mere theoretical hypothesis. Fascism is real and has restored a bourgeois-dominated 'balance', albeit a weak and problematic one. Gramsci still denies that Fascism can really be hegemonic (although with less and less conviction, especially from the beginning of 1925).

It is precisely on this restored balance that Gramsci focuses in the writings of 1924–26. He insists on the recovered unity of the dominant groups that, in this way, are able to resist the attacks of the subaltern classes, and allow the bourgeois state to survive beyond its political crisis.[57] See for instance the piece of 9 May 1925, in which he states:

> Once again it is clear that the very essence of the present crisis consists in giving a shape to the bourgeois order. Fascism had to restore the balance

---

55   On this point, see also McNally 2008.
56   'Class Struggle' ['Lotta di classe'], *L'Unità*, 24 June 1924 (CPC, p. 191).
57   On this point, see Paggi 1970, p. 377.

of Italian capitalist society, but with its action it made the stability of the capitalist order even more uncertain.[58]

Despite the criticism of the 'illegality and violence' adopted by the fascists 'to conquer the power and to keep it', Gramsci's concerns about the future of Italy emerge clearly.

It should be noted that Gramsci's interest in the topic of the 'balance' and its different 'phases' also stands out through the terminology that he used, which is significantly enriched between 1925 and 1926. At this stage he employs the phrase 'unstable balance' [*equilibrio instabile*] to describe the post-war Italian panorama, in opposition to the pre-war liberal (parliamentary) balance. See the following quotations: 'the hope for a liberal balance between the two contenders – labour movement and fascist movement – had disappeared in 1921';[59] 'in Italy there was an unstable balance between the struggling social forces'.[60]

Given that, the way in which the unstable balance of 1920–21 was resolved by the fascists in their favour can be defined as the creation of an 'illiberal balance'. This formula summarises well the compromise between the petty bourgeoisie and the big agricultural and industrial bourgeoisie which, under the auspices of fascist ideology, allows them to reconstruct the 'historical' base of the state.[61] In other words, the Italian bourgeois ruling class found a new unity around and through Fascism. As Paggi observes, the reference to the situation of equilib-

---

58 'Mussolini or Albertini?' ['Mussolini o Albertini?'], *L'Unità*, 9 May 1925 (CPC, p. 551). In this article, Gramsci ironically criticises the role of Senator Luigi Albertini (1871–1941), a bourgeois opponent of Fascism and editor of the *Corriere della Sera*. He writes: 'the things Albertini said and the reply made by Minister Federzoni characterise the crisis of bourgeois power and indicate the position the working class must choose to defend its freedoms and interests … The revolutionary proletariat … is therefore always the most vigorous force against which both Albertini and Mussolini fight, albeit with opposing methods. Examining the political situation now, it is to be expected that the bourgeoisie will adhere with more stubborn attachment to the method of Mussolini. So, the effect to be expected, after Albertini's discourse, is precisely the opposite of what he has invoked, asking for a "loosening of restraints" in the name of order and constitution' (CPC, pp. 550–1).
59 'Gatto Roissard (Anando)', *L'Unità*, 25 July 1925 (PV, p. 322).
60 'Russia, Italy, and other Countries' ['Russia, Italia e altri paesi'], under the column 'The United Front "Mondo" – "Tribuna"' ['Il fronte unico "Mondo" – "Tribuna"'] [III], *L'Unità*, 26 September 1926 (CPC, p. 343).
61 On compromise and unity understood as the 'translation in terms of political activity of the concept of hegemony, which applies both to Fascism and to the tasks of the Communist Party', see Paggi 1984, pp. 236–46 and pp. 267 ff. On the 'historical basis of the state' and on its shift, see Buci-Glucksmann 1980, pp. 93 ff.

rium, in this context, does 'draw attention to the phenomena of disaggregation and re-aggregation of superstructures that accompany the constitution of a new form of power and state'.[62]

Therefore, we can say that the formula of the balance of class forces is investigated and deepened in parallel with Gramsci's reflection on the crisis of the liberal state and on Fascism. A few months before Gramsci's arrest, the balance of class forces has become an interpretative model, suggesting a reading based on the interaction between historical, political and ideological elements, as evidenced by this text of September 1926:

> In Italy there was an unstable balance between the social forces in contention. The proletariat was too strong in 1919–20 to continue to subject itself passively to capitalist oppression. But, its organised forces were uncertain, hesitant, inwardly weak, because the Socialist Party was only an amalgam of at least three parties; because it was missing in Italy in 1919–20 a revolutionary party well organised and ready to fight. From this unstable balance the forces of Italian Fascism were born, which was organised and took power with methods and systems which, if they had an Italian peculiarity and were linked to all of the Italian tradition and to the immediate situation of our country, nevertheless they had and have a certain resemblance to the methods and systems described by Karl Marx in the *Eighteenth Brumaire of Louis Bonaparte*, that is, with the general tactic of the bourgeoisie in danger, in all countries.[63]

To conclude, it is important to note the affinity between this way of employing the model of the balance of class forces and the formula of the 'relations of force', developed by Gramsci in the *Prison Notebooks*.[64]

In my opinion there is a connection between the two formulas, on many levels. The imagery of the balance implies a many-sided socio-political concept of class (and not a mainly economic one, as in the model of the catastrophic crisis), as in the 'relations of force': the resolution of the situation of unstable balance appears as the result of the interaction between different elements of political, cultural and ideological nature. Moreover, the model of the balance emphasises the importance of the petty bourgeoisie, which seems to anticipate Gramsci's later observations on the role of intermediate classes. Finally, yet

---

62 Paggi 1970, p. 91.
63 'Russia, Italy, and other Countries', cit. (CPC, p. 343).
64 For a general description of the category (surprisingly still under-investigated), see the entry by Coutinho in Liguori and Voza 2009.

importantly, both the model of balance and that of the relations of force seem to share (albeit very distantly) the same 'scientific' language, that of the analysis of forces (vectors) drawn from analytical geometry.[65] It is possible that Gramsci had chosen to use this vocabulary to give the idea of the 'addition' of forces, an idea which explicitly contrasts with the simple 'juxtaposition' between the different components of the oversimplified 'sociological' approach.

In short, the balance formula appears as the 'incunabulum' of that of the relations of force. To that extent, it casts a significant light on the evolution of Gramsci's thought and on the genesis of his interpretative categories.

---

[65] On Gramsci and science, see e.g. Thomas 2009 and Antonini 2014b.

CHAPTER 5

Bonapartism, Caesarism and Fascism in Gramsci's Journalistic Works

1   The Crisis of the Liberal Order and the Rise of Fascism

As emerged in previous chapters, the core of Gramsci's political reflections in the 1920s deals with the crisis of the liberal state and the parallel development of a new form of (illiberal) order, embodied by Fascism.[1] The formula of the balance of class forces is crucial in this respect, insofar as it describes all the stages of this process.

In this framework, two elements are fundamental: on the one hand, the transformation of state apparatuses; on the other, the changing role of the different class forces, and in particular of the petty bourgeoisie. These aspects are strictly intermingled in Gramsci's analysis, as it developed from the beginning of the decade. The above-mentioned 1921 article *The Monkey People*, for instance, depicts in an extremely clear way the role of the petty bourgeoisie in the establishment of the fascist movement; see also the numerous pieces in which he highlights the changes that had occurred in liberal institutions (parliament, parties, etc.) in the post-war scenario.

For reasons of space, a thorough reconstruction of Gramsci's political reflections in his journalistic works cannot be developed here. I will thus only briefly focus on an excellent example in this respect. It is a text that contains his first and only speech at the Chamber of Deputies. The context is the parliamentary debate on the law against secret associations and especially against freemasonry in May 1925.

In the related article published in *Lo Stato Operaio* and entitled *The Fascist Conquest of the State* [*La conquista fascista dello Stato*], Gramsci investigates the relations between bureaucracy, freemasonry and the new fascist order. He states:

> What does it mean to fight against freemasonry in Italy? It means fighting the bureaucracy, which, as it stands, constitutes an essential factor in the balance achieved by the bourgeoisie in the slow construction of the

---

1   See Chapter 4, in particular sections 3.2 and 3.3.

unified state. To change the political and territorial recruiting criteria of the bureaucracy – this is precisely the aim of the anti-masonry law – it means to change fundamentally the relations of the social forces in balance.[2]

What Gramsci defines as the 'only organised party of the Italian bourgeoisie' (freemasonry) is attacked by Fascism in order to create a new power bloc, in which the petty bourgeoisie was trying to recapture a leading role. Thus, the bureaucratic apparatus, as institutional 'partner' of freemasonry, is also no longer considered as 'detached and opposed to civil society', but, on the contrary, as an 'essential form of internal organization of the dominant bloc'.[3] The nature of state and parastatal (i.e. state-related) apparatuses is then essential to understand where the 'centre of gravity' of the new fascist balance is located. We can therefore conclude that Gramsci's political theory, as it unfolds in the pre-prison writings analysed here, consists fundamentally in a critical reflection on the state, on society and on their transformations, in the troubled framework of the collapse of an old system of power and of the rise of a new one.

2 A (Critical) Theory of State and Politics

But on what basis does Gramsci develop this conception of politics? If different elements contributed to the development of his position (last but not least, his stay in Moscow and his exchanges of ideas with the Bolshevik leaders), from the theoretical point of view Gramsci's reflections rely on two main sources: Hegel's *Philosophy of Right* and Marx's *Eighteenth Brumaire*.

Regarding the former work, the influence of Hegel's text was already recognised by Leonardo Paggi in his pioneering 1970 study.[4] As Paggi argues, by

---

2 'The Fascist Conquest of the State', *Lo Stato Operaio*, 21 May 1925 (PV, pp. 303–4).
3 Paggi 1984, p. 378. On this topic, see especially Paggi 1984, pp. 269–72, and Buci-Glucksmann 1980, pp. 102 ff.
4 For obvious reasons, a detailed analysis of the role of Hegel's *Philosophy of Right* in Gramsci's thought cannot be provided here. Among the most recent contributions on the topic, see for instance the entry on Hegel by Roberto Finelli in Liguori and Voza 2009, pp. 389–91 and Thomas 2009, pp. 159 ff. A useful summary of the debate around Gramsci's conception of civil society (and Bobbio's reading of it) can be found in Gramsci 2012, pp. 155–6, n. 6; see also Panichi 2019. In this chapter, I will offer only a few hints in order to compare the influence of this text with that of Marx's *Eighteenth Brumaire*. As for its focus on the pre-prison writings, I rely in particular on Leonardo Paggi's account.

building on Hegel's category of civil society (initially through the mediation of Georges Sorel (1847–1922)),[5] Gramsci develops an 'autonomous conceptualisation of real social and political processes' that allows him to overcome the limits of 'philosophical Marxism' and to analyse the crisis of the Italian liberal government in the post-war period.[6]

Gramsci takes his cue from Hegel's theses on corporations as nascent forms of political organisation to reflect on parties and trade unions, conceived of as contemporary forms of associations arising from civil society. At a broader level, this reflection leads him to highlight the essential connection between state and society. If the latter is the '"private" fabric' of the state (as he will say explicitly in the *Prison Notebooks*),[7] the former intervenes actively in the social dynamic. As Paggi writes, on the one hand, Hegel's reflections provide Gramsci with the tools to understand the 'irreducibility of the social phenomenon to the mere economic factor' and, on the other, these observations illuminate the 'potentially repressive aspects of the state machine'.[8]

In this framework, the investigation of the role of the middle class is crucial. Following Hegel's *Philosophy of Right*, Gramsci focuses on state employees (who mostly belong to the middle class) as the true 'basis of the state' and, at the same time, as the key element of civil society.[9] A further step in this sense is represented by the analysis of bureaucracy: as Paggi affirms, there are some elements of Gramsci's analysis that echo explicitly Hegel's thoughts on the topic.[10]

The Hegelian model is also relevant with regard to Gramsci's understanding of the Italian crisis. His analysis of the dialectical relation between state and society leads him to a deep reflection on the parliamentary representative state and on its limits.[11] In 1921 this reflection significantly influences

---

5   See Paggi 1970, pp. 391–2: 'the most important cultural suggestion for this new definition of the concept of civil society is surely to be identified with Sorel's criticism of the materialistic conception of history ... a significant witness of this different attitude towards the workers' movement is the claim of the importance of Hegel's philosophy for Marx's thought, which Sorel puts forward repeatedly in his *Critical Essays on Marxism* [*Saggi di critica del marxismo*]'. On Gramsci and Sorel, see now Frosini 2020.

6   Paggi 1970, p. 391.

7   Q 1, § 47, p. 56; PN, vol. 1, p. 153 (in Italian: '*trama "privata" dello Stato*'). As Paggi has noted also, there are many affinities between these aspects of Gramsci's reflections in the pre-prison writings and those in the *Prison Notebooks* (see Paggi 1970, pp. 391 ff.).

8   See Paggi 1970, pp. 392 and 395, respectively.

9   These observations already evoke (albeit in embryonic form) Gramsci's reflections on the intellectuals in the *Prison Notebooks* – see Paggi 1970, pp. 393–4.

10 See Paggi 1970, pp. 395–6.

11 As Paggi writes, 'in the light of the crisis of the liberal state, Sorel's suggestion leads to a more general use of Hegel's text that ends up focusing on that part devoted to high-

Gramsci's political strategy, which urges the workers' movement to make the most of the situation of balance between the political forces by changing the political system from the inside (in line with his strategy of the factory councils).[12]

Later, these 'Hegel-inspired' formulations will also allow Gramsci to highlight the novelty of the fascist movement. Far from being simply the reaction of the bourgeoisie, the 'armed violence of a dying capitalism', Fascism is understood as the 'process of de-composition and re-composition of society and State'.[13] The investigation of the crisis of the liberal State represents therefore the occasion for an analysis of the deeper mechanisms of politics and its transformations, beyond any schematism. Finally, it is to be noted that Hegel's *Philosophy of Right* adopts a realistic and concrete method of analysis of the various historical and political contexts and the resulting theory of politics.[14]

Such an approach is in line with the conception of Marxism that Gramsci was developing in the same years and that clearly differs from other contemporary (and, in his view, misleading) interpretations of it. As Gramsci writes in two articles of 1926, Marx is not the founder of the 'historical materialism', conceived of as a 'purely speculative fact' or as a teleology.[15] He is rather the creator

---

lighting the forms in which a political constitution reflects in its internal articulations the real distinctions of society'. And, furthermore: 'the representative state can "bear" only a civil society that has not yet released from its breast all its political potentials' (Paggi 1970, pp. 393 and 401). See, in this regard, the already mentioned article on legality (Chapter 4, section 3.2).

12   See Paggi 1970, p. 405, who quotes from the theses on the syndical issue prepared for the second congress of the PCd'I in March 1922 (the so-called Rome theses): 'the trade-union organisation, embryo of a workers' state within the bourgeois state, can be endured only temporarily by the capitalist system' (SF, p. 500).

13   Paggi 1970, p. 407.

14   See Paggi 1970, p. 396: 'the Hegelian text appears to be the point of reference ... of an interpretation of the concept of civil society that solves in the concrete analysis all the difficulties of the philosophical battle'; 'once abandoned the traditional equation between structure-superstructure and state-civil society, [Gramsci] rediscovers the determinate and non-decisive character of the political state by emphasising the metamorphoses related to the great social processes of the country'.

15   'Mr. Arturo Labriola's Screams, Sighs and Tears' ['Strilli, sospiri e lacrime del signor Arturo Labriola'], *L'Unità*, 1 August 1926 (CPC, p. 439). See the following quotations: 'Arturo Labriola cannot ignore that Marx, in his letters to Engels, claims repeatedly that the main feature of all his scientific and practical activity is not historical materialism, not the theory of surplus value, but the demonstration of the historical necessity of the dictatorship of the proletariat. To forget or to hide this position of Marx means not only to be politically reactionary; but it also means not to understand the central point of Marxist doctrine'

of a critical theory of politics and of the state, which aims to actively intervene into real dynamics and to modify the political scenario (and, notably, to realise the dictatorship of the proletariat).[16]

This reading is supported by some specific texts by Marx and Engels, such as the *Critique of Hegel's Philosophy of Right* [*Zur Kritik der Hegelschen Rechtsphilosophie*], the *Critique of the Gotha Programme* [*Kritik des Gothaer Programms*] and *The Class Struggles in France*.[17] More generally speaking, the historical works by Marx play a pivotal role in this context, since they represent a powerful application of historical materialism's method of analysis to concrete historical cases.

('Disorder and Intellectual Dishonesty', cit; CPC, p. 423); 'What consequence would a serious scholar have drawn from this statement by F. Engels? Nothing but this: that in the complex of Marxist doctrine, which is not a mushroom born after an autumn drizzle, but a system that has its roots in the history of human civilisation, historical materialism and the theory of surplus value are original discoveries of Karl Marx. Instead, what conclusion does Mr. [Arturo] Labriola draw? That Marxism consists only in historical materialism and in the theory of surplus value, that is to say that Marxism is a purely speculative fact and not even and especially a practical fact, a political programme of the working class that aims to establish the proletarian dictatorship ... For us and not only for us but also for Engels and Marx, Marxism is not only historical materialism and the theory of surplus value, but also and especially the Marxist doctrine of the State, the demonstration of the historical necessity of the advent of the dictatorship of the proletariat' ('Mr. Arturo Labriola's Screams, Sighs and Tears', cit.; CPC, pp. 439–40). Arturo Labriola (1873–1959) was one of the leaders of the socialist stream of revolutionary syndicalism at the beginning of the twentieth century; he turned later to more moderate positions and he entered into the government led by Giovanni Giolitti in 1920. He wrote extensively on Marx's economic thought and notably on the theory of surplus value, here mentioned by Gramsci as one of the two elements of his misleading conception of Marxism – the other one is 'historical materialism', conceived as the interpretation of historical development from a materialistic (economic) point of view. On a more general level, it is interesting to note the opposition between Labriola's 'theoretical' approach towards Marxism and Gramsci's concrete, strategical conception of it ('speculative fact' vs 'practical fact').

16 From this perspective, it is interesting to note that, by formulating this definition of Marxism, Gramsci is implicitly posing, and also replying to, the question of whether a Marxist theory of the state exists and, if so, what its features are – of course, this is a much-debated issue in twentieth-century Marxism, especially in more recent decades (on this theme, see Van den Berg 1988 but also, for instance, Wetherly 2005 and Jessop 2007).

17 Paggi 1970, pp. 398–403.

3   Marx's *Eighteenth Brumaire*: Analogies and Analyses

Despite this, Gramsci's interest in *The Eighteenth Brumaire* in the pre-prison writings has thus far not been fully appreciated. With a few, partial exceptions, the scholarship has not recognised the importance of Marx's historical masterpiece in shaping Gramsci's theory.[18]

Nevertheless, its relevance stands out clearly from an article, written in September 1926, which has already been quoted. Here he hints for the first time at a 'certain resemblance to the methods and systems described by Karl Marx in the *Eighteenth Brumaire of Louis Bonaparte*', by affirming that they describe 'the general tactic of the bourgeoisie in danger, in all countries'.[19] The fact that this is the only explicit reference to Marx's book in Gramsci's pre-prison writings does not undermine its importance; on the contrary, it is precisely its uniqueness that makes it so meaningful.

We should make clear right at the outset what the role played by historical analogies in Gramsci's texts was.[20] While there is a constant tension between the investigation of a phenomenon in its singularity and the formulation of a historical law in Gramsci's thought as a whole, the typologising element is predominant in the journalistic writings. The reason for this is simple: in the *Notebooks* the call to concrete political action is present only indirectly and, consequently, a prudent use of the analogies prevails, whereas in Gramsci's pre-prison writings his reflections are focused more strongly on the present situation. This also makes clear his primary strategic interest: it is no coincidence that in the most important moments, from a political point of view, analogy is more frequently used, even at the expense of a simplification of the historical analysis. The use of historical parallels greatly amplifies the rhetorical force of Gramsci's argumentation, by strengthening in this way its tactical position.[21]

This is the context in which Gramsci's use of the Marxian model as a term of comparison in the text quoted before should be understood. In this text written after the Lyon theses and in the light of the most recent political directives of the PCd'I, Gramsci establishes a parallel between the unstable equilibrium

---

18   See the contributions by Paggi and Buci-Glucksmann already quoted above. In the following pages, my aim is to fill this gap and to provide a thorough analysis of the role of *The Eighteenth Brumaire* and, more generally, of Marx's historical texts on Gramsci's thought before his imprisonment.
19   'Russia, Italy, and other Countries', cit. (CPC, p. 343).
20   On this topic, see also Antonini 2019b.
21   In general, on the political meaning of analogies, see e.g. Musolff 2004, Canfora 2010 and Mumford 2015.

realised in Italy in the post-war period and the situation in France after 1848. Thus, he achieves a twofold objective. On the one hand, he shows that the current Italian situation is not a form of collective 'psychosis', but the result of a precise relation of forces; on the other hand, he points out the inability of a part of Italian socialism to oppose Fascism.[22]

On a more general level, by defining the modalities of the bourgeois reaction to the hegemonic crisis of the post-war period, Gramsci aims to support the workers' movement in elaborating both a theory and a practice able to undermine the fascist dictatorship. From this perspective, by creating a historical analogy between Fascism and the Bonapartist regime, Gramsci's writings presage the overcoming of Fascism itself and leave a ray of hope shining in dark times.

But, beyond its rhetorical and strategic dimension, the content of the comparison is also of relevance: the historical analogy reveals a deeper (and until now almost totally neglected) consonance between Gramsci's and Marx's historical thought. This is of great importance to the evaluation of Gramsci's political thinking in the pre-prison writings. In fact, some of the key aspects of Gramsci's analysis of the Italian situation in the post-war period clearly derive from a close reading of Marx's *Eighteenth Brumaire*. Three elements, in particular, must be highlighted.

The first and most important point is the issue of 'constitutional legality' and its breakdown during periods of political impasses. It represents a *Leitmotiv* of Marx's historical works as a whole, and especially of the text on Louis Napoleon's *coup d'État*; moreover, 'legality' returns also in Engels's texts (see in particular his famous introduction to the third edition of *The Class Struggles in*

---

22 See the following quotations: 'It is said that in the island of Martinique there is a curious competition between creole and mulatto women. The creoles have very small feet, for which very elegant and graceful shoes are made. The mulattos have very big and knobbly feet and they could not wear the creole shoes. They therefore go to the cafe and the boardwalk, bringing elegant shoes in their hands. The writer of *Il Mondo* resembles strangely the mulatto women of the island of Martinique. Historical materialism, socialism, and reformism are not shoes for his feet. Why, then, does he pin them to the lobes of his pronounced democratic ears?' ('Russia, Italy, and other Countries', cit.; CPC, pp. 341–2). 'The "psychosis" formula has been used for Italy. In 1919–20 it was said that there was a maximalist "psychosis"; in 1921–22 "fascist psychosis" was spoken of. But recently, Mr. Franco Clerici had emerged, claiming that in 1924 there was the democratic "psychosis" of the Aventine, which did not please the writers of *Il Mondo*. In this way, all of Italy's three fundamental factors – proletariat, capitalism, small and middle-class bourgeoisie – have become a madhouse: the whole of Italian politics is "psychosis". We do not believe in interpretations based on "psychosis"' (CPC, p. 343).

France).²³ In Gramsci, this is a recurring theme in his journalistic writings and will also be a central issue in the *Notebooks*.²⁴

In his pre-prison articles, there are numerous occurrences of the term 'legality' (*'legalità'*) and of its related adjectives.²⁵ It is worth noting that the most explicit references underline some of the main turning points in recent Italian history. In 1921, during the very moment of the fiercest struggle between proletariat and bourgeoisie, Gramsci dedicates to this topic one of his most striking and illuminating pieces on nascent Fascism. In another article written in 1924 (after the murder of the deputy Matteotti) and attributed for the first time by Paggi to Gramsci, he draws an explicit comparison between the breakdown of constitutional legality in Italy in the early 1920s and the situation in France at the time of the events described in Marx's *Eighteenth Brumaire*. Here Gramsci writes:

> When legality is not enough to guarantee the power of the bourgeois class, when the bourgeoisie suffocates within the limits of its law, it takes the initiative to violate it [legality]. That happened at the time of the Bona-

---

23   Here Engels recalls the famous exclamation by Odilon Barrot (1791–1873), Prime Minister of France between 1848 and 1849 ('legality kills us', *'la légalité nous tue'*) – see MECW, vol. 27, p. 522; a direct reference to this phrase can also be found in *The Class Struggle in France* (MECW, vol. 10, p. 89). From the same text, see also the following quotation: 'And the party of Order speaks its last word: "The iron ring of suffocating legality must be broken. *The constitutional republic is impossible.* We must fight with our true weapons; since February 1848, we have fought the revolution with *its* weapon and on *its* terrain. We have accepted *its* institutions; the constitution is a fortress which safeguards only the besiegers, not the besieged! By smuggling ourselves into holy Ilion in the belly of the Trojan horse, we have, unlike our forefathers, the *Grecs*, not conquered the hostile town, but made prisoners of ourselves" ... *"Our dictatorship has hitherto existed by the will of the people; it must now be consolidated against the will of the people"'* (MECW, vol. 10, pp. 130–1). And from *The Eighteenth Brumaire*: 'The law of May 31, 1850, was the *coup d'État* of the bourgeoisie. All its conquests over the revolution hitherto had only a provisional character and were endangered as soon as the existing National Assembly retired from the stage. They depended on the hazards of a new general election, and the history of elections since 1848 irrefutably proved that the bourgeoisie's moral sway over the mass of the people was lost in the same measure as its actual domination developed. On March 10 universal suffrage declared itself directly against the domination of the bourgeoisie; the bourgeoisie answered by outlawing universal suffrage. The law of May 31 was, therefore, one of the necessities of the class struggle' (MECW, vol. 11, p. 148).
24   See Chapter 11, section 2.1 *et passim*.
25   This is a very interesting element, which deserves to be investigated further. Generally speaking, the references to legality and its breakdown are connected to the issue of the 'decomposition' of the state as a manifestation of the post-war political crisis (see for instance 'The "conspiracy"' ['La "congiura"'], under the column 'The Week in Politics' [XXIV], *L'Ordine Nuovo*, 31 July 1920; ON, pp. 596–8).

partist *coup d'État*. That has occurred in all countries, where the working class, as a result of its growth in strength, has put forward its candidacy for power. And that has also happened in Italy in recent years.[26]

These affirmations clearly anticipate Gramsci's observations on 'the general tactic of the bourgeoisie in danger, in all countries' of 1926 and provide the reader with a meaningful perspective on the birth and development of the fascist movement. Indeed, the parallel with the breakdown of legality realised by the French bourgeoisie with the electoral law of 31 May 1850 and the subsequent advent of the Bonapartist dictatorship puts a particular emphasis on the contiguity between liberalism and Fascism, and underlines the share of responsibility of the bourgeoisie for the constitution of Mussolini's regime.

If this aspect explicitly echoes Marx, there are two other features of Gramsci's investigation that show implicitly the influence of Marx's *Eighteenth Brumaire*. Developing further some elements of Hegel's *Philosophy of Right*, Marx's historical works provide a refined analysis of politics and class alliances, both in a progressive and in a regressive sense (in particular, Marx displays a special interest for the *Lumpenproletariat*, whose description recalls, in a different guise, Gramsci's conception of the petty bourgeoisie). Another pivotal theme of Marx's (but also of Hegel's) analysis is that of the role of the state and parastatal apparatuses, and in particular of the army and bureaucracy, to which Gramsci pays great attention in his newspaper articles. The texts investigated in the previous chapters are eloquent from this point of view.

4   On the Gramsci-Marx Relationship in the Pre-prison Writings

With the influence of Marx in mind, the only explicit reference to *The Eighteenth Brumaire* (in the piece of September 1926) acquires a highly emblematic value. Far from diminishing the role of Marx's reflections for Gramsci's thought, I would argue that such a declaration of his 'debt' towards Marx is the signal of a complete integration of the categories of *The Eighteenth Brumaire* by Gramsci, i.e. of the internalisation of the principles of Marx's historico-political analysis.

In summary, we can distinguish two different ways in which Gramsci employs the categories of Caesarism and Bonapartism. On the one hand, in his pre-prison writings there are examples of an explicit adoption of these concepts (see Bonapartism and 'Cadornism'; Bonapartism with reference to the

---

26   'At the Basis of the Liberal Crisis' ['Alla base della crisi liberale'], *L'Unità*, 3 October 1924. See Paggi 1984, p. 278. Here in particular Gramsci provocatively opposes senator Albertini

Socialist Party/trade union; Mussolini's Caesarist attitude). On the other hand, Gramsci capitalises on some of the main achievements of Marxist political theory (more or less directly) connected to the categories of Bonapartism and Caesarism, by developing them further within the framework of his analysis of the Italian situation.

It is interesting to note that, generally speaking, the more explicit is the reference, the more superficial and polemical is the meaning; moreover, the explicit references are concentrated mostly in the early stages of Gramsci's journalistic production. There is, however, a clear development in Gramsci's use of the categories of Caesarism and Bonapartism that reflects the general evolution of his political thought as well as his process of reassessing Marx's historical materialism.

The first occurrence of the categories appears in 1921, in connection both with Gramsci's day-to-day political engagement and with his broader investigation of the post-war crisis (see for instance the famous piece on the 'monkey people'). In this phase, the polemical use of the Bonapartist model prevails, in order to underline the distance between rulers and ruled within state institutions – from this point of view, taking up again the Marxist interpretative key of parliamentary cretinism is important too.

A passage to a higher level in Gramsci's analysis occurs in 1924. Back in Italy after his long stay abroad and after his assumption of the party's leadership, Gramsci now develops a more detailed political and historical investigation. On the one hand, he elaborates a polemical interpretation of Fascism as a form of romanticism, with Mussolini as a new Caesar, clearly inspired by some Marxian readings (a pastiche of *The Holy Family* and *The Eighteenth Brumaire*). On the other hand, Gramsci's attention is increasingly focused on the issue of relations between classes, a lens through which he fruitfully reads the Italian and European scenario.

The following years, until his arrest in 1926, constitute the more mature phase of Gramsci's journalistic activity. At that time, Gramsci develops an in-depth analysis of the fascist regime that succeeds in capturing some of its most salient features. In this regard, Gramsci's further reflection on the formula of balance of class forces is crucial, since it allows him to explain Fascism in terms of the relations between classes, by emphasising the role of the masses in its historical development. Moreover, this class-focused investigation is combined with a thorough reflection on the nature of the state and parastatal apparatuses.

(already elsewhere a victim of Gramsci's mockery; cf. Chapter 4, section 3.3), and his vain appeals for a return to a liberal-democratic system.

This is, in short, the evolution of Gramsci's reflections on the categories of Caesarism and Bonapartism. The transformation of the balance formula is without doubt exemplary: it gradually evolves from a purely evocative and collateral hint towards a sort of historical law, and finally, a valuable key for interpreting the many-sided phenomenon of Fascism.

If this chronology parallels some crucial turning points in post-war Italian history as well as in Gramsci's personal history, it is also important as regards the development of his relationship with the thought of Marx and Engels. From a certain point of view, the reflections on Caesarism and Bonapartism offer us an insight into Gramsci's approach towards historical materialism; they also help us to shed some light on the encounter between Gramsci and other texts by Marx and Engels.

In this respect, one of the most recent accounts of Gramsci and Marx, provided by Francesca Izzo, may be reconsidered and further expanded.[27] As she writes, 'at least until 1922' Gramsci mainly uses Marx's thought in a polemical way, to fight his enemies, intellectuals and politicians.[28] Based on the previous analysis, I can say that such a polemical use of Marx's categories also persists beyond that date: it is indeed a salient feature of Gramsci's journalistic writings. But I would also argue that in 1922 (or even before, in 1920–21) Gramsci had already started a serious confrontation with some of Marx's texts, and in particular with *The Eighteenth Brumaire*, as a source of inspiration for his analysis of the crisis of the liberal state.[29]

Around the middle of the decade, a significant refinement of Gramsci's theory took place as a consequence of his renewed approach to Marx's and Engels's works. This was stimulated by the lively debate on Marxism that took place in Russia at the time of his stay.[30] Between 1924 and 1926, he engages in a close 'dialogue' with Marx's texts. While deepening his knowledge of Marxist thought, at the same time he distances himself from its deterministic and economistic readings widespread in socialist and communist milieus. On this basis he develops an original interpretation of historical materialism, laying the foundation for his future reflections on state and society.

---

27   Izzo 2009, pp. 23–74. The divergences between the chronology proposed by Izzo and the one displayed here can be explained (at least partially) by the fact that she deals with a number of Marx's works. My chronology takes its cue from a single text (*The Eighteenth Brumaire*), but I would argue that it sheds a meaningful light on some crucial turning points of Gramsci's relationship to Marx's thought as a whole.

28   Izzo 2009, p. 23.

29   Leonardo Paggi also supported this hypothesis in a private discussion with me.

30   Izzo does not discuss in detail the period 1924–26, that, I argue, is the most important in Gramsci's engagement with Marx's texts (on this point, see again Antonini 2018).

Using a seemingly contradictory expression, we can therefore say that Gramsci enriches Marx's model with elements derived from the direct reading of his works. In other words, he is 'correcting' Marx (i.e. a 'vulgar' Marx) with Marx himself.

It is clear that in Gramsci's articles the weight of Marx's reflections is greater than it seems. If we pay attention not only to the explicit references but also to the interpretative categories inspired by Marx's thought, Gramsci's journalistic articles are shot through with 'quotations' from Marx. The encounter with Marx, in some respects, marks the very development of Gramsci's thinking, silently but continually inspiring its internal evolution.

The Eighteenth Brumaire has a special place in this framework. It is one of Gramsci's favourite readings, because of its expressive and interpretative richness. What is more, this historical work can be actualised and adopted to understand Gramsci's political and historical situation. First of all, Marx's text is a goldmine of polemical hints (for the sake of clarity: from Marx's reference to the *feuilleton* to parliamentary cretinism, to Bonapartism itself) that could not fail to capture Gramsci's attention, as a ruthless critic of his contemporaries. Furthermore, the model of the balance of class forces represents somehow the 'programmatic' platform on which Gramsci elaborates his concrete political action between 1920 and 1926. This formula provides him with the conceptual tools to make an original and fruitful interpretation of the crisis of the liberal State and the subsequent rise of the fascist regime. The result is one of the most striking analyses of the post-First World War period.

CHAPTER 6

Towards the *Prison Notebooks*

1   Continuity and Novelty

From the analysis that I have carried out so far, it emerges that the concepts of Caesarism and Bonapartism play a significant role in Gramsci's thought before 1926. They are even more important in the prison writings. Unlike the journalistic articles, the significance of these categories in the *Notebooks* was already acknowledged by Luisa Mangoni and Franco De Felice in the 1970s.[1] Nevertheless, very little attention was devoted to these concepts in the following decades. This attitude began to shift only in the 2000s with the revival of Gramsci studies.[2]

In spite of this renewal of interest, a systematic discussion of Gramsci's use of such concepts is missing, as well as an in-depth examination of Gramsci's reassessment of Marx's original reflection. As a consequence, an adequate investigation of the relation between Gramsci's reflections on the topic before and after his imprisonment is also still a *desideratum*.

Such a gap in the literature is likely due to the fact that the terms 'Caesarism' and 'Bonapartism' do not occur frequently in the *Notebooks*, especially when compared to other categories. However, lack of frequency does not imply a lack of interest by Gramsci. This can be demonstrated, for instance, by the case of 'passive revolution', whose explicit occurrences are very rare, despite the absolute importance of the category for Gramsci's thought.

At the same time, Gramsci's interest in Caesarism and Bonapartism clearly stands out through the explicit references to *The Eighteenth Brumaire* that can be found in the notebooks. Two notes in particular should be mentioned: Q 3, § 51 and Q 7, § 24.

In the short text Q 3, § 51 (*Past and Present* [*Passato e presente*], single draft) written between June and July 1930, Gramsci paraphrases the famous open-

---

1 See Mangoni 1976, 1977 and 1979 and De Felice 1977; some useful hints can also be retraced in Buci-Glucksmann 1980. On the figures of Mangoni and De Felice, see, respectively, the special issue of *Studi storici* dedicated to her (3, 2015) and Sorgonà and Taviani 2016.
2 See, in particular, the works by Alberto Burgio (2003, esp. pp. 206–10; 2007a and 2007b; 2014, pp. 107–19), Benedetto Fontana (2004), David D. Roberts (2011), Lorenzo Santoro (2012) and Giuseppe Cospito (2016, pp. 207–17). See also the entries in Liguori and Voza 2009, pp. 73–4 and 123–5. On recent developments in the Gramsci scholarship, in addition to what has been said in the preface to this volume, see also Liguori 2012.

ing of Marx's historical masterpiece, which echoes, in turn, Hegel's *Lectures on the Philosophy of History* [*Vorlesungen über die Philosophie der Geschichte*].[3] Here Gramsci evokes explicitly Hegel's saying that everything in history appears twice, and the gloss by Marx that 'the first time the event occurs as tragedy and the second time as farce'.[4] Gramsci also refers to a previous use of this model by Marx. He quotes a passage from the *Introduction* to the *Critique of Hegel's Philosophy of Right*, in which Marx also adopts the 'tragedy-farce' couple, in relation to the representation of the divine characters in Aeschylus and Lucian.[5]

In Q 7, § 24 (*Structure and superstructure* [*Struttura e superstruttura*], single draft, February 1931) Gramsci deals with the issue of the relation between structure and superstructures, a key element of his reflections. As a response to the claim '(put forward as an essential postulate of historical materialism) that one can present and explain every political and ideological fluctuation as a direct expression of the structure', Gramsci evokes Marx as 'author of concrete political and historical works' and sketches a short list of the most important texts in this sense.[6] In the first place he mentions *The Eighteenth Brumaire* and then 'the writings on the Eastern Question but also others (*Revolution and Counter-Revolution in Germany*, *The Civil War in France* and minor works')'.[7] He argues that the 'analysis of these works allows one to get a better grasp of Marx's historical method, integrating, illuminating, and interpreting the theoretical affirmations scattered throughout his works', because here can be found those 'real cautions' that can help fight the 'primitive infantilism' that belongs to the

---

3   It should be remembered that Marx gets the idea from a letter from Engels (3 December 1851). On the 'genealogy' of Marx's opening, see Mazlish 1972; see also Tomba 2013.
4   Q 3, § 51, p. 334; PN, vol. 2, p. 53.
5   It is interesting to note that references to Marx's works (in particular to *The Holy Family*) also return in the two notes that immediately follow (Q 3, §§ 52 and 53; on these notes see Chapter 9, section 1.1). It is evident, in any case, that in this passage of notebook 3 Gramsci is reflecting on some key texts by Marx. In my opinion, it is no coincidence that the works on which he relies in particular are those on which he worked closely in his pre-prison writings.
6   Q 7, § 24, p. 871; PN, vol. 3, p. 173.
7   Q 7, § 24, p. 871; PN, vol. 3, p. 173. The writings on the Eastern question are Marx's articles published in the *New York Daily Tribune* between 1853 and 1857; the 'Eastern Question' concerns the complex of problems relating to the crisis of the Ottoman Empire and to the growing expansionism of European powers. The texts were first published in Italian in 1903 under the title *La questione orientale – Lettere di Carlo Marx*. *Revolution and Counter-revolution, or 1848 in Germany* [*Revolution und Konterrevolution in Deutschland*], as the exact title reads, is a series of essays written by Engels between August 1851 and September 1852, concerning the events of 1848 in Germany (first Italian edition: 1899). *The Civil War in France* is Marx's famous pamphlet on the Paris Commune of 1871 (first Italian edition: 1871). All these works are included in volumes 1 and 2 of the *Works of Marx, Engels and Lassalle* owned by Gramsci.

mechanistic conception of the relation between structure and superstructure.[8] The text as a whole is very rich and it deals with some crucial aspects of Gramsci's theory. In this respect, it is noteworthy the fact that he clearly binds them to the historical works by Marx, that becomes in this way a kind of 'tutelary deity' of the *Prison Notebooks*.

Further occurrences have to be added to these two texts. Marx's work is indeed mentioned in two notes of notebook 13 (Q 13, §§ 18 and 23; both the references are the result of additions to the first drafts). Finally, it has to be noted that also in Q 9, § 133 and in its second draft (Q 13, § 27) Gramsci evokes the '18 Brumaire'. However, he is not hinting here at Marx's text, but, rather, at the historical events represented by Napoleon I's *coup d'État* (9 November 1799) and by his nephew's *putsch* (2 December 1851).[9]

2   The Editions of Marx's Texts

Before sketching an overview of the occurrences of the categories of Caesarism and Bonapartism in the *Prison Notebooks*, we should focus briefly on the sources by Marx available to Gramsci in prison. If the readings that he made in the early 1920s represent the core of Gramsci's knowledge of Marx, during his imprisonment he also had at his disposal some further editions, provided by his sister-in-law Tatiana.[10]

He had access to the volumes of Marx's works published by the Parisian publisher Costes between 1927 and 1930. Among them, in particular, he had some volumes of the *Philosophical Works* [*Oeuvres philosophiques*] (vols. I, II and III) and some of the *Political Works* [*Oeuvres politiques*] (vols. I and VIII).[11] He also owned the three volumes of the *Complete Works* [*Oeuvres complètes*] that cover Marx's controversy with Karl Vogt (*Herr Vogt*). The second part of the third volume is devoted to *The Eighteenth Brumaire*. Regarding Marx's *Correspondence* [*Correspondance*], published in 1931 by Costes, Gramsci had the second and the third volumes, but probably never read them.

---

8   Q 7, § 24, pp. 871–2; PN, vol. 3, pp. 173–4.
9   On this last point, see also Chapter 9, section 4.2.
10   This list is based on the books held at the Fondazione Istituto Gramsci in Rome. As Giasi noted, however, 'to enter Gramsci's prison library ... is not a risk-free operation' (2011b, p. 60). This means, for instance, that we cannot exclude that he had at his disposal more books than those we have (on this point, see Giasi 2011b, *passim*).
11   In the list of volumes of the *Fondo Gramsci* the first volume of the *Oeuvres politiques* devoted to Palmerston does not appear; however, Gramsci explicitly quotes it in a letter to his sister-in-law Tatiana Schucht (see LL, p. 432).

As emerges from the exchange of letters with Tatiana, these texts were not the best editions on the market and Gramsci complains explicitly about the poor quality of Jacques Molitor's translations – they are rather the material that was able to get through the controls of the prison administration.[12]

In addition to the aforementioned volumes, Gramsci also owned a French edition of the *Letters to Kugelmann* and an anthology of Marx's early writings in German.[13] The latter, in particular, is important since it represents one of the texts that Gramsci translated before starting to write the theoretical notes of the *Prison Notebooks* (and, for a short period of time, the two phases overlap). This is most relevant from the point of view of his 'translation exercises', as has been recently emphasised in the new critical edition.[14]

3   Overview of the Occurrences

On this basis, Gramsci develops his analysis of the categories of Caesarism and Bonapartism in the *Prison Notebooks*. Before investigating these notes in detail, it is important to list his explicit references to the two concepts, in order to develop a general idea of their presence within his prison reflections.

The earliest explicit occurrences can be traced to the initial stages of the writing of the notebooks. The terms 'Bonapartism' and 'Caesarism' occur between May and November 1930 and are distributed in notebooks 1, 3 and 4, mostly concentrated in the latter.[15] After these first examples, for a certain period of time there are only 'weak' occurrences, in which these terms appear

---

12   Among the books requested by Gramsci that never arrived, see especially the *History of Economic Doctrines* [*Histoire des doctrines économiques*] (8 vols.; on this point, see Giasi 2011b, pp. 61–2 and 64). Furthermore, new prison regulations were introduced in June 1931 and the controls became more severe. As a consequence, Gramsci wrote to Tatiana, asking her to stop sending 'suspicious' books, which might have attracted the attention of the government.

13   K. Marx, *Lettres à Kugelmann: 1862–1874*, Paris: Editions Sociales Internationales, 1930; K. Marx, *Lohnarbeit und Kapital: Zur Judenfrage und Schriften aus der Frühzeit*, ausgewählt und eingeleitet von E. Drahn, Leipzig: Reclam, 1925².

14   Cf. QNaz, 2. I, in particular the introduction by G. Cospito (pp. 11–40, and especially pp. 25 ff.).

15   Q 1, § 158, *'Animality' and Industrialism* [*'Animalità' e industrialismo*], first draft; Q 2, § 75, *R. Michels, Les Partis politiques et la contrainte sociale*, single draft; Q 3, § 119, *Past and Present. Agitation and Propaganda* [*Passato e presente. Agitazione e propaganda*], single draft; Q 4, § 52, *Americanism and Fordism* [*Americanismo e Fordismo*], first draft; Q 4, § 66, *The Military Element in Politics* [*L'elemento militare in politica*], first draft; Q 4, § 69, *On Political Parties* [*Sui partiti*], first draft.

as 'incidental' formulations – see in this regard the occurrences contained in notebook 6.¹⁶ A 'renewed' interest in these concepts emerges clearly from November 1932 onwards, shortly after the beginning of the second and most intense stage of Gramsci's work in prison. Notes from notebook 9 date back to that period; then we find some references also in miscellaneous notebooks 14, 15 and 17.¹⁷ The highest point of Gramsci's reflections on the topic, however, is represented by famous notes from the 'special' notebook 13.¹⁸

Notwithstanding the small number of recorded occurrences, a precise trajectory stands out. References to the categories of Caesarism and Bonapartism accompany the most prolific creative phase of Gramsci's work in prison (1930–33). What emerges is therefore a non-occasional interest by Gramsci in these categories, which play an important and still underestimated role within Gramsci's political thought.

---

16   These occurrences date between December 1930 and August 1931 and are all concentrated in notebook 6 (§ 40, *Past and Present. The English Government* [*Passato e presente. Il governo inglese*], single draft; § 84, *Past and Present. Continuity and Tradition* [*Passato e presente. Continuità e tradizione*], single draft; § 93, *Encyclopedic Notions* [*Nozioni enciclopediche*], single draft; § 97, *Past and Present. Lofty Ambition and Petty Ambitions* [*Passato e presente. Grande ambizione e piccole ambizioni*], single draft). However, one must recognise a slight difference in degree within this group: while two occurrences are indeed of little importance (§§ 84 and 93), the other two are more significant (§§ 40 and 97). In any case, none of the four notes plays an important role within Gramsci's thought.

17   Q 9, § 133, *Machiavelli. Caesarism* [*Machiavelli. Il cesarismo*], first draft; Q 9, § 136 *Machiavelli. Caesarism* [*Machiavelli. Il cesarismo*], first draft; Q 14, § 23, *Machiavelli. Caesarism and the 'Catastrophic' Balance of Socio-political Forces* [*Machiavelli. Cesarismo ed equilibrio 'catastrofico' delle forze politico-sociali*], single draft; Q 14, § 65, *Popular Literature* [*Letteratura popolare*], single draft; Q 15, § 60, *Italian Risorgimento. Cavour* [*Risorgimento italiano. Cavour*], single draft; Q 17, § 21, *Cultural Topics. Caesar and Caesarism* [*Argomenti di cultura. Cesare e il cesarismo*], single draft.

18   Q 13, § 23, *Observations on Certain Aspects of the Structure of Political Parties in Periods of Organic Crisis* [*Osservazioni su alcuni aspetti della struttura dei partiti politici nei periodi di crisi organica*], second draft; Q 13, § 27, *Caesarism* [*Il cesarismo*], second draft; Q 13, § 37, *Notes on French National Life* [*Note sulla vita nazionale francese*], second draft. Notebook 13 is the last of the first group of special notebooks to be terminated (the *ante quem* date for this notebook is the 19 November 1933, the date of Gramsci's departure from the prison at Turi for transfer to the clinic in Formia – on this point see QAnast, vol. 14, pp. 153–4). As regards the chronology of the different notes and their relationships, see the observations disseminated in this book.

CHAPTER 7

The Meanings of 'Bonapartism'

1   Bonapartism in the *Prison Notebooks*

To a certain extent, in the *Notebooks* Gramsci's reflections on Bonapartism precede those on Caesarism. This had already happened in the pre-prison writings. However, while, in those earlier writings, Gramsci uses the category in fewer cases and in a more defined sense, in the *Prison Notebooks* 'Bonapartism' appears many times, in many different contexts and with various meanings. Nonetheless, it is possible to classify and organise these occurrences.

If we pay attention to the various texts in which the term appears, it will be noted that there is a group of notes in which 'Bonapartism' is used (at least apparently) in a generic way, as synonymous with Caesarism – I will focus on these notes in due course. In other texts, the concept is autonomous and has its own meaning (see in particular Q 1, § 158, *'Animality' and Industrialism*; Q 3, § 119, *Past and Present. Agitation and Propaganda*; Q 4, § 52, *Americanism and Fordism*).[1] Even among these, however, we can determine two different groups. In Q 1, § 158 and Q 4, § 52 the occurrences of Bonapartism have a similar meaning, more or less comparable with the meaning in the pre-prison writings; in Q 3, § 119 the use of the term has a different purpose: the concept refers to a different (broader and more complex) theoretical framework, complementary to that of Caesarism.

The notes Q 1, § 158 and Q 4, § 52 are similar in terms of their content. It is not by chance that note § 52 of notebook 4 was originally called *'Animality' and Fordism* [*'Animalità' e Fordismo*]; the title was changed only afterwards to the current title, *Americanism and Fordism*.[2]

Written more or less within the same months, the two texts deal with the issue of the industrialisation of production processes and the effects of this transformation on workers. 'Industrialism', Gramsci asserts, 'is a continual victory over man's animality, an uninterrupted and painful process of subjugating the instincts to new and rigid habits of order, exactitude, precision'.[3] Such

---

1   Q 1, § 158 and Q 4, § 52 are the first drafts of two texts from notebook 22 (§§ 10, 11 and 12). For the analysis of the second drafts, see Chapter 12, section 2.4.
2   On the change of the title, see QAnast, vol. 8, pp. 1–13.
3   Q 1, § 158, p. 138; PN, vol. 1, p. 235. In notebook 4 Gramsci capitalises on the note in notebook 1. Thus, he concentrates on the development of this issue, focusing precisely on the topic of

a transformation is implemented usually through the imposition of a 'puritan' ideology and, precisely for this reason, society is confronted with a periodic 'crisis of *libertinism*' (which, however, does not affect the new life system, already adopted by the masses).[4]

Gramsci focuses then on how this phenomenon takes shape in contemporary society, investigating, on the one hand, Americanism and, on the other, the situation in Russia – indeed, the double reference to the post-war period and to the state in which class division does not exist is clear and it is confirmed by the allusion to Trotsky in Q 1, § 158.[5]

If the American case falls into the more general model outlined above, in Russia the dynamics are somewhat different. Since the social basis is homogeneous, there is not a class that imposes the new style of life on the rest of the population.[6] This means that what happens is what Gramsci calls a 'great totalitarian social hypocrisy' which results in a '"permanent" crisis'.[7] At this point, there are two possible solutions: either a form of self-discipline is realised, or 'some form of Bonapartism will emerge, or there will be a foreign invasion; in other words, the condition will be created for an external force which will terminate the crisis by its authority'.[8]

2   Militarism and War of Movement

2.1   *Cadornism and Bonapartism*

But what does this reference to the Bonapartist phenomenon mean? What role does this category play in this context? And what does Gramsci have in mind when he talks about Trotsky? It is clear that the text needs further explanation; a comparison with the pre-prison writings can be (again) of some utility from this point of view.

Americanism. On this theme, among the most important ones of the *Notebooks*, see Gramsci 1978, De Felice 1977 and 1978, Baratta 2004, pp. 15–34, Coutinho 2012, esp. pp. 100–5, Schwarzmantel 2015, pp. 123 ff., Fonseca 2016, *passim*.

4   Q 1, § 158, p. 138; PN, vol. 1, p. 235.
5   Cospito (2016) also affirms that in Q 1, § 158 there is a clear reference to the USSR. De Felice explicitly links this note to the 'criticism of economism and of Trotsky' (1977, p. 172) and, more generally, to Gramsci's reflection on passive revolution and the war of position.
6   Or rather, this seems to be Gramsci's presupposition – this is, of course, a very disputed question.
7   Q 1, § 158, p. 138; PN, vol. 1, p. 236.
8   Q 1, § 158, p. 138; PN, vol. 1, p. 236.

In Gramsci's journalistic articles, the category of Bonapartism was closely related to that of Cadornism (*avant la lettre*) and aimed to criticise the distance between leaders and led within the workers' movement. In the *Prison Notebooks*, 'Bonapartism' seems to have a vaguer meaning, whereas the reference to Cadorna gained a more specific meaning, by describing more precisely a form of authoritarian (and potentially catastrophic) leadership of the masses.

Indeed, Cadornism is now associated by Gramsci with the adjective 'political' (see Q 7, §10, *Structure and Superstructure* [*Struttura e superstruttura*], November 1930, where Gramsci mentions the 'strategists of political Cadornism', and its second draft, Q 13, §24).[9] In this context, see also Q 2, §121, *Cadorna* (single draft, October–November 1930). Here Gramsci, discussing an article of Mario Missiroli (1886–1974) on Cadorna, links his reflections on the Italian general and on the defeat at Caporetto with the issue of political and military leadership, and he establishes an important comparison with Napoleon I:

> The Napoleonic model cannot be brought back: Napoleon represented the civil society and the militarism of France, he united within himself the two functions of head of government and head of the army. The Italian dominant class has not known how to prepare military leaders, that is all. Why should great political ability be expected of Cadorna, if a corresponding military ability is not expected of political leaders? Certainly, the military chief because of his function must have political ability, but the political attitude toward the mass of the military and military policy must be determined by the government, as its responsibility.[10]

Thus, the reason for the (formal) separation between the two categories and, in particular, for the autonomisation of that of Cadornism, is to be found, in my opinion, in the greater political effectiveness of the 'exclusive' hint to Cadorna and, implicitly, to the defeat of Caporetto – which also explains the use of the adjective 'political'.

However, a significant continuity between Bonapartism and Cadornism still exists. Bonapartism is defined as 'external coercive force' [*coazione esterna*] and acceleration 'through coercive means' [*con mezzi coercitivi*].[11] Moreover,

---

9   Q 7, §10, p. 860; PN, vol. 3, p. 163.
10 Q 2, §121, pp. 259–60; PN, vol. 1, p. 344.
11 Q 1, §158, p. 139; PN, vol. 1, p. 236 (translation modified); Q 4, §52, p. 489; PN, vol. 2, p. 216.

Bonapartism is also connected with a military model (echoing even more explicitly Cadornism), compared to a 'foreign invasion'.[12] As well as for Cadornism, the main features of Bonapartism in this context are then its 'extrinsicality' and 'verticality'. Gramsci focuses on the way in which the political leadership is realised. Bonapartism is therefore conceived of as a form of violent imposition of a higher will, the 'solution of force' to a crisis otherwise unresolvable.

On this basis, I would argue that there is a kind of 'division of labour' between the categories of Cadornism and Bonapartism in the *Prison Notebooks*. On the one hand, when talking about political Cadornism, Gramsci emphasises the 'relational' dimension, or, rather, the lack of relationship between rulers and ruled. On the other hand, Bonapartism highlights the brutality of the way in which the will of the leaders is imposed on the masses.

2.2 *Trotsky and the War of Movement*

Some pointers on the meaning of the category of Bonapartism also come from the historical and political context of Gramsci's analysis. Trotsky is taken by Gramsci – implicitly in Q 1, §158 and explicitly in Q 4, §52 – as an example of a figure who acts in an authoritarian way, by imposing his own decisions on others.[13]

> The tendency exhibited by Leon Davidovich was related to this problem. Its essential content was based on the 'will' to give supremacy to industry and industrial methods, to accelerate the growth of discipline and orderliness in production through coercive means, to adapt customs to the necessities of work. It would have ended up, necessarily, in a form of Bonapartism; hence it was necessary to break it up inexorably. His practical solutions were wrong, but his concerns were correct. The danger inhered in this imbalance between theory and practice. This had already manifested itself earlier, in 1921. The principle of coercion in the sphere of work was correct (the speech against Martov, reproduced in the book on *Terrorism*), but the form it assumed was wrong: the military 'model' had become a baneful prejudice, and the labor armies ended in failure.[14]

---

12 Q 1, §158, p. 139; PN, vol. 1, p. 236.
13 In the judgement on Trotsky, however, is probably embedded a more general reflection on the recent political development in Russia. On this double level of reading of Gramsci's texts, see Chapter 12, section 2.4.
14 Q 4, §52, p. 489; PN, vol. 2, p. 215.

The historical reference of Gramsci's statements is represented by the proposal, advanced by Trotsky at the time of the civil war in Russia, to transform the Red Army into a 'labour army', in order to accelerate the modernisation of the Soviet productive system by supporting its industrialisation.[15] On this basis, Gramsci immediately points out the paradigmatic nature of Soviet revolutionary attempts, opening the way for a broader interpretation of the category of Bonapartism.

The militarisation of labour and the industrialism desired by Trotsky are part of a more general attitude defined by Gramsci as 'economism'. It consists in considering mechanically and deterministically the relations between structure and superstructure, in the simplistic conviction that the transformation of the means of production necessarily brings with it a political and ideological change, too.[16]

Furthermore, the connection between industrialism, economism and authoritarianism sketched here with regard to the figure of Trotsky sheds a meaningful light also on the category of political Cadornism, whose relation to Bonapartism appears even clearer. Significantly, in Q 13, § 24 (the second draft of the note on Cadornism from notebook 7), Gramsci returns to the topic, in the framework of a discussion on the double concept of war of position-war of manoeuvre. Here he writes:

> On the subject of parallels between on the one hand the concepts of war of manoeuvre and war of position in military science, and on the other the corresponding concepts in political science, Rosa [Luxemburg]'s little book ... should be recalled. In this book, Rosa ... theorised the historical experiences of 1905. She in fact disregarded the 'voluntary' and organisational elements which were far more extensive and important in those events than – thanks to a certain 'economistic' and spontaneist prejudice – she tended to believe ... This view was a form of iron economic determinism, with the aggravating factor that it was conceived of as operating with lightning speed in time and in space. It was thus out and out historical mysticism, the awaiting of a sort of miraculous illumination ... The same reduction must take place in the art and science of politics, at least in the case of the most advanced States, where 'civil society' has

---

15   On Trotsky's positions, see in particular Swain 2014, pp. 80 ff. and Twiss 2014, *passim* (more generally on the economy of revolutionary Russia, see Barnett 2004). On Gramsci's criticism of it, see Benvenuti and Pons 1999, p. 99. For an updated biographical profile of the figure of Trotsky, see Patenaude 2017.

16   On this point, see Liguori and Voza 2009, pp. 258–62.

become a very complex structure and one which is resistant to the catastrophic 'incursions' of the immediate economic element (crises, depressions, etc.). The superstructures of civil society are like the trench-systems of modern warfare ... Of course, things do not remain exactly as they were; but it is certain that one will not find the element of speed, of accelerated time, of the definitive forward march expected by the strategists of political Cadornism. The last occurrence of the kind in the history of politics was the events of 1917. They marked a decisive turning-point in the history of the art and science of politics ... One attempt to begin a revision of the current tactical methods was perhaps that outlined by L. Dav. Br. [Trotsky] at the fourth meeting, when he made a comparison between the Eastern and Western fronts. The former had fallen at once, but unprecedented struggles had then ensued; in the case of the latter, the struggles would take place 'beforehand'. The question, therefore, was whether civil society resists before or after the attempt to seize power; where the latter takes place, etc. However, the question was outlined only in a brilliant, literary form, without directives of a practical character.[17]

It is evident that the judgement contained in the final section of this note (present exclusively in this second draft) is only apparently positive. Gramsci acknowledges Trotsky's merit of having raised the issue of the difference between East and West; immediately after, however, the inadequacy of his proposal is declared – Trotsky's theory is just a brilliant literary exposition. Trotsky, according to Gramsci, still remains the theorist of the permanent revolution and, as a consequence, he is much closer to economistic positions such as those derived from Luxemburg's analysis.[18]

Beyond any political controversy, the link between Trotsky's industrialism and economism on the one hand, and the reflection on the categories of war of position and war of manoeuvre on the other, is crucial. Generally speak-

---

17   Q 13, § 24, pp. 1613–16; SPN, pp. 233–6. Only the redrafted text (first draft: Q 7, § 10) contains the reference to Trotsky. As Catone affirmed, this underlining of the purely theoretical and 'literary' nature of Trotsky's theory of permanent revolution evokes the judgement already expressed by Bukharin (Bukharin criticised Trotsky for the *'rationalistic-formal, literary way of dealing with the issues'* – see Liguori and Voza 2009, p. 863). On Q 13, § 24, see QAnast, vol. 14, p. 157, Benvenuti and Pons 1999, p. 108 and Gramsci 2012, pp. 195–201 (this volume is for the most part a reprint of the book edited by Donzelli in 1981 – the two editions have different introductions; as for me, I continue to consider the interpretation suggested in the 1980s more convincing).

18   On the Gramsci-Trotsky relationship, see Rosengarten 1984–85 and 2014, Bianchi 2008 (also in relation to the issue of the 'war of position'), Thomas 2015c, Dal Maso 2018.

ing, Gramsci distinguishes between the two concepts (war of position and war of movement) on the basis of their historico-political nature. If the war of movement is characterised by its focus on the 'immediate economic element' and the 'war of manoeuvre', characterised by a 'lightninglike' organisation 'in time and in space', the war of position highlights the 'elements of civil society [that] correspond to the defensive systems', which implies a wider vision and a slower development.[19] Moreover, each concept corresponds to a precise moment of recent European history, where the watershed is clearly identified by Gramsci with the events of 1917, according to a recurring periodisation in the *Prison Notebooks*.[20] Connecting the war of movement with categories usually associated with Trotsky as well as (indirectly) with Cadornism and Bonapartism is an element of great interest in the definition of Gramsci's political thought.

Eventually, another term that belongs to the same 'conceptual cluster' is represented by the category of 'Napoleonism'. It appears only in two notes, Q 1, § 150 (*The Conception of the State from the Standpoint of the Productivity [Function] of Social Classes* [*La concezione dello Stato secondo la produttività [funzione] delle classi sociali*]; May 1930)[21] and Q 14, § 68 (*Machiavelli*; February 1933, single draft)[22] – but see also Q 2, § 60 (*On Emmanuel Philibert* [*Su Emanuele Filiberto* ...]; August–September 1930, single draft), where the figure of Napoleon as a military leader is emphasised.[23] This concept, akin to Cadornism and Bonapartism, contributes to define the features of the war of manoeuvre, by further characterising it from both the historical and the theoretical point of view. In

---

19 Q 13, § 24, pp. 1615–16; SPN, pp. 233–5 (translation slightly modified). In this paragraph, Gramsci's use of the military lexicon is particularly remarkable. Not only does he dwell on the theoretical aspect of the 'art of war', but he also recalls two famous episodes of recent military history – to be noted also the affinity, from this point of view, with Q 7, § 16. On Gramsci's military metaphors, see Egan 2016.
20 On this chronology, see Chapter 10, section 2.1.
21 The text is redrafted in Q 10, II, § 61.
22 On the chronology of notebook 14, see now Francioni 2020, who states that the entire notebook was completed by February 1933 (and not by March 1935, as previously reputed).
23 In Q 1, § 150 Gramsci links Napoleonism to the French Revolution, discussing their overcoming thanks to a '"reaction-national transcendence"' (p. 133; curiously, in the English critical edition, instead of the word 'Napoleonism', that would represent the correct translation of the Italian *'napoleonismo'*, we read 'Bonapartism' – cf. PN, vol. 1, p. 230). It is no coincidence that the text is subsequently revised by Gramsci, who replaces the second part of the sentence – and so also the term 'Napoleonism' – with 'passive revolution' (variant in the margin – see QAnast, vol. 2, pp. 1–5). On the connection between passivity and personality in Trotsky, see the aforementioned entry by Catone in Liguori and Voza 2009, p. 864. On the topic, see also Cospito 2016, p. 208, n. 4 and p. 215, especially n. 16.

particular, Napoleonism represents a reference to Napoleon Bonaparte (rather than to his nephew), whose strong personality and military achievements are well known: he is therefore a perfect representative of the war of movement model.

We may conclude that, despite the apparent shallowness of the references to Bonapartism, this concept has a definite meaning, closely related to that of Napoleonism and, above all, to that of Cadornism. Along with these categories, Bonapartism also helps to characterise the category of the war of manoeuvre. In this context, special attention is devoted to the new Bonaparte or new Cadorna, i.e. Trotsky. This also demonstrates that the category of Bonapartism still represents for Gramsci a key to interpreting the developments of the workers' movement, although now on an international level.

3   Gramsci and the So-called 'Dictatorships of Depretis, Crispi and Giolitti'

The context in which we find the other major occurrences of the term Bonapartism (Q 3, § 119) is different from many points of view. This text, a single draft written in August–September 1930, is collected under the heading *Past and Present* and is entitled *Agitation and Propaganda*. Here Gramsci deals with Italian political history from the Unification onwards, focusing on some distinctive aspects of the *Risorgimento*.[24]

The argument in general is clear. Gramsci 'diagnoses' a structural weakness of Italian parties, which is caused by an 'imbalance between agitation and propaganda', that means by the lack of a coherent political strategy and by the opportunism that characterises Italian politicians.[25] The formula used by Gramsci is very interesting too, since it revisits a phrase already present in the pre-prison writings.

In a piece on the principles of Leninism published in *L'Unità* on 10 September 1925, Gramsci states:

> The dictatorship of the proletariat constitutes for Leninism the strategic goal to reach in the present phase by the revolutionary proletariat of

---

24   Gramsci did not copy this text into the monographic notebook on the Italian *Risorgimento* (Q 19), despite the perfect fit between the topic developed here and the notes of notebook 19. On this notebook, see the still valuable introduction by Corrado Vivanti in Gramsci 1977 and, more recently, QAnast, vol. 17, pp. 1–12.

25   Q 3, § 119, p. 386; PN, vol. 2, p. 105.

all countries ... [S]trategy is conceived as the art of winning, i.e. to gain power, and tactics as the art of conducting individual operations aimed to facilitate and hasten victory. It can be said that propaganda corresponds to strategy and agitation to tactics.[26]

The two terms (often combined also with 'organisation') appear several times in Gramsci's pre-prison writings, even if with a vaguer meaning than the one illustrated here. Sometimes they indicate, in a positive sense, the premises of the revolution; at other times, they describe, in a negative sense, the ineffective nature of parliamentary action.[27] In the *Prison Notebooks*, the agitation-propaganda polarity also appears in Q 8, § 86, *Machiavelli* (written in September 1932; first draft of Q 13, § 14) and in Q 19, § 24, *The Problem of Political Leadership in the Formation and Development of the Nation and the Modern State in Italy* [*Il problema della direzione politica nella formazione e nello sviluppo della nazione e dello Stato moderno in Italia*] – here in particular we again find a connection between these two concepts and Gramsci's reflection on the *Risorgimento*.[28]

In the context of Q 3, § 119, these categories help to define the weakness of Italian politics. This is due, on the one hand, to the chronic failing of the bourgeoisie – as Gramsci writes, to the 'deliquescence of the economic classes' and to the 'gelatinous economic and social structure of the country'.[29] On the other hand, a role is played also by the nature of what Gramsci calls the 'state-government' (that is, in Gramscian terms, political society, conceived of as separated from civil society),[30] which acts according to its own interests and not according to the interests of the whole nation.

He dwells for a long time on this second element of weakness, claiming that this 'party-government' is supported by masses not linked to any polit-

---

26   *Leninism* [*Leninismo*], L'Unità, 10 September 1925 (PV, p. 335).
27   See, for instance, 'Workers' Control' ['Controllo operaio'], *L'Ordine Nuovo*, 10 February 1921 (SF, p. 68; SPW-2, pp. 10–11) and 'The Italian Crisis' ['La crisi italiana'], *L'Ordine Nuovo*, 1 September 1924 (CPC, pp. 28–39, SPW-2, pp. 255–66).
28   In Q 13, § 14 this conceptual couple appears in the framework of the '"dual perspective"' symbolised by Machiavelli's Centaur, alongside with other conceptual pairs such as 'force–consent', 'authority–hegemony', 'violence–civilisation', 'individual moment–universal moment', 'tactics–strategy' (p. 1576; SPN, p. 170). In the text of notebook 19, written between July–August 1934 and February 1935, Gramsci is speaking about the weakness of the Action Party and states: 'In essence it was always, more than anything else, an agitational and propagandist body in the service of the Moderates' (p. 2014; SPN, p. 62).
29   Q 3, § 119, pp. 386–7; PN, vol. 2, p. 105.
30   See Liguori and Voza 2009, p. 367.

ical party and therefore bound to the government only through 'paternalistic bonds of Bonapartist-Caesarist type'.[31]

To describe this self-oriented attitude, Gramsci mentions two very precise historico-political events: the governments of the three main representatives of the 'Historical Left' (the '*dictatorships* of Depretis, Crispi, and Giolitti') and the phenomenon of transformism [*trasformismo*], which gained a particular importance under these governments.[32] In this context, the definition of dictatorship stands out. As emphasised by Gramsci, albeit with the addition of the modifier 'so-called', these governments are not dictatorships in a traditional sense, with their violent and despotic actions. Depretis, Crispi and Giolitti are all dictators insofar as they do not take into account the popular masses, their desires and their needs – they act as a father might towards his (inferior and immature) children, as suggested by the adjective 'paternalistic'.[33] This separation between rulers and ruled turns into a widespread practice of political transformism, as pointed out by Gramsci in several of his prison notes.[34]

After giving this example, Gramsci describes the flawed relationship between government, parties and social classes in this framework, by defining, in turn, the correct and virtuous form of this relation. Gramsci, in short, presents a nation that, in its political pettiness and intellectual poverty, looks like a 'parody', a 'caricature' of the state, rather than a real state. He deepens further this dismal description by referring to the 'non-national', extraneous and selfish

---

31 Q 3, § 119, p. 387; PN, vol. 2, p. 106. See the whole passage: 'the government, in fact, has functioned as a "party": it has placed itself above the parties not in order to harmonize their interests and activity within the permanent frameworks of the life and interests of nation and state but rather in order to disunite them, to separate them from the great masses, and to gain "a force of nonpartisans who are attached to the government by paternalistic bonds of Bonapartist-Caesarist type". This is how one should analyze the so-called *dictatorships* of Depretis, Crispi, and Giolitti, as well as the parliamentary phenomenon of transformism' (PN, vol. 2, pp. 105–6).

32 For a detailed introduction to the Italian *Risorgimento*, see Davis 2000 and Cammarano 2011. 'Historical Left' and 'Historical Right' are terms used by the historians to distinguish, respectively, the left-wing and right-wing groups of the twentieth century from the political organisations of the nineteenth century. While the 'Historical Left' represents the liberal and reformist faction, 'Historical Right' is the name usually attributed to the Conservatives.

33 As Burgio writes, 'the "so-called dictatorship" of Crispi fits perfectly in the frame of Italian modernisation, characterized by a detachment between society and the state and by the inertia of the parties, which neglect their fundamental task, i.e. to organise the classes politically, to civilise them and to make them aware of their not merely corporate interests' (2014, p. 269).

34 See, for instance, Q 8, § 36; on the topic, see also Liguori and Voza 2009, pp. 860–2.

character of Italian bureaucracy, which, as 'state-Bonapartist party', plays a pivotal role in maintaining this state of affairs.[35]

The note ends with a reference to Max Weber's *Parliament and Government in Germany under a new Political Order* [*Parlament und Regierung im neugeordneten Deutschland*] (1918). This is significant for two reasons: first, because it represents (albeit in a compressed form) a type of comparative analysis, and, second, because it puts great emphasis on the bureaucratic element, which has a prominent role in both the Weberian and the Gramscian frameworks.[36]

Numerous observations arise from this analysis. First, there is the paradigmatic character of Gramsci's reflection on the Italian *Risorgimento*. As Vivanti has noted, if there is a 'link between the ideological interpretation of the past and the historical perspective of political action' in the *Prison Notebooks*, this is particularly true in the case of the notes on the *Risorgimento*.[37] The events gathered under this historiographic category represent a crucial turning point in the political history of the peninsula: by (literally) creating modern Italy, the *Risorgimento* embodies Italy's fundamental features. The study of this dynamics thus offers a privileged point of view on recent Italian history (and, last but not least, on the rise of the fascist dictatorship). However, if the *Risorgimento* is an exemplary case study from a 'diachronic' perspective,[38] it is equally important from the 'synchronic' one, since it represents a perfect example of the tendency towards passive revolution common in the entire European continent at that time.[39]

---

35 See Q 3, §119, p. 387; PN, vol. 2, p. 106: 'Thus the bureaucracy estranged itself from the people and through its administrative positions it became a true political party, the worst of all, because the bureaucratic hierarchy replaced the intellectual and political hierarchy: the bureaucracy became precisely the state-Bonapartist party'.

36 As Gerratana noted, Gramsci owned Weber's book (see Q1975, p. 2614). Among Weber's works, Gramsci also knew *The Protestant Ethic and the Spirit of Capitalism* [*Die protestantische Ethik und der Geist des Kapitalismus*], published between 1931 and 1932 in the journal *Nuovi studi di diritto, economia e politica*. On Gramsci's reading of Weber's *Protestant Ethic*, see Frosini 2008. Concerning the other texts by Weber (1864–1920), it is unlikely that Gramsci knew them (I disagree with Michele Filippini on this count – see Liguori and Voza 2009, p. 905 and Filippini 2015). It cannot be excluded that Gramsci's knowledge of Weber's thought is for the most part 'indirect', mediated by thinkers like Mosca, Michels or the followers of Croce (e.g. De Ruggiero). On Michels, in particular, see Chapter 9, section 1.

37 Gramsci 1977, p. xiv. However, Gramsci was not the only one that looked at the *Risorgimento* with a 'political' eye. See, for instance, Benedetto Croce's *A History of Italy. 1871–1915* [*Storia d'Italia dal 1871 al 1915*] or (from a different angle) Gioacchino Volpe's *Italy on the Road* [*L'Italia in cammino*], or Giovanni Gentile, who depicts Fascism as the fulfilment of the *Risorgimento*, and so on.

38 I adopt here the adjective 'diachronic', aptly applied to the *Prison Notebooks* by Cospito (Cospito 2016, *passim*).

39 On the connection between passive revolution and Italian *Risorgimento*, see, for instance,

Given this perspective, the two occurrences of Bonapartism contained in this note assume a paradigmatic character (although the text is unique in the *Notebooks*). In short, Bonapartism describes the exercise of power for personal and private purposes or, in any case, not in favour of the whole national community. Furthermore, it highlights the key role of bureaucracy within national politics and the conservative nature of this state apparatus.

There is a clear, if subtle, difference between the meaning of Bonapartism thus conceived and the occurrences investigated previously. While in notebooks 1 and 4 Gramsci focuses on the imbalance between theory and practice in political leadership, in notebook 3 this category underlines the non-universal, non-national and, hence, non-progressive character of Italian politics (as Gramsci argues at length in the *Notebooks*, the necessary condition for real progress in history is the universalisation of the interests of a class, i.e. their adoption also by the other social groups and, therefore, the creation of hegemony).[40] Thus, the two meanings deal with two different levels of analysis.

Moreover, it should be noted that while Q 1, § 158 and Q 4, § 52 (in continuity with the pre-prison writings)[41] are related to Gramsci's reflections on his contemporary historico-political context rather than to *The Eighteenth Brumaire*, Q 3, § 119 shows instead a clear influence of Marx's thought. This note, in fact, recalls and amplifies some of the salient aspects of Marx's investigation and, specifically, his reflection on the role of the middle classes and on bureaucracy.

4   Bonapartism and Bureaucracy

4.1   *At the Origin of the Relationship*

The focus on bureaucracy is no doubt one of the most important elements of Q 3, § 119 (*Past and Present. Agitation and Propaganda*, August–September 1930). Gramsci had already analysed the nature and the role of this state appar-

---

Q 1, § 44, *Political Class Leadership Before and After Assuming Government Power* [*Direzione politica di classe prima e dopo l'andata al governo*], where, however, the expression 'passive revolution' was added in a second moment (see QAnast, vol. 2, pp. 1–5) – the note was then redrafted in Q 19, § 24. See also Q 15, § 11 and Q 15, § 59. On this point, see also Thomas 2018a.

40 On this process of universalisation, see Frosini 2016a, *passim*.

41 It is interesting to note that another Gramscian category taken from Marx and adopted in the pre-prison writings, that of 'parliamentary cretinism', in the *Prison Notebooks* is, in a certain sense, rejected. There are only two notes in which Gramsci speaks about '"economic cretinism"' with reference to Luigi Einaudi's theory (see Q 7, § 13, p. 864; PN, vol. 3, p. 166, and its second draft Q 10, II, § 39, p. 1290; FSPN, p. 423: 'economistic "cretinism"', according to Boothman's translation).

atus in the pre-prison writings, by describing it as the 'essential form of organisation of the dominant social bloc'.[42] In the *Prison Notebooks*, these observations are taken up and extended. Q 3, § 119 is exemplary from this point of view: here Gramsci highlights the deep bureaucratisation of modern states (see the striking definition of the 'state-Bonapartist party') and describes bureaucracy as an institution detached from the 'real' country and hostile to any change. As Burgio sums up, 'the very features highlighted (separatism, conservatism and, above all, privatisation, exclusive care of their particular interests) lead Gramsci to classify the bureaucratic group as a ... Bonapartist subject', in the sense specified above.[43] Regarding Gramsci's sources of inspiration, he fruitfully combines Hegel's *Philosophy of Right* and Marx's *Eighteenth Brumaire*, while a role is also played by Weber, whose work is mentioned at the end of the note.[44]

The text from notebook 3 represents therefore an excellent example of the Gramscian conception of bureaucracy. Although written in the early stage of his prison work, the text anticipates many aspects of Gramsci's most mature reflection on the topic.[45]

On this basis, I want to sketch briefly the development of his analysis of the bureaucratic apparatus, from the first notebooks onwards, by highlighting in particular the influence of Marx's thought and its connection with the category of Bonapartism.

One of the main aspects to stress is that the term 'bureaucracy' does not describe only the ordinary administrative apparatus, but also, especially, the military one. In fact, Gramsci speaks often of 'civil and military bureaucracy'.[46] Furthermore, he puts great emphasis on the distinction between strategy and military technique within this second field, whereas the strategic aspect is assimilated, basically, to politics.[47] In Q 1, § 114, entitled *The Risorgimento. Polit-*

---

42   Paggi 1970, p. 378.
43   Burgio 2007, p. 259.
44   A clear demonstration of the relevance of Hegel's thought for Gramsci's conception of politics and society emerges, for instance, in Q 8, § 187, p. 1054 (see PN, vol. 3, p. 343: 'the position that Hegel ascribed to the intellectuals has been of great importance, not only in the conception of politics [political science] but also in the entire conception of cultural and spiritual life ... With the advent of Hegel, thinking in terms of castes and "states" started to give way to thinking in terms of the "state", and the aristocrats of the state are precisely the intellectuals'). In what follows, I will especially investigate Marx's influence, in accordance with the general aims of my work.
45   As demonstrated by Cospito (2016, p. 209), Q 3, § 119 shows a great maturity, a theoretical elaboration that also exceeds most of the texts of notebook 4.
46   Q 9, § 89, p. 1156, but see also, for instance: Q 1, § 148; Q 6, § 81; Q 13, § 37; Q 19, § 5.
47   Q 4, § 66, p. 510.

ical and Military Leadership [*Risorgimento. Direzione politica e militare*], speaking about the *Risorgimento*, he writes:

> Military leadership should not be understood only as military leadership in the strict, technical sense, that is, as a reference to the strategy and tactics of the Piedmontese army, or of Garibaldi's troops, or of the various militias that were improvised during local uprisings (the five Days of Milan, the defense of Venice, the defense of the Roman Republic, the Palermo insurrection in 1848, etc.). Rather, it should be understood in a much broader sense, and in a sense that is more closely connected with real political leadership.[48]

In another note (Q 1, § 117, *Political and Military Leadership during the Risorgimento* [*Direzione politica e militare nel Risorgimento*]), Gramsci further specifies the relationship between military direction and political direction, taking his cue from the cases of Julius Caesar, Napoleon I and Bismarck (this text anticipates to some extent the historical comparisons with regard to Caesarism in Q 9, § 133).

> Military leadership must always be subordinated to political leadership, that is, army commands must always be a military expression of a particular policy. Naturally, it may be the case that the politicians are worthless, while in the army there are commanders who combine military skill with political skill. Such is the case with Caesar and Napoleon; but in Napoleon's case one can see how the change of policy together with the presumption of possessing a military instrument which was military in the abstract led to his downfall: in other words, even in these instances of political and military leadership united in the same person, politics was more important than military leadership. Caesar's books, especially *De bello civili*, are a classic example of the display of a wise combination of politics and military art: soldiers saw in Caesar not only a great military

---

48   Q 1, § 114, p. 101; PN, vol. 1, p. 198 (translation slightly modified). The text, written in February–March 1930, was redrafted in Q 19, §§ 27–8. In addition to this, Gramsci also raises the issue of the people's involvement and, ultimately, of the 'national' character of the military action: 'Military leadership, then, is a much larger issue than the leadership of the army as such and the establishment of the strategic plan which the army has to carry out: military leadership is concerned with the mobilization of popular forces who would rebel at the enemy's back and impede his movement, it tends to create mass auxiliary and reserve forces from which new armies could be drawn and which would provide the "technical" army with an atmosphere of enthusiasm and zeal' (PN, vol. 1, p. 199).

leader, but also a great political leader. Remember that Bismarck upheld the primacy of politics over the military, whereas Wilhelm II, according to Ludwig's account, scribbled angrily on a newspaper which had either quoted or echoed Bismarck's views. Thus the Germans won almost all the battles brilliantly, but lost the war.[49]

The military element (understood both as technical-military and military-political) is an essential feature also of the 'classic' conception of Bonapartism.[50]

In Gramsci's view, however, what counts for the definition of bureaucracy is especially the military-political aspect, as emerges clearly from an important text on the topic, Q 4, § 66, *The Military Element in Politics* [*L'elemento militare in politica*] (November 1930). The note opens with an observation on the importance of the historico-political analysis of the military and civil bureaucracy, which has to be considered both 'actually' and 'potentially'. Indeed,

> an analysis of the set of social forces that have operated in history and are at work in the political activity of a state structure should give due attention to the military and the bureaucratic element, and this includes not just the military and bureaucratic elements that are actually in place but also the social strata in the particular state structure from which these elements are traditionally recruited.[51]

Gramsci demonstrates that 'military' is not just what is presented explicitly as such, but also refers to the social group from which the majority of the members of the army and of the military bureaucracy originate. He develops then what we could define as a 'sociology of the army', wondering: 'does a given country have an extensive social stratum for which a military or bureaucratic career is an important element in economic life and political self-assertion'?[52]

The answer is positive and he identifies in the 'medium and small rural bourgeoisie' the class that contributed most to 'nourishing' the civil and military

---

49 Q 1, § 117, pp. 110–11; PN, vol. 1, pp. 207–8. This note, written in February–March 1930, is redrafted in Q 19, § 28.
50 On this point, see Groh 1972. While in Q 4, § 66, p. 511 (PN, vol. 2, p. 239) Gramsci used the expression 'countries that are, so to speak, "Caesarist"' to describe countries in which there are military regimes, in the second draft he substitutes this expression with the phrase 'countries which are, so to speak, potentially Bonapartist' (Q 13, § 23, p. 1609; SPN, p. 216).
51 Q 4, § 66, p. 509; PN, vol. 2, p. 237.
52 Q 4, § 66, p. 509; PN, vol. 2, p. 237.

bureaucracy, for psychological and socio-political reasons.[53] In particular, in Q 3, § 46, *Past and Present* (single draft, June–July 1930), Gramsci specifies that it is mainly the 'petty bourgeois "starveling"' (i.e. the impoverished part of the rural bourgeoisie) that aims to become a state employee.[54]

The rural bourgeoisie is used to giving orders; if threatened, it can react ferociously and with a 'strong sense of purpose' – it is even bloodier than the big bourgeoisie, due to its willingness to distinguish itself from the peasantry.[55] As Gramsci writes, the rural bourgeoisie 'lives off the chronic poverty and prolonged labor of the peasant': 'it has an income because it owns some "brutish" land and prevents the peasant from improving his own existence'.[56] In turn, it is politically and economically subjected to the 'upper classes'; nevertheless the rural bourgeoisie seeks to control the big bourgeoisie in times of crisis, repressing on its behalf the revolts which break in the countryside and thus obtaining an 'effective participation in power, even if only indirectly, by "blackmail"'.[57] In short, the rural bourgeoisie is a parasitical and ambiguously subversive group. It has a relative 'leading function', that, however, 'is no small thing'.[58]

4.2   *Between Marx and the* Southern Question

From this perspective, it is interesting to compare Gramsci's affirmations in the *Notebooks* with the last text that he wrote before his imprisonment, the famous essay on the southern question.[59] As Elisabetta Gallo has pointed out, although the category of the rural bourgeoisie does not appear often in the *Notebooks*, 'it refers to concepts that return frequently in Gramsci and it implies the analysis of the specific Italian situation', by containing a clear reference to the pre-carceral text of 1926.[60]

---

53   Q 4, § 66, p. 509; PN, vol. 2, p. 237.
54   Q 3, § 46, p. 323; PN, vol. 2, p. 45. It should be noted, however, that Gramsci is not particularly interested in creating a precise social taxonomy; he points out rather the specific functions that the various groups play in the historical and political context.
55   Q 4, § 66, p. 510; PN, vol. 2, p. 238.
56   Q 4, § 66, p. 510; PN, vol. 2, p. 238.
57   Q 4, § 66, pp. 509–11; PN, vol. 2, pp. 237–40. The relation between city and countryside is closely related to the question of the rural bourgeoisie – on this point see Liguori and Voza 2009, pp. 130–2. On the city-countryside relation, see also Ekers et al. 2012, *passim*.
58   Q 4, § 66, p. 510; PN, vol. 2, p. 238.
59   Cf. *Some Aspects of the Southern Question*, PPW, pp. 313–37 (a definitive version of the Italian text was established by Biscione – see Biscione 1990). In spite of what is usually said (cf. for instance PPW, p. 313), the text is not unfinished.
60   Liguori and Voza 2009, p. 78. On this point see, for instance, the following quotation: 'The southern intellectuals are one of the most interesting and important social strata

Returning to Q 4, § 66, *The Military Element in Politics*, Gramsci ends this description of the rural bourgeoisie by making explicit the connection between the bureaucratic-military apparatus and Bonapartism, which is here, for the first time, explicitly associated with Caesarism:[61]

> In a number of countries, then, the influence of the military element in politics does not mean simply the influence and weight of the military in the technical sense but the influence and weight of the social stratum that is the primary source of the technical military element (especially of subaltern officers). This criterion, I believe, is quite useful for analyzing the most hidden aspect of that specific political form usually known as Caesarism or Bonapartism and for distinguishing it from other political forms in which the technical military element predominates, perhaps in ways that are even more conspicuous and exclusive.[62]

This in-depth sociological investigation is accompanied by a double historical example. Gramsci observes that in Spain and Greece – two military regimes at that time – the rural bourgeoisie has no way of showing its strength to the upper bourgeoisie, due to the passivity of the peasantry.[63] As a consequence, in both cases (albeit with specific features relating to the different contexts), the upper class holds its primacy firmly and the army is under the strict con-

---

in national Italian life. One has only to think that more than three-fifths of the State bureaucracy is made up by Southerners to realize how true this is ... The southern intellectual comes in the main from a class which is still very strong in the South: the rural bourgeoisie. This means the small or medium landowner who is not a peasant, who does not work the land, who would find it shameful to farm his own land but who wants to extract from the little land he has – leased out either for rent or on a share-cropping basis – enough to live respectably, to send his sons to university or to seminary and to give a dowry to his daughters, who must marry an officer or a civil functionary of the State. From this class background, the intellectuals derive a fierce antipathy to the working peasant, considered as a work machine that can be bled dry and then replaced, given the excess working population. They also derive from their class an atavistic, instinctual feeling of blind fear of the peasants and their destructive violence; and from this, in turn, they derive the habit of refined hypocrisy and an extremely refined art of deceiving and subduing the peasant masses' (PPW, pp. 328–9).

61 In Q 3, §119, however, Gramsci has already coined the adjective '*bonapartistico-cesareo*' (p. 387; 'a Bonapartist-Caesarist type'; PN, vol. 2, p. 106).
62 Q 4, § 66, p. 510; PN, vol. 2, p. 238.
63 See Q 4, § 66, p. 511; PN, vol. 2, p. 239: 'In Spain, the countryside, being totally passive, permits the generals of the landed aristocracy to make political use of the army to reestablish order – that is, the supremacy of the upper classes – while giving the transitional military government a deceptively different appearance'.

trol of its generals. The activity of the military troops is therefore exclusively of a technical-military nature. The complex play of interaction between the military element and the socio-political element described above, the subtle plot of obedience and blackmail that characterises the relations between the various social groups is absent ('the experience of military government did not create a permanent political and social ideology').[64] To these cases, Gramsci then opposes more complex historical phenomena and offers a summary of his conception of Bonapartism:

> In other countries, the countryside is not passive, but its movement is not politically coordinated with the urban movement: the army must remain neutral for as long as possible in order to avoid being broken up horizontally. The 'military-bureaucratic class', the rural bourgeoisie, enters the scene and uses military means to stifle the (more immediately dangerous) movement in the countryside. In this struggle it finds a certain political and ideological consolidation; it finds allies among the middle class in the city (the role of students of rural origin living in the cities); it imposes its own political methods on the upper classes, which must make many concessions to it and permit the passage of specific legislation in its favor. In short, it manages to permeate the state with its interests (up to a point) and to replace the leading personnel, while continuing to keep itself armed during a general disarmament and incessantly threatening civil wars between its own armed bands and the national army if the upper class fails to comply with certain demands.[65]

What emerges is therefore the fact that a military nature is not immediately Bonapartist; the essential condition for the establishment of a Bonapartist regime is the existence of a well-developed bureaucratic apparatus, which is able to play a decisive role in the context of political crises.

Finally, Gramsci's analysis echoes the understanding of nineteenth-century France in *The Eighteenth Brumaire*, and in particular Marx's description of the *Lumpenproletariat*.[66] Despite their evident differences (above all: the *Lumpenproletariat* lives in the city, while the rural bourgeoisie lives in the countryside), there are many points of contact between the descriptions of these two groups.

First, Gramsci's rural bourgeoisie is a 'non-class', in a similar manner to Marx's sub-proletariat: 'this stratum has no economic functions in the mod-

---

64   Q 4, § 66, p. 511; PN, vol. 2, p. 239.
65   Q 4, § 66, p. 511; PN, vol. 2, pp. 239–40.
66   On Marx's *Lumpenproletariat*, see Hayes 1988, Cowling 2008, pp. 149 ff. and Antonini 2013b.

ern sense of the term'. It is economically unproductive. This is also the reason for its parasitic nature, its seeking of public jobs.⁶⁷ The direct consequence of this lack of economic roots is the political volatility, the opportunism of these groups: whilst Gramsci speaks of a 'double-headed' subversiveness, Marx shows how the *Lumpenproletariat* chooses its political allies from time to time based on its own advantage.⁶⁸ Moreover, the *Lumpenproletariat*, and in particular the so-called 'Society of December 10', is the armed wing of Louis Bonaparte's supporters. In like manner, the rural bourgeoisie is the strong arm of the upper classes in Gramsci's view. Finally, both Marx's and Gramsci's bureaucracy are characterised by a high degree of independence *vis-à-vis* the rest of society (towards which they do not have any solidarity) and, in turn, by a close connection with the state and the government. Given these points, Marx's influence on Gramsci's thought is very clear.

---

67   Q 4, § 66, p. 510; PN, vol. 2, p. 238.
68   As for Gramsci, see in particular Q 3, § 46; on this topic, see Frosini 2016a.

CHAPTER 8

Between Bonapartism and Caesarism

1   Anachronistic Revival or Useful Analytical Tool?

It is clear that Gramsci's study of the issue of bureaucracy through the category of Bonapartism intersects with one of the fundamental themes of his reflections in prison: the relation between political society and civil society and, more generally, the complex theme of 'relations of force'. This enquiry thus represents a valuable addition to Gramsci's analysis of Caesarism in a context of hegemonic crisis. The bureaucracy's attitude to the maintenance of order and conservatism in fact plays a role in the rise of a charismatic leader.

But why does Gramsci persist in talking about Bonapartism, if Caesarism lies at the centre of these reflections? The reason why he continues to use the concept of Bonapartism, in my opinion, is that his reflections on bureaucracy are linked to Marx's model, which is an indispensable point of reference for him. Without exaggerating, it can be said that the reference to Bonapartism, albeit attenuated by its frequent association with the category of Caesarism, represents a sort of 'tribute' to Marx, a testimony to Gramsci's connection with the analysis of *The Eighteenth Brumaire*. This aspect has been so far underestimated in the Gramscian scholarship.

From this perspective, the reason for the 'split' within the concept of Bonapartism also becomes clearer. The first meaning of the term represents an element of substantial continuity with his pre-prison reflections, by highlighting a significant reference to the contemporary debate; the second sense relies on Marx's analysis of bureaucracy and serves as a complement to his investigation of Caesarism. Yet the relations between Marx and Gramsci are far more complex than they may appear at first glance.

If Gramsci uses 'conventional' Marxist formulas and phrases, he renews them from the inside, by recovering their meaning and adapting them to his needs. This 'freedom' is, at least partially, a direct consequence of Gramsci's deepening of Marx's thinking: his awareness of the meaning of Marx's categories in their historical context allows him to better integrate them into the general framework of his thought, that, in the *Notebooks*, has definitively gained its theoretical autonomy. In other words, in the *Prison Notebooks* Gramsci can grasp the deepest sense of Marx's analysis, but the analysis of Marx has to fit within Gramsci's conceptual framework, and not vice versa.

Gramsci's interest in the category of Caesarism is evident from the numerous notes in which this and related formulas are adopted. Despite such (relative) abundance, however, only a few texts deal exclusively with the phenomenology of Caesarism (§§ 23 and 27 of notebook 13 stand out among them). In the following pages, I will focus on this small group of notes that represents the core of Gramsci's analysis, by studying the differences between first and second drafts, and, thus, by laying the foundations for their further theoretical examination.

Before turning to this investigation, however, I want to discuss briefly an important contribution on this topic, namely Giuseppe Cospito's theses on Caesarism in the chapter on Gramsci and the Marxist tradition in his recent monograph.[1] Taking his cue from the analysis of a central element of Gramsci's prison writings – the relation between structure and superstructure – Cospito aims to describe the 'diachronical' development of Gramsci's thought. According to Cospito, we can summarise the various phases of Gramsci's thought as follows. While up to about the middle of 1930 Gramsci adopts an orthodox position, characterised by a certain mechanicism and determinism, from 1932 onwards he progressively overcomes the dogmatism of official Marxism and develops a more autonomous and critical conception (passing through some intermediate positions – see the reference to centrism). In this later phase, Gramsci wrote the 'special' notebooks, but also the last series of miscellaneous notebooks (notebooks 14, 15, and 17). The latter testify the emergence of new conceptions and show that Gramsci's research remains, so to speak, open and productive. The former systematise what has already been elaborated, although with a certain 'intolerance' towards the inertia of old formulations.[2] In this framework, Cospito also argues that Gramsci's notes on Caesarism in the 'special' notebook 13 contain a certain 'anachronism' – Cospito affirms that Q 13, §§ 23, 27 and 32 are 'in sharp contrast with the overall progress of Gramsci's investigation'.[3]

---

1   Cospito 2016, pp. 207–17.
2   Cospito 2016, p. 216.
3   Cospito 2016, p. 212. Cospito, in particular, tends to strongly separate the notes of notebook 4 (and of previous notebooks) from the later texts, and in particular from those of notebook 13. According to Cospito, in the early texts Gramsci adheres sincerely to the model of Caesarism-Bonapartism; this adhesion, however, takes place in 'a somewhat schematic framework common to that of Gramsci's other "arrangements" at the end of 1930' (Cospito 2016, p. 211). As regards the later texts, he emphasises their anachronistic and conservative character, in contrast with the 'increasingly flexible and elastic formulations' developed by Gramsci starting from the end of 1931 onwards (Cospito 2016, p. 211). In my view, however, such an interpretation is at times simplistic, especially regarding the texts after notebook 4. First of all, he does not explain why Gramsci, in November 1932, felt the need to write *ex novo*

Without engaging in a close reading of Cospito's analysis as a whole (which is illuminating in many respects), I would maintain that this chronological development has to be at least partially revised in light of the concrete analysis of the references to Caesarism and Bonapartism carried out so far (and, even more, on the basis of the following chapters).[4] It is true that Gramsci, in the sections devoted to these categories, warns against undue sociological schematisation, and invites us to concentrate on 'concrete historical-political analysis', as Cospito highlights.[5] Nevertheless, if we focus solely on these elements, we overlook the intrinsic value of such reflections. References to the Caesarist-Bonapartist phenomenon played a role in orienting Gramsci's reflection, alongside other references to Marx's texts or to other Marxian categories; furthermore, the deepening of the theory of Bonapartism and of Caesarism significantly contributed to the development of some central themes in the *Notebooks*. Given these points, it does not seem to me entirely correct to say, with Cospito, that Gramsci first adopts the category of Caesarism but then rejects it, despite continuing to use it on occasion. I think that there is a strong degree of continuity in Gramsci's reflections, despite (or, better, because of) the progressive evolution of his thought.

2 Q 13, §§ 23 and 27 and Their First Drafts

Against this alleged 'anachronism', I will focus on these texts from a philological and textual point of view, by contextualising them in the framework of notebook 13.

---

two important notes on Caesarism (Q 9, §§ 133 and 136) if this category appears now to Gramsci as a 'rigid position ... inappropriate to the changed general conditions of society' (Cospito 2016, pp. 212–13). Furthermore, I disagree with Cospito's judgement on the texts of notebook 13, which, in my opinion, represent the highest point of Gramsci's reflections on Caesarism. In this context, the fact that Gramsci does not merge all the observations on Caesarism contained in the *Prison Notebooks* in one single note, does not seem to me a sign of Gramsci's general lack of interest in the theme (as Cospito claims). In addition to the fact that §§ 23 and 27 of notebook 13 already collect many of the previous notes on the theme, I believe that we can say for the categories of Bonapartism and Caesarism what was said about Machiavelli's figure: while many texts relating to the figure of the Florentine secretary or to the *Prince* exist only in their first draft, 'the overall reading ... confirms and makes important the approach disseminated in the first draft texts' (QAnast, vol. 14, p. 158).

4 More generally, the question is whether a sort of 'teleological' narrative of Gramsci's 'purification' of his former 'orthodoxy' (such as the one presented in Cospito's book) can really comprehend the complexity of the development of Gramsci's thought. I would argue that a more flexible approach is required.

5 Q 4, § 66, p. 511; PN, vol. 2, p. 240. See Chapter 10, section 1.

The first text to be dealt with is Q 13, § 23, entitled *Observations on Certain Aspects of the Structure of Political Parties in Periods of Organic Crisis* [*Osservazioni su alcuni aspetti della struttura dei partiti politici nei periodi di crisi organica*].[6] This note, due to its length and complexity, is certainly one of the most significant of the notebook, perhaps even of Gramsci's entire prison writings. Q 13, § 23 is made up of the following notes, in order: Q 4, § 69 (*On Political Parties*, November 1930); Q 7, § 77 (*The Intellectuals. Political Parties* [*Gli intellettuali. I partiti politici*], December 1931); Q 4, § 66 (*The Military Element in Politics*, November 1930); Q 9, § 40 (*Machiavelli. Relations of Force, etc.* [*Machiavelli. Rapporti di forza ecc.*], June 1932); Q 9, § 22 (*Past and Present*, May 1932); Q 9, § 40 (again).[7] By adopting a famous saying, we can affirm that the whole is greater than the sum of its parts: the combination of the individual texts results in an effective synergy, which gives to the final text a much greater conceptual maturity. From this perspective, the title of the paragraph is noteworthy. The phrase chosen by Gramsci seems to embrace all the titles of the first drafts, merging them into a single, highly significant formula. Moreover, the order of the texts that constitute Q 13, § 23 is also remarkable. It does not correspond to the order in which the notes were written; it shows rather Gramsci's need to reorganise his argument and to make it more effective. In Q 13, § 23 there are also numerous stylistic and formal variants that contribute significantly to overcoming some of the 'uncertainties' of the first drafts. But Gramsci also made some changes with regard to the content – although such changes have never been analysed by commentators.[8] Generally speaking, we can say that in Q 13, § 23 Gramsci

---

6 This note, like the rest of notebook 13, is dated, quite generically, to May 1932–November 1933 (see Cospito 2011a). On the basis of the chronology of the texts of which it is comprised, however, we should argue that Q 13, § 23 was written at least after June 1932.

7 Q 9, § 40 is composed of two distinct parts. In the first section (first redrafted), Gramsci is dwelling on the 'third' moment of the relations of force. In the second section (second redrafted) he concentrates on the issue of the 'economism'. On the philological issues related to notebook 13, see QAnast, vol. 14, pp. 153–9.

8 For reasons of space, I do not list here all the changes made by Gramsci (I will refer to others in due course). See, for example, the following additions: the implicit reference to Q 13, § 17 ('(to connect with the notes on the situations and relations of power)' – Q 13, § 23, p. 1602; my translation – the sentence is omitted in SPN); the reference to Churchill and to the battle of Jutland ('An example of "preparation of the strategic conjuncture" is to be found in Churchill's *Memoirs*, where he speaks of the battle of Jutland'; Q 13, § 23, p. 1602; SPN, p. 218). See also how Gramsci rewrites this passage by adding a mention of the historical bloc: 'to change the traditional direction with a new direction in accordance with the economic content developed in a more progressive phase' (Q 9, § 40, p. 1120) – 'to change ... the political direction of certain forces that must be absorbed in order to achieve a new, homogeneous, economic-political

defines many expressions used in the first drafts more precisely, and gives a sharper tone to the whole discussion, by underlining the historically identified character of the Caesarist regimes (see, in particular, the double parallelism between Caesar-Napoleon I and De Rivera-Živković).⁹

The analysis of the Caesarist-Bonapartist phenomenon contained in § 23 is 'completed' by § 27 (*Caesarism*), which has a more theoretical nature. The latter note comprises two texts, namely Q 9, § 133 and § 136 (both entitled *Machiavelli. Caesarism*).¹⁰ In this case Gramsci did not make any particularly notable changes, but worked on the text by refining his formulations and making his thinking more precise (if Q 13, § 23 has many more – even substantive – corrections, this is due to the fact that the texts collected in § 23 are more numerous and less homogeneous, as well as the fact they were written at different times).¹¹ It seems to me that, although the variations made to the first drafts reinforce Gramsci's caution against a misuse of the concepts of Bonapartism and Caesarism, they do not diminish the significance of these categories within his discussion.

---

historical bloc, without internal contradictions' (Q 13, § 23, p. 1612; my translation – the sentence is omitted in SPN).

9   See, for instance: Q 4, § 66, p. 509; PN, vol. 2, p. 240: 'None of these observations is absolute; they have to be "relativized" according to the various moments of history and different states'; Q 13, § 23, p. 1605; SPN, p. 212: 'Obviously, none of these observations is absolute; at various moments of history and in various countries they have widely differing significance'.

10 Q 13, § 27 is part of a block of notes which resume the paragraphs of the final miscellaneous section of notebook 9. After having redrafted Q 9, § 40 in Q 13, § 23 (and after the 'break' between §§ 24 and 25; cf. what follows), Gramsci concentrates on the notes from the last pages of notebook 9, following a precise order (Q 13, § 26 corresponds to Q 9, § 132; Q 13, § 27, as already said, corresponds to Q 9, §§ 133 and 136; Q 13, § 28 corresponds to Q 9, § 137; Q 13, § 29 corresponds to Q 9, § 142). Only once he had completed the redrafting of these last miscellaneous notes did he return to his sorting of the political notes after Q 9, § 40 (without a clear order now). On the structure of notebook 9, see QAnast, vol. 6, pp. 5–6. Note also that Gramsci chooses only the texts from notebook 9 that deal with political issues, and he leaves out most of the notes not strictly related to the subject (which remain in their first draft, with only one exception).

11 It is significant to note that Gramsci, in Q 13, § 27, adds terms like 'very' ('*molto*') and 'always' ('*sempre*') in strategic positions. In this way, he accentuates the sharpness of his judgement on Caesarism (from this point of view, in continuity with Q 13, § 23). Moreover, the title of the second draft (in Italian: *Il cesarismo*), only partially reproduces the (identical) titles of the two first drafts (*Machiavelli. Caesarism*), by removing the reference to the Florentine secretary which also motivated the redrafting of these notes in Q 13.

We might wonder about the reason why Gramsci split the analysis of Caesarism and Bonapartism into two different but closely related texts (§§ 23 and 27). The chronology of notebook 13, although very vague, might offer an explanation for this: as Francioni has argued, we could put forward the hypothesis that there is a 'break' between § 24 and § 25, even if we do not know how significant (chronologically speaking) this break might be.[12] In any case, it should be noted that the texts placed between §§ 23 and 27 do not really interrupt Gramsci's train of thought on the Caesarist-Bonapartist model, which finds in notebook 13 a very consistent reading.[13]

3   Further Occurrences

Other texts from notebook 13 also contribute, albeit less immediately, to Gramsci's analysis of the Bonapartist-Caesarist model. Among these, § 37 is particularly significant. This note, entitled *Notes on French National Life* [*Note sulla vita nazionale francese*], consists of an in-depth analysis of French political history between the nineteenth and twentieth centuries, with particular attention to the development of the group *Action Française* (this paragraph is closely related to the next one, *Maurras and 'Organic Centralism'* [*Maurras e il 'central-*

---

12   In Q 13, § 25 we can find the main chronological hint contained in the notebook (as well as the only single draft). It contains a reference to an interpretation of Machiavelli's thought provided in the journal *La cultura*, in the issue of October–December 1933, which should be more or less contemporary to the writing of the note (it seems as if, while reading the article on Machiavelli, Gramsci felt the need to take some notes in order not to forget some important thoughts). Moreover, we have good reasons to affirm that the notebook was completed before Gramsci's departure from Turi in November 1933. On these points, see QAnast, vol. 14, pp. 153–9. As regards the 'break' between § 24 and § 25, there is a change in the script's *ductus* (i.e. in Gramsci's way of writing), which often signals an interruption in his work, as Francioni highlights (for these methodological considerations, see Francioni 2009). More generally, it has to be observed that, despite the limited number of notes (only forty), Gramsci took more than a year (May 1932–November 1933) to complete notebook 13. As a consequence, it is very hard to say with what 'speed' he wrote the notes and how much time passed between Q 13, § 23 and § 27.

13   A few words should be said on §§ 24–6. As shown before, Q 13, § 24 (which has no title) focuses on the concepts of war of manoeuvre and war of position (both literally and metaphorically conceived) and, therefore, it seems to develop the theme of the organic crisis that arises in § 23. Regarding § 25 (*Machiavelli's 'Duplicity' and 'Naivety'* ['*Doppiezza' e 'ingenuità' del Machiavelli*]), see the previous note. Q 13, § 26 (*Politico-cultural Hegemony* [*Egemonia politico-culturale*]) is a brief commentary on political-cultural hegemony in the twentieth century, which seems to introduce the topic of § 27. The latter is largely concerned with the substantial difference between 'pre-modernity' and 'modernity'.

ismo organico'], dedicated to Charles Maurras (1868–1952) and his 'organic centralism'). The second draft note is the result of the merging and of the redrafting of numerous texts from notebook 1 (in order: §§ 18, 48, 53, 131 and 106).[14] Thus, as with Q 13, § 23, § 37 also ends up being something far more significant than the individual parts of which it is formed. With regard to the categories of Caesarism and Bonapartism, this second draft shows an interesting variant, which thoroughly modifies the argument of Q 1, § 131, i.e. the addition of a reference to the Caesarist phenomenon.[15] The change is meaningful, as regards both the content and the position; it is very likely that this addition was influenced by the presence of §§ 23 and 27, where the phenomenology of Caesarism is examined in detail.

Alongside the texts in notebook 13, there are a number of 'minor' paragraphs that complete the framework outlined in Gramsci's analysis, exploring individual aspects of the topic and linking it with some of the key themes of his prison writings. On the historical aspect of the Caesarist-Bonapartist phenomenon, Gramsci investigates, respectively: the political and military genius of Caesar and 'ancient' Caesarism (see Q 1, § 117; Q 19, § 28 and Q 17, § 21);[16] the figure of Napoleon I, as well as that of Napoleon III and their role in the history of modern France, with particular attention to the issue of suffrage and the involvement of the masses in political life (among others: Q 1, §§ 130 and 131; Q 13, § 37; Q 19, §§ 24 and 28);[17] political characters linked in various ways

14 Q 1, § 18, *Maurras' Error. Notes on the French Monarchist Party* [*L'errore di Maurras. Note sul partito monarchico francese*], July–October 1929; Q 1, § 48, *Charles Maurras' Reverse Jacobinism* [*Il giacobinismo a rovescio di Carlo Maurras*], February–March 1930; Q 1, § 53, *Maurrasianism and Syndicalism* [*Maurrasianismo e sindacalismo*], February–March 1930; Q 1, § 131, *Bainville and Universal Suffrage in France* [*Bainville e il suffragio universale in Francia*], February–March 1930; Q 1, § 106, *Maurras' Concept of Religion* [*La concezione religiosa di Maurras*], February–March 1930.

15 In Q 13, § 37, Gramsci writes: 'every sanction given by universal suffrage and by the plebiscite took place after the fundamental class had focused heavily around a "Caesarist" personality, either in the political field or even more in the political-military field, or after a war that had created a situation of national emergency' (pp. 1647–8; this passage has not previously been translated into English; in FSPN, pp. 92–4, there is only an excerpt of the long note that does not include these sentences). In Q 1, § 131, the formulation is completely different and the reference to Caesarism is missing. On the topics of this note, see Bechelloni 1988 and, now, Lucas 2020.

16 Q 1, § 117, *Political and Military Leadership During the Risorgimento*; Q 19, § 28, second draft, *Political-military Leadership of the Italian National Uprising* [*Direzione politico-militare del moto nazionale italiano*], July/August 1934–February 1935; Q 17, § 21, *Cultural Topics. Caesar and Caesarism*, single draft, September–18 November 1933.

17 Q 1, § 130, *Real Italy and Legal Italy* [*Italia reale e Italia legale*], first draft, February–March 1930; Q 1, § 131, *Bainville and Universal Suffrage in France*, first draft, February–March 1930; Q 13, § 37, *Notes on French National Life*, second draft, May 1932–November 1933; Q 19, § 24,

to the categories of Bonapartism and Caesarism (Disraeli: Q 17, § 53, Boulanger: Q 8, § 21; Q 13, § 1; Q 4, § 38; Q 13, § 18, Dreyfus: Q 13, § 18; Q 14, § 23 – these occurrences have to be added to the references to Cromwell, MacDonald, De Rivera, Tsankov, Živković and, implicitly, also to Mussolini contained in Q 13, § 23 and Q 13, § 27 and in the related texts in their first drafts).[18] Other texts investigate the theoretical features of Caesarism and Bonapartism: the issue of the balance of class forces;[19] of catastrophe;[20] of the civil and military bureaucracy (see the notes analysed in the previous chapter); of the charismatic leader.[21]

Lastly, we can observe a peculiar concentration of occurrences in notebook 6 – there are four occurrences here. Two of them are 'weak' and do not play a significant role. Their weakness arises from the fact that the terms Caesarism and Bonapartism are conceptually and formally 'contaminated' or 'distorted'. In the first case, Gramsci speaks of '"juridical" continuity ... of the Byzantine-Napoleonic type' (Q 6, § 84); in the second case he tries to define the category of 'Caesaropapism' (Q 6, § 93).[22] The other two (Q 6, §§ 40 and 97), however, are more relevant, as I will show in my analysis.[23]

The Problem of Political Leadership in the Formation and Development of the Nation and the Modern State in Italy, second draft, July/August 1934–February 1935; Q 19, § 28 (cf. previous note).

18   Q 17, § 53, *Cultural Questions. Disraeli* [*Problemi di cultura. Disraeli*], single draft, after 19 June 1935; Q 8, § 21, *The Modern Prince* [*Il moderno principe*], first draft, January–February 1932; Q 13, § 1, no title, second draft, May 1932–November 1933; Q 4, § 38, *Relations between Structure and Superstructures* [*Rapporti tra struttura e soprastrutture*], first draft, October 1930; Q 13, § 18, *Some Theoretical and Practical Aspects of 'Economism'* [*Alcuni aspetti teorici e pratici dell'"economismo"*], second draft, May 1932–November 1933; Q 14, § 23, *Machiavelli. Caesarism and the 'Catastrophic' Balance of Socio-political Forces*, first draft, January 1933; Q 13, § 23, *Observations on Certain Aspects of the Structure of Political Parties in Periods of Organic Crisis*, second draft, May 1932–November 1933; Q 13, § 27, *Caesarism*, second draft, May 1932–November 1933.

19   See, among others, Q 3, § 34; Q 13, § 17; Q 13, § 31; Q 14, § 23; Q 14, § 76; Q 15, § 17; Q 16, § 5.

20   See, among others, Q 3, § 44.

21   See, among others, Q 2, § 75; Q 6, § 97.

22   Q 6, § 84, *Past and Present. Continuity and Tradition*, single draft, March 1931; Q 6, § 93, *Encyclopedic Notions*, single draft, March–August 1931. Regarding the quotation: Q 6, § 84, p. 757; PN, vol. 3, p. 69.

23   Q 6, § 40, *Past and Present. The English Government*, single draft, December 1930; § 97, *Past and Present. Lofty Ambition and Petty Ambitions*, single draft, March–August 1931. I disagree on this point with Cospito, who, on the basis of his own interpretation of the development of Gramsci's thought, underestimates these occurrences in notebook 6 (cf. Cospito 2016, p. 211).

CHAPTER 9

Gramsci and the Theory of Caesarism

1 Michels and 'Charismatic Leadership'

1.1 *Q 2, § 75*

If we compare Gramsci's analysis of the Caesarist phenomenon in the pre-prison writings to that of the *Prison Notebooks*, the main novelty is to be found in the figure of the strong man, i.e. a 'Caesar', who takes over the situation in the context of a political crisis.

In Gramsci's journalistic texts the analysis of the leaders does not play a significant role, even if there are a few exceptions. The most relevant one is *Leader* [*Capo*], the 1924 article that inaugurates the third series of *L'Ordine Nuovo*, where Gramsci compares the figures of Lenin and Mussolini, anticipating many issues later developed in the *Notebooks*.[1] While Gramsci does not analyse leaders in a constructive sense, there are numerous polemical references to 'missed' or 'failed' political leaders.[2] Indeed, he is more interested in understanding the transformations that take place within society, the breaking up and the rebuilding of social blocs.

Why, then, does Gramsci turn to the study of Caesar and his 'successors' in the *Prison Notebooks*? I would suggest that, in doing this, Gramsci was influenced by contemporary political theory, and in particular by Robert Michels' conception of charismatic leadership.[3] In fact, Michels' thought is discussed at length in Gramsci's prison writings, and Michels (1876–1936) is one of Gramsci's

---

1 'Leader' ['Capo'], *L'Ordine Nuovo*, 1 March 1924 (CPC, pp. 12–16; SPW-2, pp. 209–12).
2 In the *Notebooks* we can find an echo of the sole discussion on the Caesarist leader that took place in the pre-prison writings. Cf. Q 3, § 53 (*Past and Present. Influence of the Romanticism of French Serials* [*Passato e presente. Influsso del romanticismo francese d'appendice*], single draft, June–July 1930), where Gramsci returns to the comparison between Mussolini and Sue's Prince Rudolph. In closing the note, Gramsci makes an interesting, highly sarcastic addition (in brackets): 'Besides, nobody knows whether in the dim past there may not have been a princely ancestor in his pedigree' (Q 3, § 53, p. 335; PN, vol. 2, p. 55).
3 On Gramsci and Michels, see Medici 2000, pp. 111–23, Malandrino 2001, Santoro 2012, Bellamy 2013, Salamini 2014, Filippini 2015; especially on Michels' theory of charismatic leadership and on Gramsci's criticism of it, see Basile 2016. Some hints can also be found in the entries *Capo*, *Capo carismatico* and *Michels* of the *Dizionario gramsciano* (Liguori and Voza 2009, pp. 101 and 540–1) and in Cospito 2016, pp. 207–9.

favourite polemical targets.[4] This criticism, however, can also be fruitful, insofar as it paves the way for a thorough investigation of the nature of the political party and leadership.

Q 2, § 75 (*R. Michels, Les Partis politiques et la contrainte sociale*) is no doubt the most significant text in this regard. Here Gramsci takes his cue from an essay published by Michels in the journal *Mercure de France* in May 1928 to engage in a close confrontation with the German-born sociologist.[5] This note had a troubled genesis, since it was written in two phases.[6] The content of the note consists in a brief quotation followed by a quite detailed account of Michels' article. This is intertwined with Gramsci's observations, which become more extensive as the note develops.[7] He first focuses on the causes of the genesis of a party according to Weber (quoted by Michels), and on the nature of the political organisation resulting therefrom.[8] He then concentrates on the first type of party, that of the personal party. There follow numerous

---

4   See, in particular, the following notes: Q 2, §§ 45, 75 and 93; Q 3, § 59; Q 6, § 97; Q 7, §§ 12 and 64; Q 8, § 148; Q 9, § 142; Q 11, §§ 25, 26 and 66; Q 13, §§ 29 and 33.

5   Gramsci read a number of works by Michels in the 1910s and 1920s, even if the only reference to Michels in the pre-prison writings is not particularly remarkable ('The Capintesta' ['Il capintesta'], *Avanti!*, 20 January 1916; CT, pp. 86–7). He owned, in particular, a French edition of Michels' *Political Parties* (*Zur Soziologie des Parteiwesens in der modernen Demokratie*, first published in German in 1911) and the second Italian edition of 1924. As he writes in a letter to Tatiana: 'In Rome I would like you to take two or three volumes of my books: ... Michels' volume on *The political party and the oligarchic tendencies of modern democracy* [sic; he is referring to Michels' 1911 *Political Parties*] that I possess in the pre-war French translation and in the much-augmented and enriched new 1924 Italian edition' (letter of 26 august 1929 – LL, p. 280; in the *Fondo Gramsci* held at the Fondazione Gramsci in Rome, there is an underlined reprint of the French edition of Michels' book, which dates to 1919). On the basis of this previous knowledge of Michels' thought (but also of some further reading made in prison in early 1928 – see the letters of 9 and 30 January 1928, respectively to Tania – LL, p. 150 – and to Berti; LL, p. 154), the aforementioned article could have offered him the opportunity to reflect extensively on Michels' thought.

6   As has been demonstrated, the note consists of two parts. The break should be placed after this sentence: 'For this reason we see how the charismatic parties are led to rest their psychological (!) values upon the more lasting structures of human interests' (PN, vol. 1, p. 321). The first part of the text was written in 1929, perhaps in February or in the following months, while the second, likely, in August–September 1930 (see QAnast, vol. 5, pp. 3–5).

7   From a certain point on, Gramsci's comments are no longer enclosed within brackets; progressively, they take over the description of the content of the article. Moreover, Gramsci often uses exclamation and question marks to express his disagreement, and quotation marks to make clear the distinction between Michels' thought and his own thought.

8   The Weber-Michels relation is a complex issue, which I cannot deal with here – on the topic, see in particular Tuccari 1993, but also Mitzman 1970 and Mommsen 1981 and 1987, pp. 121–38. In general, as far as Gramsci's knowledge of the Weberian conception of charismatic leadership is concerned, this is largely mediated by Michels (but hints at the topic are also in Weber's volume of 1919 already cited).

historical examples, among them the workers' movement at the time of the Second International.⁹ The first, long comment by Gramsci (enclosed in brackets) is closely linked to the last of these examples, Mussolini's Fascism. Gramsci argues that Michels' judgement on Fascism is 'historically inaccurate', since 'Mussolini uses the state to dominate the party and he uses the party only to some extent, during difficult times, to dominate the state'.¹⁰ Gramsci then returns to the question of charisma. He expresses a sharp judgement by defining Michels' reasoning 'infantile' and 'primitive'.¹¹ The stress on the fragility of the 'most powerful' political dynamism of charismatic leader closes the first part of the note.¹²

In the second part of it, written eighteen months later, Gramsci puts forward three different elements that integrate his previous analysis. After having investigated (and criticised) the classification of the parties proposed by

---

9   These observations are interspersed with more general allusions to the role of the 'charismatic' leader, and, moreover, with a significant philological consideration. The textual observation is as follows (Q 2, § 75, p. 231; PN, vol. 1, p. 319): '(This note is numbered 4 bis, which means it was inserted in the proofs; certainly not for the translation of "χάρισμα", but perhaps for the reference to Weber. Michels had made a lot of noise in Italy with "his" discovery of the "charismatic leader" which, probably, was already in Weber [one should make a comparison]; one must also check Michels' 1927 book on political sociology – he does not even mention that a conception of the leader by divine grace has already been in existence, and how!)'. This notation shows Gramsci's interest in Weber's thinking; furthermore, it highlights the fact that he recognises the Weberian matrix of the theory of the charismatic leader, and, therefore, he is aware of the gap between this very account and Michels' interpretation of it. The fact that the adjective '*charismatico*' (clearly, a transliteration from ancient Greek) can be found only in the first part of Q 2, § 75 is noteworthy. In the second part of the note and throughout the rest of the *Notebooks*, this variant is not used; it is replaced by the more common '*carismatico*'.
10 Q 2, § 75, p. 233; PN, vol. 1, p. 320.
11 Q 2, § 75, pp. 233–4; PN, vol. 1, pp. 320–1. See also, in this regard, Q 10, II, § 41, II, pp. 1301–2; FSPN, p. 405 – that of assessing historico-political movements on the basis of their 'genius' and not of their 'historical necessity and political science', 'this is also a popular prejudice at certain stages of political organisation (the stage of the charismatic man) and is often confused with the prejudice for the "orator": the politician must be a great orator or great intellectual, must have the "consecration" of genius, etc., etc. One next arrives at the lower stage of some regions populated by peasants and negroes, in which you get followed if you have a beard'. The text redrafts (with significant additions, like the hint at the stage of the charismatic man) Q 7, § 8: the allusion to Michels' theory seems to me clear. On Michels' 'primitivism', see Basile 2016. In the *Prison Notebooks*, the term 'primitivism' is mainly applied to economics, always describing a situation of immaturity. See Q 9, § 26 ('they will have to be "explained" realistically as the two aspects of the same immatureness and of the same primitivism', p. 1112), but above all Q 8, § 185, where the term describes the economic-corporative level of politics.
12 Q 2, § 75, p. 234; PN, vol. 1, p. 321.

Michels, he formulates a rather negative judgement on his theory of charismatic leader. According to Gramsci, he did not understand the complexity of the party system (he uses a 'hollow and vague language') and he adopts the method of the old positivist sociology, falling into what he defines a 'superficiality of a reactionary salon'.[13] Finally, he speaks briefly about the relationship between Michels and Sorel, referring to the letter of the French thinker to Michels published in the journal *Nuovi studi di diritto, economia, politica* of September–October 1929.

1.2   A 'Programmatic' Ambivalence

This note is emblematic of the way in which Gramsci reflects on the question of the charismatic leader, which immediately comes across as 'programmatically' ambivalent. On the one hand, Michels' doctrine is a controversial object for Gramsci; on the other, it provides Gramsci with some valuable reflections, which draw his attention to some crucial aspects of contemporary politics. In the light of this fundamental ambiguity, it is interesting to return to the discussion of Michels' theory, focusing on the affinities and differences between Michels' account of the charismatic leader and Gramsci's theory of Caesarism. Without going into minute detail, it is enough to touch on some points.

First, I will look at Michels' method. In fact, Gramsci's critique of positivist sociology contained in Q 2, § 75 returns (amplified and deepened) in § 25 (*Reduction of the Philosophy of Praxis to a Sociology* [*Riduzione della filosofia della praxis a una sociologia*]) and § 26 (*General Questions* [*Quistioni generali*]) of notebook 11.[14] Here Gramsci complains about the lack of historicisation in sociological schemes and the superficiality of many generalising criteria, by adding that 'in Michels' treatises one can find a whole catalogue of similar tautological generalisations, the last and most famous being that about the "charismatic" leader'.[15]

---

13   Q 2, § 75, pp. 235 and 238; PN, vol. 1, pp. 322–5; translation slightly modified.

14   Gramsci's opposition to sociology is well known and constitutes an important theme of the *Notebooks* and in particular Q 11, in which Gramsci deals with Bukharin's *Popular Manual* (on this point, see Francioni 1987, Tuccari 2001, Liguori and Voza 2009 (entry *Bucharin*, by F. Frosini, pp. 85–8)). On Gramsci's criticism of sociology in general, see Razeto Migliaro and Misuraca 1978, but see also Salamini 1974, Morera 1990, pp. 68 ff., Frosini 2007, Liguori and Voza 2009 (entry *Sociologia*, by M. Filippini, pp. 774–8), Filippini and Rosati 2013.

15   Q 11, § 26, p. 1434 (the note is the second draft of §§ 11, 13, 14, 23 and 33 of notebook 4); SPN, p. 430. Gramsci is here alluding to the conception of charismatic leadership that Michels developed in his later fascist writings (from the mid-1920s to the mid-1930s) – see for instance the 1927 volume *First lectures in political sociology* (*Corso di sociologia politica*). See also Q 11, § 25, p. 1430; SPN, p. 429: 'A further element which, in the art of politics,

The impression is that Gramsci's growing opposition to the methodology of the German-born scholar plays a primary role in his dismissal of the category of the charismatic leader and, in turn, in his affirmation of the category of Caesarism. This concept also represents a 'generic hypothesis ... (convenient for the art of politics)' but, unlike charismatic leadership, it cannot be conceived apart from its various historical manifestations, that is to say, without seeking an 'ever greater degree of approximation to concrete historical reality'.[16]

As regards the content, by synthesising Michels' thought in Q 2, § 75, Gramsci realises an extremely meaningful shift. While accusing Michels of 'primitivism', Gramsci stresses the weakness of the dominant class which, having exhausted its 'propulsive' force, puts itself under the protection of a leader in order to remain in power and to defer (at least temporarily) its defeat. The charismatic leader no longer represents the first stage of a political party, but, on the contrary, the last one.

The reliability of this reading is demonstrated also by § 21 of notebook 8 (*The Modern Prince*, January–February 1932, later redrafted in Q 13, § 1), where Gramsci makes some very interesting observations about the figure of the *condottiere*, in particular on its short-lived and 'defensive' nature:

> Only an immediate historico-political action that necessitates moving at lightning speed can be embodied by a concrete individual. Such speed can only be generated by a great and imminent danger, precisely the kind of great danger that, in an instant, generates flaming passions and fanaticism, annihilating the critical sense and irony that can destroy the 'charismatic' character of the *condottiere* (Boulanger as an example). By its very nature, however, an immediate action of this sort cannot be long lasting; neither can it have an organic character. In almost every case, it typifies a restoration or reorganization; it is not typical of the founding of new states or new national and social structures ... It is a 'defensive' rather than creative type of action. It is based on the assumption that an already existing 'collective will' has dispersed, lost its nerve, and needs to be regrouped and reinforced.[17]

---

leads to the overthrow of the old naturalistic schema is the replacement by political organisms (parties) of single individuals and individual (or charismatic, as Michels calls them) leaders' (the text is the second draft of Q 7, § 6). In both cases, the references to Michels' thought were added in the passage from the first draft to the second one.

16   Q 13, § 27, p. 1621; SPN, p. 221.
17   Q 8, § 21, pp. 951–2; PN, vol. 3, p. 247. In PN, the term '*condottiere*' is used – this is a more frequent English variant of the Italian '*condottiero*' (adopted by Gramsci).

Thus, rather than a situation of primitivism *ipso facto*, Gramsci seems to describe a form of 'returning' primitivism, or, in other words, of anachronism. In short, the 'not yet' (i.e. the immaturity of the political party according to Michels) has been replaced by the 'no longer' (i.e. the exhaustion of the dominant class in Gramsci's view). From this perspective, it is significant to recall the commentary put into brackets by Gramsci just after the reference to Mussolini as a charismatic figure in Q 2, § 75. Here he hints at the

> sentiments and emotions which have not yet reached the final point of dissolution, because the classes (or the class) of which it is an expression, although in dissolution historically, still have a certain base and attach themselves to the glories of the past as shield against the future.[18]

2 'The Old Is Dying and the New Cannot Be Born'

2.1 *The Balance Formula in the* Prison Notebooks

Hence, if Gramsci discards the theory of charismatic leadership to develop the Caesarist model, the reason can be found in its capacity to better fulfil Gramsci's analytical demands, in its being more apt to describe contemporary political phenomena. Not by chance, a 'Caesarism without a Caesar' will be imagined by Gramsci to describe politics in impersonal mass societies; on the other hand, one cannot imagine a charismatic situation without an exceptional man that carries the charisma.[19]

Moreover, while the meaning of Michels' theory of charismatic leadership (in Gramsci's reading) is uniquely negative, Caesarism, as Alberto Burgio has noted, is a *vox media*, a multi-sided concept that can fit different, even opposing, solutions.[20]

---

18   Q 2, § 75, p. 233; PN, vol. 1, p. 320.
19   On 'Caesarism without a Caesar', see Chapter 12, section 4. It should be noted that the two formulas (charismatic leadership and Caesarism) never appear in the same note. There is only one exception, represented by the aforementioned § 23 of notebook 13. Here their coexistence is explained by the fact that, in Q 13, § 23, §§ 66 and 69 of notebook 4 are merged: while in the former there are many references to Caesarism, the latter deals with the actions of the 'man sent by providence', making a clear reference to Michels' conception – p. 513; PN, vol. 2, p. 242.
20   See Burgio 2014, pp. 274 ff. It is necessary, however, to distance ourselves from Burgio's thesis. Indeed, he clearly opposes the category of Bonapartism (conceived of as entirely negative) to the one of Caesarism (neutral, in his view). On the basis of the investigation carried out so far, however, Bonapartism appears as a complementary and unavoidable

The origin of this 'neutrality' is to be found in the formula of the balance of class forces implied by the Caesarist model. This formula represents an element of strong continuity with the pre-prison writings, as well as a real *Leitmotiv* of Gramsci's *Prison Notebooks*. As shown previously, the importance of this category is due to its connection to the 'relations of force', itself a category that deeply structures Gramsci's analysis of the different moments or degrees of reality.

Unlike in his journalistic writings, where the model of balance anticipated, so to speak, that of the relations of force, in the *Prison Notebooks* the connection between the two categories is more complex, but still very close.[21] The category of relations of force describes Gramsci's 'analysis of situations' (hence the title of Q 13, § 17: *Analysis of the Situation: Relations of Force* [*Analisi delle situazioni. Rapporti di forza*]).[22] The balance formula, in this framework, assumes a more specific meaning, by defining a stalemate in the struggle between the bourgeoisie and the proletariat. Generally speaking, the reference to the notion of balance represents an important element of Gramsci's thought in prison, which allows him to reflect on the nature of political crises and on the possibilities that they open up.[23]

---

aspect of Gramsci's analysis of Caesarism, and, as a consequence, it is not negative *tout court*: it is an analytical category focused on the function (under certain conditions and circumstances) of bureaucracy. As shown before, the true opposition is precisely the one between Michels' account of the charismatic leader (which is entirely negative) and a more open and flexible conception such as the Caesarist one.

21   The impression is that, in the pre-prison writings, Gramsci tries to cover the full spectrum of possible political scenarios by pointing to the different declinations of the balance theme. On the category of 'relations of force' in the *Prison Notebooks* see the entry by C.N. Coutinho in Liguori and Voza 2009, pp. 686–90, but also Mancina 1980, Showstack Sassoon 1980 (esp. pp. 180–93) and, more recently, Morton 2007 (pp. 93 ff.) and Cospito 2016, *passim*.

22   Q 13, § 17, p. 1578; SPN, p. 175.

23   In the *Notebooks* the term 'balance' is used in different ways and with different purposes. Gramsci adopts it sometimes in a geopolitical context in order to define the relations between different powers within the same nation or between different nations (see for instance Q 9, § 99). In other cases, when he speaks of the balance of forces, it is a synonym of the socio-political situation (a 'situation' or an 'equilibrium of forces' – Q 15, § 17, p. 1774; SPN, p. 107); there is also a demographic (Q 2, § 124), a psycho-physical (Q 4, § 52), and an economic balance (Q 4, § 42). The most widespread use, however, is no doubt the one analysed in this chapter, in connection to the imagery of the catastrophe (and its 'forerunners'). If we stick to the explicit interpretations of the term, he speaks of 'static equilibrium' [*equilibrio statico*] (Q 2, § 75, p. 234; PN, vol. 1, p. 322; also Q 4, § 69, then redrafted in Q 13, § 23), 'deadly equilibrium' [*equilibrio mortale*] (Q 2, § 75, p. 234), 'equilibrium of the urban classes struggling with each other' [*equilibrio delle classi urbane in lotta*] (Q 4, § 66, p. 511; PN, vol. 2, p. 239; in the second version, Q 13, § 23, 'groups' instead

From the first notebooks onwards, there are references to the balance between classes. The earliest occurrences date back to the summer of 1930 and can be found in the second part of Q 2, §75 and in Q 3, §34 (*Past and Present*, single draft, June–July 1930). Here Gramsci mentions, respectively, the 'deadly equilibrium' and the 'static equilibrium of the conflicting forces' and, in the second text, the 'interregnum' due to the fact that 'the old is dying and the new cannot be born', and thus 'morbid phenomena of the most varied kind come to pass'.[24] Even if very synthetically, the double metaphor (the biological – death/birth – and the architectural one – static/dynamic direction) highlights the salient aspects of Gramsci's conception: the polarisation of the socio-political scenario and the (apparent) 'immobilism' that characterises it.[25] In this framework, the characterisation of this stillness as 'deadly' is particularly remarkable, since it anticipates the 'catastrophic' dimension that will be the core element of the following occurrences of the balance formula (from notebook 9 onwards).

2.2 Balance and Catastrophe

In relation to this theme, it should be noted that (unlike in the pre-prison writings) Gramsci's references to catastrophe are a constant factor in the *Notebooks*.

Here, of course, the terms 'catastrophe' and 'catastrophic' no longer have a specific strategic meaning: they have long lost their old, Third Internationalist nuance. Having once dismissed all predictions of the imminent crisis of the capitalist system, the hint to the catastrophic ending is, first and foremost, a way to criticise theoretical positions that attribute an excessive weight to the

---

of 'classes'), 'equilibrium of forces heading towards catastrophe' [*equilibrio delle forze a tendenza catastrofica*] (Q 9, §133, p. 1194, then taken up again in Q 13, §27, p. 1619; SPN, p. 219); 'equilibrium with catastrophic prospects' [*equilibrio a prospettive catastrofiche*] (Q 9, §136, p. 1198, then repeated in Q 13, §27, p. 1622; SPN, p. 222), 'catastrophic balance of socio-political forces' [*equilibrio catastrofico delle forze politico-sociali*] (in the title of Q 14, §23, p. 1680) 'equilibrium of the "fundamental" forces' [*equilibrio delle forze fondamentali*] (Q 14, §23, p. 1680; SPN, p. 222; in this case there are no adjectives that specify that the balance is 'catastrophic', but that stands out clearly from the context). On this theme, see also McNally 2008.

24   Q 2, §75, p. 234; PN, vol. 1, p. 322; Q 3, §34, p. 311; PN, vol. 2, p. 33. Gramsci also ruminates on the old/new couple in Q 4, §3, p. 425 ('what exists is a "combination" of old and new, a temporary equilibrium corresponding to the equilibrium of social relations'; PN, vol. 2, p. 144). The text reappears with some modifications in Q 16, §9, p. 1863 (SPN, p. 398: 'what exists at any given time is a variable combination of old and new, a momentary equilibrium of cultural relations corresponding to the equilibrium of social relations').

25   Burgio 2014, p. 243. On Gramsci's biological metaphor, see Ciliberto 1989, Di Meo 2012, Jackson 2016 and (especially) 2019.

role of the 'immediate economic factor'.²⁶ More generally, it represents a critique of those positions which, by highlighting the structural and 'mechanical' dimension of the conflict between the forces, end up in a form of political (and parliamentary) abstentionism.²⁷

Even more widespread is his interpretation of the catastrophe as a particularly profound and long-lasting crisis, which threatens the very existence of the social groups in combat. It is noteworthy that, if, in principle, any crisis 'can become "permanent" – that is, potentially catastrophic', this is a distinctive feature of situations of balance.²⁸ Since neither of the two factions is able to win over the other, the stalemate does not find a quick solution and degenerates into a catastrophic crisis.²⁹ The catastrophe then turns into a tautology of sorts: it describes a crisis without (real) solutions, a permanent but 'unstable' balance that can give birth to a variety of political scenarios – last but not least, a Caesarist one.

The occurrences of the balance formula that come after Q 3, § 34 fit perfectly into this scheme and, so to speak, refine it. Among them, the best-known formulations are undoubtedly those contained in Q 13, § 27, which takes up the notes of notebook 9 on Caesarism (§§ 133 and 136), as well as in Q 13, § 23, extensively rewritten from its first draft, Q 4, § 69, *On Political Parties*. For example, in the following passages, he says:

> Caesarism can be said to express a situation in which the forces in conflict balance each other in a catastrophic manner; that is to say, they balance

---

26 Q 7, § 10, p. 859; PN, vol. 3, p. 161. Here, Gramsci defines Rosa Luxemburg's thought as the 'prototype' of these catastrophic interpretations (on the figure of Rosa Luxemburg (1871–1919) in Gramsci's thought, see Liguori and Voza 2009, pp. 491–3). In this regard see also Q 1, § 63 (second draft: Q 28, § 11).

27 See, for instance, Q 1, § 53 (second draft: Q 13, § 37). Here Gramsci refers to the political abstention of Italian Catholics as a consequence of the *non expedit* of Pius IX; he also hints at the doctrine of Maurras and, indirectly, to Bordiga (see Q1975, p. 1647).

28 Q 22, § 10, p. 2163; SPN, p. 300. This reading emerges from various notes: see, among others, Q 15, § 5; Q 19, § 6 (second draft of Q 9, § 105) and Q 22, § 1. On this point, see also Liguori and Voza 2009, p. 107.

29 Incidentally, note that the term 'catastrophe' also has a (loose) historical meaning. Contrastingly, Gramsci also uses the term while talking about historical phases associated with radical transformations. In particular, he recalls the term in relation to the Renaissance and the Restoration (see Q 5, § 139, p. 669; second draft: Q 26, § 11). In the second draft of this note, by associating catastrophe with lethargy, he creates a meaningful chiasmus. The Restoration overcomes the catastrophe represented by the French Revolution; likewise, the Renaissance overcomes the lethargic and barbaric Middle Ages. On the categories of Reformation, Renaissance, etc., see Thomas 2009, pp. 423 ff., and especially Frosini 2004, 2008 and 2012c.

each other in such a way that a continuation of the conflict can only terminate in their reciprocal destruction ... It always expresses the particular solution in which a great personality is entrusted with the task of 'arbitration' over a historico-political situation characterised by an equilibrium of forces heading towards catastrophe.[30]

The generic schema of forces A and B in conflict with catastrophic prospects – i.e. with the prospect that neither A nor B will be victorious, in the struggle to constitute (or reconstitute) an organic equilibrium ... In the modern world, Caesarist phenomena are quite different, both from those of the progressive Caesar/Napoleon I type, and from those of the Napoleon III type – although they tend towards the latter. In the modern world, the equilibrium with catastrophic prospects occurs not between forces which could in the last analysis fuse and unite – albeit after a wearying and bloody process – but between forces whose opposition is historically incurable and indeed becomes especially acute with the advent of Caesarist forms.[31]

When the crisis does not find this organic solution, but that of the charismatic leader, it means that a static equilibrium exists (whose factors may be disparate, but in which the decisive one is the immaturity of the progressive forces); it means that no group, neither the conservatives nor the progressives, has the strength for victory, and that even the conservative group needs a master. See *The Eighteenth Brumaire of Louis Bonaparte*.[32]

---

30   Q 13, § 27, p. 1619; SPN, p. 219. In the redrafted text, Gramsci removes a reference to Bonapartism (Q 9, § 133, p. 1194: '*Il cesarismo o bonapartismo esprime* ...'; Q 13, § 27, p. 1619: '*Il cesarismo esprime* ...') and substitutes the word 'tendency' [*tendenza*] with 'perspective' [*prospettiva*] (Q 9, § 133, p. 1194: '*a tendenza catastrofica*'; Q 13, § 27, p. 1619: '*a prospettiva catastrofica*').
31   Q 13, § 27, pp. 1621–2; SPN, pp. 221–2. In the formulation of Q 13, § 27 the first part of this text is more explicit, e.g. the meaning of the phrase 'organic equilibrium' is clearer. On the shift in the meaning of the adjective 'organic' (first negative, then positive, in connection to the issue of the party 'centralism') in the *Prison Notebooks*, see Cospito 2016, pp. 169 ff.
32   Q 13, § 23, p. 1604; SPN, p. 211. In this redrafted version, Gramsci added an observation on the immaturity of the progressive forces (this aspect is particularly emphasised in the second draft). The explicit reference to Marx's historical masterpiece is also new. Regarding the meaning of this addition, I would argue that it refers specifically to Gramsci's remarks on the conservative group that 'needs a master' (the reference to *The Eighteenth Brumaire* therefore represents a kind of historical exemplification).

Gramsci clearly depicts two opposing fronts, gathered around the two fundamental forces (bourgeoisie and proletariat). They engage in an 'all out fight' with the opponent, but neither is stronger than the other: the risk is their mutual destruction. In this context, a third force could intervene: by breaking up the legally constituted order and taking control of the situation, the Caesar may unlock this 'apocalyptic' scenario and open the way for an (at least temporary) overcoming of the crisis.

I would also argue that, in this framework, it is not by chance that Gramsci, in these notes of notebook 9 and 13, does not employ the adjective 'static' as a *quasi*-synonym of 'catastrophic' as in Q 2, § 75 and in Q 4, § 69.[33] This term no longer fits in with the conception of history and politics that Gramsci has since developed, a conception that understands history as a *continuum*, which can never be genuinely 'blocked' or interrupted, 'for it is certain that in the movement of history there is never any turning back, and that restorations *in toto* do not exist'.[34]

3   The Dreyfus Affair and the 'Tendential' Character of the Catastrophic Crisis

In its various formulations, the formula of the catastrophic balance thus has a clear meaning, which is functional in describing the context in which a Caesarist phenomenon may occur. However, the existence of a situation of balance of forces is a necessary but not sufficient condition for the advent of Caesarism, whose realisation can be foiled thanks to the (hidden or residual) capacity for resistance of a specific political and social configuration.

This emerges distinctly from Q 14, § 23. In spite of the title of the note *Machiavelli, Caesarism and the 'Catastrophic' Balance of Socio-political Forces* [*Machiavelli. Cesarismo ed equilibrio 'catastrofico' delle forze politico-sociali*], the text deals with the situations in which the balance between the classes does not result in a personal dictatorship.[35] The primary scope of the text, dating to January 1933, is to show how, in assessing a particular historical-social framework, not only the 'fundamental' forces, but also the secondary ones must be taken into account – in fact, their intervention can be essential in order to avoid a Caesarist drift. To support this thesis, Gramsci refers to the situation in France at the time of the Dreyfus Affair:

---

33   The only exception is Q 13, § 23, for the reasons of composition previously mentioned.
34   Q 13, § 27, p. 1619; SPN, pp. 219–20.
35   Interestingly, Gramsci puts the word 'catastrophic' into inverted commas.

A very important historical episode from this point of view is the so-called Dreyfus affair in France. This too belongs to the present series of observations, not because it led to 'Caesarism', indeed precisely for the opposite reason: because it prevented the advent of a Caesarism in gestation, of a clearly reactionary nature. Nevertheless, the Dreyfus movement is characteristic, since it was a case in which elements of the dominant social bloc itself thwarted the Caesarism of the most reactionary part of that same bloc. And they did so by relying for support not on the peasantry and the countryside, but on the subordinate strata in the towns under the leadership of reformist socialists (though they did in fact draw support from the most advanced part of the peasantry as well).[36]

Hence, a socio-political formation cannot be considered exhausted until there is a certain 'margin for manoeuvre', that is, until the dominant group is able to maintain control of the situation (even if this capacity is largely determined by the organisational weakness of the opposing force).[37] As Gramsci writes:

> There are other modern historico-political movements of the Dreyfus type to be found, which are certainly not revolutions, but which are not entirely reactionary either – at least in the sense that they shatter stifling and ossified State structures in the dominant camp as well, and introduce into national life and social activity a different and more numerous personnel. These movements too can have a relatively 'progressive' content, in so far as they indicate that there were effective forces latent in the old society which the old leaders did not know how to exploit – perhaps even 'marginal forces'.[38]

Consequently, Gramsci also sheds light on the issue of the catastrophe, by providing us with very useful indications on the way to conceive of the 'catastrophic' situations he refers to in the *Prison Notebooks*.

Indeed, Q 14, § 23 represents a further step in the re-semanticisation of the category of catastrophe. As emerges from the text, the catastrophic balance

---

36   Q 14, § 23, p. 1681; SPN, p. 223. On Gramsci's analysis of the Dreyfus case, see Antonini 2020.
37   It seems to me that these thoughts echo Gramsci's reflections on the two methodological canons of Marx's *Preface* of 1859, fully developed in notebook 15 (on this issue, see Chapter 10, section 3.2). On Gramsci's approach to these 'canons' (in the context of his reflection on the categories of permanent revolution and passive revolution), see Thomas 2018a.
38   Q 14, § 23, p. 1681; SPN, p. 223.

is not absolute; the conflict can be reabsorbed and the crisis recedes. As with the French case described here, the reciprocal ruin of the contending classes is not an inevitable outcome, a real development towards the dissolution of the society. It is rather the perspective of a threat, an impending (but not unavoidable) outcome. In this sense Gramsci's connected reflections on the distinction between 'to be epoch-making' [*fare epoca*] and 'to last' [*durare*] are highly significant.[39]

This makes the 'tendential' or 'perspective' character of Gramsci's catastrophism, repeatedly evoked in the *Notebooks*, clearer. As he writes in Q 10, II, § 36 (June–August 1932),

> it seems that the meaning of 'tendential' must, on this account, be of a real 'historical' and not a methodological, nature: the term serves in fact to indicate the dialectical process by which the molecular progressive thrust leads to a tendentially catastrophic result in the social ensemble, a result from which other individual progressive thrusts set off in a continual overhauling process which cannot however be reckoned as infinite, even if it does break up into a very large number of intermediate stages of different size and importance.[40]

As in the case of the tendency of the rate of profit to fall, also in the case of the catastrophic development of the situation of balance, Gramsci is suggesting that there are two tendencies that 'oppose and contrast [each other], partially annulling [themselves]'.[41] Moreover, this tendential dimension, far from implying any form of abstract or formal necessity, has to be understood historically, by carefully considering the context and the contingent variables that define it.

---

39 Q 14, § 23, p. 1681: '*non possono "fare epoca"*'; SPN, p. 223: 'they are not "epochal"'. In Q 14, § 23, the first of these expressions is used in a negative sense. A clear, 'positive' opposition between the two categories can be found only in Q 14, § 76, p. 1744; SPN, p. 256: 'it should be noted that the fact of "not constituting an epoch" is too often confused with brief "temporal" duration: it is possible to "last" a long time, relatively, and yet not "constitute an epoch": the viscous forces of certain régimes are often unsuspected, especially if they are "strong" as a result of the weakness of others' (as for the content, § 76 evokes clearly the argument of § 23). Apart from its employment in Q 14, the category of 'being epoch-making' occurs only one other time in the *Prison Notebooks*, i.e. in Q 10, II, § 48. On this point, see also Burgio 2014, pp. 112–16 *et passim*.

40 Q 10, II, § 36, p. 1283; FSPN, p. 432.

41 Liguori and Voza 2009, p. 456 (but see the entire entries – both by F. Frosini – *Caduta tendenziale del saggio di profitto* and *Leggi di tendenza*, respectively pp. 94–7 and 455–6).

From this perspective, 'catastrophic' and 'molecular' are also no longer antithetical categories; rather, both concepts emphasise (even if from different points of view) the 'historicity of the processes of transformation'.[42] In particular, the reference to the catastrophe has to be read as a structural element that highlights a fundamental feature of contemporary politics, i.e. the difficulties in overcoming the organic crisis of modernity. In this framework, the solution represented by the Caesarist dictatorship also assumes a different and more complex meaning. When it does not give birth to a different 'type of state' (which rarely happens), Caesarism represents a form of molecular transformation of society, which postpones its catastrophic collapse.[43]

In conclusion, Gramsci is already thinking within a new perspective, characterised by an interweaving of revolution and reaction, where there are no sudden changes but, instead, transformations follow slow and tortuous pathways. Only in this framework is it possible to understand contemporary Caesarist phenomena of the 1930s.

4   The 'Taxonomy' of Caesarism

4.1   *Great Personalities and Historical Analogies*

Before dwelling on the specific features of modern Caesarism, however, it is necessary to illustrate the phenomenology of Caesarism as sketched by Gramsci in the *Prison Notebooks* through concrete historical examples. Indeed, he starts one of the core texts on Caesarism (Q 13, § 27) with an observation about the need to 'compile a catalogue of the historical events which have culminated in a great "heroic" personality'.[44]

---

42 Liguori and Voza 2009, p. 554 (entry *Molecolare*; but see also the entry *Catastrofe, catastrofico*, written by E. Forenza, pp. 107–9).

43 Q 13, § 27, p. 1622; SPN, p. 222. In this note, Gramsci also affirms that molecular transformations, though not always possible, are a better alternative to Caesarist solutions strictly conceived (as a radical change).

44 Q 13, § 27, p. 1619; SPN, p. 219. The four personalities that Gramsci cites at the opening of this paragraph (as well as at the beginning of its first draft) are Caesar, Napoleon I, Napoleon III, and Cromwell. This affirmation evokes another passage from the *Notebooks* (Q 7, § 20; second draft Q 11, § 22), where Gramsci, by rejecting every mechanicist, miracle-based approach, reflects on how 'the historical movement arise[s]'; in this context, he insists also on the necessity to investigate the 'problem of the formation of social groups and of political parties and, in the final analysis, of the function of the great personalities in history' (PN, vol. 3, p. 171).

The connection between the historical and the theoretical aspect is one of the main features of the articulation of the category. As Gramsci states at the beginning of the note, he is aware of the distinction between Caesarism as a theoretical category and Caesarism as a historical event – as he writes, 'Caesarism ... does not in all cases have the same historical significance'.⁴⁵

The 'heuristic technique' through which he combines these two aspects of his analysis is represented by historical analogies.⁴⁶ Whilst avoiding a careless and naive use of parallels, Gramsci combines historical comparisons with the use of antithetical conceptual couples: analogies stress both affinities and dissimilarities between the different cases of Caesarism, and therefore open the door to a conceptual assessment.⁴⁷

This technique emerges distinctly in Q 13, § 23, where Gramsci establishes an illuminating multiple comparison between different forms of Caesarism. In § 27 of the same notebook this pivotal role of analogy stands out through the multifaceted description of the historical situations taken into account, which are portrayed from different points of view. The result is the creation of a 'taxonomy' of Caesarism that demonstrates the great theoretical potential of his historical analyses.⁴⁸

---

45   Q 13, § 27, p. 1619; SPN, p. 219. Gramsci makes some historical examples to clarify this general principle – Renaissance Italy 'after the death of Lorenzo il Magnifico' (p. 1619; p. 219), as well as the 'ancient world after the barbarian invasions' (p. 1619 – this second example is missing in the English translation).
46   On the use of historical analogies in the *Prison Notebooks*, especially with regard to the categories of Caesarism and Bonapartism, see Antonini 2019b.
47   Gramsci's train of thought often relies on the use of opposing conceptual couples, by revealing a 'dilemmatic' or 'binary' way of reasoning (see Thomas 2009, *passim*). Moreover, it is noteworthy that Gramsci's reassessment of Caesarism seems to take its cue from Marx's own style of 'comparative' analysis (see Antonini 2019b).
48   Burgio affirms that Gramsci traces a 'complex combinatorics' by describing 'the intertwining ... between causes ..., historical times and ... results of the Caesarist intervention' (Burgio 2014, p. 276). On a general level, I agree with Burgio's description of these three main aspects of Gramsci's taxonomy of Caesarism; however, it should be remembered that these distinctions have a mere heuristic value in Gramsci's view. Not only do these theoretical categories (at least partially) overlap, but they also cannot substitute for the concrete analyses of the historical cases, which maintain their primacy (therefore, in a certain sense, talking about a 'combinatorics' could be misleading, insofar as a combinatorics is always formal and abstract). Furthermore, Gramsci does not proceed systematically in his exploration of the theoretical articulation of the category of Caesarism, which remains, as it were, 'incomplete', as I will show in Chapter 9, section 4.3.

4.2   The Articulation of the Category

The first and most general distinction that Gramsci introduces on the basis of these historical comparisons is that of progressive and regressive Caesarism. According to Gramsci's formulation, 'Caesarism is progressive' when the power that unlocks the situation of balance 'helps the progressive force to triumph, albeit with its victory tempered by certain compromises and limitations'.[49] On the other hand, Caesarism is regressive 'when its intervention helps the reactionary force to triumph – in this case too with certain compromises and limitations, which have, however, a different value, extent, and significance than in the former'.[50] In both of these cases, the balance situation is resolved (albeit with some restrictions, as Gramsci noted) in favour of one of the two contenders. The two solutions are differentiated on the basis of the progressive or, alternatively, the reactionary character of the force supported by the Caesar. Despite the apparent obviousness of this reasoning, this is far from being trivial; it contextualises Gramsci's reflection on Caesarism within a more complex historico-political dynamic centred on the category of 'revolution-restoration'.[51]

After this preliminary distinction, illustrated through the reference to Caesar and Napoleon I (as examples of progressive Caesarism) and to Napoleon III and Bismarck (as regressive Caesarism), Gramsci continues the 'approximation to concrete historical reality' of the generic Caesarist 'hypothesis'.[52] In particular, he focuses on the forms assumed by Caesarism, respectively, in the pre-modern and modern world. The difference between the contemporary phenomena and those which belong to the previous historical phase ('pre-modernity', in Gramsci's words)[53] is primarily identified by Gramsci in their genesis, meaning in the times and in the ways in which the Caesarist development is realised.

Until the 1870s, the military element had played a decisive role: the rise of a Caesar was the result of a *coup d'État* (like 'the Caesar or 18 Brumaire type').[54]

---

49   Q 13, § 27, p. 1619; SPN, p. 219.
50   Q 13, § 27, p. 1619; SPN, p. 219.
51   Cf. Q 13, § 27, p. 1619; SPN, p. 219: 'The problem is to see whether in the dialectic "revolution-restoration" it is revolution or restoration which predominates'.
52   Q 13, § 27, p. 1621; SPN, p. 221.
53   As regards the chronology of the categories of Caesarism and Bonapartism, and, in particular, for the distinction between pre-modern and modern phenomena, see Chapter 10, section 2.
54   Q 13, § 27, p. 1620; SPN, p. 220. Famously, Julius Caesar's crossing of the river Rubicon in 49 BC with the army represented the first step of the Civil War and played a role in his rise to power. Military apparatuses were also important in Napoleon Bonaparte's *putsch* and in his nephew's *coup d'État* (on the latter, see McMillan 1991). I would argue that both these historical events can be comprehended in terms of the '18 Brumaire *type*'.

Afterwards, the army lost its primacy and the establishment of a Caesarist dictatorship was the consequence of a deeper and more thoroughgoing reorganisation of the state.

> In the modern world, with its great economic-trade-union and party-political coalitions, the mechanism of the Caesarist phenomenon is very different from what it was up to the time of Napoleon III. In the period up to Napoleon III, the regular military forces or soldiers of the line were a decisive element in the advent of Caesarism, and this came about through quite precise *coups d'État*, through military actions, etc. In the modern world trade-union and political forces, with the limitless financial means which may be at the disposal of small groups of citizens, complicate the problem. The functionaries of the parties and economic unions can be corrupted or terrorised, without any need for military action in the grand style – of the Caesar or 18 Brumaire type. The same situation recurs in this field as was examined in connection with the Jacobin/Forty-eightist formula of the so-called 'Permanent Revolution'. Modern political technique became totally transformed after Forty-eight; after the expansion of parliamentarism and of the associative systems of union and party, and the growth in the formation of vast State and 'private' bureaucracies (i.e. politico-private, belonging to parties and trade unions); and after the transformations which took place in the organisation of the forces of order in the wide sense – i.e. not only the public service designed for the repression of crime, but the totality of forces organised by the State and by private individuals to safeguard the political and economic domination of the ruling classes. In this sense, entire 'political' parties and other organisations – economic or otherwise – must be considered as organs of political order, of an investigational and preventive character.[55]

This passage clearly relates to remarks already made in Q 13, § 23 and, before, in its first draft texts (in this case, Q 4, § 66). In these notes, Gramsci points to the opposition between narrow-minded military governments and 'true' Bonapartist regimes. We can see, in this regard, the comparison that Gramsci makes between Petar Živković and Primo de Rivera on the one hand, and, again, Caesar and Napoleon I on the other.[56] While Živković and De Rivera embody

---

55   Q 13, § 27, pp. 1620–1; SPN, pp. 220–1.
56   Petar Živković (1879–1947) was a Yugoslav general and politician. Between 1929 and 1932 he was prime minister of the Kingdom of Yugoslavia where he realised a form of dictatorship supported by the monarchy. Miguel Primo de Rivera (1870–1930) was a Span-

two cases of proper military regimes (albeit very different from each other), Caesar and Napoleon I know how to combine military and political capabilities. Thus, they are able to achieve a more solid rule, which can consequently be qualified as 'real' Bonapartism.[57] In Q 13, § 27, Gramsci distinguishes between Caesarist regimes that arise thanks to the direct intervention of the army, and dictatorships in which the main role is played by police apparatuses, widely understood.[58]

Some structural elements allow us to distinguish between modern Caesarism and its pre-modern version. Even more than military intervention, the crucial element of distinction between the two types of Caesarism is represented by the different relations between the two struggling social blocs, and by the outcomes of their balance (and, consequently of the Caesarist solution). In both cases Caesarism originates from a situation of balance between the classes, i.e. from a context in which neither of the two forces in the field (by immaturity or weakness) is able to take control of the situation.

In the modern scenario, however, this situation of balance is far from being resolved by the intervention of a Caesar. Thus, it acquires a sort of 'tragic' dimension:

> The equilibrium with catastrophic prospects occurs not between forces which could in the last analysis fuse and unite – albeit after a wearying and bloody process – but between forces whose opposition is historically incurable and indeed becomes especially acute with the advent of Caesarist forms.[59]

---

ish politician and military leader. He took power after a *coup* supported by the army in 1923 and retained it until 1930. In the first draft (Q 4, § 66), instead of Rivera, Gramsci mentions Zankof (sic), i.e. Aleksander Tsolov Tsankov (1879–1959), prime minister of the Kingdom of Bulgaria between 1923 and 1926. His government was also the result of a *putsch* and was characterised by internal struggles and fierce repression of its opponents. Gramsci could likely have gathered information on Živković and Tsankov thanks to his contacts with Bulgarian anti-fascists and Yugoslav students during his stay in Vienna (on this point, see Giasi 2009, p. 188). It should also be remembered that Gramsci took part in the conference of the Balkan Communist Federation in November 1923 (cf. QNaz, 2.I, p. 839).

57 There is no contradiction between the double description of Caesar and Napoleon I, first, as Bonapartist figures (Q 13, § 23) and, then, as Caesarist characters (Q 13, § 27). This double classification is because the two categories (Bonapartism and Caesarism) have different analytical aims.

58 On this enlarged conception of police, see Chapter 11, section 3.3.

59 Q 13, § 27, p. 1622; SPN, p. 222.

This did not happen in the pre-modern context. As a matter of fact, although the struggle was fierce, the two opposing forces

> were nevertheless not such as to be 'absolutely' incapable of arriving, after a molecular process, at a reciprocal fusion and assimilation. And this was what in fact happened, at least to a certain degree (sufficient, however, for the historico-political objectives in question – i.e. the halting of the fundamental organic struggle, and hence the transcendence of the catastrophic phase).[60]

Gramsci does not insist too much on this issue here, but it is clear that the possibility of finding a compromise between the forces (albeit molecularly and after a bloody fight) greatly reduces the dramatic nature of the conflict. It also clearly underlines the gap between pre-modern and modernity – the latter is in fact characterised by a slow agony of bourgeois society and by an uncertain future.

There follows a discussion of the various types of political crisis that give rise to the Caesarist phenomena. Caesarism, Gramsci asserts, may be the result either of a 'necessarily insuperable organic deficiency' (that is, of an organic crisis), or it can derive from a '"momentary" political deficiency'.[61] In the first case, the Caesarist regime represents the conclusion of a historical phase and the opening of a new one; it is therefore of a 'quantitative-qualitative' type and it makes possible the creation of a new form of state.[62] In the second case, Caesarism is the result of a peculiar historical conjuncture, i.e. of the contingent weakness of the dominant force. Thus, the emergence of Caesarist government does not imply a general crisis of the previous system; it represents rather a prolongation of the existing power scheme, albeit under a different form. Exemplary in this respect is, for instance, the regime of Louis Bonaparte, which embodies a merely 'quantitative' Caesarism.[63]

---

60   Q 13, § 27, p. 1621; SPN, p. 221. Once again, the case studies mentioned by Gramsci are Caesar and Napoleon I.
61   Q 13, § 27, p. 1621; SPN, p. 222.
62   Cf. Q 13, § 27, p. 1622; SPN, p. 222: 'the Caesarism of Caesar and Napoleon I was, so to speak, of a quantitative-qualitative character; in other words it represented the historical phase of passage from one type of State to another type – a passage in which the innovations were so numerous, and of such a nature, that they represented a complete revolution'. In this case, the qualitative passage is not the consequence of a process of 'molecular' transformation of reality, but rather the effect of a quick and effective political metamorphosis (see the entry *Quantità-qualità* by G. Prestipino in Liguori and Voza 2009, pp. 677–8).
63   Cf. Q 13, § 27, pp. 1621–2; SPN, pp. 221–2: 'This [the fact that Caesarism arises from a

4.3 An 'Incomplete' Scheme

Nevertheless, the 'qualitative-quantitative' couple should not be confused with the 'progressive-regressive' one. While it is true that 'qualitative' dictatorships such as Caesar and Napoleon I are absolutely progressive, the Caesarism of Napoleon III is also relatively (or 'objectively', as Gramsci says) progressive. This is precisely because Napoleon III represents the expression of the latent forces of development of a social system.[64]

Interestingly, a case that Gramsci defines first as regressive (Napoleon III) becomes, in the course of the note, a relatively or 'objectively progressive' version of Caesarism. It is not by chance that, when in Q 14, § 23 Gramsci speaks of Caesarism of an 'intermediate and episodic character', he clearly hints at Louis Bonaparte's regime.[65] In addition to this, the scarcity and the problematic nature of the examples used by Gramsci to illustrate regressive Caesarism may also give us food for thought.[66] I would argue that regressive Caesarism strictly conceived is, for Gramsci, only a 'limit case', a theoretical option necessary to complete the scheme but that, in historical reality, does not exist. In fact, as Gramsci writes in this very same Q 13, § 27, 'in the movement of history there is never any turning back, and that restorations *in toto* do not exist'.[67]

The 'incompleteness' of Gramsci's scheme also manifests itself from another point of view. Gramsci aims to analyse contemporary Caesarist phenomena, although he does not take a clear position in this regard. Precisely because of the dramatic ('catastrophic', in the sense explained above) clash between the bourgeoisie and the proletariat in the modern world, there is no such thing as a truly progressive (or, as we saw, regressive) Caesarism. Moreover, in Gramsci's

---

"momentary" political deficiency of the dominant force] was true in the case of Napoleon III ... The internal faction struggle was such as to make possible the advance of the rival force B (progressive) in a precocious form; however, the existing social form had not yet exhausted its possibilities for development, as subsequent history abundantly demonstrated. Napoleon III represented (in his own manner, as fitted the stature of the man, which was not great) these latent and immanent possibilities: his Caesarism therefore has a particular coloration ... The Caesarism of Napoleon III was merely, and in a limited fashion, quantitative; there was no passage from one type of State to another, but only "evolution" of the same type along unbroken lines'.

64 Strangely, a crucial sentence of Q 13, § 27 is missing in the English edition of the text. In Q 13, § 27, p. 1621, Gramsci is talking about the regime of Napoleon III and he writes: 'It is objectively progressive though not like that of Caesar and Napoleon' [*È obbiettivamente progressivo sebbene non come quello di Cesare e di Napoleone*].
65 Q 14, § 23, p. 1680; SPN, p. 222.
66 If we exclude the reference to the Second French Empire, only a fleeting cross-reference to Bismarck in Q 4, § 66 remains, which is not resumed in the second version (Q 13, § 23).
67 Q 13, § 27, p. 1619; SPN, pp. 219–20.

times, the only 'objectively' progressive Caesarism also does not seem to be a truly feasible option. As he affirms, 'in the modern world, Caesarist phenomena are quite different, both from those of the progressive Caesar/Napoleon I type, and from those of the Napoleon III type – although they tend towards the latter'.[68] The affinities between the relatively progressive Caesarism of Napoleon III and the Caesarist phenomena of modernity also appear limited; the pre-modern and the modern cases of Caesarism are only partly comparable, and, from a certain point of view, immeasurable. Rather than a developed assessment of modern Caesarism, the analysis appears to be barely suggested or, so to speak, 'commenced' by Gramsci in these notes – the reference to the contemporary coalition governments as the 'degree o', i.e. 'ground level' of Caesarism is eloquent in this sense.[69]

To conclude, the reading proposed here has demonstrated that Caesarism, in Gramscian terms, is not something monolithic, but rather represents a multifaceted phenomenon, able to describe an extremely broad and varied spectrum of political events. The case studies mentioned by Gramsci were essential in orienting his inquiry; the observation in the catalogue of 'heroic' personalities at the outset of Q 13, § 27 is confirmed by this interpretation.

This prominent role of the historiographical dimension (compounded by the peculiar features of Gramsci's writing in prison) explains the character of Gramsci's taxonomy. Far from establishing a systematic catalogue of the various forms of Caesarism, Gramsci's notes draw simply a sketch, however rich and articulated it may be. It is clear that the distinction between progressive and regressive Caesarism and the ones which follow (in short: military or police Caesarism, pre-modern or modern Caesarism, Caesarism as a result of an organic crisis or a momentary crisis, qualitative or quantitative Caesarism) do not cover all the possible Caesarist forms, and especially do not fully explain its most recent manifestations.

---

68 Q 13, § 27, p. 1622; SPN, p. 222.
69 On this point, see Chapter 11, section 1.1.

CHAPTER 10

Caesarism and Historical Analysis

1   Gramscian 'Concerns'

1.1   *Practical Criteria of Interpretation*

In the previous chapter, I focused on the articulation of the Caesarist phenomenon as it is described in Q 13, §§ 23 and 27. However, in these notes, Gramsci repeatedly warns himself (or perhaps warns the reader) not to take this taxonomy too literally and to avoid an uncritical use of the category. These notes are therefore a powerful illustration of how Gramsci conceives of the concepts of Caesarism and Bonapartism, showing their fundamental ambivalence.

Indeed, there are numerous warnings against lingering excessively on the formula of the balance of class forces, or of treating the Caesarist solution as an exclusively theoretical formulation. While, in the case of Q 13, § 23, the number of 'meta-textual' observations is also due to the composite nature of the note (which, as we saw previously, is the result of the merging of several first draft texts), I would argue that these warnings are a core element of Gramsci's reflection on Caesarism. Consequently, they have to be considered as such. See the following passages:[1]

> None of these observations is absolute; at various moments of history and in various countries they have widely differing significance ... These observations must not be conceived of as rigid schemata, but merely as practical criteria of historical and political interpretation. In concrete analyses of real events, the historical forms are individualised and can almost be called 'unique'.[2]

---

1   See also this passage from Q 14, § 23 (p. 1680; SPN, p. 222): 'It would be an error of method (an aspect of sociological mechanicism) to believe that in Caesarism – whether progressive, reactionary, or of an intermediate and episodic character – the entire new historical phenomenon is due to the equilibrium of the "fundamental" forces'. On the relationship between Q 13 and Q 14, see Chapter 10, section 3.2.

2   Q 13, § 23, pp. 1605–10; SPN, pp. 212–17. Cf. the first draft: 'None of these observations is absolute: they have to be "relativized" according to the various moments of history and different states ... This phenomenon always assumes historically specific forms ... In other words, these observations are not sociological schemata; they are practical criteria of historical and political interpretation which must always be removed from schematic generalizations and

> But Caesarism – although it always expresses the particular solution in which a great personality is entrusted with the task of 'arbitration' over a historico-political situation characterised by an equilibrium of forces heading towards catastrophe – does not in all cases have the same historical significance ... the exact significance of each form can, in the last analysis, be reconstructed only through concrete history, and not by means of any sociological rule of thumb ... Besides, Caesarism is a polemical-ideological formula, and not a canon of historical interpretation.[3]

> The generic schema of forces A and B in conflict with catastrophic prospects ... is precisely a generic hypothesis, a sociological schema (convenient for the art of politics). It is possible to render the hypothesis ever more concrete, to carry it to an ever greater degree of approximation to concrete historical reality, and this can be achieved by defining certain fundamental elements. Thus, in speaking of A and B, it has merely been asserted that they are respectively a generically progressive, and a generically reactionary, force. But one might specify the type of progressive and reactionary force involved, and so obtain closer approximations.[4]

In addition to these methodological 'caveats', it should also be noted that Gramsci adopts some typical 'precautions of writings', such as the use of quotation marks and other cautionary formulas, as pointed out by Dario Ragazzini and, more recently, by Giuseppe Cospito.[5] But how should we interpret these obser-

---

incorporated into a concrete historico-political analysis' (Q 4, §66, pp. 509–11; PN, vol. 2, pp. 239–42).

3 Q 13, §27, p. 1619; SPN, pp. 219–20. Cf. the first draft: 'But Caesarism, if it always expresses the "arbitrary" solution, entrusted to a great personality, of a historical-political situation of a balance of forces with a catastrophic tendency, does not always have the same historical meaning ... The exact meaning of every form of Caesarism can be reconstructed, ultimately, from the concrete history and not from a sociological scheme ... Moreover, the "Caesarist" phenomenon is a polemical-ideological formula rather than a historical-political one' (Q 9, §133, pp. 1194–5).

4 Q 13, §27, p. 1621. Cf. the first draft: 'The generic scheme of the A and B forces in struggle with catastrophic prospects, ... is in fact a generic hypothesis, a sociological scheme of a mathematical type ([a scheme] of political science). The hypothesis can still be made more concrete, [it can be] brought to a greater degree of approximation to concrete historical reality. This can be achieved by better specifying some fundamental elements. Thus, speaking of A and B, we have only said that they are a generically progressive force and a generically regressive force: we can specify what kind of regressive and progressive force we are dealing with and, thus, we can obtain a greater approximation' (Q 9, §136, p. 1197).

5 See Ragazzini 2002 and Cospito 2015. By applying these general observations of Cospito in

vations by Gramsci? Far from representing a 'definitive abandonment' of the concept of Caesarism,[6] Gramsci's methodological concerns should be understood in light of the general framework of his thought.

From his vocabulary, it emerges that Gramsci's scope is twofold. On the one hand, he rejects a purely sociological approach to the issue. On the other, his reflections on Caesarism reiterate the indissolubility of the intertwining of theoretical formulation and historical reality. While it is well known that 'sociologism' (a 'degeneration' of sociological thought) is one of Gramsci's main polemical targets, his second aim is directly connected to my prior observations on the 'incompleteness' of his taxonomy of Caesarism. This is also related to the link between the different theoretical variants and their historical examples (the references to the 'practical criteria of historical and political interpretation' and to the 'approximation to concrete historical reality' of the 'generic hypothesis' do not seem to me to leave room for doubt).[7]

Hence, Gramsci's apparently harsh formulations should not be taken too literally. For instance, the statement that 'Caesarism is a polemical-ideological formula, and not a canon of historical interpretation' does not imply a refusal of its analytical value, but rather, as clearly emerges from the context, it is a way to warn against a preconceived interpretation of it (although based on a constitutive element of the category such as the reference to the Caesar – not by chance immediately after that he adds: 'a Caesarist solution can exist even without a Caesar, without any great, "heroic" and representative personality').[8]

---

the specific case of the notes on Caesarism, we can state that Gramsci attenuates his observations through phrases such as 'so to speak' or through the combination of strong expressions with more 'delicate' terms, often between brackets. He also makes extensive use of quotation marks, even if their number progressively decreases. I would argue that, if at the beginning he feels the need to underline the fact that his conception of Caesarism detaches itself from the *vulgata*, as his thought develops there is no longer any need to highlight this originality. From this perspective, it should be noted that initial terminological uncertainties often disappear in the second drafts. Numerous cases in which, in the first drafts, Gramsci speaks of Caesarism or Bonapartism are replaced in the redrafted texts by an unequivocal reference to Caesarism only.

6   Cospito 2016, p. 215. Previously, Luisa Mangoni addressed this issue, although she did not discuss it in detail (cf. Mangoni 1976, p. 39 and Mangoni 1977, p. 412 *et passim*).
7   The same expressions mentioned here constitute indeed intermediate formulas between the two opposite poles of 'concrete history' and 'sociological scheme'. In short, I would argue that Gramsci's attempt here is to avoid a unilateral interpretation of the question, both in one sense and in the other.
8   Q 13, § 27, p. 1619; SPN, p. 220.

1.2 Julius Caesar and Caesarism

On the basis of these points, we can also clarify the meaning of one of the last notes of the *Notebooks* dealing with a Caesarist theme. Here, in particular, the figure of the 'eponymous hero' of the category, Julius Caesar, is at stake.[9] In §21 of notebook 17, (*Cultural Topics. Caesar and Caesarism*, single draft, September–18 November 1933), Gramsci writes:

> The theory of Caesarism, which predominates today (see the speech of Emilio Bodrero *The Humanity of Julius Caesar* [*L'umanità di Giulio Cesare*], in the *Nuova Antologia* of 16 September 1933), was introduced into the political language by Napoleon III, who was certainly not a great historian or philosopher or political theorist. It is certain that in Roman history the figure of Caesar is not characterised only or principally by 'Caesarism' in this narrow sense.[10]

Indeed,

> the historical development of which Caesar was the expression assumes in the 'Italian peninsula', i.e. in Rome, the form of 'Caesarism'; but its framework is the entire imperial territory and it actually consists in the 'denationalisation' of Italy and in its subordination to the interests of the Empire … Rome became a cosmopolitan city, and the whole of Italy became the centre of a cosmopolis.[11]

There follows a critical discussion of Bodrero's intervention in which Gramsci states that the main historical legacy of Caesar is to be found, rather than in the creation of an authoritarian form of government, in shifting the struggle for political domination from the national level to the international one. Consequently, this opens up the theme of cosmopolitanism, which will become a major feature of Gramsci's analysis of Italy and of Italian intellectuals.[12]

With regard to this issue, I would also recall Gramsci's discussion in Q 17, §53, entitled *Cultural Questions. Disraeli* [*Problemi di cultura. Disraeli*].[13] This

---

[9] On this point, see Fontana 2004, pp. 187–8 and Liguori and Voza 2009, pp. 122–3. On the reference to the historical figure of Julius Caesar and on Gramsci's interest in the classical world, see respectively Santangelo 2020 and Fonzo 2019.

[10] Q 17, §21, p. 1924.

[11] Q 17, §21, p. 1924. The term 'cosmopolis' indicates here a supra-national political community.

[12] On the category of cosmopolitanism in Gramsci's thought, see in particular Izzo 2009, but see also Ciliberto 1999, Basile 2009, and Frosini 2017a.

[13] This single draft was written after 19 June 1935 and it is the last note of the notebook.

text contains a number of observations on the politics of Benjamin Disraeli and on his attempt to achieve an 'organic English imperialism'.[14] Disraeli is here compared to Caesar, because of his supra-national political project.[15] This confirms how, from Gramsci's perspective, the historical figure of Julius Caesar is closely connected to Roman imperial politics.

It cannot be denied that Q 17, § 21 is particularly clear in discarding the concept of Caesarism as defined by Bodrero. However, it is also evident that this is not a rejection of the Caesarist model as a whole. In fact, in this case, the rejection of Caesarism is closely linked to the context in which it is placed, i.e. to the redefinition of Caesar's historical role, and above all to Gramsci's critique of the contemporary developments of the 'theories of Caesarism', exemplified by Bodrero.

The conclusion of the note, on the other hand, clearly shows that Gramsci pays attention to the history of the concept, to the events that have determined its genesis and development: 'From the cultural point of view, it is interesting [to note that] the current myth of "Caesar" has no historical basis, just as the exaltation of the Roman republic as a democratic and popular institution etc. had no basis in the eighteenth century'.[16]

2   The Historico-political Framework of the *Prison Notebooks*

2.1   *Gramsci's 'Plural Temporalities' and the Case of France*

Thus, Gramsci's first concern is to warn against a simplification of the concept of Caesarism and to condemn the purely ideological and propagandistic uses of the term. Given that, it is necessary to focus on the origin of the concept,

---

14   Q 17, § 53, p. 1949; FSPN, p. 261. Benjamin Disraeli (1804–81) was a conservative politician; he was twice Prime Minister of the United Kingdom, in 1868 and in 1874–80.

15   See the text: 'Why is it that Disraeli understood imperial necessities better than any other British head of government? Comparison may be made between Disraeli and Caesar. But Disraeli did not successfully pose the question of the British Empire's transformation and had no one to continue his work: Englishness prevented the fusion into a single unified imperial class of the national groups that of necessity were being formed throughout the Empire. It is self-evident that the British Empire could not be founded on a bureaucratic-military structure, as happened in the Roman case; fruitfulness of the programme of an "imperial parliament" as conceived by Disraeli. That imperial parliament would however have had to legislate for Britain too, which for a Briton is an absurdity: only a semite, free of preconceptions, like Disraeli, could be the expression of organic British imperialism. Analogous modern historical phenomena' (Q 17, § 53, p. 1949; FSPN, p. 261).

16   Q 17, § 21, pp. 1924–5.

by analysing its connection with nineteenth-century French history and with the category of passive revolution within the general framework of Gramsci's historical view.

As Alberto Burgio wrote, the *Prison Notebooks* represent in a certain sense 'a great history book: a history of the bourgeois West or, as Gramsci writes more simply, of the "modern world"'.[17] Indeed, if his ultimate goal is to interpret the tumultuous historical situation in which he lives and, at the same time, to lay the foundations for a recovery of the workers' movement, Gramsci's attention is not limited to the contemporary situation. He searches in the past for the deep roots of current phenomena, by formulating a fascinating critical theory of modernity as a whole.

On a general level, it should be noted that there is not a unique timeframe in the *Prison Notebooks*. Gramsci's conception of historical times is 'plural' in its very essence, as has been recently argued by Peter Thomas.[18] Historically speaking, Gramsci's 'multiple temporalities' correspond to the various times of the European countries, which follow different rhythms and display different dynamics.[19] In spite of the national variants, however, there is a common *motif* in the history of modern Europe. This is constituted by the rise and decline of the bourgeois class, i.e. by the (more or less successful) establishment of bourgeois hegemony over society and by the efforts to maintain its primacy in the changing political panorama (by controlling the politicisation and 'insubordination' of the masses, through new hegemonic strategies).

The history of France undoubtedly represents the main point of reference for the categories of Caesarism and Bonapartism. This has emerged already from my previous analysis. Without assuming the pre-eminence of French history over the history of the other European countries, I would like to focus briefly on the development of bourgeois hegemony in France, by highlighting the 'milestones' identified by Gramsci. Although it is more of a suggestion than

---

17   Burgio 2003, p. 3.
18   See Thomas 2017a (but see also Thomas 2017c).
19   The most significant example is represented, of course, by Italy. As regards the German case, its singularity emerges clearly from Gramsci's observations on Hegel's *Philosophy of Right*, which highlights how, in the nineteenth century, a passive revolution took place in the German states (see, on this point, Frosini 2016a). Moreover, as regards England, the combination of elements, such as the advanced capitalist system and the development of classical political economy (Ricardo, etc.), reflects another different temporality. Each of these situations is equally important in the framework of Gramsci's conception of 'translatability' (on this pivotal Gramscian category and on its broader meaning, see Frosini 2010a and Descendre and Zancarini 2016).

formally established, a precise 'chronology' can be retraced in the prison writings, where Gramsci distinguishes between three different historical periods.[20]

The first phase embraces all the events that occur in France from the end of the Middle Ages up to the French Revolution, during which the bourgeoisie gradually gained importance. The outbreak of the Revolution of 1789, in particular, represented the open breach with the ancient order (feudal and medieval) and deeply and quickly transformed politics and society. The second stage opens in 1789 and goes up to 1870, by extending far beyond the formal end of the revolutionary period. It represents the most profound and radical phase of transformation, during which, in France, the bourgeoisie took control of the political, social and economic system. The third phase is characterised by a general 'retreat of the bourgeoisie', that shortens the distance between France and the other European nations. This stage began in 1870–71, with the experience of the Paris Commune of 1871 and the end of the Second French Empire, substituted by the Third Republic. It describes the end of the expansion of the bourgeoisie and its settling on more conservative positions. It is noteworthy that Gramsci makes a further distinction within this third stage. He introduces another 'historical fracture' represented by the First World War, conceived of as an explicit expression of the crisis of the authority of the bourgeoisie. See, in this regard, Q 15, § 59, where he writes that 'everybody recognises that the war of 1914–18 represents an historical break, in the sense that a whole series of questions which piled up individually before 1914 have precisely formed a "mound", modifying the general structure of the previous process'.[21] Thus, the period after 1918 represents 'fully developed modernity'.

On this basis, the terminology adopted by Gramsci can also be better understood. In fact, although in some texts he refers to the second stage as the 'modern' stage,[22] in the majority of the notes (including those on Caesarism) 'real'

---

20 On this tripartition, see Burgio 2014, pp. 157–64.
21 Q 15, § 59, p. 1824; SPN, p. 106. Giuseppe Vacca convincingly explained why Gramsci did not choose 1917 (i.e. the Russian Revolution) as a threshold, although he had done so previously (see Vacca 1988, pp. 129–31). In particular Vacca highlights the pivotal role of the category of passive revolution, and the social and economic analysis that it entails. See Vacca 1988, p. 131: 'It seems to me that the notion of "passive revolution" changes the chronologising value of the "historical fracture" represented by the war of 1914–1918, not only because of the connection of crisis-war-topicality of the revolution ..., but with reference to the whole transition from "market economy" to "corporate society". More generally, in the chronology of twentieth century the accent shifts from the October revolution to the "Great War"'. On this question, see also Benvenuti and Pons 1999, p. 115 *et passim* (and, more recently, Pons 2017, pp. 920 ff.), and Burgio 2014, pp. 157–93.
22 See the entry *Modernità*, by G. Prestipino, in Liguori and Voza 2009, pp. 547–8.

modernity is represented by the third phase, by which he means the current period in which he is living – his coining of the 'modern prince' is eloquent from this point of view. Therefore, we should define the previous stage, as it were, as 'pre-modern'. Furthermore, Gramsci never speaks of 'contemporaneity'. While he uses the adjective 'contemporary' infrequently, contemporaneity as a chronological label appears only in two notes, where it is rejected as a superficial and ridiculous category.[23]

2.2 The 'Waves' of History

The most important phase for Gramsci is certainly the second one, which is characterised by the progressive and expansive attitude of the French bourgeoisie, whose political dynamic both subsumes and includes other groups. In fact, in this phase the bourgeoisie capitalised on its hegemonic capacity (in a more or less effective way) to gather around itself the other social classes; it convinces them of the need for a common action aimed at achieving a 'superior' interest, embodied by the bourgeois state.

This emerges distinctly from his analysis of the revolutionary events that took place in France between 1789 and 1870. As Burgio writes, they represent a 'dialectical structure with progressive dominance'.[24] As Gramsci observes in Q 13, § 17, *Analysis of the Situation: Relations of Force*,

> the internal contradictions which develop after 1789 in the structure of French society are resolved to a relative degree only with the Third Republic; and France has now enjoyed sixty years of stable political life only after eighty years of convulsions at ever longer intervals: 1789, 1794, 1799, 1804, 1815, 1830, 1848, 1870.[25]

Far from representing a monotonous *continuum*, this historical period shows a 'fluctuating' trend. On the one hand, there are moments in which the most progressive political instances are openly expressed and sustained. On the other hand, during other phases these instances are repressed and the bourgeois strategy becomes clearly conservative. In fact, if the bourgeoisie exploits the most advanced groupings to break the old system, when the goal is achieved, it rejects their too modern demands and adopts a more 'centrist' behaviour, which better corresponds to its real needs.[26] In fact,

---

23 See Q 8, § 232, redrafted in Q 11, § 18.
24 Burgio 2014, p. 159.
25 Q 13, § 17, p. 1582; SPN, p. 180.
26 Burgio also argued that there might be a possible connection between the Gramscian

the new bourgeois class struggling for power defeated not only the representatives of the old society unwilling to admit that it had been definitively superseded, but also the still newer groups who maintained that the new structure created by the 1789 revolution was itself already outdated; by this victory the bourgeoisie demonstrated its vitality *vis-à-vis* both the old and the very new.[27]

These observations also evoke the themes of Jacobinism and of permanent revolution, insofar as real or 'substantial' Jacobinism, which is opposed to 'superficial' Jacobinism, makes a leap forward in history, by adopting the programme of a true revolutionary strategy.[28] From this perspective, we also can read Q 13, § 37, *Notes on French National Life*, where Gramsci affirms:

> The development of Jacobinism (of content), and of the formula of Permanent Revolution put into practice in the active phase of the French Revolution, found its juridical-constitutional 'completion' in the parliamentary regime. The latter, in the period in which 'private' energies in society were most plentiful, realised the permanent hegemony of the urban class over the entire population in the Hegelian form of government with permanently organised consent.[29]

---

theses and some observations by Labriola on the non-linear development of the rule of the bourgeoisie (see Burgio 2014, pp. 159–60 *et passim*; on Gramsci and Labriola, more generally, see Burgio 2014, pp. 414–47).

27 Q 13, § 17, pp. 1581–2; SPN, p. 179.
28 Thomas 2018a now offers a fresh insight into this theme. For a synthetic description of the distinction between the 'substantial' Jacobinism (*'giacobinismo di contenuto'*) and the 'superficial' Jacobinism (*'giacobinismo deteriore'*, *'esteriore'*, or *'formale'*), see Martin 2002, vol. 2, p. 24. See also Q 16, § 9, p. 1864, where the opposition is between 'the utopian character of the mummified Jacobin ideologies' and Jacobinism as 'circumscribed activity in specific circumstances and not as something ideologised' (SPN, p. 399). On this topic, see also Medici 2004 and the entry *Rivoluzione permanente* (by R. Ciccarelli) in Liguori and Voza 2009, pp. 728–31. The best example of 'superficial' Jacobinism is represented by Francesco Crispi (1818–1901), prime minister of the Kingdom of Italy in 1887–91 and 1893–96. Because of his ability to hold together a moderate political content with a wholly formal Jacobinism, he is symbolic of a selfish political direction, which does not take into account the real interests of the country. As Gramsci remarks, he is 'energetic and resolute because fanatically convinced of the thaumaturgical power of his ideas' (Q 1, § 44, pp. 44–5; PN, vol. 1, p. 141). On Crispi, see also the entry by S. Suppa in Liguori and Voza 2009, p. 182.
29 Q 13, § 37, p. 1636; SPN, p. 80, n. 49.

This 'alternation of assimilating dynamics ... and disruptive phases', i.e. the 'continuous oscillation between liberal moments and repressive breaks', is embodied perfectly by the metaphor of the 'waves' adopted by Gramsci. This image is particularly suitable to illustrate the 'oscillating' nature of historical movement (see Q 2, § 32, *Augur*, single draft, May–15 June 1930: 'waves ... which come and go capriciously')[30] and it returns many times in the *Notebooks*. In Q 13, § 17, for instance, he uses this metaphor to describe the different phases of the revolutionary and post-revolutionary process in France.[31] In Q 10, II, § 61, the waves describe more precisely the 'reformist' moments of the history of France, in opposition to the 'revolutionary explosions like the original French one'.[32] The 'waves' represent here the phases of molecular transformation as opposed to sudden changes resulting from popular uprisings; in this sense, the metaphor of the waves has to be connected with Gramsci's analysis of passive revolution.

2.3   *Napoleon III as Archetype of Caesarism*

We should understand the figure of Louis Bonaparte in this context. The empire of Napoleon III, made possible by the *coup d'État* of 2 December 1851, represents the conservative 'wave' that followed the revolutionary outbreak of 1848. Indeed, during the Second Empire the bourgeoisie restored order within a political framework shaken by popular insurrections, while the second Bonaparte realised his personal domination.

The figure of Louis Napoleon himself is discussed in a number of notes in the *Prison Notebooks*. In Q 6, § 65 (*Journalism* [*Giornalismo*], single draft, December 1930–13 March 1931), for instance, Gramsci mentions Napoleon III's opinions about journalism. In Q 15, § 36 (*Past and Present*, single draft, May 1933), his sympathies for Proudhon are evoked. Elsewhere, Gramsci speaks of the 'invectives *à la* Victor [Hugo] against Napoleon III',[33] by hinting at the famous remark by Victor Hugo on Louis Bonaparte, which is also mentioned by Marx. This

---

30   Q 2, § 32, p. 190; PN, vol. 1, p. 281.
31   See the following quotation: 'It is precisely the study of these "waves" of varying frequency which enables one to reconstruct the relations on the one hand between structure and superstructure, and on the other between the development of organic movement and conjunctural movement in the structure. One might say in the meantime that the dialectical mediation between the two methodological principles formulated at the beginning of this note is to be found in the historico-political formula of Permanent Revolution' (Q 13, § 17, p. 1582; SPN, p. 180). The translation has been modified, since in the English version the term 'waves' is translated as 'intervals'.
32   Q 10, II, § 61, p. 1358; SPN, p. 115.
33   Q 9, § 42, p. 1122; the text is redrafted in Q 23, § 8.

passage also anticipates Gramsci's allusion to the 'pettiness' of Napoleon III contained in Q 9, § 136, redrafted in Q 13, § 27 (see also, in this respect, Q 17, § 21). Moreover, other notes deal with Louis Napoleon's political strategy, in particular his use of universal suffrage.[34]

Beyond the purely quantitative consideration of the number of texts dedicated to Napoleon III, it is clear that Louis Bonaparte's Caesarism is characterised in a far more historical manner than the other examples mentioned by Gramsci – in most cases they represent little more than 'labels'. This stands out clearly, for instance, in Q 13, § 27, where Gramsci carefully reconstructs the French political landscape at the middle of the nineteenth century, by underlining the (relative) weakness of the bourgeoisie due to its fragmentation into different 'parties':

> The dominant force in France from 1815 up to 1848 had split politically (factiously) into four camps: legitimists, Orleanists, Bonapartists, Jacobin-republicans. The internal faction struggle was such as to make possible the advance of the rival force B (progressive) in a precocious form; however, the existing social form had not yet exhausted its possibilities for development, as subsequent history abundantly demonstrated.[35]

From the theoretical point of view, the theory of Caesarism took shape around the case of Napoleon III, who acts as a 'centre of gravity' for the whole Gramscian scheme. As previously demonstrated, if we go beyond the generic definition of Louis Napoleon as an example of 'regressive Caesarism', and if we pay attention to the passages in which the 'relatively progressive' character of his regime is described, it is clear that Gramsci is sketching a spectrum of possible Caesarist manifestations. Thus, the case of the Second Empire represents the point of mediation between opposing tendencies.

---

34 Cf. Q 1, § 130, redrafted in Q 19, § 31; Q 1, § 131, redrafted in Q 13, § 37.
35 Q 13, § 27, p. 1621; SPN, pp. 221–2. It is likely that Gramsci had taken over the categories of 'legitimist', 'Orleanist', 'Bonapartist' and 'Jacobin-Republican' from *The Eighteenth Brumaire*, where they are explicitly mentioned and where the analysis of the troubled relations within the bourgeois bloc is a crucial element of Marx's reflection. However, we should not think that Gramsci's knowledge of the history of nineteenth-century France derives exclusively from Marx (see on this point Gervasoni 1998 and Descendre and Zancarini 2020). Thanks also to his longstanding interest in French culture, politics, and society, Gramsci's historical knowledge is broad and he makes use of a variety of sources (some hints can be found in Baldan 1978; however, the theme deserves a proper investigation – in this regard, see also Antonini 2020, which focuses in particular on Gramsci's thoughts on the Third French Republic).

From this perspective, it is worth briefly focusing on a passage from Q 13, § 23 and its first drafts.[36] In once more taking up Q 4, § 66 (November 1930), Gramsci deeply modifies the text, by adding and removing elements and by inverting the order of the argumentation (while in the first draft the theoretical observation followed the historical analysis, in the second draft it is the opposite). In particular, in its second version, the note is characterised by a double parallel, where two episodes of pre-modern, progressive Caesarism (Caesar and Napoleon I) are opposed to two cases of post-1870, regressive Caesarism (Primo De Rivera and Živković).[37] From this point of view, the removal of the reference to Napoleon III is meaningful. Due to its 'intermediate' character, it did not fit very well within the scheme drafted in Gramsci's note, which emphasises the distance between the pre-modern, progressive phenomena and the modern, regressive ones. In this sense, the removal of the reference to Bismarckism also makes sense, since Bismarck too, like Louis Napoleon, embodies a form of 'objectively progressive' Caesarism (indeed, his political results 'contradict' the definition given by Gramsci in Q 13, § 27 of Bismarckism as a form of regressive Caesarism).

However, precisely due to its 'intermediate' nature, the Caesarist regime of Napoleon III represents a precious benchmark with which to compare pre-modern, modern and 'contemporary' Caesarist phenomena. It is especially useful in order to highlight the gap between situations and events happening before and after the First World War. While late nineteenth-century Caesarisms are closer to the (in Gramsci's terms) objectively progressive regime of Louis Bonaparte, twentieth-century phenomena occur in a 'grey area' that lies between the intermediate Caesarism *à la* Napoleon III and the 'limit case' of regressive Caesarism, with a tendency to slip towards the second.

---

36 Compare the first and second drafts: 'This phenomenon always assumes historically specific forms: Caesar represents a different combination of elements from that represented by Napoleon I, and the latter is different from that of Napoleon III, or from Bismarck's, etc. In the modern world, Zivkovic resembles the Spanish type (and Zankov [sic] resembles Caesarism?), etc. In other words, these observations are not sociological schemata; they are practical criteria of historical and political interpretation which must always be removed from schematic generalizations and incorporated into a concrete historico-political analysis' (Q 4, § 66; PN, vol. 2, p. 240); 'These observations must not be conceived of as rigid schemata, but merely as practical criteria of historical and political interpretation. In concrete analyses of real events, the historical forms are individualised and can almost be called "unique". Caesar represents a very different combination of real circumstances from that represented by Napoleon I, as does Primo de Rivera from that of Zivkovic, etc.' (Q 13, § 23; SPN, p. 217).

37 The reference to Primo de Rivera replaced that to Tsankov contained in the first draft (cf. Chapter 8, section 2).

Moreover, these (implicit or mediated) historical analogies raise a series of questions in relation to Gramsci's theory of history and, above all, to the connection between his conception of Caesarism, passive revolution and hegemony. To what extent, for instance, are the governments of Italy's Historical Left or that of Bismarck Caesarist and, at the same time, do they represent a form of the passive revolution that characterises nineteenth-century Italy and Germany? And how do these categories apply to the deeply changed socio-political framework of the twentieth century? What kind of hegemony do they support in this new context?

3   Caesarism and Passive Revolution

3.1   *The Meanings of a Category*

In recent years Gramscian scholarship has dwelt extensively on the category of passive revolution, by investigating its 'historical narrative' as well as its relation to Gramsci's 'theory of state formation and transformation'.[38] I will quote a well-known passage on the topic, contained in Q 8, § 25 (*Risorgimento*, first draft, January–February 1932). Here, in discussing the case of Italy, Gramsci defines passive revolution as

> the historical fact that popular initiative is missing from the development of Italian history, as well as the fact that 'progress' occurs as the reaction of the dominant classes to the sporadic and incoherent rebelliousness of the popular masses – a reaction consisting of 'restorations' that agree to some part of the popular demands and are therefore 'progressive restorations,' or 'revolutions-restorations,' or even 'passive revolutions'.[39]

---

38 Thomas 2018a, p. 3. Among the most recent Italian bibliography on the theme, see Voza 2004 (redrafted in Voza 2008); Di Meo 2015; Vacca 2017. For a story of the debate on the topic, see Liguori 2012 and Frosini 2017c, which deals with the scholarly discourse in the 1970s, by focusing on the path-breaking contribution of De Felice 1977. Regarding the Anglophone literature, see in particular Morton 2007 and the numerous contributions of Thomas (in particular: 2006, 2009 and 2018a). In his last essay, in particular, Thomas suggests a challenging, new perspective on the issue, which highlights the 'strategic role' of the category of passive revolution in the 'lexical architecture of the *Prison Notebooks*' (Thomas 2018a, p. 22). In this framework, Thomas stresses the connection with the categories of 'permanent revolution' and 'Jacobinism' and with Gramsci's political strategy in the 1930s.

39 Q 8, § 25, p. 957; PN, vol. 3, p. 252.

This famous definition includes the two key elements of Gramsci's conception. The first is the weakness of the antagonistic force (the 'sporadic and incoherent rebelliousness' of the masses is the counterpart of this absence of an organised popular initiative, led by the vanguard of the peasants' and workers' movement). The second is the dominant bloc's acceptance (albeit partial) of some 'popular demands', which is constrained by the need to maintain order. In this way we can read the passage of Q 13, § 27, where Gramsci claims: 'In the movement of history there is never any turning back, and that restorations *in toto* do not exist'.[40]

In other words, passive revolution is a 'molecular' metamorphosis of reality.[41] Despite the absence of clearly revolutionary conjunctures, it is still possible for an effective transformation of the socio-political framework to take place, by capitalising on the marginal opportunities offered by the system – hence the proximity of this discussion to the concept of 'war of position/manoeuvre'. Moreover, the great 'flexibility' and many-sidedness of this category (as it emerges from Gramsci's analysis) makes it suitable to be applied to different historical contexts and to outline a broader historical dynamic.[42]

Against this background, it is interesting to investigate the connection between passive revolution and (modern) Caesarism, insofar as both of these concepts describe a situation in which progressive and regressive elements are entangled and the course of historical development is anything but simple and straightforward.[43]

---

40   Q 13, § 27, p. 1619; SPN, pp. 219–20. Given this, a reading of passive revolution as a merely conservative phenomenon, such as the one proposed by Burgio (2014, pp. 257–61), must be rejected. In fact, Burgio considers passive revolution as a mere 'morphological category', i.e., a formula that aims primarily at highlighting the intrinsic weakness of the antagonistic force, by stressing the element of the passivity of popular masses; this interpretation is consistent with Burgio's own 'catastrophic' interpretation of Gramsci's view. It is a mistake, indeed, to ignore the revolutionary element embedded in the category of passive revolution and, consequently, the development of history – although it must not be conceived, of course, in a linear and, so to speak, teleological way.

41   On the issue of 'molecular transformation', see the entry by E. Forenza in Liguori and Voza 2009, pp. 551–5, Ragazzini 2002, pp. 36–7, Voza 2008, pp. 15–16. Regarding the English bibliography, see Fonseca 2016, pp. 119–21 *et passim*, and especially Thomas 2009, pp. 373–4, n. 194 and pp. 398–410.

42   This progressive enlargement of the category is well described in Voza 2004. As a consequence, this also highlights the strategic significance of the category as well as its importance in elaborating a concrete programme of political action for the present (see, in this regard, Thomas 2018a).

43   From this perspective, see Modonesi 2018, pp. 114–22, who also connects passive revolution and the Caesarist-Bonapartist model, by investigating the role of Caesarism as a 'device' of the 'passivisation that accompan[ies] and characterise[s] all passive revolu-

The first and most obvious remark is that passive revolution appears often as a 'revolution from above', by significantly echoing Caesarist dynamics.[44] In fact, it is not uncommon for a 'Caesar' to take over the molecular transformation; similarly, charismatic figures often dominate the political framework in which passive revolution takes place. However, a deeper affinity can be retraced in the theoretical premises of both categories, as well as in their historiographical applications.

3.2 Marx's 'Canons' and the Issue of the Marginal Forces

Concerning the first aspect, Q 14, § 23, *Machiavelli. Caesarism and the 'Catastrophic' Balance of Socio-political Forces*, is a pivotal text. As I have already shown, in this note Gramsci takes his cue from the analysis of the Dreyfus Affair and the 'failed' Caesarism of General Georges Boulanger (1837–91) to stigmatise the 'sociological mechanicism', which believes that 'in Caesarism ... the entire new historical phenomenon is due to the equilibrium of the "fundamental" forces', and which, therefore, forgets to investigate the 'interplay of relations between the principal groups ... of the fundamental classes and the auxiliary forces directed by, or subjected to, their hegemonic influence'.[45]

Precisely this text (quite paradoxically, since it deals with 'Caesarisms that have been missed') contains one of the most significant descriptions of the Caesarist phenomenon. Moreover, while talking about 'modern historico-political movements of the Dreyfus type to be found, which are certainly not revolutions, but which are not entirely reactionary either', a meaningful

---

tions' (Modonesi 2018, p. 114). In spite of the differences between my interpretation and Modonesi's reading (which critically capitalises on Burgio's understanding of passive revolution), it is worth noting the similarity of the approach to this issue. On Modonesi's account, see also Modonesi 2014.

44 See for instance Q 10, II, § 61, p. 1358, where Gramsci alludes precisely to 'interventions from above' (SPN, p. 115).

45 Q 14, § 23, p. 1680; SPN, p. 222. On Gramsci's analysis of Boulanger and Dreyfus, see Antonini 2020. In Q 13, § 18, two other historical figures of the Boulanger type are mentioned. First, Gramsci mentions General Radola Gajda (1892–1948): head of the 'Czechoslovak national fascist community', in 1926 Gajda was the main political opponent of President Thomas Masaryk; due to the spread of rumours about the preparation of a *coup d'État*, Gajda was removed from his position and expelled from the army. Second, Gramsci evokes the figure of Georges Valois (1878–1945), former member of *Action française* and, between 1925 and 1928, leader of a French fascist movement (*Faisceau*). While Gajda is mentioned only in Q 4, § 38 and Q 13, § 18, references to Valois also feature in other notes, although mainly with reference to *Action française* and his relationship with Charles Maurras (cf. Q 1, § 48, Q 2, § 74, Q 4, § 44, Q 11, § 66). It is interesting to note that Gramsci assembles suggestions coming from different historico-political contexts to support his theoretical reflection.

consonance emerges between the category of passive revolution and that of Caesarism.[46]

Indeed, Gramsci states that historical episodes such as the Dreyfus Affair play a role in the analysis of Caesarist movements, since they highlight the necessity of considering all the elements of a historico-political situation, and not simply the (apparently) main ones. In other words, he is suggesting that 'intermediate' Caesarism is far more common than openly progressive (or regressive) Caesarism and that Caesarist phenomena usually appear as a 'compromise' between revolutionary and reactionary tendencies. From this perspective, they show a significant 'kinship' with the movements of passive revolution, whose main feature is exactly this combination of revolution and restoration (the example of the Dreyfus case is meaningful).

Q 14, §23 contains therefore an analysis of *both* Caesarism *and* passive revolution. In this regard, an extremely valuable linguistic 'clue' is represented by the use of the adverb 'too' (*'anche'*), which appears twice in this note and reveals how Gramsci is developing here an implicit comparison between the category of Caesarism and that of passive revolution.[47]

In this sense, I would argue that Q 14, § 23 is a real turning point in Gramsci's thought. It represents somehow a 'summary' of the reflections on Caesarism that he had conducted up to this point. At the same time, it is a crucial stage in the investigation of passive revolution. But what are the common elements that are mentioned by Gramsci? And what are the theoretical premises that ground both Caesarism and passive revolutions?

Gramsci talks about the 'relatively "progressive" content' of the historical movement; the activation of 'latent', '"marginal forces"' of the dominant social bloc; the weakness of the subaltern groups; the peculiar historical conjuncture in which there is not a group that has sufficient strength to prevail over its opponent (i.e. the 'stifling and ossified State structures' which cannot be overcome).[48]

---

46   In this framework, it is interesting to note that Francioni, in the introductory note to the anastatic edition of notebook 4, also brings Q 4, § 57 (on passive revolution) and Q 4, § 52 (on Bonapartism) into close proximity with each other – see QAnast, vol. 8, pp. 11–12.

47   See the following quotations: 'a very important historical episode from this point of view is the so-called Dreyfus affair in France. This *too* belongs to the present series of observations, not because it led to "Caesarism", indeed precisely for the opposite reason' (Q 14, § 23, p. 1681; SPN, p. 223; emphasis mine); 'These movements *too* can have a relatively "progressive" content, in so far as they indicate that there were effective forces latent in the old society which the old leaders did not know how to exploit – perhaps even "marginal forces"' (Q 14, § 23, p. 1681; SPN, p. 223; emphasis mine).

48   Q 14, § 23, p. 1681; SPN, p. 223. In Italian, Gramsci speaks of *'cristallizzazioni statali soffoc-*

Among these elements, the most interesting one is the second, which relates to the margins for manoeuvre of the old dominant group, the forces that allow it to maintain its primacy within the system despite being in decline. Indeed, these observations openly connect with Gramsci's 'theory of historical transitions', i.e. to Gramsci's conception of historico-political development that takes its cue from his reassessment of Marx's *Preface* to *A Contribution to the Critique of Political Economy*.

The Gramscian interpretation of Marx's two 'canons' has been widely investigated by scholars.[49] The fact that these two principles (particularly the first one) are implicitly but clearly recalled in Q 14, § 23 is, in my opinion, the most effective demonstration of the fact that the category of Caesarism and that of passive revolution belong to the same historico-theoretical framework, thus revealing the same intellectual 'root'.[50]

The very same 'canons' are also mentioned in Q 4, § 38, *Relations between Structure and Superstructures*, a key text of the *Notebooks*.[51] In its second version, the note was 'split' into different parts, in order to create more coherent texts: among them Q 13, § 17, which focuses on the issue of the relations of force, and Q 13, § 18, which dwells on the shortcomings of the economistic method of analysis, are particularly important.[52]

As I have tried to demonstrate elsewhere, I would argue that § 18 of notebook 13 is strictly connected (thematically and also chronologically) to Q 14, § 23, as the addition of the reference to the Dreyfus Affair in the redrafted version of the text of notebook 4 shows.[53] Moreover, it seems to me that the two notes investigate the same issue of the complexity of socio-political systems from different points of view (theoretical in Q 13, § 18, historical in Q 14, § 23).

---

anti' (it seems to me that the English translation does not render perfectly the expression used by Gramsci; a better translation could be 'suffocating crystallisations of the state').

49 This issue has been thoroughly analysed, e.g., by Frosini in numerous contributions (see, for instance, Frosini 2009).

50 Cf. Q 15, § 17, p. 1774; SPN, pp. 106–7: 'the concept of "passive revolution" must be rigorously derived from the two fundamental principles of political science: 1. that no social formation disappears as long as the productive forces which have developed within it still find room for further forward movement; 2. that a society does not set itself tasks for whose solution the necessary conditions have not already been incubated, etc. It goes without saying that these principles must first be developed critically in all their implications, and purged of every residue of mechanicism and fatalism'. Regarding Caesarism, the connection emerges mainly from reflecting on the issue of the marginal forces, as I have shown previously.

51 On this famous text, see in particular Cospito 2016, *passim*.

52 Other passages of Q 4, § 38 are redrafted in Q 10, II, § 11.

53 See Antonini 2020.

Although it is not possible to establish a precise order of composition of the texts,[54] it should be noted that the relation between these two paragraphs has to be placed within the context of the connection between Gramsci's famous notebook on Machiavelli's politics and the political theory that he develops in the miscellaneous notebooks 14, 15, and 17.[55] This represents an important element of the link between the category of Caesarism and that of passive revolution – the arguments on these two topics partially overlap (see Q 14, § 23 but not only there). The analysis of passive revolution that unfolds in the final miscellaneous notebooks seems to bring Gramsci's reflections on the topic of 'crisis' to a higher level than already thematised in his notes on Caesarism.[56]

Without going into detail, I will focus briefly on the aforementioned *motif* of the 'marginal forces'. This *motif*, for instance, appears in Q 13, § 27, one of the key texts on Caesarism, where Gramsci writes:

> In the modern world Caesarism also has a certain margin – larger or smaller, depending on the country and its relative weight in the global context. For a social form 'always' has marginal possibilities for further development and organisational improvement, and in particular can count on the relative weakness of the rival progressive force as a result of its specific character and way of life. It is necessary for the dominant social form to preserve this weakness.[57]

Furthermore, in Q 14, § 76 (*Past and Present*, single draft),[58] there is a passage that alludes clearly to Q 14, § 23 and the issues developed there, when Gramsci writes that Caesarism must be interpreted in the framework of the dialectic revolution-restoration.[59] Gramsci writes:

---

54   On this basis, we might only observe that Q 13, § 18 may have been written around January 1933 (to which Q 14, § 23 is dated). However, I would argue that this is already a significant finding, inasmuch as the chronology of notebook 13 is extremely vague (in fact, the only 'clue' is represented by Q 13, § 25, which contains a reference to an article published in autumn 1933; on this point, see Chapter 8, section 2).
55   On this issue, see the arguments proposed in Antonini 2019a and 2020.
56   On this point, see, again, Antonini 2019a.
57   Q 13, § 27, p. 1622; SPN, p. 222.
58   On the chronology of this note (probably written by February 1933), see now Francioni 2020.
59   See Q 14, § 23, p. 1681; SPN, p. 223.

It should be noted that the fact of 'not constituting an epoch' is too often confused with brief 'temporal' duration: it is possible to 'last' a long time, relatively, and yet not 'constitute an epoch': the viscous forces of certain regimes are often unsuspected, especially if they are 'strong' as a result of the weakness of others (including where this has been procured).[60]

3.3 'Effectual Reality' and New Instruments of Analysis

With regard to the historical events that are interpreted by Gramsci through the categories of Caesarism and of passive revolution, the most important cases are without doubt Italy and Germany in the nineteenth century.

The Italian *Risorgimento* has been conceived of by Gramsci as a phenomenon of revolution-reaction.[61] However, as I explained previously, in Q 3, § 119 he adopts the concept of Bonapartism in order to highlight the elements of backwardness in the Italian context, and therefore the limits of its ongoing socio-political transformation.[62] While he does not explicitly mention Bonapartism any further, I would argue that this text has had an enduring influence on Gramsci's reflections on Italy in the *Risorgimento*, as demonstrated by his later statements.

Germany is the other main European nation in which a passive revolution occurs. Bismarck was the main political 'player' of that time.[63] We find few explicit references to the Chancellor in the *Notebooks*. However, they are relevant, since they connect closely with Gramsci's analysis of the Caesarist features of Bismarck's government.[64] In fact, in Q 9, § 133 and even more clearly in Q 13,

---

60 Q 14, § 76, p. 1744; SPN, p. 256.
61 See Chapter 7, section 3. With regard to Gramsci's judgement on the Italian *Risorgimento*, the introduction by Corrado Vivanti to the monographic edition of notebook 19 is still valuable (see Gramsci 1977). On the topic, see more recently Albarani 2008, the entry *Risorgimento* by P. Voza in Liguori and Voza 2009, pp. 716–20, Carlucci 2013c.
62 Regarding the Italian *Risorgimento*, the bibliography is vast and extensive. As a point of departure, see Riall 1994, Patriarca and Riall 2012, and Banti 2008.
63 On the figure of Bismarck (1815–98), see Steinberg 2011; on his 'legacy', see Frankel 2005. As regards his Caesaristic attitude, see in particular Rusconi 2011 (but numerous hints are also contained in the bibliography specifically devoted to the categories of Caesarism and Bonapartism).
64 However, the figure of Bismarck is also evoked in the *Prison Notebooks* with regard to his attitude towards the Holy See, in the framework of the reflections on the German *Kulturkampf* (see Q 2, § 20; Q 8, § 129; Q 16, § 11). Furthermore, in other notes Gramsci deals with Bismarck's foreign policy (Q 9, § 93 and Q 14, § 70) and with his conception of the state (Q 26, § 2 – the text is the second version of Q 5, § 69, which, however, does not contain the reference to Bismarck); a fairly superficial reference is contained in Q 7, § 43.

§27, Bismarckism is classified as a Caesarist regime, and, in particular, as a Caesarism of a regressive type.[65] However, its steady association with Napoleon III seems to suggest that this regressive characterisation does not have to be understood as absolute, but rather as relative (the aforementioned removal of the reference to Bismarck in Q 13, §23 is telling in this respect). In addition, Bismarck's rule is 'objectively progressive', although certainly to a lesser extent than that of Louis Napoleon. In this context, the references to Bismarck's conception of the relation between military leadership and politics are distinctive, as also are those concerning the relations between internal and foreign political strategy.[66] In short, by defining Bismarck as a Caesarist figure, Gramsci is underlining the conservative aspect of the transformation going on in Germany. Thus, there is no contradiction between this and his analysis of the German situation in terms of revolution-restoration.

To conclude, the impression is that there is a partial 'overlap' between Caesarism and passive revolution, as far as both concepts are valuable for understanding situations that cannot be explained through the classical tools of sociological and political analysis, which do not grasp the nuances of 'actual' reality (or, in Gramsci's words, 'effectual reality' [*realtà effettuale*]).[67] Despite the broader meaning of the formula of revolution-restoration (which applies to a variety of situations), however, we cannot talk of a 'subordination' of Caesarism to the category of passive revolution. A hierarchical relation of this type would not make sense in the conceptual framework of the *Notebooks*.[68] Rather,

---

65   See Q 9, §133, p. 1194: 'Caesar and Napoleon I are examples of progressive Caesarism. Napoleon III (and also Bismarck) of reactionary Caesarism'; Q 13 §27, p. 1619; SPN, p. 219: 'Caesar and Napoleon I are examples of progressive Caesarism. Napoleon III and Bismark [*sic*] of reactionary Caesarism'.

66   See Q 1, §117. The note is redrafted in Q 19, §28, p. 2052; SPN, p. 88: 'It should be recalled how Bismarck, following Clausewitz, maintained the supremacy of the political moment over the military; whereas Wilhelm II, as Ludwig records, scribbled furious notes on a newspaper in which Bismarck's opinion was quoted. Thus the Germans won almost all the battles brilliantly, but lost the war'.

67   This Machiavellian expression is used several times by Gramsci to refer to the concrete historical reality in opposition to more or less imaginative reconstructions of philosophers, historians, or, generally speaking, intellectuals. See, for instance, Q 8, §84, p. 990; PN, vol. 3, p. 283: 'The question is more complex: one must determine whether the "ought to be" is an arbitrary act or a necessary fact, whether it is concrete will or passing fancy, desire, daydream. The active politician is a creator, but he does not create out of nothing, and neither does he draw his creations out of his brain. He bases himself on effectual reality; but what is this effectual reality? Could it be something static and immobile? Is it not, rather, a reality in motion, a relation of forces in continuous shifts of equilibrium?'

68   On the relations between different categories in the *Prison Notebooks*, see Mangoni 1987.

Caesarism and passive revolution represent two different but 'complementary' instruments for investigating how specific politico-social transformations unfold in a context of uncertain and contested hegemony or, in other words, of crisis. For this reason, both concepts are useful for conceiving the historical dynamics of the pre-modern period, but they are even more important for the modern one and its enduring 'crisis of authority'.

CHAPTER 11

Hegemony and Modernity

1   Twentieth-Century Caesarism

1.1   *MacDonald, the Labour Party and the Coalition Governments*

It is clear that 'modern' Caesarisms are Gramsci's primary target. While this category emerges from the nineteenth century, its potential fully unfolds only in the twentieth. In what follows, I will show that the Caesarist-Bonapartist paradigm is, in Gramsci's view, on the one hand, a valuable tool for describing the framework of the organic crisis of modernity, and, on the other, a helpful model for deciphering the unprecedented state forms that appear on the European scene. It is, therefore, vital for interpreting the new features of hegemony in the post-war period.

I will take my cue from Gramsci's brief analysis of two historical cases that are recalled in Q 9, § 133, to which he then returns in Q 13, § 27. Here he compares the British governments presided over by Ramsay MacDonald to the first phase of the fascist regime in Italy.[1]

> The parliamentary system has also provided a mechanism for such compromise solutions. The 'Labour' governments of MacDonald were to a certain degree solutions of this kind; and the degree of Caesarism increased when the government was formed which had MacDonald as its head and a Conservative majority. Similarly in Italy from October 1922 until the defection of the 'Popolari', and then by stages until 3 January 1925, and then until 8 November 1926, there was a politico-historical movement in which various gradations of Caesarism succeeded each other, culminating in a more pure and permanent form – though even this was not static or immobile. Every coalition government is a first stage of Caesarism, which either may or may not develop to more significant stages (the

---

1   James Ramsay MacDonald (1866–1937) was a Labour Party politician. He was prime minister of the United Kingdom three times. In 1924, he led a minority government for nine months. He would later be prime minister again in two separate parliaments during the period 1929–35. MacDonald was a highly controversial figure. Between 1931 and 1935, he headed a government of national unity, which is also mentioned by Gramsci. On the Labour Party during MacDonald's time, see Howell 2002 and Morgan 2006.

common opinion of course is that coalition governments, on the contrary, are the most 'solid bulwark' against Caesarism).[2]

The passage is very interesting, as it aims to show that coalition governments can also represent initial forms of Caesarism. More specifically, Gramsci distinguishes between a first 'crypto-Caesarist' phase of MacDonald's governments and a second phase in which the political coalition between Conservatives and Labour has taken place.[3] Moreover, while sketching a brief history of Italy between 1922 and 1926, he suggests the existence of a multiplicity of intermediate forms of Caesarism, each corresponding to a moment in the construction of the fascist regime.

Thus, these observations enlarge the taxonomy of the forms of Caesarism illustrated before, by confirming its 'incomplete' character.[4] In particular, the coalition government seems to represent, so to speak, the 'degree 0' of Caesarism.

With regard to the historical analysis, it is worthwhile considering the British case (I will come back to Fascism, which, obviously, is the most directly relevant reference for Gramsci).[5] Indeed, the brief reference to MacDonald in Q 9, § 133 acquires a greater significance when connected to the other notes on the British politician and on the Labour Party contained in the *Notebooks*. Beside the aforementioned passage, the other references can be found in Q 3, § 55; Q 7, § 30; Q 15, § 2; an indirect reference is then contained in Q 6, § 40.

The first text, *Past and Present. Otto Kahn*, is a single draft written in June–July 1930. Interestingly, here Gramsci already compares the English and the Italian cases by defining both 'regime[s]'.[6] The content of the note clarifies Gramsci's judgement of MacDonald (and, indirectly, of Fascism). In fact, he mentions the sympathies that Otto Kahn and Paul Warburg, two representat-

---

2 Q 13, § 27, pp. 1619–20; SPN, p. 220. I quote here from the second draft of the text (the first one is Q 9, § 133), in which Gramsci's thought is expressed more clearly and in a more defined manner, and where his theoretical reflections are more precise and refined. As for the spelling of MacDonald, Gramsci usually writes 'Mac Donald'.
3 The first phase is identified with the Labour governments presided over by MacDonald before 1931; Gramsci is suggesting that they represented *de facto* a form of coalition government and therefore, precisely, of crypto-Caesarism.
4 These statements are also accompanied by a strong emphasis on the dynamism and flexibility of the category, according to Gramsci's rejection of Caesarism as a mere sociological scheme and, on the contrary, his attention to their concrete historical manifestations.
5 See Chapter 11, section 1.2.
6 Q 3, § 55, p. 366, my translation. In the English edition, '*regime*' is translated as 'government', which does not grasp the precise 'authoritarian nuance' of Gramsci's term (cf. PN, vol. 1, p. 56).

ives of American financial lobbies, had for MacDonald's government.[7] In this way, Gramsci seems to suggest that the high financial bourgeoisie is supportive of MacDonald's rule, thus revealing its capitalist character.[8]

Furthermore, in Q 7, § 30 (*On Graziadei* [*Su Graziadei*], single draft, February 1931), Gramsci, in criticising Antonio Graziadei as one of the 'most right-wing and opportunistic' representatives of the Socialist Party in the pre-First World War period (he even defines him as 'liquidator of the party'), states that his 'model' is precisely the 'English labor movement'.[9]

In this context, it seems interesting also to recall a note (*Past and Present. The English Government*, single draft) from notebook 6 in which Gramsci comments on an article published in December 1930 in the *Rassegna settimanale della stampa estera*. Here he makes some telling observations on the British parliamentary government and on the shortcomings that characterised it in the post-war period.[10] Despite the absence of precise historical references, it is likely that Gramsci, in dealing with these issues, was thinking about the case of MacDonald – note in particular the end of the paragraph, where Gramsci writes: 'Muir overlooks other phenomena: within the government, there is a restricted group that dominates the whole cabinet, and, furthermore, there is a bigwig who exercises a Bonapartist role'.[11]

---

7   See Q 3, § 55, p. 366; PN, vol. 1, p. 56: '*Otto Kahn*. His European journey in 1924. His statements about the Italian regime and MacDonald's regime in England. Analogous statements by Paul Warburg (Otto Kahn and Paul Warburg both belong to the big American company Kuhn-Loeb and Co.), by Judge Gary, by the delegates of the American Chamber of Commerce, and by other important financiers. International high finance favorably disposed towards the English and Italian regimes'. I have modified the English translation according to what was said in the previous note.

8   Indeed, Gramsci is critical of the British Labour Party and particularly of MacDonald – on this point, see the entry *Inghilterra* by D. Boothman in Liguori and Voza 2009, p. 424.

9   Q 7, § 30, p. 878; PN, vol. 3, p. 180. Antonio Graziadei (1873–1953) was an Italian economist and politician. He was a member of the Socialist Party from 1893 and in 1921 he was one of the founders of the PCd'I (he was expelled in 1928, though, on account of his revisionism). On the Labour Party, see also Q 7, § 94.

10 See Q 6, § 40, p. 714; PN, vol. 3, p. 31: 'Muir maintains that one cannot speak of a parliamentary regime in England, since parliament has no control over government or the bureaucracy; one can speak only of a party dictatorship or, rather, of an inorganic dictatorship, since power oscillates between extreme parties ... The deficiencies of the English system of government were harshly revealed after the war by the huge problems of reconstruction and adaptation to the new situation'.

11 Q 6, § 40, p. 715; PN, vol. 3, p. 31. Ramsey Muir (1872–1941), the author of the piece, was a British historian and member of the Liberal Party.

1.2   Italy in the 1920s

Gramsci refers to Fascism in two notes that I have already mentioned. In Q 3, §55, he highlights the support given by the financial lobbies to the fascist movement. In Q 9, §133 (and, then, in Q 13, §27), he refers to the development of Italian politics after 1922, by mentioning some turning points during that period, relevant both to general history and to Gramsci's personal life – indeed, the note contains a veiled reference to his own arrest, and as such it takes on a particularly dramatic tone.

These passages are noteworthy for two reasons. First, Gramsci explicitly declares the Caesarist character of Fascism (at least until 1926) by referencing the coalition governments.[12] Second, the parallel with the English model draws attention to the forces that exist behind charismatic leadership (and, in these cases, to their conservative nature). From this perspective, Fascism, as a solution to the 'unstable balance' that characterises Italy after the First World War, is revealed as a socio-political construction that functions to consolidate the existing power system and protect the interests of the ruling classes.[13]

Another explicit reference to Fascism as a Caesarist-Bonapartist phenomenon can be found in a passage from a text that has also already been discussed, §75 of notebook 2. In this passage, Gramsci dwells on the figure of Mussolini as a charismatic personality:

> Mussolini is another example of a party leader who has something of the seer and the believer in him. Moreover, he is not only the sole leader of a great party, but he is also the sole leader of a great country. In his case, the concept of the axiom 'I am the party' has also had its fullest development in the sense of responsibility and hard work ... To those who are familiar with the susceptibility of Italian crowds to sentimental exaggeration and 'emotional' enthusiasm, the example offered by Michels as proof of the resonance of this conception among the masses is infantile. According to Michels, a voice out of a crowd of ten thousand standing outside Palazzo Chigi shouted: 'No, you are Italy' – this on an occasion when the emotion

---

12   However, I would argue that Fascism could still be defined as Caesarist even after 1926, as far as the highest form of Caesarism (or, as Gramsci writes, its 'more pure and permanent form' – Q 13, §27, p. 1620; SPN, p. 220) could be identified with Fascism in its 'mature' (or 'totalitarian') phase.

13   Historically speaking, Mussolini's rise to power was favoured and supported by important parts of the dominant bloc. As regards the development of the fascist regime, it transformed the parliamentary system from within, up to the creation of an openly dictatorial political form (though not without internal problems and contradictions). On these themes, see, for instance, Gentile 2002 and Paxton 2004.

of the fascist crowd was objectively real. Moreover, according to Michels, Mussolini displayed the charismatic essence of his character in the telegram sent to Bologna in which he stated that he was sure, absolutely sure (and surely he was, *pour cause*) that nothing bad could happen to him before he had completed his mission.[14]

Despite the absence of proper historical contextualisation, it is clear that Gramsci is describing here Benito Mussolini as the leader of a 'solid' regime, and not simply as the leader of a movement that has yet to find its place within the political panorama. Furthermore, this allusion to a one-party state does not fit with the depiction of a rising fascist movement, but rather with the established fascist system of the 1930s.

With regard to Gramsci's remarks on the 'charismatic essence' of Mussolini's character, on the one hand, they meaningfully anticipate his observations on the 'reprehensible "demagogue"' in Q 6, § 97, *Past and Present. Lofty Ambition and Petty Ambitions* (which, for their part, recall similar reflections contained in the journalistic writings).[15] On the other hand, underlining the collective and 'emotional' dimension of early twentieth-century politics makes clear the novelty of the political scenario in which fascist Caesarism takes place.

1.3   Fascism and Caesarism: A Controversial Match

If we add to the above-mentioned texts the passages in which Gramsci refers to contemporary examples of Caesarist-Bonapartist phenomena, we have a complete list of his explicit references to twentieth-century Caesarisms. However, Gramsci's analysis of Caesarist dynamics is not restricted to the investigation of specific historical examples. It goes far beyond this, by connecting with a broader reflection on the salient features of modernity.

This is particularly true if we take Fascism into account: in spite of the relatively limited number of direct references, Gramsci's reflections on the fascist

---

14   Q 2, § 75, pp. 232–3; PN, vol. 1, pp. 319–20.
15   Q 6, § 97, p. 772 (in Italian, *"demagogo" deteriore*'); PN, vol. 3, p. 83. Cf. the entire passage: 'The reprehensible "demagogue" posits himself as irreplaceable, he creates a desert around himself, he systematically crushes and eliminates potential rivals, he wants to establish a direct relationship with the masses (plebiscite, etc., grandiose rhetoric, stage effects, spectacular phantasmagoric displays – what Michels called "charismatic leader")' (Q 6, § 97, p. 772). It seems to me that this text recalls the description of the figure of Mussolini contained in the two articles of the second half of 1924 and previously analysed (see Chapter 3, section 2). In fact, despite the absence of explicit references, the vocabulary used by Gramsci evokes the same 'decadent' atmosphere described there (see, in particular, the exasperated romanticism of the French *feuilletons*).

phenomenon and, more generally speaking, on recent Italian history are his unavoidable point of reference for the development of his theoretical reflections. In a certain sense, it can be said that the entire analysis in the *Prison Notebooks* is shaped by Gramsci's will to understand the causes of the success of Mussolini's dictatorship (and, as a consequence, of the failure of the workers' movement).

These two elements (the intertwining of historical investigation and theoretical arguments; the 'pervasive' nature of his reflections on the fascist regime) are, in my opinion, the reasons for the absence of a comprehensive analysis of Gramsci's account of Fascism. In fact, while many scholars have dealt with this issue in a number of contributions and from different point of views, a thorough investigation is still lacking.[16]

It should be noted that the connection between Fascism and the Caesarist-Bonapartist model has also generally passed unnoticed by Gramscian scholarship and, even when raised, has been a controversial issue for scholars.[17] I will focus briefly on the essays by Walter L. Adamson and David D. Roberts, since they combine the analysis of Fascism and that of Caesarism-Bonapartism, giving us the opportunity to reflect further on the topic.[18]

16 I will mention here only the most relevant titles of the huge bibliography on Gramsci's analysis of Fascism (mostly in Italian). With regard to the pre-prison writings, see Paggi 1970 and 1984, Bergami 1978, Sillanpoa 1983, Ciliberto 1987, Zunino 1988a and 1988b, Garzarelli 2007 and 2008 (in a number of contributions the discussion turns around the interpretation of Gramsci's article 'The Monkey People'). Those specifically devoted to the *Prison Notebooks* are Colarizi 2008 and Accardo and Fresu 2009 – the latter book, however, is disappointing in many respects, as noted by Rapone 2010. A more comprehensive approach (in the chronological and/or analytical sense) was adopted by Mangoni 1976 and 1977, De Felice 1977, Adamson 1980, Roberts 2011 and Gagliardi 2016a (but see also, more recently, Gagliardi 2017, who offers a survey of previous interpretations of Gramsci's account of Fascism, as well as a few suggestions for further investigations). A special role is played in this context by the works of Fabio Frosini, which in recent years have investigated a number of aspects of Gramsci's understanding of Fascism, by connecting it with his broader reflections on Italian history as well as on historical materialism (see Frosini 2011, 2012a, 2012b, 2014, 2016c, 2017b, 2018). Finally, some significant references can also be found in the bibliography specifically devoted to the analysis of Caesarism and Bonapartism (see, in particular, Fontana 2004) and in the main works by Burgio (2003, 2014).
17 Only a few authors connect the two categories: see especially the above-mentioned essays by Mangoni, Adamson and Roberts. Frosini mentions the category of Caesarism only tangentially. Gagliardi limits the application of the category of Caesarism to the first phase of the construction of the fascist regime, while De Felice explicitly affirms the inadequacy of the Caesarist-Bonapartist model to understand Fascism, preferring the totalitarian model (I will return in a while to Gagliardi's and De Felice's judgements).
18 Roberts, in particular, capitalises on Adamson's account, by 'reconsidering' his view on this aspect of Gramsci's thought (see the title of Roberts' essay). Alongside the work by

These two texts are devoted primarily to Gramsci's understanding of Fascism, both in the pre-prison and in the prison writings, both from the historical and from the theoretical point of view.[19] As regards the *Notebooks*, in particular, both scholars rely on three categories: 'Caesarism'; 'passive revolution'; 'war of attrition' (this represents an unattested variant of the concept of 'war of position', which aims to highlight the features of modern class struggle).[20] Hence, Fascism is considered as a form of Caesarism. But what does Caesarism mean in this context?

First, Adamson and Roberts refuse to combine Caesarism and Bonapartism. Roberts does not use the latter term at all, while Adamson conceives the category as a purely Marxist, class-based concept and, for this reason, discards it.[21] As regards Caesarism, they underline almost exclusively its 'balance aspect'. Roberts, for instance, describes it as 'a term [Gramsci] uses to encompass an array of *ad hoc*, provisional outcomes that had emerged throughout history in response to a threat of systemic crisis'.[22] In this framework, Fascism is conceived of as a fragile, temporary Caesarist solution to the crisis of authority of

---

Adamson, his other main source is a book by Michele Maggi (2008), which, although very rich and informative, adopts a partially misleading interpretation of Gramsci's thought (due to a 'Gentilian' reading of Gramsci).

19 Each essay also has a (more or less direct) historiographical scope, which goes beyond the analysis of Gramsci's thought. On the one hand, Adamson aims to demonstrate that Gramsci's conception of Fascism cannot be reduced to the loose Comintern *vulgata* ('Fascism as the last stage of capitalism', Adamson 1980, p. 616) – see also, in this sense, the (critical) comparison with Trotsky's and Thalheimer's heterodox conceptions (Adamson 1980, *passim*). On the other hand, Roberts focuses on the issue of the 'modernity' of Fascism (he follows contemporary historians such as Payne, Griffin and Gentile), by evaluating Gramsci's view on this basis (see Roberts 2011, *passim*).

20 See Adamson 1980, p. 628; Roberts 2011, p. 247. In fact, Gramsci does not use the expression 'war of attrition', but he only talks about the 'war of position'.

21 See Adamson 1980, pp. 630–1. In doing that, Adamson follows a misleading interpretation that is also evident in the work of Fontana (2004, p. 193 and *passim*). As I demonstrate in my analysis, in fact, such an interpretation does not grasp the strong conceptual connection between the categories of Bonapartism and Caesarism and, furthermore, their close relation within Gramsci's thought. As regards Caesarism, it is described as a balance, which 'results not so much from an equilibrium of rival class forces [that is, according to Adamson, Bonapartism] but from the defeat of one and the intrinsic weakness of the other' (Adamson 1980, p. 628, n. 57).

22 Roberts 2011, p. 246. Even if the connection of Caesarism with the balance formula and with the theme of the 'catastrophe' is correct, I think that Roberts takes it too literally. He underestimates Gramsci's awareness of the 'hegemonic' elements embedded in the Caesarist-fascist solution to the post-war crisis (as he writes, Gramsci 'continued to sidestep aspects of the fascist challenge'; Roberts 2011, p. 252); in this sense, Roberts' account recalls Burgio's 'catastrophic' interpretation.

modernity. If Adamson writes that 'Fascism is a Caesarism because of its imbalance between domination and hegemony',[23] Roberts affirms:

> Even as he implicitly conceded that he had previously underestimated Fascism, Gramsci did not find it an organic solution, a viable alternative revolution in the wake of proletarian failure … The Caesarist force manages to dominate the situation, producing a kind of equilibrium but without providing a new hegemony. So the equilibrium is inherently provisional and unstable.[24]

I think that the two essays offer a useful, albeit partial analysis of the relation between Caesarism and Fascism. On the one hand, Adamson's and Roberts' readings of the category of Caesarism are in many respects limited (see, for instance, the 'absence' of the Caesarist leader) and somehow also biased. Moreover, I would argue that their interpretation of Fascism is questionable insofar as it implies that Gramsci failed to grasp the complexity of the fascist regime and its internal 'cleavages', due to his own strategical (up to 1926) and conceptual limitations.[25]

On the other hand, however, these analyses point towards a correct comprehension of the dynamics of Fascism, since they highlight its historical novelty and contextualise the Caesarist phenomena within the more general framework of the contemporary political, social and economic transformations.[26]

---

23   Adamson 1980, p. 629.
24   Roberts 2011, p. 247. Regarding the judgement on the pre-prison writings evoked here, both Adamson and Roberts claim that Gramsci underestimated Fascism in the period before his imprisonment due to strategic and tactical reasons (and this is, partially, true).
25   It appears to me that both scholars underestimate the depth of Gramsci's analysis of Fascism, as it unfolds both prior to and in the *Prison Notebooks* (on Gramsci's pre-carceral awareness of the 'fissures' within the fascist regime in 1924–26, see Garzarelli 2008). The richness and complexity of Gramsci's account of Fascism is demonstrated clearly, for instance, in the essay by Gagliardi (2016a), but also in more conceptually oriented works (see, above all, De Felice 1977 and the previously mentioned contributions by Frosini).
26   In this respect, it is noteworthy that both scholars recognise that there is a constant effort to strengthen Caesarist hegemony: 'Caesarism always involves a perpetual struggle for the hearts and minds of the population beyond that usually associated with processes of legitimation in "normal politics"' (Adamson 1980, p. 629); 'Still, any mode of Caesarism seeks to strengthen itself by trying, at least, to build up its hegemony, making mere domination less evident and less necessary … Caesarism always entails a certain margin for development, varying depending on the country and its weight on the international level' (Roberts 2011, pp. 247–8; he is referring to the issue of the 'marginal forces' raised by Gramsci in Q 14, § 23).

From this perspective, there is a crucial connection between the category of Caesarism and that of passive revolution, whose twentieth-century representative is Fascism.[27]

In short, rather than complaining about the limitations of an analysis of Fascism conceived of as Caesarism, I believe that such a 'Caesarist reading' allows us to investigate fruitfully the 'new' hegemonic features of Fascism. This line of investigation emerges with Gramsci's reflections on totalitarian issues, at the socio-political level, or on Americanism, Fordism and corporatism, at the economic one.[28] In my analysis, I will try to deepen further the useful indications (in this respect) provided by some recent (and not so recent) contributions.[29]

2 Crisis of Authority and Caesarist-Bonapartist Solutions

2.1 *The Organic Crisis*

The first element that has to be considered is that of the 'organic crisis' or, according to the different expressions used by Gramsci, of the 'crisis of hegemony' or 'crisis of authority'.[30] This is an important theme of the *Prison Note-*

---

27 This relation has already been detected by a number of studies (also without an explicit reference to Fascism): see especially Mangoni 1976, Buci-Glucksmann 1980, Gagliardi 2016a. Regarding the 'hierarchy' between the two concepts, there is no agreement among scholars. As I stated previously, however, it seems to me very difficult (and, to a certain extent, even useless) to speculate on this point.

28 From this perspective, I disagree with Gagliardi when he says that '[the concept of Caesarism] can well describe the first phase of the fascist dictatorship, that of the conquest of power and of the construction of the regime, no longer that of maturity, which opened in the late 1920s' (Gagliardi 2016a, p. 10). Equally, I disagree with the rejection of the category of Caesarism by De Felice: 'it seems to me undoubted, however, that Caesarism can express only partially the wealth of implications connected to the evaluation of Fascism as a passive revolution ... with the category of Caesarism Gramsci does not go beyond the results achieved before the arrest' (De Felice 1977, p. 187). Specifically, De Felice blames the Gramscian category of Caesarism for 'failing to deepen the implications connected to the new instruments of political direction and organisation born with Fascism and therefore for a constant tendency to overestimate the internal ruptures of Fascism' (De Felice 1977, p. 188). It is interesting to note that De Felice says exactly the opposite of what is claimed by Adamson and Roberts about the cleavages within Fascism (!). I will try to show in what follows why the category of Caesarism is invaluable for analysing the hegemonic dynamics of the interwar period and how it connects with a 'totalitarian' interpretation of Gramsci's time.

29 See especially the works by Frosini, but also Mangoni 1976, De Felice 1977, and Gagliardi 2016a.

30 See, in this regard, also the entry *Crisi* by F. Frosini in Liguori and Voza 2009, pp. 175–9 and Burgio 2014, pp. 161ff.

books and is connected closely to his 'theory of historical transitions'. To understand the organic crisis means to understand when and why the transition from one historico-political configuration to another takes place and, above all, what happens in the critical moment in which 'the old is dying and the new cannot be born'.[31]

The 'organic crisis' is twofold, since it involves at the same time the structural and the superstructural dimension. At first, the crisis reflects the contradictions of the productive system, and shows the separation between rulers and ruled, i.e. the shortcomings on the political and cultural level. The crisis manifests itself in growing political ungovernability and in the shattering of the hegemonic apparatus, which means in the disintegration of the network of relations and influences, which in turn assures the primacy of one social class over the others.[32] In this context, the crisis of the political leadership describes the 'crisis of authority' or 'crisis of hegemony', which represents a specific aspect of the more general phenomenon of the crumbling of a given historical bloc.[33]

If this process is somehow typical of all phases of transition from one historical epoch to another, however, Gramsci's conceptualisation is clearly shaped around modernity, i.e. around the decline of the bourgeois-capitalist system after the expansive period of the 'long nineteenth century'. In the twentieth century, in fact, the crisis is organic to the highest degree. While in previous historical epochs an 'organic solution' was ready in advance for the collapse of the old system, in the contemporary age this does not occur and the crisis appears to be radical and deep – on several occasions Gramsci highlights the 'catastrophic' nature of this process, where this adjective, as I have previously demonstrated, strongly emphasises the drama of the conjuncture.[34] On the dif-

---

31   Q 3, § 34, p. 311; PN, vol. 1, p. 33.
32   Cf. Q 13, § 37, p. 1639: 'The crisis displays itself in the ever increasing difficulty of forming governments and in the ever increasing instability of the governments themselves: it has its immediate origin in the multiplication of parliamentary parties, and in the permanent internal crises of each of these parties'. On the causes of the organic crisis of modernity, among which the politicisation of the masses, the so-called 'question of the young' (Q 3, § 34, p. 311; PN, vol. 1, p. 33), the war, and so on, see the aforementioned entry by F. Frosini in Liguori and Voza 2009. Regarding the distinction between structure and superstructure and its 'methodological' character, see Cospito 2016, pp. 3 ff.
33   See the entries *Crisi di autorità* (by M. Filippini) and *Crisi organica* (by L. La Porta) in Liguori and Voza 2009, pp. 179–82.
34   Q 13, § 23, p. 1604; SPN, p. 211. On the 'catastrophic' character of the crisis of hegemony in modernity, see Q 13, § 23, pp. 1604–5; SPN, p. 211: 'Their crisis [of the French parties] could become even more catastrophic than that of the German parties'; see also Q 19, § 6, p. 1989; FSPN, p. 237: 'Political expression of the general post-war crisis, which in 1929 deepened to the point of near catastrophe'.

ference between the organic crises of modernity and the earlier crises, see in particular Q 6, § 10 (*Past and Present*, single draft, November–December 1930), where Gramsci affirms:

> One can say that, generally speaking, the modern world is currently experiencing a phenomenon similar to the split between the 'spiritual' and the 'temporal' in the Middle Ages, a phenomenon that is more complex now than it was then, to the extent that modern life has become more complex ... This [process of] disintegration of the modern state is far more catastrophic than the medieval [historical process], which was simultaneously disintegrative and integrative, given the particular grouping that was the motor of the historical process itself and given the type of state that had existed after the year 1000 in Europe, a state that knew nothing of modern centralization and could be described as 'federative of the dominant classes' rather than the state of a single dominant class.[35]

The formula of the balance of class forces is essential in this framework. As Gramsci writes in Q 13, § 23, after having explained of what the hegemonic crisis consists, and having investigated its causes:

> The crisis creates situations which are dangerous in the short run, since the various strata of the population are not all capable of orienting themselves equally swiftly, or of reorganizing with the same rhythm. The traditional ruling class, which has numerous trained cadres, changes men and programmes and, with greater speed than is achieved by the subordinate classes, reabsorbs the control that was slipping from its grasp. Perhaps it may make sacrifices, and expose itself to an uncertain future by demagogic promises; but it retains power, reinforces it for the time being, and uses it to crush its adversary and disperse his leading cadres, who cannot be very numerous or highly trained. The passage of the troops of many different parties under the banner of a single party, which better represents and resumes the needs of the entire class, is an organic and normal phenomenon, even if its rhythm is very swift – indeed almost like lightning

---

35   Q 6, § 10, pp. 690–1; PN, vol. 3, pp. 8–9. In the central part of the text, omitted here, Gramsci focuses on the intellectuals, whose detachment from 'the social grouping to which they have hitherto given the highest, most comprehensive form and hence the most extensive and complete consciousness of the modern state' (p. 9) plays a decisive part in precipitating the situation and in determining the opening of the crisis, by highlighting their fundamental role in the creation of hegemony.

in comparison with periods of calm. It represents the fusion of an entire social class under a single leadership, which alone is held to be capable of solving an overriding problem of its existence and of fending off a mortal danger. When the crisis does not find this organic solution, but that of the charismatic leader, it means that a static equilibrium exists (whose factors may be disparate, but in which the decisive one is the immaturity of the progressive forces); it means that no group, neither the conservatives nor the progressives, has the strength for victory, and that even the conservative group needs a master. See *The Eighteenth Brumaire of Louis Bonaparte*.[36]

Therefore, the organic crisis is the result of a situation of balance that seems almost impossible to unlock. As a consequence, the situation of balance represents much more than a simple Marxian *motif*: by describing the 'siege' that characterises the European socio-political context, it becomes a valuable formula for the understanding of the very essence of modernity.[37]

2.2   The 'Massive Structure of the Modern Democracies'

What form does this crisis assume? Moreover, how quickly does it develop? In a passage of Q 13, § 17, *Analysis of the Situation: Relations of Force*, Gramsci focuses on the distinction between 'organic' and 'conjunctural' movements. He observes:

> In studying a structure, it is necessary to distinguish organic movements (relatively permanent) from movements which may be termed 'conjunctural' (and which appear as occasional, immediate, almost accidental). Conjunctural phenomena too depend on organic movements to be sure, but they do not have any very far-reaching historical significance; they give rise to political criticism of a minor, day-to-day character, which has as its subject top political leaders and personalities with direct governmental responsibilities. Organic phenomena on the other hand give rise to socio-historical criticism, whose subject is wider social groupings – beyond the public figures and beyond the top leaders. When an

---

36   Q 13, § 23, pp. 1603–4; SPN, pp. 210–11. This passage is the result of a significant extension of the first draft text. Thanks also to the explicit reference to Marx's text, Q 13, § 23 seems also to echo the article written by Gramsci in 1926 on the issue of the balance of forces in the post-war framework ('Russia, Italy, and other Countries'; see Chapter 4, section 3.3 and Chapter 5, section 3).

37   As for the image of the 'siege' and its totalitarian implications, see Chapter 12, section 1.1.

historical period comes to be studied, the great importance of this distinction becomes clear. A crisis occurs, sometimes lasting for decades. This exceptional duration means that incurable structural contradictions have revealed themselves (reached maturity), and that, despite this, the political forces which are struggling to conserve and defend the existing structure itself are making every effort to cure them, within certain limits, and to overcome them. These incessant and persistent efforts ... form the terrain of the 'conjunctural', and it is upon this terrain that the forces of opposition organise. These forces seek to demonstrate that the necessary and sufficient conditions already exist to make possible, and hence imperative, the accomplishment of certain historical tasks (imperative, because any falling short before an historical duty increases the necessary disorder, and prepares more serious catastrophes).[38]

In this text, Gramsci does not oppose the 'occasional' aspect to the 'organic' one: rather, he demonstrates how the former finds a place within the latter, by representing a sort of internal articulation of the organic crisis. Gramsci is more interested in the intertwining of these two elements, insofar as it shows that the organic crisis does not automatically lead to the overthrow of the old system and to the creation of a new one. In fact, it might produce an 'interregnum', as brilliantly defined in Q 3, §34, *Past and Present*,[39] that in certain cases can be of 'exceptional duration', thanks to the resilience of society as a whole (involving economic, political and cultural aspects).[40]

This issue is analysed well in Gramsci's reflection on the 'massive structure of the modern democracies' in Q 13, §7, where the term 'democracy' simply indicates a form of state, without further characterisations.

The massive structures of the modern democracies, both as State organisations, and as complexes of associations in civil society, constitute for the art of politics as it were the 'trenches' and the permanent fortifications of the front in the war of position: they render merely 'partial' the element of movement which before used to be 'the whole' of war, etc.[41]

It is interesting to note that, in the rest of the *Prison Notebooks*, the adjective 'massive' is mainly employed to describe the organisational capacity of the reli-

---

38 Q 13, §17, pp. 1579–80; SPN, pp. 177–8.
39 Q 3, §34, p. 311; PN, vol. 1, p. 33.
40 Q 13, §17, pp. 1579–80; SPN, p. 178.
41 Q 13, §7, p. 1567; SPN, p. 243.

gious institutions (and in particular the Catholic Church) and, therefore, their hegemony over the popular masses.[42] In two cases the adjective is not used in this sense, when it defines the complex of French intellectuality in the pre-modern era, by describing its effective and progressive expansive capacity – *versus* the 'incapacity' of Italian intellectuals.[43]

In modernity, this term synthesises the strength of the bourgeois-capitalist system and its long-lasting influence on state and society. Furthermore, I think that this element can be linked to what was previously said about the exploitation of the marginal forces of a political formation. On this basis, I will investigate the distinctive way in which this 'hegemonic extension' takes place in the context of the organic crisis.

3   A New Form of Hegemony

3.1   *A Post-Jacobin Framework*

I will dwell first on a distinction recently put forward by Fabio Frosini: he distinguishes between a 'classical', pre-1848 or 'Jacobin' conception of hegemony and a modern, 'post-Jacobin' one.[44] If hegemony is 'one of the possible articulations of the relationships between the classes', its Jacobin or, as an alternative, post-Jacobin nature will depend on the specific class relations that characterise each historical period.[45]

In the contemporary world, these relations are framed in terms of 'mobilisation' and 'involvement' of the masses, but also (and, perhaps, above all) in terms of a strict control of them, in order to prevent the emergence of autonomous initiatives of the subordinate groups – in other words, in modernity 'the passage of the bourgeoisie from an attitude of expansive democratisation to [an attitude] of control of the population' takes place.[46]

---

42   Cf. Q 2, § 90; Q 5, § 134; Q 10, I, § 1; Q 16, § 11.

43   Cf. Q 4, § 49, p. 479; PN, vol. 2, p. 204: 'This massive intellectual establishment explains the intellectual function of France in the second half of the eighteenth century and throughout the nineteenth century; an international and cosmopolitan function of irradiation and of an expansion which had the character of organic imperialism – therefore, quite different from the intellectual function of Italy which was characterized by a haphazard personal migration whose effect was to preclude rather than enable the development of the national base' (the text is redrafted in Q 12, § 1).

44   See, in particular, Frosini 2016a.

45   Frosini 2016a, p. 129.

46   Frosini 2016a, p. 131.

HEGEMONY AND MODERNITY 161

If the 'direction' remains a pivotal element in the crisis of the bourgeois system (whence the specific character of the 'struggle between hegemonies' of the present war of position), it can be achieved, however, at the price of an unprecedented and 'frantic' centralisation of forces, i.e. of the progressive absorption by the state of all the elements of civil society able to 'educate' the population and to organise the consensus.[47] This interpenetration between public and private, this 'democratic-bureaucratic' character of contemporary regimes finds its highest expression in Italian Fascism, which, as Frosini affirms, represents 'the laboratory in which the most advanced forms of bourgeois hegemony in Europe are being tested'.[48]

The explicit references to the Italian regime that I investigated in the previous chapters have already partly raised these 'neo-hegemonic' aspects, by emphasising how, through Fascism, the traditional ruling classes attempt to recover the lost ground in the hegemonic field. However, there are also other elements that deserve to be analysed.

3.2 The Issue of the 'Dark Powers'

I will examine, first, the following passage from Q 13, § 23. In dealing with crises of authority, Gramsci writes:

> When such crises occur, the immediate situation becomes delicate and dangerous, because the field is open for violent solutions, for the activities of dark powers, represented by charismatic 'men of destiny'.[49]

I would stress here that the expression 'dark powers' [*potenze oscure*], thanks to its evocativeness, perfectly fits with the 'atmosphere' of Gramsci's description of the organic crisis.[50] This is a phrase that occurs only once in the *Notebooks*, as a variant in the second draft of Q 4, § 69.[51] The expression describes the

---

47 Frosini also underlines how this new form of hegemony implies a 'broadening of the mass of intellectuals', and a 'multiplication of their functions' (Frosini 2016a, p. 135).
48 Frosini 2016a, p. 133. As regards the expression 'democratic-bureaucratic', see Frosini 2016a, *passim*.
49 Q 13, § 23, p. 1603; SPN, p. 210.
50 I have modified the current English translation of the Gramscian expression '*potenze oscure*' (in the version by Hoare and Nowell Smith: 'unknown forces'). In fact, I think the existing translation does not really render the sense of Gramsci's words. Moreover, it does not take into account the previous occurrences, which are fundamental to understanding the meaning of the expression in this context.
51 See the first draft note, which is much more synthetic: 'This conflict between the represented and the representatives which takes place on the terrain of private organizations

forces that, without showing themselves directly, control the political system, i.e. forces that are concerned with the maintenance of their privileges and of their dominance over society.

From this perspective, it is noteworthy that the same expression can be found in an article on the failed *putsch* of Cadorna in 1917: here Gramsci analyses precisely the 'dark forces' that supported him on that occasion.[52] In particular, in the 1920 article, Gramsci refers to the 'industrial plutocracy', hence suggesting an economico-political interpretation of the dark forces (the expression is otherwise rather vague, by evoking a generic form of conspiracy). It is therefore very likely that the expression in the *Notebooks* represents the legacy of his spirited journalistic language.

In Q 13, § 23, Gramsci expands the list of the organisms that embody the 'dark powers', by including now also the Church, high finance and 'all bodies relatively independent of the fluctuations of public opinion', which are strengthened in the context of a hegemonic crisis.[53] This grouping of institutions is symptomatic of the Gramscian vision of those apparatuses: although they do not have an explicit political characterisation, they are constitutively on the side of those in power and play a fundamental role in difficult times. In fact, it is precisely their 'relative independence', emphasised in these situations, which allows them to react quickly and effectively, by working against the collapse of the system.

Arguably, these observations also illuminate the other reference to the 'obscurity' of the political leadership contained in Q 13, § 23: the 'uncertain future by demagogic promises'.[54] On this basis, the charismatic leader appears as the representative of the conservative forces that rule 'from the shadows', thus not revealing the real political dynamics.

[ ] (parties or trade unions) inevitably has repercussions on the state, reinforcing in a formidable way the power of the bureaucracy (in the broad sense: military and civil). How does this situation of conflict arise in the first place?' (Q 4, § 69, p. 513; PN, vol. 2, p. 243).

52 Cf. 'Chiaroscuro', cit.; for a quotation from this text, see Chapter 3, section 1.1.

53 Q 13, § 23, p. 1603; SPN, p. 210. On this theme see, also Q 6, § 166, p. 819 (PN, vol. 3, p. 124), where Gramsci speaks of the negative effects of indifference towards politics in the *Risorgimento*, and asserts that 'from the point of view of the "forces of order," this was an ideal state of affairs: the less people participated in the political life of the state, the more powerful these forces became ... What is said about the army can be extended to the entire personnel employed by the state apparatus: the bureaucracy, the justice system, the police, etc.'.

54 Q 13, § 23, p. 1603; SPN, p. 210.

3.3   Bureaucracy, Military Associations, Police

In Q 13, § 23 bureaucracy plays then a crucial role, due also to the numerous changes made by Gramsci. First of all, in the above-mentioned passage on 'dark powers', the reactionary features of bureaucracy stand out: it is described as a 'hidebound' and dangerously 'conservative' force, hostile towards broad strata of society and very interested in the maintenance of the constituted order.[55]

The redrafted text, however, also offers a further element of analysis. As I demonstrated previously, the focus of Gramsci's reflection is on investigating the social origin of the bureaucrats (both civil and military), which is mainly the rural bourgeoisie and the petty bourgeois '*morto di fame*' deriving from it.[56] In concluding this argument, in Q 13, § 23, Gramsci takes his cue from a book of Gaetano Mosca and restates the '"military" character of the social group in question'.[57] Far from simply describing the affinity of a social group with a state apparatus, he also provides a brief description of the ultimate political aim of bureaucracy. In this regard, Gramsci makes observations on the 'ideological activity of the conservative intellectuals of the Right' and on the role of the associations of soldiers on leave or of former combatants.[58] These associations, in particular, are excellent instruments to control the popular masses and, more generally, of bringing civil society 'into line'.[59]

A third important element is represented by Gramsci's remarks on the police, which directly connect to the issue of the character of the Caesarist phenomena of modernity, as written by Gramsci in Q 13, § 27 ('modern Caesarism

---

[55]   Q 13, § 23, pp. 1603–4; SPN, p. 211. Elsewhere Gramsci underlines the 'caste' and not national nature of bureaucracy, as well as its parasitism, making specific reference to the Italian case – see Q 5, § 38, p. 571; PN, vol. 2, p. 300 ('the bureaucracy, in other words, does not have a national character; it has the character of a caste') and above all Q 14, § 47 (p. 1705), where the Italian bureaucracy of the *Risorgimento* is compared to the papal bureaucracy and to the Chinese mandarins. On Gramsci's conception of bureaucracy (with special attention given to its development in the miscellaneous notebooks 14, 15 and 17), see Antonini 2019a.

[56]   Regarding the phrase '*morto di fame*' (i.e. extremely poor), see SPN, p. 272, n. 76.

[57]   Q 13, § 23, p. 1607; SPN, p. 214 (this passage on Mosca is an innovation in the second draft text). The book of Mosca, *Theory of Governments and Parliamentary Government* [*Sulla teorica dei governi e governo parlamentare*], was previously quoted by Gramsci in Q 9, § 89 – we could argue that Gramsci had in mind § 89 of notebook 9 while writing Q 13, § 23.

[58]   Q 13, § 23, p. 1607; SPN, p. 214. As for the *excursus* on the combatants' associations, a part of it was already added by Gramsci in a footnote to the first draft (Q 4, § 66, p. 509; PN, vol. 2, p. 239). In the second draft of the text, this addition is refined and expanded (see Q 13, § 23, pp. 1607–8).

[59]   More generally, on the expansion of the state and para-statal apparatus, on the multiplication of the number and types of intellectual figures and on the transformation of the State-civil society relationship in the conditions of modernity, see Frosini 2016a.

is more a police than a military system').⁶⁰ As Guido Liguori has pointed out, the extension of the category of police runs parallel to the enlargement of the concept of the state and, therefore, to Gramsci's reflection on contemporary socio-political phenomena.⁶¹ In the *Prison Notebooks*, in fact, if the police, as a term, does not stop at defining the 'public service designed for the repression of crime', but also describes all those organisations that control and 'contain' the social body – first and foremost the political party.⁶² This point of view is also expressed pertinently in Q 2, §150 (*Cultural Topics [Argomenti di cultura]*).⁶³ Here, Gramsci writes:

> 'What is the police?' It certainly is not just that particular official organization which is juridically recognized and empowered to carry out the public function of public safety, as it is normally understood. This organism is the central and formally responsible nucleus of the "police", which is a much larger organization in which a large part of a state's population participates directly or indirectly through links that are more or less precise and limited, permanent or occasional, etc.⁶⁴

In short, the picture that emerges from the analysis of these elements matches the one described above in more general terms: in modernity, hegemony is the result of a new combination of direction and coercion, which is made possible both by new organisations and by a transformation (of greater or lesser depth) of the old ones.

---

60 Q 13, § 27, p. 1622; SPN, p. 222.
61 See the entry *Polizia* by G. Liguori in Liguori and Voza 2009, pp. 651–2.
62 Q 13, § 27, p. 1620; SPN, p. 221. On the connection with the political party, see in particular Q 14, § 34, significantly entitled *Machiavelli. Political Parties and Police Functions [Machiavelli. Partiti politici e funzioni di polizia]*. On this theme, see again Antonini 2019a.
63 The text is a single draft written in January 1933 (on this text, see QAnast, vol. 5, p. 5). Q 9, § 133 is therefore the very first paragraph dedicated by Gramsci to the theme of police. Consequently, when Gramsci talks about the other notes written on the topic ('"What is the police?" (This question has been mentioned in other notes dealing with the real function of political parties.)'; Q 2, § 150, p. 278; PN, vol. 1, p. 361), he is referring exactly to the texts in notebooks 9 and 13. Moreover, the 'primacy' of Q 9, § 133 (and of its second draft, Q 13, § 27) allows us to establish a close and direct connection between this reflection on the police and that on Caesarism.
64 Q 2, § 150, pp. 278–9; PN, vol. 1, p. 361. A similar reflection is contained in Q 14, § 34, where Gramsci distinguishes between a progressive form and a regressive form of the (broadly conceived) policy control put into practice by the contemporary political parties.

3.4 Bonapartism, Caesarism and Fascism

As a result of these reflections on the police, the relationship between Caesarism and Bonapartism also has to be (partially) reassessed. If Bonapartism, in its second, deeper meaning, focuses on the shortcomings of political leadership and provides us with an analysis of bureaucratic phenomena, now the two concepts of Caesarism and Bonapartism appear even closer and both contribute to the characterisation of the complex political landscape of the twentieth century. It is perhaps no coincidence that Q 13, § 23 is the only text in which the category of Caesarism and that of Bonapartism appear, so to say, side by side, and not in 'hybrid' compounds.[65]

This also illuminates the 'so-called dictatorships of Depretis, Crispi and Giolitti', and the definition of bureaucracy as a 'state-Bonapartist party'.[66] Rather than representing a purely negative characterisation, these elements emphasise how, even in a non-progressive political context such as the *Risorgimento*, the dominant groups exercise a form of political direction that allows them to maintain control of the state (*trasformismo* is crucial in this sense).

The most relevant historical example, however, is obviously Fascism, which, according to Gramsci, in a famous passage from the *Prison Notebooks*, is the paradigm of twentieth-century passive revolution (Q 8, § 236; April 1932).[67] As I have shown in this chapter, Gramsci addresses the transformations underway in Italy during the turbulent post-war period, i.e. the disintegration of the post-unification liberal hegemonic framework and the attempts to substitute an alternative to it (from the left) or to restore it (from the right). Fascism is seen therefore as a political solution (although a limited and problematic one)

---

[65] In Q 13, § 23 Gramsci does not use the adjective '*bonapartistico-cesareo*' ('of a Bonapartist-Caesarist type'), as he did, for example, in Q 3, § 119 (p. 387; PN, vol. 2, p. 106); he speaks of 'Caesarism or Bonapartism' (Q 13, § 23, p. 1608; SPN, p. 215). As I have shown previously, it should be considered that Q 13, § 23 is the result of the fusion of a number of first draft texts that used different terms. In spite of that, I would argue that there might be a reason why, while redrafting the notes, Gramsci did not pursue any sort of conceptual 'homogeneity' (by substituting the term Bonapartism with Caesarism or vice versa) and keeps the two categories separated. Moreover, as I pointed out elsewhere, the original expression 'so to speak, "Caesarist"' (Q 4, § 66, p. 511; PN, vol. 2, p. 241) is substituted in the second draft with a 'so to speak, potentially Bonapartist' (Q 13, § 23, p. 1609; SPN, p. 216), confirming the fact that, in Q 13, § 23, Gramsci is seeking closer terminological precision.

[66] Q 3, § 119, p. 387; PN, vol. 2, p. 106.

[67] Cf. Q 8, § 236, p. 1089 (then redrafted in Q 10, I, 9): 'A new "liberalism" under modern conditions – wouldn't that be, precisely, "fascism"? If liberalism was the form of "passive revolution" specific to the 19th century, wouldn't fascism be, precisely, the form of "passive revolution" specific to the 20th century?' (PN, vol. 3, p. 378). On this issue, see Frosini 2017b.

to the organic crisis, as an effort to restore the 'broken' bourgeois hegemony. The bureaucracy, the military associations, the police (broadly conceived), and so on are the instruments through which the fascist regime realises its control over the masses and, more generally, over civil society.

Insofar as these aspects are connected to Gramsci's analysis of the Caesarist-Bonapartist phenomena, it follows that an analysis of Fascism in a Caesarist-Bonapartist key is not only possible, but even necessary.

CHAPTER 12

Contemporary Caesarism(s)

1   Totalitarian Trends

1.1   *War of Position, Siege, and Concentration*

According to Gramsci, modernity appears as a 'new' and more decisive war of position. Indeed, the transition between the war of movement and the war of position is

> the most important postwar problem of political theory; it is also the most difficult problem to solve correctly ... The war of position calls on enormous masses of people to make huge sacrifices; that is why an unprecedented concentration of hegemony is required and hence a more 'interventionist' kind of government that will engage more openly in the offensive against the opponents and ensure, once and for all, the 'impossibility' of internal disintegration by putting in place controls of all kinds – political, administrative, etc., reinforcement of the hegemonic positions of the dominant group, etc. All of this indicates that the culminating phase of the politico-historical situation has begun, for, in politics, once the 'war of position' is won, it is definitively decisive. In politics, in other words, the war of maneuver drags on as long as the positions being won are not decisive and the resources of hegemony and the state are not fully mobilized. But when, for some reason or another, these positions have lost their value and only the decisive positions matter, then one shifts to siege warfare – compact, difficult, requiring exceptional abilities of patience and inventiveness. In politics, the siege is reciprocal, whatever the appearances; the mere fact that the ruling power has to parade all its resources reveals its estimate of the adversary.[1]

This note, *Past and Present. Transition from the War of Manoeuvre (and Frontal Assault) to the War of Position – in the Political Field as well* [*Passato e presente. Passaggio dalla guerra manovrata (e dall'attacco frontale) alla guerra di posizione anche nel campo politico*], a single draft written in August 1931, is significant in terms of its conception of Caesarism.[2] It describes the 'polarised' political

---

1 Q 6, § 138, pp. 801–2; PN, vol. 3, p. 109.
2 On this note, see also QAnast, vol. 12, pp. 10 ff. As regards the political reflections in notebook

scenario in which two hostile and opposing blocs (the bourgeois and the proletarian) compete to win power, in a fight to the death.³ Such a polarisation is exactly what makes the post-war period the 'culminating phase of the politico-historical situation'. Moreover, this also explains features of the current war of position, which culminates in the powerful image of the reciprocal 'siege' (a further 'dramatic' element is represented by Gramsci's observation that the resolution of this conflict will be permanent, meaning that one of the two blocs will be radically destroyed).⁴

The practical consequence of this contraposition is the 'unprecedented concentration of hegemony' evoked by Gramsci in §138 of notebook 6. However, we cannot comprehend this new form of hegemony without considering the radical transformations taking place within society. In fact, as Gramsci asserts, one of the main causes of this situation is the politicisation of the masses, or, in Gramsci's words, the 'trade-union phenomenon' [*fenomeno sindacale*].⁵ This should not be 'understood in its elementary sense of associationalism of all social groups and for any purpose', but, as he specifies, as the gathering 'of the newly formed social elements, which previously had no voice, and which, if unified, are able to change the political structure of society'.⁶

The mobilisation of classes previously excluded from political life implies a radical rethinking of the ways in which a group assures its own primacy over others, by making an involvement of all the social strata necessary. It follows that, in the twentieth century, the rule of the dominant groups is no longer the result of an alliance between small, well-defined groups of power (the 'trusts' and the 'camarillias', the parties of 'notables' on which the political life of the liberal state was based). The rule of a class is made possible through the

---

6, which partially anticipate Gramsci's later thoughts on the 'totalitarian' state, see QAnast, vol. 12, pp. 1–13.

3 With regard to the issue of polarisation, see also what I said previously about the differences between modern and pre-modern Caesarisms and the existence, in the pre-modern era, of a variety of forces that were able to defuse the social conflicts.

4 Gramsci adopts the term 'siege' as a synonym of 'position' already in Q 1, §133, p. 120 ('*guerra d'assedio o di posizione*'; 'war by siege or war of position'; PN, vol. 1, p. 217). However, the term is regularly used in this sense only from Q 6, §138 onwards; see Q 7, §10; Q 9, §137; Q 13, §§24 and 28; Q 17, §28. Generally speaking, I would argue that, at least in the context of Q 6, §138, the term 'siege' expresses far more emphatically the difficulties of the ongoing class struggle.

5 Q 15, §59, p. 1824; SPN, p. 106.

6 Q 15, §47, p. 1088. See also Q 15, §59, p. 1824: this is 'a general term in which various problems and processes of development, of differing importance and significance, are lumped together ..., but which objectively reflects the fact that a new social force has been constituted, and has a weight which can no longer be ignored, etc.' (SPN, p. 106).

affirmation of its own conception of the world over the others, i.e. through the suppression of autonomies and the 'saturation' of the ideological framework.[7]

This reasoning also emerges clearly from a note in notebook 25, which redrafts two texts from notebook 3 (§ 16, *Political Development of the Popular Class in the Medieval Commune* [*Sviluppo politico della classe popolare nel Comune medioevale*], June 1930; § 18, *History of the Subaltern Classes* [*Storia delle classi subalterne*], June 1930). Here, with a synthetic but highly evocative historical comparison between modern states and contemporary authoritarian regimes, it is affirmed that

> the modern state substitutes the mechanical bloc of social groups with their subordination to the active hegemony of the ruling and dominant group, and therefore it abolishes some autonomies, which however are reborn in other forms, such as parties, trade unions, associations of culture. Contemporary dictatorships also legally abolish these new forms of autonomy and strive to incorporate them into state activity: the legal centralisation of all national life in the hands of the dominant group becomes 'totalitarian'.[8]

The strengthening of the hegemonic position of the dominant group goes hand in hand with a variety of forms of surveillance aimed at eliminating the opponents and avoiding internal upheavals. The search for the inclusion of the masses in the political project of the ruling class is inextricably linked to their containment, in the context of an unprecedented centralising 'grip', of an oppressive, almost suffocating ideological pervasiveness. To sum up, the atmosphere became '"totalitarian"', as Gramsci says at the very end of the note, substituting for the couple of adjectives 'frenetic and all-consuming' that appear in the first draft text.[9]

---

7 See in this sense the essential role of the intellectuals and of the 'neutral' state apparatuses like bureaucracy. For some hints in this direction, see also Vacca 2017.
8 Q 25, § 4, p. 2287. The note is entitled *Some General Notes on the Historical Development of Subordinate Social Groups in the Middle Ages and in Rome* [*Alcune note generali sullo sviluppo storico dei gruppi sociali subalterni nel Medio Evo e a Roma*] and it is dated between August 1934 and the first months of 1935. As is well known, this text is also crucial for Gramsci's reflections on the subaltern groups and subalternity (on this theme, see Green 2002).
9 Q 3, § 18, p. 303; PN, vol. 2, p. 25.

1.2   A 'Totalitarian' Conception of the World

It is no accident that Gramsci uses the adjective 'totalitarian' in this text. On the contrary, this represents an important category in the *Prison Notebooks*, which deserves thorough investigation.[10]

The term has two meanings.[11] First, 'totalitarian' is opposed to 'partial' and describes all those 'conceptions of the world' that aspire to be 'universal'.[12] Gramsci adopts the adjective 'totalitarian' in a number of notes in the sense of 'total', 'totalising' or 'absolute'. This meaning emerges clearly in Q 20, § 2 (*Catholic Action and the French tertiaries [L'Azione Cattolica e i terziari francesi]*), where Gramsci redrafts and significantly expands a text from notebook 1 (§ 139, *Catholic Action [Azione Cattolica]*, February–March 1930): 'Catholic Action marked the beginning of a new era in the history of the Catholic religion – the moment when, from a totalitarian conception (in the dual sense – that it was a total world-conception of a society in its entirety) it became partial (that too in the dual sense) and had to have its own party'.[13] It is noteworthy that his reference to the 'totalising' features of the Catholic Church recurs in a few notes.[14] In fact, Gramsci is interested primarily in Catholicism due to its being an 'ideology' capable of permeating the entire society.[15]

However, Gramsci makes analogous reflections also with regard to historical materialism. If historical materialism is to have a real effectiveness and give rise to a radical transformation of society, Gramsci claims, it must indeed be all-encompassing. Thus, in Q 4, § 75 (*Past and Present*, single draft, November

---

10   We can trace some useful hints in the entry *Totalitario* by R. Caputo in Liguori and Voza 2009, pp. 851–3. On this issue, see Kalyvas 2000 and Gagliardi 2017.

11   We should not confuse Gramsci's use of the adjective 'totalitarian' with the development of the category of 'totalitarianism' after World War II. These conceptualisations include the famous analysis by Hannah Arendt in *The Origins of Totalitarianism* up to the most recent discussion on the topic. We should contextualise Gramsci's account within the contemporary debate, in order to avoid undue anachronisms. On early twentieth-century interpretations of totalitarianism, see Petersen 1975; more generally, see Jay 1984 and Traverso 2001.

12   'Totalitarian conception' includes the sense that today might be referred to in English as a 'holistic conception'. As G. Liguori pointed out (entry *Concezione del mondo*, in Liguori and Voza 2009), the expression 'conception of the world' is used by Gramsci as a synonym of 'ideology', 'but in an even broader sense, to indicate the connective ground on which different degrees of the capacity of the subject for the elaboration of reality arise' (p. 148).

13   Q 20, § 2, p. 2086; FSPN, p. 34 – translation slightly modified. In the FSPN, the Italian expression *'concezione totalitaria'* is (too vaguely, I would argue) translated as 'all-embracing conception'. See also below, fn. 21.

14   See, for instance, Q 6, § 188 and Q 7, § 98.

15   On the 'totalising', hegemonic role of the Catholic Church, see now in particular Descendre 2019.

1930), he says: 'Historical materialism will have or may have this function which is not only totalitarian as a conception of the world, but also in that it will permeate all of society down to its deepest roots'.[16]

In a more specific sense, Gramsci uses the adjective to analyse the contemporary socio-political situation, i.e. the single-party systems that arose in the interwar period.[17] This emerges clearly from Q 6, §136 (*Organization of National Societies* [*Organizzazione delle società nazionali*], single draft, August 1931), where Gramsci stresses the differences between traditional and totalitarian politics.

> In any given society nobody is unorganized and without a party, provided that organization and party are understood broadly, in a nonformal sense. The numerous private associations are of two kinds: natural and contractual or voluntary. In this multiplicity of private associations, one or more prevails, relatively or absolutely, constituting the hegemonic apparatus of one social group over the rest of the population (civil society), which is the basis for the state in the narrow sense of governmental-coercive apparatus. There are always cases of individuals belonging to more than one private association, and often they belong to associations that are essentially in conflict with one another. A totalitarian policy in fact attempts: (1) to ensure that the members of a particular party find in that one party all the satisfactions that they had previously found in a multiplicity of organizations, that is, to sever all ties these members have with extraneous cultural organisms; (2) to destroy all other organizations or to incorporate them into a system regulated solely by the party.[18]

---

16   Q 4, §75, p. 515; PN, vol. 2, p. 244; translation slightly modified. See also Q 8, §182, p. 1051: 'Only a totalitarian system of ideologies rationally reflects the contradiction of the structure and represents the existence of the objective conditions for revolutionizing praxis' (PN, vol. 3, p. 340; I have modified the English translation, since the Italian expression '*sistema di ideologie totalitario*' is misleadingly translated as 'comprehensive system of ideologies' – it is clear that the essence of the expression lies in the adjective 'totalitarian' and the English translation does not perfectly grasp it). Q 15, § 6 also refers to historical materialism, albeit in a more indirect manner – see the following passage: 'Hence the conclusion that in building a party, it is necessary to give it a "monolithic" character rather than base it on secondary questions; therefore, painstaking care that there should be homogeneity between the leadership and the rank and file, between the leaders and their mass following' (15, §6, p. 1760; SPN, p. 158).
17   On this second, more specific meaning of the adjective 'totalitarian', some useful hints are contained already in De Felice 1977 and, more recently, in Frosini 2016a.
18   Q 6, §136, p. 800; PN, vol. 3, pp. 107–8.

Q 6, §136 evokes the observations on the trade associations as 'private bodies' or '"private" fabric of the State' mentioned in Q 1, §47, *Hegel and Associationism* [*Hegel e l'associazionismo*] (single draft, February–March 1930).[19] More importantly, it is connected to his reflections on the elimination of the autonomy of the different groups further developed in Q 6, §138.

Generally speaking, Gramsci is trying to show that a totalitarian politics implies a radical reconsideration of the relationship between state and society, as well as a new conception of the party, conceived of as the main author of this 'totalitarian' turn. If, in the premodern era, there could be more 'private associations' [*società particolari*] without endangering the domination of one class over the others, in the post-war context, there is no longer any room for the expression of interests other than those of the group that holds power. Hence, on the one hand, there is a suppression of all antagonistic organisations while, on the other, there are efforts to 'ensure that the members of a particular party find in that one party all the satisfactions that they had previously found in a multiplicity of organisations'.[20] In short, civil society is 'absorbed' by political society, and the 'integral' character of the state appears in its harsh reality.

In this framework, Gramsci makes pivotal observations that elaborate the 'new integral and totalitarian intelligentsia'.[21] Yet, even more important, Gramsci says that the creator of this new 'typology' of intellectuals is the party.[22]

1.3   The Role of the Party

The party is the cornerstone of the system, the centre of the new post-war order. The totalitarian party has occupied the place which, before the advent of the parliamentary system, belonged to the Crown. Moreover, the party has also developed crown-like prerogatives.[23] As Gramsci writes, for instance, in Q 7, §93 (*Political Terminology. Privileges and Prerogatives* [*Nomenclatura politica. Privilegi e prerogative*], December 1931),

---

19   Cf. Q1975, p. 2730.
20   Q 6, §136, p. 800; PN, vol. 3, p. 108.
21   Q 8, §169, p. 1042; PN, vol. 3, p. 331, translation modified. In the English translation, the adjective '*totalitario*' is not rendered accurately – it is substituted with the adjective 'all-embracing', perhaps to reclaim some of the non-pejorative aspects of the meaning that Gramsci is trying to convey. However, I would argue that it is important to use the term 'totalitarian' in order to grasp the connection with Gramsci's broader reflection on the totalitarian tendencies in his times. The note is redrafted in Q 11, §12, p. 1387 ('new integral and totalitarian intelligentsias'; SPN, p. 335). Here the term is correctly translated; on the meaning of the term 'totalitarian', see also SPN, p. 335, n. 20.
22   See Q 8, §169, p. 1042; Q 11, §12, p. 1387.
23   Some hints on this issue are contained in Frosini 2016a, p. 145.

according to one constitutional theory, the function of the Crown – i.e., to embody sovereignty both in the sense of state and in the sense of cultural-political administration (in other words, to be the arbiter in the internal conflicts of the dominant groups, the hegemonic class and its allies) – is now being transferred to the big, 'totalitarian' types of parties. If this theory is correct, then it is obvious that the corresponding prerogatives are also handed over to such parties.[24]

And, again, in Q 13, § 21: 'In those regimes which call themselves totalitarian, the traditional function of the institution of the Crown is in fact taken over by the particular party in question, which indeed is totalitarian precisely in that it fulfils this function'.[25] As a 'substitute' for the Crown, the totalitarian party has two main tasks: to represent formally the institutions of a state, and to provide the 'political-cultural direction' of the state.

The second task is, without doubt, the pivotal one. It refers to the function of 'arbitration' traditionally played by the Crown. To play a role of arbitration means to mediate between the different elements of the dominant bloc in

---

24   Q 7, § 93, p. 992; PN, vol. 3, p. 219. As an example of this transfer of powers Gramsci mentions the fascist state – see the conclusion of the note: 'For this reason, one must study the function of the Grand Council, which aims to become a "council of state" in the old sense (that is, with the old attributes) but with a much more radical and decisive function' (PN, vol. 3, p. 220). The Grand Council of Fascism, created as supreme body of the National Fascist Party in 1923, was transformed into an institution of the Kingdom of Italy in 1928. Because of this 'institutionalisation', the fascist case is a significant example not only with regard to the identification between the government and the party, but also with regard to the relation between the private sphere (which also includes the parties) and the public sphere in modern dictatorships and, in particular, to the totalising hegemonic dynamics taking place in Gramsci's time. On the 'council of state' mentioned by Gramsci, see Q 6, § 185, p. 830, where he shows how such a council was not always a 'judicial body that deals with administrative affairs' (as it was in Italy), but an institution that supports the executive power in the framework of a 'regime of absolute monarchy or a dictatorship of the Right' (PN, vol. 3, p. 134). In the same note he also states that something similar to the original council of state can be represented in Italy by the senate, since it is 'not elected, not even indirectly' and since it is 'selected by the executive branch from among people who are loyal to the authority of a particular power, in order to stem the spread of democracy and interference by the people' (PN, vol. 3, p. 135). On the fascist structure of state, see Aquarone 1965.
25   Q 13, § 21, p. 1601; SPN, pp. 147–8. The text redrafts Q 4, § 10 and modifies it significantly – cf. Q 4, § 10, p. 432; PN, vol. 2, p. 153: 'In dictatorial states the traditional function of the institution of the Crown is performed by the parties: they are the ones who while representing a class, and only one class, nevertheless maintain an equilibrium with the other allied, unhostile classes and ensure that the development of the represented class takes place with the consent and the assistance of the allied classes'.

order to reconcile and balance their interests, and, above all, to gain the consent of the opposing forces to the actions of the ruling class. In other words, it consists in the creation of a hegemonic relationship that is able to involve (more or less actively) all of the elements of society in the development of a 'shared' socio-political platform.

However, when the task of mediation between the interests of the dominant group and those of the other groups is not carried out by a *super partes* body (the Crown), but by a defined party, both the form and the substance of this arbitration undergo a deep change. In fact, it is evident that, if the exclusive interests of a party are raised to the plane of the interests of society as a whole, the precautions previously adopted to ensure the impartiality of the king or of the president become redundant. Furthermore, in order to establish the primacy of a group, a 'surplus' of domination is required; this surplus is embodied necessarily in the forms of pervasive control of society proper to modernity.

The shared features of monarchical institutions and totalitarian parties are, therefore, not the effective independence of the arbitrator (impossible in one-party regimes, in spite of propaganda efforts). It is rather the 'absolutising' character of the action pursued, namely the fact that the established power relations leave no room for any alternative conception of the world.

> Although every party is the expression of a social group, and of one social group only, nevertheless in certain given conditions certain parties represent a single social group precisely in so far as they exercise a balancing and arbitrating function between the interests of their group and those of other groups, and succeed in securing the development of the group which they represent with the consent and assistance of the allied groups – if not out and out with that of groups which are definitely hostile. The constitutional formula of the king, or president of the republic, who 'reigns but does not govern' is the juridical expression of this function of arbitration, the concern of the constitutional parties not to 'unmask' the Crown or the president. The formulae stating that it is not the head of State who is responsible for the actions of the government, but his ministers, are the casuistry behind which lies the general principle of safeguarding certain conceptions – the unity of the State; the consent of the governed to State action – whatever the current personnel of the government, and whichever party may be in power. With the totalitarian party, these formulae lose their meaning; hence the institutions which functioned within the context of such formulae become less important. But the function itself is incorporated in the party, which will

exalt the abstract concept of the 'State', and seek by various means to give the impression that it is working actively and effectively as an 'impartial force'.²⁶

This final reference to the (merely apparently) 'impartial force' seems to echo expressly Q 9, § 133 redrafted in Q 13, § 27, where Gramsci identifies the 'arbitral' solution with Caesarism.

I will also focus briefly on the functioning of the totalitarian party in this framework.²⁷ First, the 'single, totalitarian, governing party' is a 'party of masses', which, as such, 'have no other political function than a generic loyalty, of a military kind, to a visible or invisible political centre'.²⁸ Likewise, Gramsci adds, 'the visible centre [of this party] is the mechanism of command of forces which are unwilling to show themselves in the open, but only operate indirectly, through proxies and a "proxy ideology"'.²⁹

Moreover, even the struggle within the party, i.e. the contraposition between the different members of the party, can no longer find an explicit expression, for the sake of the unity of the political movement. Thus, these contrasts are 'sublimated' in a contraposition of principles, which, even if it is fought with the weapons of polemics, can nevertheless be resolved definitively only by violence, through the physical elimination of the members of the losing faction (such 'cultural' disputes are therefore extremely important). As Gramsci writes,

> for the functions of such a party are no longer directly political, but merely technical ones of propaganda and public order, and moral and cultural influence, the political function is indirect. For, even if no other legal parties exist, other parties in fact always do exist and other tendencies which cannot be legally coerced; and, against these, polemics are unleashed and struggles are fought as in a game of blind man's buff. In any case it is certain that in such parties cultural functions predominate, which means that political language becomes jargon. In other words, political questions are disguised as cultural ones, and as such become insoluble.³⁰

---

26   Q 13, § 21, pp. 1601–2; SPN, p. 148.
27   On this aspect, see also Antonini 2019a.
28   Q 17, § 37, pp. 1939–40; SPN, p. 150.
29   Q 17, § 37, p. 1940; SPN, p. 150. These observations evoke clearly Gramsci's reflection on the issue of the 'dark forces'.
30   Q 17, § 37, p. 1939; SPN, p. 149.

2   Between Moscow and Rome

2.1   *Progressive or Regressive Authoritarianism?*

If these are the general characteristics of modern Caesarisms, i.e. of single-party systems, it is also necessary to see how they are applied in different historical contexts – notably in fascist Italy and in the USSR.

First, it should be noted that, according to Gramsci, totalitarian phenomena are conceptually twofold: they can be either progressive or regressive (likewise, *mutatis mutandis*, Caesarism). The first type is given when the totalitarian party 'is the bearer of a new culture – this is a progressive phase'; on the contrary, 'when the party in question wants to prevent another force, bearer of a new culture, from becoming itself "totalitarian" – this is a regressive and objectively reactionary phase, even if the reaction (as always) does not admit it and tries to create the impression that it is itself the bearer of a new culture'.[31] These alternative options are clearly expressed in Q 14, § 34 (*Machiavelli. Political Parties and Police Functions*, single draft, January 1933), where Gramsci dwells on the 'police' features of the party in the totalitarian framework:

> Does [the totalitarian party] have a reactionary or a progressive character? Does the given party carry out its policing function in order to conserve an outward, extrinsic order which is a fetter on the vital forces of history; or does it carry it out in the sense of tending to raise the people to a new level of civilisation expressed programmatically in its political and legal order? … The policing function of a party can hence be either progressive or regressive. It is progressive when it tends to keep the dispossessed reactionary forces within the bounds of legality, and to raise the backward masses to the level of the new legality. It is regressive when it tends to hold back the vital forces of history and to maintain a legality which has been superseded, which is antihistorical, which has become extrinsic. Besides, the way in which the party functions provides discriminating criteria. When the party is progressive it functions 'democratically' (democratic centralism); when the party is regressive it functions 'bureaucratically' (bureaucratic centralism).[32]

---

31   Q 6, § 136, p. 800; PN, vol. 3, p. 108.
32   Q 14, § 34, pp. 363–4; SPN, p. 155; on this note, see also Antonini 2019a. The category of 'centralism' (which, historically speaking, describes the centralised organisation of the communist parties) was particularly remarkable in the Italian context, due to the use of the

'Totalitarian' appears, then, as a neutral term in itself, a term that embodies a pure morphological description. The progressive or regressive character of the totalitarian action is the result of the 'cultural' role (broadly conceived) of the party. If regressive, the state defends the interests of the reactionary classes in difficulty and it has a conservative character. If progressive, it supports instead the progressive groups and it plays a supporting role in the construction of a new socio-economic system.

Historically speaking, however, the distinction is not so cut and dried. Gramsci's judgement on both the totalitarian systems of his time is elaborate and many-sided. It cannot be reduced to a simple 'label', despite its conceptual refinement, as in the case of the progressive/regressive totalitarian attitude. Moreover, Gramsci's aim is not simply to establish a mere comparison or contraposition between Italy and Russia. His purpose is, rather, to understand what is really happening in these two 'totalitarian' countries, beyond any superficial analogy or difference between them.

Thus, by relying on a highly developed theoretical apparatus and on a broad historical knowledge, Gramsci investigates the political, social and economic dynamics that characterise the two regimes, providing the (ideal) reader of the *Prison Notebooks* with some valuable reflections both on fascist Italy and on Soviet Russia.

2.2   *Fascist Corporatism*

We can retrace both 'progressive' and 'regressive' elements in fascist Italy as well as in the USSR. Regarding the situation in Italy, Gramsci's reflections on the category of Caesarism have already shown the complexity of his analysis of Mussolini's regime and his multilayered judgement on the socio-political situation in post-war Italy.

The issue of corporatism represents without doubt the most important aspect. As scholarship has demonstrated, Gramsci reflected at length on this major theme of fascist politics, carefully investigating the debate on the topic in Italy and the positions of the main intellectual representatives of this trend (Ugo Spirito (1896–1979), Arnaldo Volpicelli (1892–1968), Massimo Fovel (1880–1941), etc.).[33]

---

expression 'organic centralism' made by Amadeo Bordiga. On Gramsci's account of centralism as well as on the changing meaning of the terms 'democratic', 'organic' and 'bureaucratic', see Cospito 2016, p. 169 ff. In this note from notebook 14, the term 'centralism' is used in a broader sense, in order to describe the different options in the functioning of a political party.

33 Gramsci's interpretation of corporatism has been analysed extensively by scholars. See Rafalski 1988, Maccabelli 2008, Gagliardi 2008 and 2016, Frosini 2011, Santoro 2012. On

After 1932, corporatism appears to Gramsci as a possible further development of the capitalist economic system. It is, indeed, presented as an economic form that is 'able to carry out a deep change without altering the preexisting social hierarchies'.[34] In this perspective, it could also guarantee Fascism a broad consensus among the masses (in particular, among the urban and rural petty bourgeoisie), as well as among the intellectuals. As Gramsci writes,

> the corporative trend, born in strict dependence on such a delicate situation whose essential equilibrium must at all costs be maintained if monstrous catastrophe is to be averted, could yet manage to proceed by very slow and almost imperceptible stages to modify the social structure without violent shocks: even the most tightly swathed baby manages nevertheless to develop and grow.[35]

In this sense, corporativist ideology plays a crucial role. If we interpret corporatism as a form of capitalist rationalisation linked to Fordism and Americanism,[36] it is accorded a leading role by Fascism, as an advanced political element of its war of position.

> The ideological hypothesis could be presented in the following terms: that there is a passive revolution involved in the fact that – through the legislative intervention of the State, and by means of the corporative organisation – relatively far-reaching modifications are being introduced into the country's economic structure in order to accentuate the 'plan of production' element; in other words, that socialisation and co-operation in the sphere of production are being increased, without however touching (or at least not going beyond the regulation and control of) individual and group appropriation of profit. In the concrete framework of Italian social relations, this could be the only solution whereby to develop the product-

---

fascist corporatism, more generally, see Santomassimo 2006 and Gagliardi 2010. On the question of the comparative approach to the topic, see Pasetti 2016, Costa Pinto 2017, Costa Pinto and Finchelstein 2018; see also Steffek and Antonini 2015.

34 Gagliardi 2008, p. 637. From this perspective, see also the telling metaphor used by Gramsci to conclude Q 1, § 135, then redrafted in Q 22, § 6 (cf. the following quotation).
35 Q 22, § 6, p. 2158; SPN, p. 294.
36 However, such an assumption is not entirely problem-free, as Gagliardi 2008 underlines.

ive forces of industry under the direction of the traditional ruling classes, in competition with the more advanced industrial formations of countries which monopolise raw materials and have accumulated massive capital sums. Whether or not such a schema could be put into practice, and to what extent, is only of relative importance. What is important from the political and ideological point of view is that it is capable of creating – and indeed does create – a period of expectation and hope, especially in certain Italian social groups such as the great mass of urban and rural petit bourgeois. It thus reinforces the hegemonic system and the forces of military and civil coercion at the disposal of the traditional ruling classes. This ideology thus serves as an element of a 'war of position' in the international economic field (free competition and free exchange here corresponding to the war of movement), just as 'passive revolution' does in the political field.[37]

However, Gramsci is aware that the practical achievements of corporatism are far more problematic and difficult to evaluate, due in part to their historical 'incompleteness'.[38] At the same time, he recognises that 'the corporative trend did not originate from the need for changes in the technical conditions of industry, or even from that of a new economic policy, but rather from the need for economic policing, a need which was aggravated by the 1929 crisis which is still going on'.[39] Such a reflection clearly expresses Gramsci's scepticism about fascist corporatism; more generally, it manifests his doubts about the 'progressive' elements embedded in Italian Fascism, by revealing a more complex judgement on Mussolini's dictatorship as a whole.[40]

2.3   'Statolatry' and the 'Return' of the Economic-Corporative Phase

The coexistence of different elements of judgement is perhaps even more evident in the case of the USSR. If, on the one hand, communist rule in Russia represented the first and greatest success of the workers' movement, on the other hand, there were a few aspects of the new Soviet state about which Gramsci is, so to speak, more 'concerned'.

---

37   Q 10, I, § 9, pp. 1228–9; SPN, pp. 119–20.
38   On the troubled issue of the 'failed' realisation of Italian corporatism, see, for instance, Baker 2006 and Gagliardi 2016b.
39   Q 22, § 6, p. 2156; SPN, p. 292. 'Economic policing' is a translation of Gramsci's notable expression 'polizia economica', where the reference to the police clearly hints at the coercive character of 1930s politics.
40   See, on this point, for instance, Gagliardi 2016a.

This is, of course, a tricky question for Gramsci's readers.[41] Here I will limit myself to a (necessarily brief) analysis of some aspects of his account of the USSR that highlight the complexity of Gramsci's judgement and that relate (more or less directly) to the issues evoked by the categories of Caesarism and Bonapartism.

In this regard, I will focus first on Gramsci's observations on the theme of 'statolatry'.[42] Gramsci uses the term in the *Prison Notebooks* to describe a situation in which the state and the civil society are identified with each other, and where the state is an 'element of active culture' which shapes society according to its own image.[43] Statolatry usually characterises a political system in its early stages, since it represents the 'initiation into autonomous state life and into the creation of a "civil society", which historically could not be created before the ascent to independent state life'.[44] However, Gramsci also adds that statolatry 'must be criticized, precisely in order for it to develop and to produce new forms of state life in which individual and group initiative has a "state" character even if it is not indebted to the "official government" (makes state life

---

41 The topicality of the theme notwithstanding, Gramsci's interpretation of Soviet Russia in the *Prison Notebooks* still requires in-depth investigation by scholars in all its facets. In fact, despite the number of articles dedicated to Gramsci's relations with the Italian Communist Party and the Comintern, a thorough analysis of his interpretation in the prison writings is still absent (Benvenuti and Pons 1999, despite being the main contribution on the topic, cannot be considered an exhaustive study; see also, more recently, Pons 2017, which is, however, mostly a survey of Gramsci's notes about Soviet Russia). The cause may be connected to the fact that it is very difficult (or even impossible) to separate Gramsci's interpretation of the events taking place in Russia from his more general theoretical and historical reflections, as well as from his political 'faith' (but see also the thesis about Gramsci's 'Aesopic' language – see Caprioglio 1991 and Thomas 2009, pp. 102 ff.). On this basis, for instance, the different opinions about the adoption of the category of Caesarism can be explained in relation to Gramsci's account of the USSR (while, e.g., De Felice 1977, pp. 109–10, clearly states that the concept of Caesarism is not adequate to explain the complex dynamics in Russia, according to Vacca 1988, pp. 137–8, this interpretation is possible; moreover, Martelli 1995 and 1999, while discussing Gramsci's account of Soviet Russia, focuses only on the category of Bonapartism, without taking into account the role of the concept of Caesarism).
42 On so-called 'statolatry', see the entry by G. Liguori in Liguori and Voza 2009, pp. 806–7. Gramsci's reflections on this category should be linked to his analysis of the nature of the state, and its relation to society (see Liguori 2015 and Cospito 2016).
43 Q 8, § 130, p. 1020; PN, vol. 3, p. 310. Besides Q 8, § 130 (a note in which Gramsci specifically investigates the concept of 'statolatry'), the term appears also in Q 8, § 142, where Gramsci explicitly hints at § 130. It should be noted that this reflection is closely connected to the development of Gramsci's reasoning on political and civil society in notebooks 5–8.
44 Q 8, § 130, p. 1020; PN, vol. 3, p. 310.

"spontaneous")'.[45] Gramsci is here alluding to the process of the establishment of hegemony, as widely thematised in his prison writings.

An analogous reflection is developed by Gramsci with regard to the concept of the 'economic-corporative'.[46] This adjective describes the initial phase of the rule of a class over society, when the dominating social group carries forward its own partial interests and it does not yet involve the entirety of civil society in its hegemonic project, which implies a 'necessary' use of coercion and violence.[47] In other words, this is a first step in the process of creation of a 'collective political consciousness', as he affirms in the famous §17 of notebook 13, *Analysis of Situation. Relations of force*.[48] Thus, the economic-corporative stage also has to be overcome (or 'criticised') in order to establish a real hegemony over society.

However, real trends are not always so linear and straightforward. In fact, Gramsci observes that contemporary one-state systems are characterised by a 'return' to the economic-corporative stage and to statolatry, since they display the close interpenetration between the private and public dimensions that was typical of the first phases of pre-modern societies (see also, from this perspective, the previous reflections on the 'returning primitivism'). We can see this, for instance, in Q 6, §88 (*Gendarme or Night-watchman State, etc. [Stato gendarme – guardiano notturno, ecc.]*, single draft, March–August 1931): Gramsci evokes the 'representation of the economic-corporative form – in other words, of the confusion between civil society and political society', where the term 'representation' has to be understood as 'recurrence'.[49]

It is clear, however, that the revival of these dynamics has a completely different meaning in the present-day political situation. In the fascist context, this return responds to the need to reaffirm the interests of the dominant group in the context of the organic crisis of the post-war period. Therefore, it is an explicitly 'conservative' dynamic. In the case of the USSR, the evaluation of this phenomenon is more problematic, inasmuch as it is connected to the issue of the

---

45 Q 8, §130, pp. 1020–1; PN, vol. 3, pp. 310–11.
46 On the topic, see the entry *Economico-corporativo* by G. Cospito in Liguori and Voza 2009, pp. 255–8.
47 Regarding the use of violence and coercion, see, for instance Q 5, §123, p. 647, where, while talking about the economic-corporative rule of the Italian bourgeoisie in the Medieval Communes (the main historical example of Gramsci's analysis of the category of 'economic-corporative'), Gramsci describes it as a government of the 'common people with raw violence' (PN, vol. 2, p. 370). On the term 'violence' in Gramsci's thought, see Jackson 2018.
48 On this crucial text of the *Prison Notebooks*, see, among others, Cospito 2016.
49 Q 6, §88, p. 763; PN, vol. 3, p. 75. In Italian the expression is unambiguous: '*ripresentarsi della forma corporativa-economica*'.

state as *veilleur de nuit* and, as a consequence, to Gramsci's reflections on the Marxist *Leitmotiv* of the 'withering away of the state' and the advent of what Gramsci calls the 'regulated society'.[50]

As he writes in Q 8, §130 (*Encyclopedic Notions and Cultural Topics. Statolatry* [*Nozioni enciclopediche e argomenti di cultura. Statolatria*], single draft, April 1932), indeed, 'some social groups rose to autonomous state life without first having had an extended period of independent cultural and moral development of their own ...; for such social groups, a period of statolatry is necessary and indeed appropriate' (Gramsci is here clearly hinting at the situation in the USSR).[51] However, 'this kind of "statolatry" must not be abandoned to itself; above all, it must not become theoretical fanaticism or come to be seen as "perpetual"'.[52]

Of course, Gramsci is not criticising the establishment of the Soviet state. However, his words sound like an invitation to overcome the mere external or formal 'adjustment' of the masses to the new political, social and productive system (this adjustment is unavoidable, given the 'premises' of the Russian revolution) and to develop, as quickly as possible, a form of hegemony that will lead to the establishment of fully realised socialism. Therefore, Gramsci is warning against the dangers of 'static' situations and of the 'lack' of revolutionary pressure.

---

50   On this theme, see in particular Q 6, §88, where Gramsci dwells on the 'conception of the state as gendarme–night watchman'. Gramsci writes: 'Isn't the conception of the state as gendarme–night watchman, etc. (setting aside the polemical nature of the terms: gendarme, night watchman, etc.), after all, the only conception of the state that goes beyond the ultimate stages of "economic-corporativism"?' (Q 6, §88, p. 763; PN, vol. 3, p. 75). And, he adds: 'In the theory of state → regulated society (from a phase in which state equals government to a phase in which state is identified with civil society), there must be a transition phase of state as night watchman, that is, of a coercive organization that will protect the development of those elements of regulated society that are continually on the rise and, precisely because they are on the rise, will gradually reduce the state's authoritarian and coercive interventions' (Q 6, §88, p. 764; PN, vol. 3, pp. 75–6). To sum up, Gramsci is sketching here a precise development, which should describe the evolution of the Soviet regime: 1) 'ultimate stages of "economic-corporativism"', i.e. 'returning' statolatry; 2) state as night watchman; 3) withering away of the state/regulated society. On the complex issue of the state *veilleur de nuit*, see the entry *Stato guardiano notturno* (by G. Liguori) in Liguori and Voza 2009, p. 806. On Gramsci's 'regulated society', see Cospito 2016, pp. 91ff.

51   Q 8, §130, p. 1020; PN, vol. 3, p. 310.

52   Q 8, §130, p. 1020; PN, vol. 3, p. 310.

2.4   Trotsky, Bonapartism and Napoleonism

With this framework in mind, the importance of Gramsci's aforementioned observations on industrialism, animalism and Bonapartism stands out more clearly. They contain an implicit, although unequivocal, reference to Trotsky. These texts raise a number of issues (which relate not only to Gramsci's judgement on Trotsky but, more generally, on political developments in Soviet Russia) that are extremely complex and still highly debated. An adequate treatment would require a more detailed analysis, which, for obvious reasons, I cannot provide here. However, I can note some significant features, which shed some light on Gramsci's reflection on the Caesarist-Bonapartist model as a whole.

In particular, I will focus briefly on Gramsci's rewriting of the first draft texts (Q 1, §158 and Q 4, §52) in notebook 22 (§§10, 11 and 12, the last two deriving from the splitting of §52 of notebook 4). In the first place, it is noteworthy that Gramsci decides to redraft the notes in the 'special' notebook dedicated to Americanism and Fordism. This element emphasises the close relationship between the question of the contemporary dynamics of production and consumption and the theme of political hegemony – the mediation is represented here by his observations on the topics of 'animalism', 'puritanism' and the 'crisis of liberalism' (and also sexual behaviour), that introduce some ideological aspects of great importance. Thus, such a reading of the categories of Taylorism and 'rationalisation' plays an important role in the framework of a comparison between liberalism and socialism, between America and the USSR, since it problematises the construction of a socialist economy (and, as a consequence, of a socialist society) in the Soviet Union, by highlighting its difficulties and 'contradictions'.

Regarding the form of the second drafts, both the number and the relevance of the changes made by Gramsci and the connection now established between the two first draft texts are significant. The resulting group of notes (Q 22, §§10, 11 and 12)[53] represents a much more impressive reflection on the topic than the one that emerges from the first draft texts (the division into three separate paragraphs is functional to a better exposition of the subject).[54] Far from

---

53   Q 22, §10, 'Animality' and Industrialism ['Animalità' e industrialismo]; Q 22, §11, Rationalisation of Production and Work [Razionalizzazione della produzione e del lavoro]; Q 22, §12, Taylorism and Mechanisation of the Worker [Taylorismo e meccanizzazione del lavoratore]. All texts were written in the second half of 1934.

54   Something similar also happened with the second draft notes on Caesarism in notebook 13.

diminishing the sharpness of the single notes, their synergy is very effective and the consistency and continuity of the argumentation stands out.[55]

With regard to the specific changes made by Gramsci, the most relevant is no doubt the addition about the 'function of the *élites*'[56] in a one-party context, in which 'the working masses are no longer subject to coercive pressure from a superior class'.[57] By underlining the importance of the leading groups for the realisation of a form of class self-discipline and for the internalisation of a new type of morality ('Alfieri tying himself to the chair'),[58] he points the finger of suspicion at those groups which were incapable of realising their 'historical task'.[59] He blames, therefore, the 'totalitarian social hypocrisy' that results from it.[60]

It seems to me that such affirmations echo and expand his observations on the 'imbalance between theory and practice' that characterises Trotsky's attitude, as he writes in Q 4, §52, *Americanism and Fordism* (and, again, in Q 22, §11, *Rationalisation of Production and Work*), on which basis Gramsci defines Trotsky as a 'Bonapartist'.[61] I would argue that, in a certain sense, in notebook 22 Gramsci develops his critique of Trotsky, contained in the texts of notebooks 1 and 4, and makes it more general.[62] He does this in order to warn against undue transformations of the economic and social system, and against the risks of an involution of the USSR in a bureaucratic sense (where the adjective 'bureaucratic' has to be conceived in the broader sense previously explained).[63]

Taking their cue from these sentences by Gramsci, Benvenuti and Pons have claimed that in these notes Trotsky would act as a substitute, as a 'screen-figure'

---

55 R. Caputo, in Liguori and Voza 2009, p. 853, has stated that the elimination of the explicit reference to Bonapartism in Q 22, §10 mitigates the critical character of Gramsci's notes. I disagree with Caputo's analysis (based on the exclusive comparison between Q 1, §158 and Q 22, §10). The removal of the reference to Bonapartism in §10 of notebook 22 is due to the 'new' closeness of Q 1, §158 and Q 4, §52, i.e. to the fact that the category of Bonapartism is at stake in Q 22, §11. The reason for the elimination of the first occurrence is therefore simply formal.
56 Q 22, §10, p. 2163; SPN, p. 301.
57 Q 22, §10, p. 2163; SPN, p. 300.
58 Q 22, §10, p. 2163; SPN, p. 300. Gramsci is hinting here at a famous episode in the life of the poet Vittorio Alfieri (1749–1803), who asked his servant to bind him to the chair in order to force him to complete a work.
59 Q 22, §10, p. 2164; SPN, p. 301.
60 Q 22, §10, p. 2163; SPN, p. 300.
61 Q 4, 52, p. 489; PN, vol. 2, p. 216 (Q 22, §11, p. 2164).
62 See Chapter 7, section 2.2.
63 See Chapter 7, section 4 and Chapter 11, section 3.3.

for the Gramscian critique of the Stalinist USSR.[64] Consequently, these scholars also claim that, while criticising the proposal to create a 'labour army' put forward by Trotsky in 1921, the Soviet policies of the 1930s represent Gramsci's real polemical objective. Thus, he is seen to be alluding to the liquidation of the New Economic Policy (NEP) and the activation of the five-year plans, but, also, on a more general level, to the increasingly openly autocratic character of Stalin's government.[65]

To interpret Gramsci's discussion as a 'coded' critique of the developments in the USSR in the 1930s (as much as he could know them) is a fascinating option, which seems to be supported by various elements – textual, but also, more generally, historical and political. It is well established that he had disagreements with the Soviet leadership on significant points, even if always in the context of membership of a unitary international communist movement.[66] In my opinion, however, it is hard to draw any definitive conclusions about his direct or indirect polemical targets. Not only should we keep in mind that, in the *Prison Notebooks*, Gramsci refers frequently to much more distant events and facts,[67] but also, especially, that there are multiple layers of reading in Gramsci's notes, whose 'validity' goes beyond contemporary polemics. Thus, it is perhaps more fruitful to stress the many-sidedness of Gramsci's reflections on the establishment of Socialism in Russia and, therefore, the richness of the conceptual 'set of tools' elaborated by him to understand this situation.

This includes, first of all, the category of Bonapartism, whose two meanings (Bonapartism as Cadornism, i.e. 'militaristic' rule of the masses; Bonapartism as a reflection on the themes of bureaucracy and state apparatuses) seem to be somehow 'subsumed' in these notes of notebook 22, written after Gramsci had fully developed his reflections on the totalitarian tendencies of modern

---

64 See Benvenuti and Pons 1999; they assert that the reference to the 'foreign invasion' contained in Q1, §158 is to be understood as a reference to the 'Stalinist arguments put forward since the summer of 1927 (but with significant precedents in 1925–26 in support of an industrialisation of the USSR for military defence)' (p. 98). On this point, see also Cospito 2016, p. 209, n. 7.

65 See Benvenuti and Pons 1999, p. 99 *et passim*. In a similar vein (albeit with a more 'nuanced' judgement), see now also Pons 2017.

66 See Benvenuti and Pons 1999. From this perspective, we should also remember Gramsci's 'critical' attitude towards the USSR before his imprisonment. On this point, see Pons 2008 and 2017, pp. 908 ff. On Gramsci's relationship to Moscow in prison, see Rossi and Vacca 2007, Vacca 2012 and Rossi 2017. On these themes, see also Francioni 2020.

67 For example, episodes from Italian and European history from the beginning of the century, or his pre-prison reading.

politics.⁶⁸ Moreover, as regards the historical aspect of the issue, it is interesting to note that in Q 22, § 10 Gramsci refers to Oliver Cromwell (1599–1658), who is one of the examples of Caesarism mentioned (the reference is a new addition to the second draft of the text).⁶⁹

From this perspective, we should recall also a famous note from the *Notebooks*, the only one in which Gramsci refers explicitly to Stalin (1878–1953), Q 14, § 68 (*Machiavelli*).⁷⁰ In this paragraph, by questioning how 'the international situation should be considered in its national aspect',⁷¹ Gramsci focuses on the wait-and-see policy that has characterised the workers' movement for a long time. The result of this situation, among other things, is 'an anachronistic and anti-natural form of "Napoleonism"'.⁷² And he adds: 'The theoretical weaknesses of this modern form of the old mechanicism are masked by the general theory of permanent revolution, which is nothing but a generic forecast presented as a dogma, and which demolishes itself by not in fact coming true'.⁷³

The category of 'Napoleonism', which is used by Gramsci only twice (the first time in Q 1, § 150), is doubly interesting in this context.⁷⁴ On the one hand, because the category is inspired by the figure of Napoleon Bonaparte, it fits very well, alongside Cromwell and Trotsky, into Gramsci's list of examples of 'coercive' political leadership. He is thus playing a fascinating game of mirrors

---

68   Chronologically speaking, notebook 22 dates to the second half of 1934, after July–August (see Cospito 2011a). Although Gramsci does not mention these issues explicitly, the rewriting of Q 1, § 158 and Q 4, § 52 in notebook 22 is influenced by his reflections on the new features of modern politics and on its totalising dimension, in which bureaucracy plays a pivotal role (on these themes, see Antonini 2019a).

69   In addition to the citations related the issue of Caesarism in Q 9, § 133 and Q 13, § 27, Oliver Cromwell is mentioned only three other times in the *Prison Notebooks*. Besides Q 22, § 10, the other two occurrences are contained in Q 1, § 44 and in its second draft text, Q 19, § 24, where Gramsci refers to Cromwell's Jacobinism *ante litteram*.

70   Here, Stalin is called '*Giuseppe Bessarione*' (Q 14, § 68, p. 1728 – in the English translation: 'Joseph Vissarionovitch'; SPN, p. 240). Gramsci uses this name due to prison censorship (on Gramsci's 'precautions', see Cospito 2015 and Frosini 2015). For the same reasons he refers to Trotsky as '*Leone Davidovi*' (Q 14, § 68, p. 1729; 'Leo Davidovitch'; SPN, p. 240).

71   Q 14, § 68, p. 1729; SPN, p. 240.

72   Q 14, § 68, p. 1730; SPN, p. 241.

73   Q 14, § 68, p. 1730; SPN, p. 241. As Peter Thomas stresses (*per litteras*), this judgement of Trotsky's theory of permanent revolution is taken almost *verbatim* from Bukharin's critique of *The Lessons of October* by Trotsky (October 1924). On Trotsky's text and on the 'literary dispute', see Corney 2015. In general, Gramsci's discussion of the category of permanent revolution in the *Prison Notebooks* is deeply shaped by that debate, and especially by Bukharin's intervention.

74   See Chapter 7, section 2.2.

between historical epochs. On the other hand, it is of interest because Napoleonism is connected with Gramsci's reflections on the categories of Bonapartism and Cadornism. It is clear, however, that its usage at this stage (Q 14, § 68 was written in February 1933) has a deeper meaning: while it evokes his reflections on statolatry and on the transformation of hegemony previously analysed, the direct reference to Stalin and to the Soviet reality makes Gramsci's observations even more urgent and dramatic.

3   'Alternative Modernities'

3.1   *Black Parliamentarism, Critique and Self-critique*

A further important aspect of the transformations that characterise the post-war political situation is the crisis of the representative principle and, therefore, of parliamentarism. Gramsci investigates this theme at length, connecting this crisis with the failure of nineteenth-century liberal states, and, more generally, with the collapse of liberalism.[75] He also focuses on the 'transformations' of parliamentarism itself, by analysing so-called 'black parliamentarism'. This concept occurs in only two notes, §§ 74 and 76 of notebook 14 (written by February 1933), and it represents, in a certain sense, a unique point in Gramsci's thought.[76]

Likewise, Q 14, §§ 74 and 76 are 'unique' texts, due to formal and thematic reasons. § 76 is an explicit continuation of § 74 and, at the same time, §§ 74 and 76 are part of a broader group of notes, which includes § 75 and § 77.[77] The two paragraphs deal in an unusually explicit (but also very complex) way with the opposing totalitarian regimes, fascist Italy and USSR.[78]

---

75 See, for instance, Q 10 II, § 41 xii, where Gramsci speaks about the 'breakdown of parliamentarism' (FSPN, p. 398), or Q 15, §§ 47 and 48, in which Gramsci discusses the debate about the 'end of parliamentarism', raised by Sergio Panunzio (1886–1944) in the fascist journal *Gerarchia* in April 1933. On this theme, see also Frosini 2011.

76 On this category, see Sotgiu 1987, pp. 115 ff., Benvenuti and Pons, 1999, pp. 103–4, Saccarelli 2008, pp. 81–2, the entries *Parlamentarismo nero* (by L. La Porta, pp. 613–14) and *Corporativismo* (by A. Gagliardi, pp. 163–6) in Liguori and Voza 2009, Frosini 2011, p. 35, Cospito 2016, pp. 74–5 and 89, Gagliardi 2017, pp. 1033–4, Pons 2017, pp. 924–5. On the chronology of Q 14, §§ 74 and 76, see Francioni 2020.

77 In fact, § 76 starts with a parenthesis in which Gramsci writes: '(it continues the second-to-last paragraph)' (Q 14 § 76, p. 1744 – in the English edition of these notes (SPN, pp. 256–7), the text is given in a continuous way). On the non-linearity of §§ 74 and 76, see QAnast, vol. 16, pp. 2–3.

78 The texts are also interesting from a linguistic point of view. Gramsci's statements are here 'raw' (so to speak) and elliptical, sometimes almost aphoristic – this is due, at least

Q 14, § 74, entitled *Self-criticism and the Hypocrisy of Self-criticism* [*L'autocritica e l'ipocrisia dell'autocritica*], opens with a reflection on the political value of self-criticism in single-party regimes:[79] 'The stated claim is that an equivalent has been found to the criticism represented by the "free" political struggle of a representative system'.[80] However, self-criticism often reveals itself as a purely superficial and rhetorical solution (cf. in this sense the 'totalitarian social hypocrisy' of Q 22, §10).[81] As Gramsci writes, 'in reality it has turned out that self-criticism offers an opportunity for fine speeches and pointless declarations, and for nothing else; self-criticism has been "parliamentarised"'.[82]

First, Gramsci establishes a connection between the category of self-criticism, its absence and his analysis of Cadornism in the *Prison Notebooks*.[83] However, a 'lack' of self-criticism is very different from the 'hypocritical' self-criticism depicted here – the obvious difference lies in the fact that the latter is aware of its falseness, although it does not admit it (and, therefore, is worse than the former). The reference to parliamentarism as a manifestation of this hypocrisy of political life is even more relevant.

The category of parliamentarism is understood here in a broad sense (as becomes clear from Gramsci's argument), as the existence of different and conflicting interests within a political community. In other words, it is the expression of individualistic and capitalistic tendencies (where individualism is the 'content', and parliamentarism represents the '"pure" form').[84]

It is evident that, in a one-party regime that aims to overcome these specific features of liberal state, the abolition of parliamentarism is a necessity.

---

partially, to Gramsci's worsening health condition, but also (I would argue) to the intrinsic complexity of the topic.

[79] It is well known that self-criticism was a 'common practice' in the USSR; see in this regard Stalin's speech of April 1928, *Against Vulgarising the Slogan of Self-Criticism* (on this point, see also SPN, pp. 254–5, n. 56). For an historical and political analysis of the phenomenon in Russia, see McLoughlin and McDermott 2003, pp. 181 ff., Pons 2014, *passim* and Pons and Smith 2017, *passim*.

[80] Q 14, § 74, p. 1742; SPN, pp. 254–5.

[81] Q 22, §10, p. 2163; SPN, p. 300.

[82] Q 14, § 74, p. 1742; SPN, p. 255.

[83] Indeed, in the rest of the *Notebooks*, the category of 'self-criticism' is mostly evoked in relation to its absence, with particular reference to the figure of Cadorna and to the political class that he represents (see Q 6, § 74, p. 742; PN, vol. 3, p. 56: 'absence of self-criticism' – in this context, the defeat of Caporetto is described as the effect of the 'misunderstanding' of the condition of Italy, and, more specifically, of the Italian army – see also Q 2, §121). This reference is even more interesting if we consider the connection between the categories of Cadornism, Bonapartism, and Napoleonism which I dealt with in the previous section.

[84] Q 14, § 74, p. 1742; SPN, p. 255.

However, the suppression of the institutional 'form' does not imply the supersession of its 'content'. Even under totalitarian forms of domination, a variety of interests continue to exist and, consequently, a kind of parliamentarism survives. Gramsci defines this odd phenomenon as 'black parliamentarism', drawing an analogy with the 'black market' and the clandestine *lotto*:[85] 'The entire subject needs re-examining, especially with respect to the "implicit" party system and parliamentarism, i.e. that which functions like "black markets" and "illegal lotteries" where and when the official market and the State lottery are for some reason kept closed'.[86]

In any case, this characterisation of a 'dark' form of parliamentarism does not imply an inevitably regressive phenomenon. According to Gramsci, black parliamentarism 'is a function of present historical necessities, is "a progress" in its way, that the return to traditional "parliamentarism" would be an antihistorical regression, since even where this "functions" publicly, the effective parliamentarism is the "black" one'.[87]

To point out the differences between the old type of absolutism and contemporary regimes, Gramsci introduces the theme of hegemony (by alluding to its different nature in the present-day situation). He refers specifically to Fascism and mentions the corporative ideology explicitly, which is the core of a fascist 'progress'.[88] Gramsci's reflections on the fascist regime continue in § 76 (cf. what I said about the connection between the two texts).[89] However, Gramsci also specifies the contingent and non-structural character of Fascism, which is 'lasting' but does not 'constitut[e] an epoch'.[90]

---

85 The *lotto* is a type of lottery widespread in Italy (right up to the present) which is regulated by the state; Gramsci is referring here to illegal sessions, and thus establishing a meaningful parallel with the black market.

86 Q 14, § 74, p. 1743; SPN, p. 255. On the question of the transition from constitutional to dictatorial regimes, and on the legal appeals offered by the constitutions of the early twentieth century, see also Q 14, § 11.

87 Q 14, § 74, p. 1743; SPN, p. 255.

88 Cf. Q 14, § 74, p. 1743; SPN, pp. 255–6: 'Theoretically it seems to me that one can explain the phenomenon with the concept of "hegemony", with a return to "corporativism" – not in the *ancien régime* sense, but in the modern sense of the word, in which the "corporation" cannot have closed and exclusivistic limits as was the case in the past. Today it is corporativism of "social function", without hereditary or any other restriction'.

89 In § 76 Mussolini's dictatorship is not directly mentioned, but is alluded to indirectly by the reference to the figure of Cesare (Cesarino) Rossi (1887–1967), one of the first members of the fascist movement, who was removed by Mussolini in 1921 because of his 'forecast' of the defeat of the fascist regime.

90 On this topic, see Chapter 9, section 3 (the meaning of these categories has already been explained by Gramsci in Q 14, § 23).

3.2   The Legal-Real Opposition and the Image of the Barometer

Taking his cue from these sketched observations, Gramsci reflects on the more general meaning of 'black parliamentarism', both in a theoretical and in a historico-political sense. His reference to the 'liquidation of Leone Davidovi'[91] as an example of the 'liquidation "also" of the "black" parliamentarism which existed after the abolition of the "legal" parliament', in particular, is extremely important. Gramsci summarises the conceptual core of the problem of black parliamentarism with the distinction between 'real fact' and 'legal fact'.[92]

This conceptual couple has a long history in Italian political debate. It refers, originally, to the opposition of clericals to national politics during the *Risorgimento*. Deriving from Stefano Jacini's opposition between '*legal Italy*' [*Italia legale*] and '*real Italy*' [*Italia reale*], the historical development of these terms emerges from numerous notes in the *Notebooks*.[93] It is without doubt that in the following note Gramsci is using the categories in a much broader sense and in an 'up-to-date' perspective, by looking at the contemporary political situation:[94]

---

91   On the 'liquidation of Leone Davidovi', see Francioni 2020. The term 'liquidation' (in Italian: '*liquidazione*') has either a (common) economic meaning or a political meaning (political defeat) throughout the *Notebooks*. It should not be read as the 'physical destruction' (assassination) of Trotsky.

92   Cf. Q 14, § 76, p. 1744; SPN, p. 256. This passage of Q 14, § 76 represents a development of what was already said on the 'lasting'/'constituting an epoch' couple in another note of the same notebook (§ 23).

93   The opposition between 'real' and 'legal' Italy was coined by Stefano Jacini (1826–91), Italian economist and liberal politician. In the text entitled *On the Conditions of Public Affairs in Italy After 1866* [*Sulle condizioni della cosa pubblica in Italia dopo il 1866*], he distinguishes between the nation as a whole (real Italy) and the small part of the population that has political rights and that rules the country (legal Italy) – see Jacini 1870. On this conceptual couple and its various interpretations, see Berselli 1965, pp. 36–70, Davis 1988, pp. 262–3 *et passim*; with specific reference to Gramsci, see QNaz, vol. 1, p. 398 *et passim*. The distinction between real and legal fact is defined by Gramsci in Q 1, § 130, p. 117 (later redrafted in Q 19, § 31), as the 'formula contrived by the clericals after 1870 to direct attention to the national political uneasiness', a formula that he defines as 'felicitous because there existed a clear disjunction between the State (legality) and civil society (reality)' (PN, vol. 1, p. 214). On the real/legal couple in the Italian *Risorgimento*, see also Q 2, § 22; Q 7, § 103; Q 13, § 18. See in particular this last note, where, while speaking about the political abstentionism of the Catholic Church before 1919, Gramsci states that 'the organic distinction which the clericals made between the real Italy and the legal Italy was a reproduction of the distinction between economic world and politico-legal world' (Q 13, § 18, p. 1591; SPN, p. 161).

94   I would argue that a role in this broadening of the categories might have been played by the way in which Marx reflects on institutional legality and on its breakdown in his historical works. On this issue, see Chapter 5, section 3.

System of forces in unstable equilibrium which find on the parliamentary terrain the 'legal' terrain of their 'more economic' equilibrium; and abolition of this legal terrain, because it becomes a source of organisation and of reawakening of latent and slumbering social forces. Hence this abolition is a symptom (and prediction) of intensifications of struggles and not vice versa. When a struggle can be resolved legally, it is certainly not dangerous; it becomes so precisely when the legal equilibrium is recognised to be impossible.[95]

Although synthetic, these affirmations are of distinct interest. First, Gramsci is hinting at the logic of the 'potential' of the latent forces that ward off a Caesarist solution, as already developed in Q 14, § 23. Capitalising on this, he makes a further step: he affirms that the abolition of the 'legal' terrain of struggle shows the 'intensifications of struggles and not vice versa'.[96] At this stage, society is not simply venturing on a dangerous path; the class struggle has already reached its highest and most decisive point – in other words, the perspective is 'catastrophic'.

The conclusion of the note represents a succint but extremely powerful metaphor, that of the barometer and the bad weather: '(Which does not mean that by abolishing the barometer one can abolish bad weather)'.[97] Scholars have discussed the meaning of this image.[98] Even if there is no doubt that Gramsci is referring to the episode of the 'liquidation' of Trotsky by Stalin in Q 14, § 77 (*Past*

---

[95] Q 14, § 76, p. 1744; SPN, pp. 256–7. From this perspective, it is worth remembering that Gramsci had already applied the couple 'real-legal' to twentieth-century politics in § 130 of notebook 1 (see Q 1, § 130, p. 118; PN, vol. 1, p. 215): 'The question (about real and legal Italy) persists, but on a higher political and historical plane – hence the events of 1924–26 up to the suppression of all the parties and the affirmation of an achieved identity between real and legal, because "civil society" in all its forms is dominated by a single State organization, a party organization'.

[96] Q 14, § 76, p. 1744; SPN, p. 256.

[97] Q 14, § 76, p. 1744; SPN, p. 257.

[98] Scholarship has traditionally identified Trotsky with the barometer. Moreover, some scholars have seen in this image a polemical ('Aesopic') reference to Stalin's regime. Saccarelli has suggested the existence of a parallel between Trotsky's use of the image of the barometer and Gramsci's metaphor in the *Prison Notebooks* (see Saccarelli 2008, p. 266; as regards his interpretation of Q 14, § 74 and 76, see pp. 81–2). Frosini (*per litteras*) puts forward a radically different reading of this image – he suggests that the sentence on the abolition of the barometer is a reference to the failure of the *costituente* (which, in Gramsci's mind, is a gathering of the anti-fascist forces aiming to overthrow Mussolini's regime; on this issue, see the entry by G. Cospito in Liguori and Voza 2009, p. 173, Vacca 2012, Frosini 2018 – some hints are also contained in Thomas 2017b).

and Present),⁹⁹ I would argue that the image of the barometer does not have to be read either as a reference to Trotsky or as a reference to Stalin's authoritarian rule. I would rather interpret it in a more general way, as the '*résumé*' of the entire logic of black parliamentarism developed in these notes.

To sum up, Gramsci is reflecting in Q 14, §§ 74 and 76 on two distinct levels. On the one hand, he is dwelling on the abolition of legal parliamentarism and, hence, on the establishment of black parliamentarism, as a 'symptom' of the intensification of class struggles (from this perspective, fascist Italy embodies closely this transformation). On the other hand, he is explaining the expulsion of Trotsky as the manifestation of the abolition of black parliamentarism in the USSR. Both abolitions are therefore 'progressive', insofar as they are the result of an historico-political 'necessity'. In spite of their obvious differences, both fascist Italy and the USSR are in fact manifestations of the new 'totalitarian' features that characterise the contemporary landscape.

In the fascist context, the different existing interests are represented above all by the corporations. However, it is the whole system that stresses the effort of Fascism to reshape Italian society. In this respect, corporatism, as a 'new economic policy', plays a pivotal role. Regarding the USSR, the 'clash' between different ideas and positions is suppressed even within the Communist Party (cf. the expulsion of Trotsky), since the class struggle is here violently 'demanding', i.e. it requires extreme actions. It does not imply, though, a negative judgement on the process of the establishment of Socialism in Russia as a whole but, rather, an acute awareness of the complexity and of the 'demands' of this process (and of the dangers of a bureaucratic-authoritarian regression of the Soviet regime).

From this perspective, it is noteworthy that Gramsci deals with Fascism and Socialism in the very same notes, constantly interweaving references to the two opposing one-party systems (cf. for instance: self-criticism, USSR; corporatism, fascist Italy; 'liquidation' of Trotsky, USSR; abolition of legal parliamentarism, fascist Italy). Indeed, alongside Americanism (also evoked in Q 22, §§ 10–12 and in their first draft texts), they represent the 'alternative modernities' on which Gramsci focuses in the *Prison Notebooks*. With this, he reaches the highest point of his carceral political reflection.¹⁰⁰

---

99   See the beginning of this meaningful but very complicated note: 'The fact is often observed as an inconsistency and a symptom of how politics itself perverts souls, that after a political split "one discovers" against the defector [*transfuga*] or the traitor a bunch of wrongdoings that previously seemed to be ignored. But the question is not so simple' (Q 14, § 77, p. 1745).

100 The expression 'alternative modernities' is taken from the title of a recent book by

4 'Caesarism without a Caesar' and the Issue of the Modern Prince

4.1 *Individual Action and Collective Will*

Despite his doubts over the categories of Caesarism and Bonapartism, it is clear why Gramsci is still willing to adopt them. These categories, and the concepts related to them, are necessary if one is to grasp some essential features of modernity. These include: the formula of the balance of class forces for the description of the situation of organic crisis; the breaking of constitutional legality as a premise for the construction of a new socio-political order; the reflections on the bureaucracy as an aspect of the analysis of the hegemonic apparatus; the question of political leadership and its connection with the popular masses; etc.

Caesarism and Bonapartism, in particular, are important for understanding the totalitarian regimes of Gramsci's time. If a study of the events that made possible the birth and development of Mussolini's regime lies at the basis of Gramsci's reflections on contemporary Caesarism, this category is then in turn reused to interpret Fascism itself, by highlighting its simultaneously conservative and progressive character – a similar logic can be used for his analysis of the USSR.

The nature of the 'Caesar' is a matter of crucial importance. Far from simply dismissing the Caesarist-Bonapartist model, Gramsci rather reflects on the new forms of leadership in the modern political scenario. Within this framework, we should conclusively discuss the question of the relationship between the categories of Caesarism and Bonapartism and one of the most celebrated and fascinating topics in the *Prison Notebooks*, the modern prince.[101]

This connection has been noted already (to a limited extent) by some scholars, although they have not grasped the full complexity of the issue, or have misrepresented its significance. I refer in particular to Burgio's reading: he interprets Gramsci's observations on the 'collective' character of the modern Caesar

---

Giuseppe Vacca (Vacca 2017). A similar reasoning can be found also in Ragazzini 2002, p. 82, where it is claimed that 'this arrangement of ideas reveals a recurring attention to the Soviet experience, to the situation in the U.S., to fascist construction, which is often found within the same note and often even entails an overlapping of the same words, which gives the effect that they have thrice the value at the same time' (the translation, modified, is taken from Cospito 2016, p. 76, n. 43).

101 On this topic, see, for a start, the entry in Liguori and Voza 2009 by L. La Porta, pp. 548–51, and the numerous contributions by Thomas (2013, 2015b, 2017b and 2018b); on the genesis of the topic, see Frosini 2013. I refer here only to the philologically oriented analyses of the issue of the modern prince in Gramsci's thought (for examples of theoretical readings of the concept, see Kalyvas 2000 or White and Ypi 2010).

in Q 13, § 27 as an allusion to a 'democratic Caesarism ... focused on the active role of collective subjectivities'; in other words, as a form of progressive Caesarism that the modern prince (i.e. the Communist Party) can and must implement if it wants to overturn the status quo.[102] However, Burgio's observations are not consistent with what is said in the *Prison Notebooks*. The meaning of Gramsci's passage should be understood as taking its cue from the context within which it is placed.

The object of debate is the issue of 'Caesarism without a Caesar', to recall Burgio's expression.[103] This topic is evoked by Gramsci in Q 9, § 133 (and then, later, in Q 13, § 27), within the framework of his analysis of coalition governments as initial forms of Caesarism. He is here underlining that, in the contemporary world, Caesarism is no longer linked to individual charismatic figures, such as Caesar or Napoleon I (but also, in a certain sense, Napoleon III and Bismarck). Caesarism is rather the result of a specific socio-political combination, which can lead all social groups to converge on a party that progressively 'saturates' the political landscape, by developing totalitarian characteristics. It is in this sense that Gramsci's affirmation that 'a Caesarist solution can exist even without a Caesar, without any great, "heroic" and representative personality' should be interpreted.[104]

These observations relate to his analysis of the collective dimension of political modernity, whose subject, in Gramsci's words, is precisely the 'collective man' or, as he says in Q 7, § 12, the 'man as mass'.[105] Despite being a single draft, this note from notebook 7 is of great relevance to this topic. Here Gramsci opposes the past, where individuality plays an important role, to the present, in which the 'tendency toward conformity ... is more widespread and deeper'.[106] Moreover, he also asks himself if a 'collective man exist[ed] in the past', and he answers that

---

102 Burgio 2014, p. 280.
103 Burgio 2014, p. 280.
104 Q 13, § 27, p. 1619; SPN, p. 220. The text reprises precisely the first version of the note.
105 Q 7, § 12, p. 861; PN, vol. 3, p. 165. The note, a single draft, is entitled *Man as Individual and Man as Mass* [*L'uomo individuo e l'uomo-massa*]. On the individual or collective character of the political dimension according to Gramsci, see Ragazzini 2002, pp. 119–35.
106 Q 7, § 12, p. 862; PN, vol. 3, p. 164. See also, in this regard, Antonini 2019a. From the historical point of view, see the fascist debate on the 'new human type' (see, for instance, Gentile 2002b, esp. pp. 235–64, and Matard-Bonucci and Milza 2004). On the issue of 'conformism', see also (in addition to Manacorda 1970) Mancina 1992, Boeri 1999, Liguori 2015, pp. 113 ff. and Maltese 2015.

he existed, as Michels would say, under the form of charismatic leadership. In other words, a collective will was attained under the impetus and direct influence of a 'hero', of a paradigmatic individual, but this collective will was produced by extraneous factors and once formed would disintegrate, repeatedly. Today, by contrast, collective man is formed essentially from the bottom up.[107]

On the politico-historical level, such an opposition between individual and collective action highlights the differences between modern and pre-modern politics already mentioned before.[108]

4.2   *Caesarism and the Modern Prince*
In this piece (Q 7, § 12, written in November–December 1930), Gramsci recalls some aspects of his previous reflections on the Caesarist-Bonapartist model to describe the features of individual action, although he does not mention them explicitly – see the references to Michels, to the theory of charismatic leadership, as well as to 'paradigmatic individual'.[109]

However, the text also anticipates some of the key elements developed later in Q 8, § 21 (January–February 1932), one of the main notes on the theme of the modern prince.[110] In particular, the section of this paragraph devoted to the 'myth-Prince' as a symbol of the collective will seems to take its cue from Q 7, § 12 and from Gramsci's reflections on the 'individual-collective' conceptual opposition:

> The modern Prince, the myth-Prince, cannot be a real person, a concrete individual. It can only be an organism, a social component in which a collective will – one that is recognized and, to some extent, has asserted itself

---

107   Q 7, § 12, p. 862; PN, vol. 3, p. 165.
108   It has to be remembered that the text also offers an interesting perspective on the issue of conformism, the rationalisation of production, and Taylorism.
109   The phrase 'paradigmatic individual' is a translation of the Italian expression '*uomo rappresentativo*' (Q 7, § 12, p. 862). At this stage, Michels' account and the issue of charismatic leadership have already been investigated by Gramsci: see Q 2, § 75 and Q 4, §§ 66 and 69. This paragraph represents, in a certain sense, a significant development of these reflections, insofar as it reassesses them in a historical and 'comparative' dimension – from this perspective, it is remarkable that § 12 of notebook 7 is chronologically very close to the already mentioned notes (in fact, Q 2, § 75 was completed in August–September 1930, while the notes from notebook 4 date back to November 1930).
110   On this key text, see the already mentioned essays by Thomas (in particular Thomas 2015b and 2017b).

in action – has already begun to take shape. Historical development has already produced this organism, and it is the political party – the modern formation that contains the partial collective wills with a propensity to become universal and total. Only an immediate historico-political action that necessitates moving at lightning speed can be embodied by a concrete individual. Such speed can only be generated by a great and imminent danger, precisely the kind of great danger that, in an instant, generates flaming passions and fanaticism, annihilating the critical sense and irony that can destroy the 'charismatic' character of the *condottiere* (Boulanger an example). By its very nature, however, an immediate action of this sort cannot be long lasting; neither can it have an organic character. In almost every case, it typifies a restoration or reorganization; it is not typical of the founding of new states or new national and social structures … It is a 'defensive' rather than creative type of action. It is based on the assumption that an already existing 'collective will' has dispersed, lost its nerve, and needs to be regrouped and reinforced, as opposed to the assumption that a 'collective will' has to be created *ex novo* and directed toward goals that are concrete, to be sure, but whose concreteness has not yet been tested by experience.[111]

Some parallels are clear: the 'extraneous factors' mentioned before are here represented by the 'great and imminent danger that … generates flaming passions and fanaticism' described by Gramsci; the 'hero' of notebook 7 is the *condottiere* that shows '"charismatic" character' in Q 8, §21.[112] However, the points of view are somehow opposite. Whereas, in Q 7, §12, Gramsci is wondering whether there is a collective will in the pre-modern scenario, in notebook 8 his scope is to dismiss any individual action in contemporary politics (the reference to Boulanger is apposite).[113]

Q 8, §21, nevertheless, goes beyond Q 7, §12, since its reflections on the individual-collective dimension are placed within the debate on the organic crisis of modernity and on the 'type[s] of action' that correspond to the different political attitudes.[114] As a matter of fact, while a 'charismatic' solution is '"defensive"' and aims to 'restore' and to 'reinforce' a 'dispersed' collective will, the organic, collective action realised by the modern prince is creative and pro-

---

111 Q 8, §21, pp. 951–2; PN, vol. 3, p. 247. Some passages of the text have been previously analysed, while dealing with Gramsci's account of Michels (see Chapter 9, section 1).
112 Q 7, §12, p. 862; PN, vol. 3, p. 165; Q 8, §21, pp. 951–2; PN, vol. 3, p. 247.
113 In this regard, see also Antonini 2020.
114 Q 8, §21, p. 952; PN, vol. 3, p. 247.

gressive.¹¹⁵ This emerges distinctly in the second draft of the text, which opens notebook 13 on Machiavelli's politics:¹¹⁶

> In the modern world, only those historico-political actions which are immediate and imminent, characterised by the necessity for lightning speed, can be incarnated mythically by a concrete individual ... But an improvised action of such a kind, by its very nature, cannot have a long-term and organic character. It will in almost all cases be appropriate to restoration and reorganisation, but not to the founding of new States or new national and social structures ... It will be defensive rather than capable of original creation. Its underlying assumption will be that a collective will, already in existence, has become nerveless and dispersed, has suffered a collapse which is dangerous and threatening but not definitive and catastrophic, and that it is necessary to reconcentrate and reinforce it – rather than that a new collective will must be created from scratch, to be directed towards goals which are concrete and rational, but whose concreteness and rationality have not yet been put to the critical test by a real and universally known historical experience.¹¹⁷

Here Gramsci, while rewriting the note, specifies that the collective will 'shaped' by the charismatic leader 'has suffered a collapse which is dangerous and threatening but not definitive and catastrophic'.¹¹⁸ There is a clear hint, in this passage, to the theme of the 'catastrophe', as well as to the issue of 'marginal forces'.

We can appreciate how deeply connected are Gramsci's reflections on the modern prince and on the Caesarist-Bonapartist model. This stands out from the text in notebook 7, as well as in Q 8, § 21. But if we reconsider briefly the notes on Caesarism and Bonapartism already analysed, the connection between the two topics appears even more evident.

Generally speaking, we could observe that there is a significant intertwining (both chronologically and thematically) between the reflections on these issues. As regards Gramsci's notes on Caesarism and Bonapartism, we can

---

115   Q 8, § 21, p. 952; PN, vol. 3, p. 247.
116   The fact that there is a short interval of time between the first draft text (Q 8, § 21) and the second draft text (Q 13, § 1) is due to the peculiar mode of composition of notebook 13, which rewrites the first draft texts starting from notes of notebook 8. On this modality, see QAnast, vol. 14, pp. 153–9. On the passage from Q 8, § 21 to Q 13, § 1, see also Thomas 2017b, esp. pp. 538–9.
117   Q 13, § 1, p. 1558; SPN, pp. 129–30.
118   Q 13, § 27, p. 1158; SPN, p. 130.

identify different stages of elaboration. As I illustrated in the previous analysis,[119] the first occurrences of these categories correspond to the notes of notebooks 1, 2, 3 and 4, and they concentrate especially between May and November 1930. The second and more important phase corresponds to the texts of notebook 9, which are dated to November 1932. In §§ 23 and 27 of notebook 13 we can then find the 'canonisation' of these reflections on the Caesarist-Bonapartist model. Further observations are contained in the texts of the later miscellaneous notebooks: among them Q 14 § 23, written in January 1933, stands out.

With regard to the chronology of the theme of the modern prince, this is a complex issue, with which we cannot deal at length here.[120] In short, we can say with Peter Thomas that the modern prince, conceived as a collective political organism, first appears in Q 8, § 21 (January–February 1932) and finds its last explicit reference in Q 13, § 1 (May 1932). After this date, the theme is still present in Gramsci's notes, but in a different way, as an instrument of the 'moral and intellectual reform' sketched by Gramsci.[121]

On this basis, we could suggest, in the first place, that the observations on Caesarism and Bonapartism developed by Gramsci in 1930 contributed (among other elements) to open the floor for his discussion of the modern prince in 1932, by stimulating the reflections on the issue of political leadership and on the nature of political parties between pre-modernity and modernity. In turn, we can say that the investigation of the modern prince also influenced Gramsci's following reflections on the Caesarist-Bonapartist model (whose highest point has to be identified with the period between November 1932 and October/November 1933).

We can indeed recognise an influence of his analysis of the modern prince in the notes on Caesarism of 1932 (notebook 9), but also in the later texts (notebooks 13 and 14).[122] In Q 9, §§ 133 and 136, and in their second draft (Q 13, § 27), we can retrace, for instance, comparable reflections on the organic crisis of modernity (but, in this regard, we should see also what Gramsci says in Q 13, § 23), as well as an analogous distinction between modern and pre-modern politics and a reference to the creation (or not) of a new 'type of state'.[123] In

---

119   See Chapter 6, section 3.
120   On the topic, see in particular Frosini 2013 and Thomas 2017b.
121   See Thomas 2017b.
122   It seems to me that, in a certain sense, the issue of the modern prince is closely connected to the 'new' conception of politics developed by Gramsci in the last miscellaneous notebooks. On this point, see Antonini 2019a.
123   We can note that in Q 9, § 133 (as well as in its second draft, Q 13, § 27) we find the expres-

various notes in notebook 13 and elsewhere (cf. in particular Q 14, § 23), Gramsci focuses on the issue of the latent forces. These are also evoked by contrast in the framework of the definition of the modern prince. On a more general level, Gramsci's analysis of the totalitarian dimension, as well as his understanding of the fascist dictatorship (not to mention the more or less explicit references to Mussolini), show an astonishing (and until now almost completely neglected) affinity between Gramsci's interpretation of the categories of Caesarism and Bonapartism and his reflections on the issue of the modern prince.

To sum up, I would argue that from these cross-references there emerges a common conceptual network. This network is constituted by some shared structural 'patterns', with which Gramsci approaches the contemporary political framework. The Caesarist-Bonapartist model and the topic of the modern prince are, however, two opposing scenarios. While the Caesarist solution represents the (more or less) reactionary and conservative response to the crisis of modernity, the modern prince is the progressive option, which contains all of Gramsci's hopes for a radical transformation of politics.

This 'proximity in the antithesis' is of distinct relevance to the current investigation, and it sheds a meaningful light on Gramsci's understanding of his own times, by showing their unique (and perhaps even contradictory) dynamics and by grasping their complexity.

4.3   The 'Party-Caesar' and the Role of Charismatic Figures

The theme of the modern prince, of course, cannot be reduced solely to these aspects. It is also composed of other elements, such as the issues of the 'myth' and of the 'moral and intellectual reform'. Or, more generally, it contains the 'dramatical' dimension of Gramsci's prince, as has been recently highlighted by Thomas.[124] So far as the transformation of the contemporary socio-political system is concerned, however, the scheme is the one sketched before (and in previous chapters).

In this framework, if the political party can become a 'new Prince', it can also turn into a 'Caesar' – and indeed it has done so, as history has demonstrated. Under the condition of modernity, Caesarism must therefore be interpreted as a Caesarism of the party: totalitarian politics is an 'up-to-date' version of nineteenth-century Caesarism, in which single-party government has replaced the individual dictatorship (this emerges clearly from previous quotations from, for example, Q 13, § 1 and § 27).

---

sion *personalità ... rappresentativa*' (p. 1195; 'representative personality'), which echoes significantly the phrase adopted in Q 7, § 12 ('*uomo rappresentativo*', p. 862).

124   See, in particular, Thomas 2018b.

However, this does not imply that there is no room at all for charismatic figures. Rather, we must reassess their role, and contextualise it within the new social and political situation. Since it connects directly to this aspect, it might be worth discussing further Gramsci's interpretation of Fascism and especially the figure of Mussolini.

Benito Mussolini's Caesaristic attitude is a long-standing theme in Gramsci's thought, from his pre-prison journalistic writings onwards. The best-known article in which Gramsci deals with this theme is *Leader*, first published in *L'Ordine Nuovo* in March 1924.[125] In this text, a eulogy to Lenin, Gramsci affirms that Mussolini is not a leader; he is rather a dictator, who 'seized governmental power and is holding onto it by means of the most violent and arbitrary repression'.[126]

In the *Prison Notebooks*, Gramsci's position regarding Mussolini is more nuanced, as is his judgement of Fascism as a whole. In modernity, autonomous initiatives promoted by individual, 'charismatic' actors are rejected as a-historical, contingent and, ultimately, pointless (as he writes clearly in Q 8, § 21).[127] However, individual 'charisma' may still contribute to develop the party's Caesarism; this is the case with Mussolini. I think that this is a likely reading of the passage from Q 7, §12 where Gramsci says that 'the paradigmatic individual still has a role in the formation of collective man, but it is a greatly diminished role, so much so that he could disappear without the collective cement disintegrating or the structure collapsing'.[128] To conclude, there is no opposition, but rather, to a certain extent, a coexistence between the two 'forms' of Caesarism (individual and collective). Mussolini's charisma represents a 'detail' of the radical fascist transformation of Italian state and society. In other words, it is an aspect of Fascism conceived of as the '"passive revolution" specific to the 20th century'.[129]

---

125 'Leader', cit. On this article, see also Chapter 9, section 1.1.
126 'Leader', cit. (CPC, p. 16; SPW-2, p. 212).
127 From this perspective, it is also worth recalling Gramsci's reflections on the issue of the '*superuomo*', which unfold largely in notebook 14 (mostly in connection with the reflections on the popular novel and, more generally, on literature) and which are strictly connected to Gramsci's analysis of the figure of Mussolini (on this theme, see also the observations on the figure of 'prince Rudolph' contained in the previous chapters as well as analogous reflections in the pre-prison writings).
128 Q 7, §12, p. 862; PN, vol. 3, p. 165.
129 Q 8, §236, p. 1089; PN, vol. 3, p. 378; see, in particular, Frosini 2017b. On this issue, see also Thomas 2018a, which highlights how the (relatively late) definition of Fascism as a form of passive revolution is overdetermined by the novelty of the figure of the modern prince.

CHAPTER 13

Caesarism, Bonapartism and the 'Return to Marx' in the Prison Writings

1 Gramsci and the Marxian Legacy

To summarise, Gramsci explicitly refers to the concepts of Bonapartism and Caesarism in relatively few notes, which, apart from the very first appearances, dating back to May–November 1930, are concentrated between the end of 1932 and the end of 1933. But in light of the analysis conducted so far, it becomes clear that there are numerous indirect or mediated references, which, added to the explicit ones, enrich the picture considerably. They show that the presence in the *Notebooks* of these two categories is both more meaningful than one might suspect, and more extended from the chronological point of view, accompanying Gramsci's reflections up to their final iteration. From prior investigations of the *Prison Notebooks*, the importance of Gramsci's references to Marx's account also emerged very clearly. These references are scattered throughout Gramsci's analysis of the categories of Caesarism and Bonapartism.

A (non-exhaustive) list of Gramsci's debts towards Marx's historical works and especially towards *The Eighteenth Brumaire* includes the following elements: the investigation of the political role of the bureaucratic apparatus and the social milieu from which the bureaucracy is drawn, the rural bourgeoisie; the role of the military element in Bonapartist situations; the 'autonomy' of state and parastatal bodies (primarily the bureaucracy) from the rest of society; the analysis of the figure of the charismatic leader and his relationship with the masses; the study of the French historico-political framework of the mid-nineteenth century (the Second French Empire, Napoleon III); the attention to electoral dynamics and to the question of universal suffrage; the centrality of the formula of the balance of class forces; the issue of the breakdown of constitutional legality.

Therefore, Marx's model represents a central point of reference in Gramsci's carceral reflection. In the *Notebooks*, in particular, he shows a deep understanding of Marx's thinking on the themes of Bonapartism and Caesarism, which is manifested in his reappraisal of the 'spirit' of Marx's texts, much more than of their 'letter'.

While in the pre-prison writings Gramsci fits his reflections into the interpretation of the Caesarist-Bonapartist model proposed by Marx in his historical works (albeit 'implemented' and modified according to Gramsci's theoretical and strategic needs), in the later writings the hierarchy is, so to speak, turned upside-down. Notwithstanding Gramsci's respect for Marx's 'paternity' of the categories, and in the framework of a faithful adoption of specific aspects of the Marxian investigation, in the *Prison Notebooks* Gramsci adapts Marx's analysis to the new conceptual horizon of his thought. Gramsci profoundly reconsiders Marx's model based on the dramatic challenges raised by twentieth-century politics and society. It is precisely in Gramsci's effort to 'emancipate' himself from Marx that he ends up being closer to him. Gramsci's firm rejection of a standard Marxist model and his attention to the historical, concrete forms of Caesarism in their potential diversity make him one of the richest inheritors of Marx's legacy.

Consequently, we can also reassess Gramsci's 'return to Marx'. Francesca Izzo adopts this expression to highlight how, in the *Prison Notebooks*, Gramsci reads Marx's texts in order to 'create a solid basis for the theoretical autonomy of the new historical subject', i.e. the political party (here Gramsci's reference is primarily to Marx's 'philosophical' writings).[1] I would argue that the 'return to Marx' is much wider and more profound, since it involves Gramsci's account of political modernity as a whole, both in its 'positive' (the project of a modern prince) and 'negative' aspects (the analysis of the contemporary crisis of hegemony, the new totalitarian trends). Such an 'enlarged' interpretation of this expression capitalises on Gramsci's reflections on the concepts of Caesarism and Bonapartism, as I aimed to demonstrate in the previous chapters.

2 Caesarism and Bonapartism in the *Prison Notebooks*

On this basis, we can finally better understand the full meaning of Gramsci's reflection on the Caesarist-Bonapartist model in his carceral writings. By taking up these concepts, Gramsci is not proposing an anachronistic and, therefore, ineffective interpretative apparatus; Caesarism and Bonapartism are up-to-date categories, which contribute to the analysis of Gramsci's time and of its challenges. In this regard, I believe I have proved that the rejection of the soci-

---

1 Izzo 2009, p. 49. Izzo also seems to suggest that there is a clear gap, as regards Gramsci's use of Marx, between his prison and pre-prison writings; she states, in fact, that 'for the predominantly controversial, negative character of his approach towards Marxian thought, Gramsci, during his youth, is driven to enhance certain aspects of Marxism to fight against his various opponents' (Izzo 2009, p. 24). I partially disagree with such interpretation, as previously explained.

ological reading of these formulas is, more than anything else, a way in which Gramsci warns against an excessive schematisation of these concepts (i.e. against their undue use in an abstract sense), rather than a dismissal of them.

It is in this perspective that the references to Bonapartism and, above all, to Caesarism in the *Prison Notebooks* should be read. Bonapartism is twofold. On the one hand (further developing Gramsci's pre-prison reading of the category), it expresses the incapacity to establish a truly hegemonic relationship, and it qualifies the 'missing' connection between leaders and masses – in this regard, the conceptual cluster of Bonapartism, Industrialism, Cadornism and Napoleonism is crucial. This militaristic rule of the masses applies to different historical and political scenarios, but it is especially in the Russian context that its meaning is most striking. In this framework, Bonapartism represents a strong (but never oversimplified) criticism of 'misleading' interpretations of a regulated society, both regarding its establishment as well its consolidation. This refers both to the political and to the economic level (cf. the reflections on 'statolatry' and on the 'economic-corporative' phase). On the other hand, Bonapartism evokes the issue of the balance of power and the growing political role of military and civil bureaucracy in contemporary societies. By connecting with categories such as that of the police (broadly understood), this concept represents a pivotal element of Gramsci's understanding of hegemony and of its new, 'post-Jacobin' meaning in the twentieth-century context.

As regards Caesarism, it is an essential part of Gramsci's thought in the *Prison Notebooks*. Gramsci investigates, at length, the features of this category, which polemically replaces Michels' formula of 'charismatic leadership'. Thanks to a brilliant use of historical analogies, he creates a multilayered theory of Caesarism, grasping each 'nuance' of the Caesarist phenomenon. The historical dimension is also extremely rich: if his investigation of the Caesarist model takes its cue from his analysis of the post-1848 French political situation, its field of application covers the entire political history of the nineteenth and the twentieth centuries, with a special focus on the interwar period. Conceptually speaking, Caesarism represents a pivot in Gramsci's lexicon: it is at the crossroads of different lines of investigation and offers a valuable insight into his very conception of political modernity. In fact, the category of Caesarism not only 'anticipates' some of the elements of his reflections on passive revolution while analysing Louis Napoleon's dictatorship, but it is also strictly connected to Gramsci's understanding of the 'organic crisis' or 'crisis of hegemony'. This crisis unfolds after 1870 and, in particular, in the aftermath of the First World War. Conceived of as a 'catastrophic balance' between opposing forces, this crisis could lead to a (more or less temporary) Caesarist solution: Caesarism appears, therefore, as an up-to-date formula for explaining the rising authoritarian tendencies in Europe, and notably in Italy, in the 1920s and 1930s. A reading of Fascism as a Caesarist regime can be traced in some highly significant notes from Gramsci's prison writings. Caesarism is a turning point for his investigation of the transformation of hegemony in the existing one-party systems or, in other words, in the 'totalitarian' framework of the contemporary war of position – in this way, we can read also his references to the crisis of parliamentarism and to 'black parliamentarism'. Finally, yet importantly, the concept of Caesarism allows us to illuminate some of the essential features of a contested issue in Gramscian scholarship, namely that of the modern prince.

Having summarised Gramsci's use of the categories of Bonapartism and Caesarism in the prison notes, I will conclude by making three observations on the wider usefulness of the analysis provided in this book.

The first relates to the link between Gramsci's newspaper articles and the *Prison Notebooks*. From Gramsci's earliest writings onwards, it emerges that the Caesarist-Bonapartist model represents a *Leitmotiv*. In spite of the significant evolution in his approach, and the obvious differences between the pre-prison texts and the notebooks, this connection is of twofold importance. On the one hand, it shows the need for a change of approach towards the pre-prison writings (which remain generally underestimated, in spite of the efforts of recent scholarship to demonstrate their value). On the other hand, more importantly, this 'continuity' allows the reader to grasp the full complexity of Gramsci's analysis of politics and society, by displaying the necessity of an all-encompassing reading of his thought.

In connecting Gramsci's pre-carceral and carceral writings, my research also emphasises the exceptional richness and originality of Gramsci's reflections, which follow their own internal 'rhythm', despite the difficulties experienced by Gramsci in his life.[2] In this framework, the most fascinating aspect is perhaps the unexhausted productivity of Gramsci's 'conceptual laboratory'. Thanks also the peculiar features of his writing (especially in the *Prison Notebooks*), he keeps returning to analyse further already investigated points. Moreover, he constantly addresses new themes and issues and shows a great intellectual strength in spite of the progressive decline of his physical forces (the considerations that Gramsci develops in the last phase of his work in prison are remarkable). The fertility of his investigation of Caesarism and Bonapartism stands out from this point of view. These categories, their clear theoretical and historical limitations notwithstanding, are valuable to our understanding of

---

2   I echo here a fascinating formula from the *Notebooks* ('the rhythm of thought in development', [*il ritmo del pensiero in isviluppo*] – Q 16, § 2, p. 1841), also adopted by Giuseppe Cospito in the title of his book (Cospito 2016).

the passage from the political circumstances of the nineteenth century to the twentieth century, and they contribute to the shaping of key concepts such as 'passive revolution' or 'modern prince'.

From this perspective, I would finally stress the methodological significance of this investigation. Although it is a study of a particular aspect of Gramsci's reflections, it demonstrates how a historico-philological approach to his writings could help in reassessing previously undervalued elements, and, ultimately, in opening the way for a new, broader reading of Gramsci's thought as a whole.

Bibliography

Abendroth, Wolfgang (ed.) 1967, *Faschismus und Kapitalismus. Theorien über die sozialen Ursprünge und die Funktion des Faschismus*, Frankfurt am Main: Europäische Verlagsanstalt.

Accardo, Aldo and Gianni Fresu 2009, *Oltre la parentesi. Fascismo e storia d'Italia nell'interpretazione gramsciana*, Rome: Carocci.

Adamson, Walter L. 1980, 'Gramsci's Interpretation of Fascism', *Journal of the History of Ideas*, 4: 615–33.

Agosti, Aldo 2009, *Il partito mondiale della rivoluzione. Saggi sul comunismo e l'Internazionale*, Milan: Unicopli.

Albarani, Giuliano 2008, 'Gramsci e il Risorgimento', in *Gramsci e la storia d'Italia*, edited by Giuliano Albarani et al., Milan: Unicopli.

Antonini, Francesca 2013a, 'Cesarismo e bonapartismo negli scritti precarcerari gramsciani', *Annali della Fondazione Luigi Einaudi*, 47: 203–24.

Antonini, Francesca 2013b, 'Il bonapartismo nel *Diciotto brumaio* di Marx tra fenomeno storico e categoria teorica', *Critica marxista*, 2: 71–9.

Antonini, Francesca 2014a, 'Autonomy or Heteronomy of the State? An Enquiry on the Political Theory of *The Eighteenth Brumaire of Louis Bonaparte* by Karl Marx', in *Actas das IV Jornadas Internacionais de Investigadores de Filosofia*, Evora: Instituto de Filosofia Prática, Pólo da Universidade de Évora (IFPPUE).

Antonini, Francesca 2014b, 'Science, History and Ideology in Gramsci's *Prison Notebooks*', *HoST – Journal of History of Science and Technology*, 9: 64–80.

Antonini, Francesca 2016, '"Il vecchio muore e il nuovo non può nascere": cesarismo ed egemonia nel contesto della crisi organica', *International Gramsci Journal*, 2, no. 1: 167–84.

Antonini, Francesca 2018, 'Gramsci, il materialismo storico e l'antologia russa del 1924', *Studi storici*, 59, no. 2: 403–35.

Antonini, Francesca 2019a, 'Pessimism of the Intellect, Optimism of the Will: Gramsci's Political Thought in the Last Miscellaneous Notebooks', *Rethinking Marxism*, 31, no. 1: 42–57.

Antonini, Francesca 2019b, 'Interpreting the Present from the Past: Gramsci, Marx and the Historical Analogy', in *Revisiting Gramsci's* Notebooks, edited by Francesca Antonini et al., Leiden-Boston: Brill.

Antonini, Francesca 2020, 'Entre Boulanger et Dreyfus: ombres et lumières de la Troisième République dans les "Cahiers de prison"', in Descendre and Zancarini 2020 [forthcoming].

Aquarone, Alberto 1965, *L'organizzazione dello Stato totalitario*, Turin: Einaudi.

Baehr, Peter 1998, *Caesar and the Fading of the Roman World: A Study in Republicanism and Caesarism*, New Brunswick: Transaction Publishers.

Baehr, Peter and Melvin Richter (eds) 2004, *Dictatorship in History and Theory: Bonapartism, Caesarism, and Totalitarianism*, Cambridge: Cambridge University Press.

Baker, David 2006, 'The Political Economy of Fascism: Myth or Reality, or Myth and Reality?', *New Political Economy*, 11, no. 2: 227–50.

Baldan, Attilio 1978, *Gramsci come storico. Studio sulle fonti dei* Quaderni del carcere, Bari: Dedalo.

Banti, Alberto Mario 2008, *Il Risorgimento italiano*, Rome-Bari: Laterza.

Baratta, Giorgio 2004, 'Americanismo e fordismo', in *Le parole di Gramsci. Per un lessico dei* Quaderni del carcere, edited by Fabio Frosini and Guido Liguori, Rome: Carocci.

Barnett, Vincent 2004, *The Revolutionary Russian Economy, 1890–1940: Ideas, Debates and Alternatives*, London-New York: Routledge.

Basile, Luca 2009, *Per una teoria del mercato. Labriola, Croce, Gramsci*, Lecce: Pensa multimedia.

Basile, Luca 2016, *Scienza politica e forme dell'egemonia. Intorno al problema della classe dirigente in Mosca, Michels, Gramsci*, Saonara: Il Prato.

Bechelloni, Antonio 1988, 'Gramsci e l'Action Française', in *Teoria politica e società industriale. Ripensare Gramsci*, edited by Franco Sbarberi, Turin: Bollati Boringhieri.

Bellamy, Richard 2013, *Croce, Gramsci, Bobbio, and the Italian Political Tradition*, Colchester: ECPR Press.

Benvenuti, Francesco and Silvio Pons 1999, 'L'Unione Sovietica nei Quaderni del carcere', in *Gramsci e il Novecento*, vol. 1, edited by Giuseppe Vacca, Rome: Carocci.

Bergami, Giancarlo 1978, 'Gramsci e il fascismo nel primo tempo del Partito Comunista d'Italia', *Belfagor*, 2: 159–72.

Bernstein, Aaron J. 2016, *From the* Theses on Feuerbach *to the Philosophy of Praxis: Marx, Gramsci, Philosophy and Politics*, PhD Dissertation, King's College London.

Berselli, Aldo 1965, *La Destra storica dopo l'Unità*, vol. II, *Italia legale e Italia reale*, Bologna: Il Mulino.

Bianchi, Alvaro 2008, *Laboratório de Gramsci: Filosofia, história e política*, São Paulo: Alameda.

Biscione, Francesco M. 1990, 'A. Gramsci, Note sul problema meridionale e sull'atteggiamento nei suoi confronti dei comunisti, dei socialisti e dei democratici', *Critica marxista*, 3: 51–78.

Bluche, Frédéric 1980, *Le bonapartisme. Aux origines de la droite autoritaire (1800–1850)*, Paris: Nouvelles Editions Latines.

Boeri, Maria Grazia 1999, 'Il "conformismo" nei *Quaderni del carcere*', *Studi sulla formazione*, 2: 125–44.

Bongiovanni, Bruno 2003, 'Rubel, Marx e il bonapartismo', in Ceretta 2003.

Botz, Gerhard 1976, 'Austro-Marxist Interpretations of Fascism', *Journal of Contemporary History*, 11: 129–56.

Bravo, Gian Mario 2003, 'Il fallimento della politica. Marx e gli altri. A proposito di Luigi Bonaparte', in Ceretta 2003.
Bravo, Gian Mario 1992, *Marx ed Engels in Italia. La fortuna, gli scritti, le relazioni, le polemiche*, Rome: Editori Riuniti.
Buci-Glucksmann, Christine 1980, *Gramsci and the State*, London: Lawrence and Wishart.
Burgio, Alberto 2003, *Gramsci storico. Una lettura dei "Quaderni del carcere"*, Rome-Bari: Laterza.
Burgio, Alberto 2007a, 'L'analisi del bonapartismo e del cesarismo nei *Quaderni* di Gramsci', in Riosa 2007.
Burgio, Alberto 2007b, *Per Gramsci. Crisi e potenza del moderno*, Rome: DeriveApprodi.
Burgio, Alberto 2014, *Gramsci. Il sistema in movimento*, Rome: DeriveApprodi.
Cammarano, Fulvio 2011, *Storia dell'Italia liberale*, Rome-Bari: Laterza.
Cammett, John M. 1967, *Antonio Gramsci and the Origins of Italian Communism*, Stanford: Stanford University Press.
Canfora, Luciano 2010, *L'uso politico dei paradigmi storici*, Rome-Bari: Laterza.
Caprioglio, Sergio 1991, 'Gramsci e l'URSS. Tre note nei *Quaderni del carcere*', *Belfagor*, 46, no. 1: 65–75.
Carlucci, Alessandro 2013a, *Gramsci and Languages: Unification, Diversity, Hegemony*, Leiden-Boston: Brill.
Carlucci, Alessandro 2013b, '"Essere superiori all'ambiente in cui si vive, senza perciò disprezzarlo". Sull'interesse di Gramsci per Kipling', *Studi storici*, 4: 897–914.
Carlucci, Alessandro 2013c, 'The Risorgimento and its Discontents. Gramsci's Reflections on Conflict and Control in the Aftermath of Italy's Unification', in *The Political Philosophies of Antonio Gramsci and B.R. Ambedkar*, edited by Cosimo Zene, London-New York: Routledge.
Carlucci, Alessandro and Caterina Balistreri 2011, 'I primi mesi di Gramsci in Russia. Giugno-Agosto 1922', *Belfagor*, 6: 645–58.
Carver, Terrell 2004, 'Marx's *Eighteenth Brumaire of Louis Bonaparte*: Democracy, Dictatorship, and the Politics of Class Struggle', in Baehr and Richter 2004.
Cassina, Cristina 2001, *Il bonapartismo o la falsa eccezione. Napoleone III, i francesi e la tradizione illiberale*, Rome: Carocci.
Ceretta, Manuela (ed.) 2003, *Bonapartismo, cesarismo e crisi della società. Luigi Napoleone e il colpo di stato del 1851*, Florence: Olschki.
Cervelli, Innocenzo 1996, 'Cesarismo: alcuni usi e significati della parola (secolo XIX)', *Annali dell'Istituto Storico Italo-Germanico in Trento*, XXII: 61–197.
Ciliberto, Michele 1987, 'Gramsci e l'analisi del fascismo', *Dimensioni*, 43: 17–26.
Ciliberto, Michele 1999, 'Cosmopolitismo e Stato nazionale nei "Quaderni del carcere"', in *Gramsci e il Novecento*, vol. 1, edited by Giuseppe Vacca with the collaboration of Marina Litri, Rome: Carocci.

Colarizi, Simona 2008, 'Gramsci e il fascismo', in Giasi 2008a, vol. 2.

Corney, Frederick 2015, *Trotsky's Challenge: The 'Literary Discussion' of 1924 and the Fight for the Bolshevik Revolution*, Leiden-Boston: Brill.

Cospito, Giuseppe 2008, 'Gramsci e Marx', in *Gramsci e la storia d'Italia*, edited by Giuliano Albarani et al., Milan: Unicopli.

Cospito, Giuseppe 2011a, 'Verso l'edizione critica e integrale dei "Quaderni del carcere"', *Studi storici*, 4: 881–904.

Cospito, Giuseppe 2011b, 'Gramsci dalla *Rivoluzione contro il "Capitale"* alla "Critica dell'Economia Politica"', in *Marx e Gramsci. Filologia, filosofia e politica allo specchio*, edited by Anna Di Bello, Naples: Liguori.

Cospito, Giuseppe 2011c, *Il ritmo del pensiero. Per una lettura diacronica dei 'Quaderni del carcere' di Gramsci*, Naples: Bibliopolis.

Cospito, Giuseppe 2015, 'Le "cautele" nella scrittura carceraria di Gramsci', *International Gramsci Journal*, 1, no. 4: 28–42.

Cospito, Giuseppe 2016, *The Rhythm of Thought in Gramsci: A Diachronic Interpretation of Prison Notebooks*, Leiden-Boston: Brill.

Costa Pinto, Antonio (ed.) 2017, *Corporatism and Fascism: The Corporatist Wave in Europe*, London-New York: Routledge.

Costa Pinto, Antonio and Federico Finchelstein (eds) 2018, *Authoritarianism and Corporatism in Europe and Latin America: Crossing Borders*, London-New York: Routledge.

Coutinho, Carlos Nelson 2012, *Gramsci's Political Thought*, Leiden-Boston: Brill.

Cowling, Mark 2008, *Marxism and Criminological Theory: A Critique and a Toolkit*, Basingstoke: Palgrave Macmillan.

D'Alessandro, Leonardo Pompeo 2011, 'Luigi Cadorna: da Caporetto al caporettismo', in *Il nostro Gramsci: Antonio Gramsci a colloquio con i protagonisti della storia d'Italia*, edited by Angelo D'Orsi, Rome: Viella.

D'Orsi, Angelo 2008, 'Gramsci e la guerra: dal giornalismo alla riflessione storica', in Giasi 2008a, vol. 1.

Dal Maso, Juan 2018, *Hegemonia y lucha de clases. Tres ensayos sobre Trotsky, Gramsci y el Marxismo*, Buenos Aires: Ediciones IPS.

Davis, John A. 1988, *Conflict and Control: Law and Order in Nineteenth-Century Italy*, Basingstoke: MacMillan.

Davis, John A. (ed.) 2000, *Italy in the Nineteenth Century: 1796–1900*, Oxford: Oxford University Press.

De Felice, Franco 1971, *Serrati, Bordiga, Gramsci e il problema della rivoluzione in Italia. 1919–1920*, Bari: De Donato.

De Felice, Franco 1977, 'Rivoluzione passiva, fascismo, americanismo in Gramsci', in *Politica e storia in Gramsci*, vol. 1, edited by Franco Ferri, Rome: Editori Riuniti.

De Felice, Franco 1978, 'I comunisti italiani e la crisi generale del capitalismo negli anni Venti', in Telò 1978.

De Grand, Alexander J. 1989, *The Italian Left in the Twentieth Century: A History of the Socialist and Communist Parties*, Bloomington: Indiana University Press.

Del Roio, Marcos 2015, *The Prisms of Gramsci: The Political Formula of the United Front*, Leiden-Boston: Brill.

Descendre, Romain 2019, '"Des prélats, c'est-à-dire des politiques": l'Église dans les *Cahiers de prison* d'Antonio Gramsci', *Revue de l'histoire des religions*, 236, no. 2: 367–94.

Descendre, Romain and Jean-Claude Zancarini 2016, 'De la traduction à la traductibilité. Un outil d'émancipation théorique', *Laboratoire italien. Politique et société*, 18, available at: http://journals.openedition.org/laboratoireitalien/1062 (accessed 13 January 2019).

Descendre, Romain and Jean-Claude Zancarini (eds) 2020, *La France d'Antonio Gramsci*, Lyon: ENS Éditions [forthcoming].

Detti, Tommaso 1972, *Serrati e la formazione del Partito comunista italiano. Storia della frazione terzinternazionalista. 1921–1924*, Rome: Editori Riuniti.

Di Meo, Antonio 2015, 'La "rivoluzione passiva": Una ricognizione sui significati', *Critica marxista*, 1: 59–67.

Durante, Lea 2004, 'Nazionale-popolare', in *Le parole di Gramsci. Per un lessico dei 'Quaderni del carcere'*, edited by Fabio Frosini and Guido Liguori, Rome: Carocci.

Egan, Daniel 2016, *The Dialectic of Position and Maneuver: Understanding Gramsci's Military Metaphor*, Leiden-Boston: Brill.

Ekers, Michael, Gillian Hart, Stefan Kipfer and Alex Loftus (eds) 2012, *Gramsci: Space, Nature, Politics*, Oxford: Wiley-Blackwell.

Elazar, Dahlia S. 2001, *The Making of Fascism: Class, State, and Counter-revolution, Italy 1919–1922*, Westport, CT: Praeger.

Eley, Geoff 2002, *Forging Democracy: The History of the Left in Europe, 1850–2000*, Oxford: Oxford University Press.

Favilli, Paolo 1996, *Storia del marxismo italiano. Dalle origini alla grande guerra*, Milan: Franco Angeli.

Filippini, Michele 2015, *Una politica di massa: Antonio Gramsci e la rivoluzione della società*, Rome: Carocci.

Filippini, Michele and Massimo Rosati (eds) 2013, *Gramsci e la sociologia*, monographic section of *Quaderni di teoria sociale*, 13.

Fonseca, Marco 2016, *Gramsci's Critique of Civil Society: Towards a New Concept of Hegemony*, London-New York: Routledge.

Fontana, Benedetto 2004, 'The Concept of Caesarism in Gramsci', in Baehr and Richter 2004.

Fonzo, Erminio 2019, *Il mondo antico negli scritti di Antonio Gramsci*, Mercato San Severino: Edizioni del Paguro.

Francioni, Gianni 1984, *L'officina gramsciana. Ipotesi sulla struttura dei 'Quaderni del carcere'*, Naples: Bibliopolis.

Francioni, Gianni 1987, 'Gramsci tra Croce e Bucharin: sulla struttura dei Quaderni 10 e 11', *Critica marxista*, 6: 19–45.

Francioni, Gianni 2009, 'Come lavorava Gramsci', in QAnast, vol. 1.

Francioni, Gianni 2016, 'Un labirinto di carta (Introduzione alla filologia gramsciana)', *International Gramsci Journal*, 2, no. 1: 7–48.

Francioni, Gianni 2020, '"La liquidazione di Leone Davidovi". Per una nuova datazione del Quaderno 14', in *Un nuovo Gramsci. Biografia, temi, interpretazioni*, edited by Gianni Francioni and Francesco Giasi, Rome: Viella.

Frankel, Richard 2005, *Bismarck's Shadow: The Cult of Leadership and the Transformation of the German Right. 1898–1945*, Oxford: Berg.

Fresu, Gianni 2005, *'Il diavolo nell'ampolla'. Antonio Gramsci, gli intellettuali e il partito*, Naples: La Città del Sole.

Frosini, Fabio 2004, 'Riforma e Rinascimento', in *Le parole di Gramsci. Per un lessico dei 'Quaderni del carcere'*, edited by Fabio Frosini and Guido Liguori, Rome: Carocci.

Frosini, Fabio 2007, 'Gramsci y la sociedad. De la crítica de la sociología marxista a la ciencia de la política', *Revista Internacional de Sociología*, 65, no. 47: 179–99.

Frosini, Fabio 2008, 'Gramsci lettore di Croce e Weber (Rinascimento, Riforma, Controriforma)', in *Réforme et Contre-Réforme à l'époque de la naissance et de l'affirmation des totalitarismes (1900–1940)*, edited by Chiara Lastraioli and Maria Rosaria Chiapparo, Turnhout: Brepols.

Frosini, Fabio 2009, *Da Gramsci a Marx. Ideologia, verità e politica*, Rome: DeriveApprodi.

Frosini, Fabio 2010a, 'On "Translatability" in Gramsci's *Prison Notebooks*', in *Gramsci, Language, and Translation*, edited by Peter Ives and Rocco Lacorte, Lanham, MD: Lexington Books.

Frosini, Fabio 2010b, *La religione dell'uomo moderno: politica e verità nei Quaderni del carcere di Antonio Gramsci*, Rome: Carocci.

Frosini, Fabio 2011, 'Fascismo, parlamentarismo e lotta per il comunismo in Gramsci', *Critica marxista*, 5: 9–35.

Frosini, Fabio 2012a, 'I "Quaderni" tra Mussolini e Croce', *Critica marxista*, 4: 60–8.

Frosini, Fabio 2012b, 'Croce, fascismo, comunismo', *Il cannocchiale. Rivista di studi filosofici*, 48, no. 3: 141–62.

Frosini, Fabio 2012c, 'Reformation, Renaissance and the State: The Hegemonic Fabric of Modern Sovereignty', *Journal of Romance Studies*, 12, no. 3: 63–77.

Frosini, Fabio 2013, 'Luigi Russo e Georges Sorel: sulla genesi del "moderno Principe" nei "Quaderni del carcere" di Antonio Gramsci', *Studi storici*, 54, no. 3: 545–90.

Frosini, Fabio 2014, 'Gramsci e il fascismo. La letteratura e il "nazionale popolare"', in *Narrazioni egemoniche. Gramsci, letteratura e società civile*, edited by Mauro Pala, Bologna: Il Mulino.

Frosini, Fabio 2015, 'Sulle "spie" dei "Quaderni del carcere"', *International Gramsci Journal*, 1, no. 4: 43–65.

Frosini, Fabio 2016a, 'L'egemonia e i "subalterni". Utopia, religione, democrazia', *International Gramsci Journal*, 2, no. 1: 126–66.

Frosini, Fabio 2016b, 'Subalterns, Religion, and the Philosophy of Praxis in Gramsci's *Prison Notebooks*', *Rethinking Marxism*, 28, nos. 3–4: 523–39.

Frosini, Fabio 2016c, 'L'eccidio di Roccagorga e la "settimana rossa": Gramsci, il "sovversivismo" e il fascismo', *Studi storici*, 57, no. 1: 137–66.

Frosini, Fabio 2017a, 'Cosmopolitanism, Nationalism and Hegemony: Antonio Gramsci's *Prison Notebooks* and the European Crisis', *International Critical Thought*, 7, no. 2: 190–204.

Frosini, Fabio 2017b, 'Rivoluzione passiva e laboratorio politico: appunti sull'analisi del fascismo nei *Quaderni del carcere*', *Studi storici*, 58, no. 2: 297–328.

Frosini, Fabio 2017c, 'Stato delle masse ed egemonia: note su Franco De Felice interprete di Gramsci', *Studi storici*, 58, no. 4: 987–1014.

Frosini, Fabio 2018, '"Politica totalitaria" e "costituentismo" nei *Quaderni del carcere* di Antonio Gramsci', *Paradigmi. Rivista di critica filosofica*, 36, no. 2: 365–80.

Frosini, Fabio 2020, 'Gramsci, Sorel, Croce: de la "passion" au "mythe"', in Romain Descendre and Zancarini 2020 [forthcoming].

Gagliardi, Alessio 2008, 'Il problema del corporativismo nel dibattito europeo e nei *Quaderni*', in Giasi 2008a, vol. 2.

Gagliardi, Alessio 2010, *Il corporativismo fascista*, Rome-Bari: Laterza.

Gagliardi, Alessio 2016a, 'Tra rivoluzione e controrivoluzione. L'interpretazione gramsciana del fascismo', *Laboratoire italien. Politique et société*, 18, available at: http://journals.openedition.org/laboratoireitalien/1062 (accessed 13 January 2019).

Gagliardi, Alessio 2016b, 'The Corporatism of Fascist Italy between Words and Reality', *Estudos Ibero-Americanos*, 42: 409–29.

Gagliardi, Alessio 2017, 'Oltre il paradigma antifascista. Gramsci e le interpretazioni del fascismo', *Studi storici*, 58, no. 4: 1015–40.

Garzarelli, Benedetta 2007, 'Il fascismo e la crisi italiana negli scritti di Antonio Gramsci del 1924–1926', *Studi storici*, 48, no. 4: 1059–90.

Garzarelli, Benedetta 2008, 'Il fascismo e la crisi italiana negli scritti del 1924–26', in Giasi 2008a, vol. 1.

Gentile, Emilio 2002, *Fascismo. Storia e interpretazione*, Rome-Bari, Laterza.

Gervasoni, Marco 1998, *Antonio Gramsci e la Francia. Dal mito della modernità alla 'scienza della politica'*, Milan: Unicopli.

Gianni, Emilio 2001, *L'editore Luigi Mongini e la diffusione del marxismo in Italia. Catalogo storico 1899–1911*, Milan: Pantarei.

Gianni, Emilio 2004, *Diffusione, popolarizzazione e volgarizzazione del marxismo in Italia. Scritti di Marx ed Engels pubblicati in italiano dal 1848 al 1926*, Milan: Pantarei.

Giasi, Francesco (ed.) 2008a, *Gramsci nel suo tempo*, 2 vols., Rome: Carocci.

Giasi, Francesco 2008b, 'Divisioni politiche e unità sindacale dopo Livorno', in Giasi 2008a, vol. 1.

Giasi, Francesco 2009, 'Gramsci a Vienna. Annotazioni su quattro lettere inedite', in *Pensare la politica. Scritti per Giuseppe Vacca*, edited by Francesco Giasi, Roberto Gualtieri and Silvio Pons, Rome: Carocci.

Giasi, Francesco 2011a, 'Problemi di edizione degli scritti precarcerari', *Studi storici*, 4: 837–58.

Giasi, Francesco 2011b, 'Marx nella biblioteca di Gramsci', in *Marx e Gramsci. Filologia, filosofia e politica allo specchio*, edited by Anna Di Bello, Naples: Liguori.

Giocanti, Stéphane 2009, *Une histoire politique de la littérature. De Victor Hugo à Richard Millet*, Paris: Flammarion.

Gollwitzer, Heinz 1952, 'Der Cäsarismus Napoleons III', *Historische Zeitschrift*, 173: 23–75.

Gramsci, Antonio 1977, *Quaderno 19*, edited by Corrado Vivanti, Turin: Einaudi.

Gramsci, Antonio 2012, *Il moderno principe. Il partito e la lotta per l'egemonia. Quaderno 13. Noterelle sulla politica del Machiavelli*, edited by Carmine Donzelli, Rome: Donzelli.

Green, Marcus E. 2002, 'Gramsci Cannot Speak: Presentations and Interpretations of Gramsci's Concept of the Subaltern', *Rethinking Marxism*, 14, no. 3: 1–24.

Griepenburg, Rüdiger and Karl Hermann Tjaden 1966, 'Faschismus und Bonapartismus. Zur Kritik der Faschismustheorie August Thalheimers', *Das Argument*, 41: 461–72.

Groh, Dieter 1972, 'Cäsarismus, Napoleonismus, Bonapartismus, Führer, Chef, Imperialismus', in *Geschichtliche Grundbegriffe*, vol. 1 (A–D), edited by Otto Brunner, Werner Konze and Reinhardt Koselleck, Stuttgart: Klett-Cotta.

Hájek, Milos 1985, 'Il fascismo nell'analisi dell'Internazionale Operaia Socialista', in *L'Internazionale Operaia Socialista fra le due guerre*, edited by Enzo Collotti, Milan: Feltrinelli.

Hamilton, Richard F. 1991, *The Bourgeois Epoch: Marx and Engels on Britain, France, and Germany*, Chapel Hill, NC: University of North Carolina Press.

Hammer, Karl and Claus Hartmann (eds) 1977, *Le Bonapartisme. Phénomène historique et mythe politique*, München: Artemis Verlag.

Hanisch, Ernst 1974, 'Otto Bauers Theorie des "Austrofaschismus"', *Zeitgeschichte*, 11–12: 251–63.

Hayes, Peter 1988, 'Utopia and the *Lumpenproletariat*: Marx's Reasoning in *The Eighteenth Brumaire of Louis Bonaparte*', *The Review of Politics*, 3: 445–65.

Howell, David 2002, *MacDonald's Party: Labour Identities and Crisis. 1922–1931*, Oxford: Oxford University Press.

Izzo, Francesca 2009, *Democrazia e cosmopolitismo in Antonio Gramsci*, Rome: Carocci.

Izzo, Francesca 2011, 'Marx dagli scritti giovanili ai "Quaderni"', in *Marx e Gramsci. Filologia, filosofia e politica allo specchio*, edited by Anna Di Bello, Naples: Liguori.

Jacini, Stefano 1870, *Sulle condizioni della cosa pubblica in Italia dopo il 1866. Lettera agli elettori di Terni del loro deputato dimissionario Stefano Jacini*, Florence: Stabilimento Giuseppe Civelli.

Jackson, Robert P. 2016, 'Subalternity and the Mummification of Culture in Gramsci's "Prison Notebooks"', *International Gramsci Journal*, 2, no. 1: 201–25.

Jackson, Robert P. 2018, 'Violence and Civilization: Gramsci, Machiavelli, and Sorel', in *The Meanings of Violence: From Critical Theory to Biopolitics*, edited by Gavin Rae and Emma Ingala, London-New York: Routledge.

Jackson, Robert P. 2019, 'The "Mummification of Culture" in Gramsci's "Prison Notebooks"', in *Revisiting Gramsci's* Notebooks, edited by Francesca Antonini et al., Leiden-Boston: Brill.

Jay, Martin 1984, *Marxism and Totality: The Adventure of a Concept from Lukács to Habermas*, Berkeley: University of California Press.

Jessop, Bob 2007, *State Power: A Strategic-relational Approach*, Cambridge: Polity Press.

Kalyvas, Andreas 2000, 'Hegemonic Sovereignty: Carl Schmitt, Antonio Gramsci and the Constituent Prince', *Journal of Political Ideologies*, 5, no. 3: 343–76.

Kitchen, Martin 1973, 'August Thalheimer's Theory of Fascism', *Journal of History of Ideas*, 1: 67–78.

Kramer, Alan 2007, *Dynamic of Destruction: Culture and Mass Killing in the First World War*, Oxford: Oxford University Press.

LaPorte, Norman, Kevin Morgan and Matthew Worley (eds) 2008, *Bolshevism, Stalinism and the Comintern: Perspectives on Stalinization, 1917–53*, Basingstoke: Palgrave Macmillan.

Liguori, Guido 2006, *Sentieri gramsciani*, Rome: Carocci.

Liguori, Guido 2012, *Gramsci conteso. Storia di un dibattito 1922–2012*, Rome: Editori Riuniti.

Liguori, Guido 2015, *Gramsci's Pathways*, Leiden-Boston: Brill.

Liguori, Guido and Pasquale Voza (eds) 2009, *Dizionario gramsciano. 1926–1937*, Rome: Carocci.

Losurdo, Domenico 1997, *Antonio Gramsci dal liberalismo al 'comunismo critico'*, Rome: Gamberetti.

Lucarini, Federico 2008, 'Socialismo, riformismo e scienze sociali nella Torino del giovane Gramsci (1914–1921)', in Giasi 2008a, vol. 1.

Lucas, Marie 2020, 'Gramsci et l'Action française: nationalisme, positivisme, catholicisme', in Descendre and Zancarini 2020 [forthcoming].

Maccabelli, Terenzio 2008, 'La "grande trasformazione". I rapporti tra Stato ed economia nei *Quaderni del carcere*', in Giasi 2008a, vol. 2.

Mackenbach, Werner 1994, 'Bonapartismus', in *Historisch-kritisches Wörterbuch des Marxismus*, vol. 1, edited by Wolfgang Fritz Haug, Hamburg: Argument-Verlag.

Maggi, Michele 2008, *La filosofia della rivoluzione. Gramsci, la cultura e la guerra europea*, Rome: Edizioni di Storia e Letteratura.

Malandrino, Corrado 2001, 'Gramsci e la "Sociologia del partito politico" di Michels', in *Gramsci: il partito politico nei 'Quaderni'*, edited by Salvo Mastellone and Giorgio Sola, Florence: Centro Editoriale Toscano.

Maltese, Pietro 2015, 'Disciplina e conformismo nelle riflessioni industrialiste di Antonio Gramsci', *Studi sulla formazione*, 18, no. 1: 65–79.

Manacorda, Mario Alighiero 1970, *Il principio educativo in Gramsci. Americanismo e conformismo*, Rome: Armando.

Mancina, Claudia 1980, 'Rapporti di forza e previsione. Il gioco della storia secondo Gramsci', *Critica marxista*, 5: 41–54.

Mancina, Claudia 1992, 'Individualité et conformisme selon Gramsci', in *Modernité de Gramsci*, edited by André Tosel, Paris: Le Belles Lettres.

Mangoni, Luisa 1976, 'Cesarismo, bonapartismo, fascismo', *Studi storici*, 17, no. 3: 41–61.

Mangoni, Luisa 1977, 'Il problema del fascismo nei "Quaderni del carcere"', in *Politica e storia in Gramsci*, vol. 1, edited by Franco Ferri, Rome: Editori Riuniti.

Mangoni, Luisa 1979, 'Per una definizione del fascismo: i concetti di bonapartismo e cesarismo', *Italia contemporanea*, 135: 17–52.

Mangoni, Luisa 1987, 'La genesi delle categorie storico-politiche nei "Quaderni del carcere"', *Studi storici*, 28, no. 3: 565–79.

Marramao, Giacomo 1977, *Austromarxismo e socialismo di sinistra fra le due guerre*, Milan: La Pietra.

Martelli, Michele 1995, 'Gramsci e l'URSS staliniana', *Marxismo oggi*, 1: 67–84.

Martelli, Michele 1999, *I filosofi e l'URSS, Per una critica del socialismo reale. Nietzsche, Marx, Gramsci, Lukács, Bloch, Marcuse, Merleau-Ponty, Sartre, Bobbio*, Naples: La Città del Sole.

Martin, James 2002, *Antonio Gramsci: Critical Assessments*, London-New York: Routledge.

Matard-Bonucci, Marie-Anne and Pierre Milza (eds) 2004, *L'homme nouveau dans l'Europe fasciste (1922–1945). Entre dictature et totalitarisme*, Paris: Fayard.

Mazlish, Bruce 1972, 'The Tragic Farce of Marx, Hegel, and Engels: A Note', *History and Theory*, 11, no. 3: 335–7.

McDaniel, Iain 2016, 'The Politics of Historical Economics: Wilhelm Roscher on Democracy, Socialism and Caesarism', *Modern Intellectual History*, 15, no. 1: 93–122.

McDaniel, Iain 2018, 'Constantin Frantz and the Intellectual History of Bonapartism and Caesarism: a Reassessment', *Intellectual History Review*, 28, no. 2: 317–38.

McDonough, Terrence 1995, 'Lenin, Imperialism, and the Stages of Capitalist Development', *Science & Society*, 59, no. 3: 339–67.

McLoughlin, Barry and Kevin McDermott (eds) 2002, *Stalin's Terror: High Politics and Mass Repression in the Soviet Union*, Basingstoke: Palgrave Macmillan.

McMillan, James F. 1991, *Napoleon III*, London: Longman.

McNally, Mark 2008, 'The Organization of Balance and Equilibrium in Gramsci's Hegemony', *History of Political Thought*, 4: 662–89.

McNally, Mark 2015, 'Gramsci, the United Front Comintern and Democratic Strategy', in *Antonio Gramsci*, edited by Mark McNally, Basingstoke: Palgrave Macmillan.

McNally, Mark 2017, 'Socialism and Democratic Strategy in Italy's *Biennio Rosso*: Gramsci *contra* Treves', *Journal of Modern Italian Studies*, 3: 314–37.

Medici, Rita 2000, *Giobbe e Prometeo. Filosofia e politica nel pensiero di Gramsci*, Florence: Alinea.

Michelini, Luca 2011, *Marxismo, liberismo, rivoluzione. Saggio sul giovane Gramsci. 1915–1920*, Naples: La Città del Sole.

Milza, Pierre, 2006, *Napoléon III*, Paris: Tempus.

Mitzman, Arthur 1970, *The Iron Cage: An Historical Interpretation of Max Weber*, New York: Kopf.

Modonesi, Massimo 2014, *Subalternity, Antagonism, Autonomy: Constructing the Political Subject*, London: Pluto Press.

Modonesi, Massimo 2018, *The Antagonistic Principle: Marxism and Political Action*, Leiden-Boston: Brill.

Momigliano, Arnaldo 1956, 'Per un riesame della storia dell'idea di cesarismo', *Rivista storica italiana*, 68, no. 2: 220–9.

Mommsen, Wolfgang J. 1981, 'Max Weber and Roberto Michels: An Asymmetrical Partnership', *European Journal of Sociology / Archives Européennes de Sociologie*, 22, no. 1: 100–16.

Mommsen, Wolfgang J. and Jürgen Osterhammel (eds) 1987, *Max Weber and His Contemporaries*, London: Allen & Unwin.

Morera, Esteve 1990, *Gramsci's Historicism: A Realist Interpretation*, London-New York: Routledge.

Morgan, Kevin 2006, *Ramsay MacDonald*, London: Haus Publishing.

Morton, Adam David 2007, *Unravelling Gramsci: Hegemony and Passive Revolution in the Global Political Economy*, London: Pluto Press.

Mumford, Andrew 2015, 'Parallels, Prescience and the Past: Analogical Reasoning and Contemporary International Politics', *International Politics*, 52, no. 1: 1–19.

Musolff, Andreas 2004, *Metaphor and Political Discourse: Analogical Reasoning in Debates about Europe*, Basingstoke: Palgrave Macmillan.

Natoli, Claudio 2000, *Fascismo, democrazia, socialismo. Comunisti e socialisti tra le due guerre*, Milan: Franco Angeli.

Natoli, Claudio 2008, 'Grande Guerra e rinnovamento del socialismo negli scritti del giovane Gramsci (1914–1919)', in Giasi 2008a, vol. 1.

Newman, John P. 2017, 'Revolution and Counterrevolution in Europe 1917–1923', in Pons and Smith 2017.

Olsaretti, Alessandro 2016, 'From the Return to Labriola to the Anti-Croce. Philosophy,

Praxis and Human Nature in Gramsci's *Prison Notebooks*', *Historical Materialism*, 24, no. 4: 193–220.

Paggi, Leonardo 1970, *Gramsci e il moderno principe. 1. Nella crisi del socialismo italiano*, Rome: Editori Riuniti.

Paggi, Leonardo 1984, *Le strategie del potere in Gramsci. Tra fascismo e socialismo in un solo paese. 1923–1926*, Rome: Editori Riuniti.

Paladini Musitelli, Marina 2004, 'Brescianesimo', in *Le parole di Gramsci. Per un lessico dei 'Quaderni del carcere'*, edited by Fabio Frosini and Guido Liguori, Rome: Carocci.

Paladini Musitelli, Marina 2008, 'La funzione della letteratura e il concetto di nazionale-popolare', in Giasi 2008a, vol. 2.

Panaccione, Andrea 2008, 'Gramsci e il socialismo europeo fra guerra e dopoguerra', in Giasi 2008a, vol. 1.

Panichi, Alessio 2019, 'Between Belonging and Originality. Norberto Bobbio's Interpretation of Gramsci', in *Revisiting Gramsci's* Notebooks, edited by Francesca Antonini et al., Leiden-Boston: Brill.

Pasetti, Matteo 2016, *L'Europa corporativa. Una storia transnazionale tra le due guerre mondiali*, Bologna: Bononia University Press.

Patenaude, Bertrand M. 2017, 'Trotsky and Trotskyism', in Pons and Smith 2017.

Patriarca, Silvana and Lucy Riall (eds) 2012, *The Risorgimento Revisited: Nationalism and Culture in Nineteenth-Century Italy*, Basingstoke: Palgrave Macmillan.

Paxton, Robert O. 2004, *The Anatomy of Fascism*, New York: Knopf.

Payne, Stanley G. 1995, *A History of Fascism, 1914–1945*, Madison: University of Wisconsin Press.

Petersen, Jens 1975, 'La nascita del concetto di "Stato totalitario" in Italia', *Annali dell'Istituto storico italo-germanico in Trento / Jahrbuch des Italienisch-Deutschen Historischen Instituts in Trient*, 1: 143–70.

Pissarello, Giulia 2008, 'Lingua e letteratura inglese negli scritti del carcere di Antonio Gramsci: "Esercizi di lingua inglese" e riletture di Rudyard Kipling', in *La lingua/le lingue di Gramsci e delle sue opere*, edited by Fiamma Lussana, Soveria Mannelli: Rubbettino.

Pons, Silvio 2008, 'Il gruppo dirigente del PCI e la "questione russa" (1924–26)', in Giasi 2008a, vol. 1.

Pons, Silvio 2014, *The Global Revolution: A History of International Communism 1917–1991*, Oxford: Oxford University Press.

Pons, Silvio 2017, 'Gramsci e la Rivoluzione russa: una riconsiderazione (1917–1935)', *Studi storici*, 58, no. 4: 883–928.

Pons, Silvio and Stephen A. Smith (eds) 2017, *The Cambridge History of Communism*, 2 vols., Cambridge: Cambridge University Press.

Poulantzas, Nicos 1970, *Fascisme et dictature. La troisième internationale face au fascisme*, Paris: François Maspero.

Prawer, Siegbert Salomon 1976, *Karl Marx and World Literature*, Oxford: Clarendon.
Price, Roger 1997, *Napoleon III and the Second Empire*, London-New York: Routledge.
Prutsch, Markus J. 2019, *Caesarism in the Post-Revolutionary Age: Crisis, Populace and Leadership*, London: Bloomsbury.
Rafalski, Traute 1991, 'Gramsci e il corporativismo', *Critica marxista*, 3: 85–116.
Ragazzini, Dario 2002, *Leonardo nella società di massa. Teoria della personalità in Gramsci*, Bergamo: Moretti-Honegger.
Rapone, Leonardo 1978, *Trotskij e il fascismo*, Rome-Bari: Laterza.
Rapone, Leonardo 2008, 'Critica dell'Italia (e degli italiani) e antigiolittismo nel giovane Gramsci', in Giasi 2008a, vol. 1.
Rapone, Leonardo 2010, Review of Accardo and Fresu 2009, *Il mestiere di storico*, 2: 135.
Rapone, Leonardo 2011a, 'Gramsci giovane: la critica e le interpretazioni', *Studi storici*, 4: 975–91.
Rapone, Leonardo 2011b, *Cinque anni che paiono secoli. Antonio Gramsci dal socialismo al comunismo (1914–1919)*, Rome: Carocci.
Razeto Migliaro, Luis and Pasquale Misuraca 1978, *Sociologia e marxismo nella critica di Gramsci. Dalla critica delle sociologie alla scienza della storia e della politica*, Bari: De Donato.
Rees, Tim and Andrew Thorpe 1998, *International Communism and the Communist International, 1919–1943*, Manchester: Manchester University Press.
Riall, Lucy 1994, *Risorgimento: The History of Italy from Napoleon to Nation State*, London: Palgrave.
Richter, Melvin 2005, 'A Family of Political Concepts: Tyranny, Despotism, Bonapartism, Caesarism, Dictatorship, 1750–1917', *European Journal of Political Theory*, 4: 221–48.
Righi, Maria Luisa 2011, 'Gramsci a Mosca tra amori e politica (1922–1923)', *Studi storici*, 52, no. 4: 1001–38.
Riosa, Alceo 2007, *Napoleone e il bonapartismo nella cultura politica italiana. 1802–2005*, Milan: Guerini e Associati.
Roberts David D. 1979, *The Syndicalist Tradition and Italian Fascism*, Chapel Hill, NC: University of North Carolina Press.
Roberts David D. 2011, 'Reconsidering Gramsci's Interpretation of Fascism', *Journal of Modern Italian Studies*, 2: 239–55.
Rosengarten, Frank 1984–85, 'The Gramsci-Trotsky Question (1922–1932)', *Social Text*, 11: 65–95.
Rosengarten, Frank 2014, *The Revolutionary Marxism of Antonio Gramsci*, Leiden-Boston: Brill.
Rubel, Maximilien 1960, *Karl Marx devant le bonapartisme*, Paris: Le Haye.
Rusconi, Gian Enrico 2011, *Cavour e Bismarck. Due leader fra liberalismo e cesarismo*, Bologna: Il Mulino.

Saccarelli, Emanuele 2008, *Gramsci and Trotsky in the Shadow of Stalinism: The Political Theory and Practice of Opposition*, London-New York: Routledge.

Salamini, Leonardo 1974, 'Gramsci and Marxist Sociology of Knowledge: An Analysis of Hegemony-Ideology-Knowledge', *Sociological Quarterly*, 15, no. 3: 359–80.

Salamini, Leonardo 2014, *The Sociology of Political Praxis: An Introduction to Gramsci's Theory*, London-New York: Routledge.

Santangelo, Federico 2020, 'Between Caesarism and Cosmopolitanism: Julius Caesar as an Historical Problem in Gramsci', in *Antonio Gramsci and the Ancient World*, edited by Roberto Ciucciovè et al., London-New York: Routledge [forthcoming].

Santomassimo, Gianpasquale 2006, *La terza via fascista. Il mito del corporativismo*, Rome: Carocci.

Santoro, Lorenzo 2012, 'Antonio Gramsci: The Fascist Leadership as Modern Reactionary Caesarism and the Novelty of the Corporative State', *Leadership*, 3: 277–86.

Schecter, Darrow 1991, *Gramsci and the Theory of Industrial Democracy*, Aldershot: Avebury.

Schwarzmantel, John 2015, *The Routledge Guidebook to Gramsci's 'Prison Notebooks'*, London-New York: Routledge.

Showstack Sassoon, Anne 1980, *Gramsci's Politics*, London: Croom Helm.

Sillanpoa, Wallace P. 1983, 'Gramsci sul fascismo italiano: il giornalismo come storia', *Rassegna degli Archivi di Stato*, 2–3: 441–53.

Smith, W. Rand 2012, *Enemy Brothers: Socialists and Communists in France, Italy, and Spain*, Lanham, MD: Rowman & Littlefield.

Somai, Giovanni 1979, *Gramsci a Vienna. Ricerche e documenti: 1922–1924*, Urbino: Argalía.

Sorgonà, Gregorio and Ermanno Taviani (eds) 2016, *Franco De Felice. Il presente come storia*, Rome: Carocci.

Sotgiu, Girolamo 1987, 'Parlamentarismo nero', in *Gramsci. Le sue idee nel nostro tempo*, Rome: Editrice L'Unità.

Spriano Paolo 1967–75, *Storia del partito comunista italiano*, 5 vols., Turin: Einaudi.

Spriano Paolo 1971, *'L'Ordine Nuovo' e i Consigli di fabbrica*, Turin: Einaudi.

Spriano Paolo 1975, *The Occupation of the Factories. Italy 1920*, London: Pluto Press.

Steffek, Jens and Francesca Antonini 2015, 'Toward Eurafrica! Fascism, Corporativism and Italy's Colonial Expansion', in *Radicals and Reactionaries in Twentieth-Century International Thought*, edited by Ian Hall, Basingstoke: Palgrave Macmillan.

Steinberg, Jonathan 2011, *Bismarck: A Life*, Oxford: Oxford University Press.

Swain, Geoffrey 2014, *Trotsky and the Russian Revolution*, London-New York: Routledge.

Telò, Mario (ed.) 1978, *La crisi del capitalismo negli anni '20. Analisi economica e dibattito strategico nella Terza Internazionale*, Bari: De Donato.

Thomas, Peter D. 2006, 'Modernity as "Passive Revolution": Gramsci and the Funda-

mental Concepts of Historical Materialism', *Journal of the Canadian Historical Association / Revue de la Société historique du Canada*, 17, no. 2: 61–78.
Thomas, Peter D. 2009, *The Gramscian Moment: Philosophy, Hegemony and Marxism*, Leiden-Boston: Brill.
Thomas, Peter D. 2013, 'Hegemony, Passive Revolution and the Modern Prince', *Thesis Eleven*, 117, no. 1: 20–39.
Thomas, Peter D. 2015a, 'Cosa rimane dei subalterni alla luce dello "Stato integrale"?', *International Gramsci Journal*, 1, no. 4: 83–93.
Thomas, Peter D. 2015b, 'Gramsci's Machiavellian Metaphor: Restaging The Prince', in *The Radical Machiavelli: Politics, Philosophy and Language*, edited by Filippo Del Lucchese, Vittorio Morfino and Fabio Frosini, Leiden-Boston: Brill.
Thomas, Peter D. 2015c, 'Uneven Developments, Combined: The First World War and Marxist Theories of Revolution', in *Cataclysm 1914: The First World War and the Making of Modern World Politics*, edited by Alexander Anievas, Leiden-Boston: Brill.
Thomas, Peter D. 2017a, 'Gramsci's Plural Temporalities', in *The Government of Time: Theories of Plural Temporality in the Marxist Tradition*, edited by Vittorio Morfino and Peter D. Thomas, Leiden-Boston: Brill.
Thomas, Peter D. 2017b, 'The Modern Prince: Gramsci's Reading of Machiavelli', *History of Political Thought*, 38, no. 3: 523–44.
Thomas, Peter D. 2017c, 'The Plural Temporalities of Hegemony', *Rethinking Marxism*, 29, no. 2: 281–302.
Thomas, Peter D. 2018a, 'Gramsci's Revolutions: Passive and Permanent', *Modern Intellectual History* (published online: 21 June 2018).
Thomas, Peter D. 2018b, 'Reverberations of The Prince: From "Heroic Fury" to "Living Philology"', *Thesis Eleven*, 147, no. 1: 76–88.
Togliatti, Palmiro 1958, 'Gramsci e il leninismo', in *Studi gramsciani*, Rome: Editori Riuniti.
Togliatti, Palmiro 1976, *Lectures on Fascism*, New York: International Publishers.
Togliatti, Palmiro 2004, *Sul fascismo*, edited by Giuseppe Vacca, Rome-Bari: Laterza.
Tomba, Massimiliano 2013, 'Marx as the Historical Materialist: Re-reading *The Eighteenth Brumaire*', *Historical Materialism*, 17, no. 4: 44–65.
Traverso, Enzo 2001, *Le Totalitarisme. Le XXe siècle en débat*, Paris: Seuil.
Tuccari, Francesco 1993, *I dilemmi della democrazia moderna. Max Weber e Robert Michels*, Rome-Bari: Laterza.
Tuccari, Francesco 2001, 'Gramsci e la sociologia marxista di Nikolaj I. Bucharin', in *Gramsci: il partito politico nei Quaderni*, edited by Salvo Mastellone and Giorgio Sola, Florence: Centro Editoriale Toscano.
Twiss, Thomas M. 2014, *Trotsky and the Problem of Soviet Bureaucracy*, Leiden-Boston: Brill.

Vacca, Giuseppe 1988, 'L'Urss staliniana nell'analisi dei "Quaderni del carcere"', *Critica marxista*, 3–4: 129–46.

Vacca, Giuseppe 2011, 'Gramsci Studies since 1989', *Journal of Modern Italian Studies*, 16, no. 2: 179–94.

Vacca, Giuseppe 2012, *Vita e pensieri di Antonio Gramsci. 1926–1937*, Turin: Einaudi.

Vacca, Giuseppe 2017, *Modernità alternative. Il Novecento di Antonio Gramsci*, Turin: Einaudi.

Van den Berg, Axel 1988, *The Immanent Utopia: From Marxism on the State to the State of Marxism*, Princeton: Princeton University Press.

Voza, Pasquale 2004, 'Rivoluzione passiva', in *Le parole di Gramsci. Per un lessico dei 'Quaderni del carcere'*, edited by Fabio Frosini and Guido Liguori, Rome: Carocci.

Voza, Pasquale 2008, *Gramsci e la 'continua crisi'*, Rome: Carocci.

Wetherly, Paul 2005, *Marxism and the State: An Analytical Approach*, Basingstoke: Palgrave Macmillan.

White, Jonathan and Lea Ypi 2010, 'Rethinking the Modern Prince: Partisanship and the Democratic Ethos', *Political Studies*, 58: 809–28.

Williams, Gwyn A. 1975, *Proletarian Order: Antonio Gramsci, Factory Councils and the Origins of Italian Communism, 1911–1921*, London: Pluto Press.

Winkler, Heinrich August 1978, *Revolution, Staat, Faschismus. Zur Revision des historischen Materialismus*, Göttingen: Vandenhoeck & Ruprecht.

Wippermann, Wolfgang 1981, *Zur Analyse des Faschismus. Die sozialistischen und kommunistischen Faschismustheorien, 1921–1945*, Frankfurt am Main: Diesterweg.

Wippermann, Wolfgang 1983, *Die Bonapartismustheorie von Marx und Engels*, Stuttgart: Klett-Cotta.

Wistrich, Robert 1976, 'Leon Trotsky's Theory of Fascism', *Journal of Contemporary History*, 11: 157–84.

Zunino, Pier Giorgio 1988a, '"Il popolo delle scimmie" e la lettura gramsciana del fascismo negli anni Venti', *Italia contemporanea*, 171: 67–85.

Zunino, Pier Giorgio 1988b, 'Gramsci e il fascismo negli anni Venti', in *Teoria politica e società industriale. Ripensare Gramsci*, edited by Franco Sbarberi, Turin: Bollati Boringhieri.

Name Index

Marx and Gramsci are not included in this index, as both names occur very frequently throughout the book.

Abendroth, Wolfgang   x
Accardo, Aldo   152n
Adamson, Walter   18n, 152n, 153n, 154n
Aeschylus   74
Agosti, Aldo   8n, 37n, 44n
Albarani, Giuliano   144n
Albertini, Luigi   58n, 69n
Alfieri, Vittorio   184n
Antonini, Francesca   x, 3n, 6n, 13n, 33n, 60n, 66n, 71n, 95n, 116n, 119n, 136n, 140n, 142n, 143n, 175n, 176n, 178n, 186n, 194n, 196n, 198n
Aquarone, Alberto   173n
Arendt, Hannah   170n

Baehr, Peter   x
Baker, David   179n
Baldan, Attilio   136n
Balistreri, Caterina   13n
Banti, Alberto Mario   144n
Baratta, Giorgio   79n
Barnett, Vincent   82n
Basile, Luca   105n, 107n, 129n
Bauer, Otto   8
Bechelloni, Antonio   103n
Bellamy, Richard   105n
Benvenuti, Francesco   82n, 83n, 132n, 180n, 184n, 185n, 187n
Bergami, Giancarlo   152n
Bernstein, Aaron   14n
Berselli, Aldo   190n
Bianchi, Alvaro   83n
Biscione, Francesco   93n
Bismarck, Otto von (Otto Eduard Leopold von Bismarck-Schönhausen)   5n, 91–2, 120, 124n, 137, 144n, 145n, 194
Bluche, Frédéric   x
Bobbio, Norberto   62n
Bodrero, Emilio   129–30
Boeri, Maria Grazia   194n
Bonaparte, Charles-Louis-Napoléon   1–7, 14, 16, 32–5, 75, 96, 103, 114, 118n, 120–1, 123–5, 129, 135–7, 145n, 194, 201, 203

Bonaparte, Napoléon   1–2, 34, 80, 85, 91, 101, 103, 114, 118n, 120–2, 123n, 124–5, 137, 145n, 186, 194
Bongiovanni, Bruno   3n
Boothman, Derek   89n, 149n
Bordiga, Amadeo   46n, 51, 113n, 177n
Borkenau, Franz   8
Botz, Gerhard   x, 8n
Boulanger, Georges   104, 109, 140n, 196
Bravo, Gian Mario   3n, 11n
Buci-Glucksmann, Christine   10, 20n, 38n, 53n, 54n, 58n, 62n, 66n, 73n, 155n
Bukharin, Nikolai Ivanovich   83n, 186n
Burckhardt, Jacob   2
Burgio, Alberto   13n, 25n, 73n, 87n, 90n, 110, 112n, 117n, 119, 131, 132n, 133, 134n, 139n, 152n, 153n, 155n, 193

Cadorna, Luigi   11, 16–9, 80, 85, 162, 188n
Caesar (Gaius Julius Caesar)   91, 101, 114, 118n, 120–2, 123n, 124–5, 128n, 129–30, 137, 145n, 194
Cammarano, Fulvio   87n
Cammett, John   18n
Canfora, Luciano   66n
Caprioglio, Sergio   180n
Caputo, Renato   170n, 184n
Carlucci, Alessandro   xi, 13n, 23n
Carver, Terrell   3n
Cassina, Cristina   x, 1, 3n
Catone, Andrea   83n, 84n
Ceretta, Manuela   x
Cervelli, Innocenzo   x, 1n, 2n, 4n
Chernov, Viktor Mikhailovich   52
Churchill, Winston   100n
Ciccarelli, Roberto   134n
Ciccotti, Ettore   11–2
Ciliberto, Michele   112n, 129n, 152n
Clausewitz, Carl Philipp Gottlieb von   145n
Clerici, Franco   67n
Colarizi, Simona   152n
Corney, Frederick   186n

NAME INDEX

Cospito, Giuseppe xi, 11n, 73n, 76n, 79n, 84n, 88n, 90n, 98–9, 100n, 104n, 105n, 111n, 114n, 127n, 128n, 142n, 156n, 180n, 181n, 182n, 185n, 186n, 187n, 191n, 204n
Costa Pinto, Antonio 178n
Courier, Paul-Louis 1
Coutinho, Carlos Nelson 59n, 79n, 111n
Cowling, Mark 95
Crispi, Francesco 87, 134n, 165
Croce, Benedetto 88n
Cromwell, Oliver 104, 118, 186

D'Alessandro, Leonardo Pompeo 17n
D'Annunzio, Gabriele 23n
D'Orsi, Angelo 17n
Dal Maso, Juan 83n
Davis, John 87n, 190n
De Felice, Franco 18n, 20n, 73, 79n, 138n, 152n, 154n, 155n, 171n, 180n
De Grand, Alexander 18n
De Rivera, Primo (Miguel Primo de Rivera y Orbaneja) 101, 104, 121, 137
De Ruggiero, Guido 88n
De Vecchi, Cesare 30n
Del Roio, Marcos 50n
Depretis, Agostino 87, 165
Descendre, Romain 131n, 136n, 170n
Detti, Tommaso 25n
Di Meo, Antonio 112n, 138n
Disraeli, Benjamin 104, 129n, 130n
Donzelli, Carmine 83n
Dreyfus, Alfred 104, 140n
Durante, Lea 28n

Egan, Daniel 84n
Einaudi, Luigi 89n
Ekers, Michael 93n
Elazar, Dahlia 18n, 50n
Eley, Geoff 18n
Engels, Friedrich 6n, 7n, 9, 11–2, 13n, 21n, 32n, 36, 64–5, 67, 68n, 74n

Favilli, Paolo 18n
Federzoni, Luigi 58n
Ferri, Enrico 26n
Filippini, Michele 88n, 105n, 108n, 156n
Finchelstein, Federico 178n
Finelli, Roberto 62n

Fonseca, Marco 79n, 139n
Fontana, Benedetto x, 73n, 129n, 152n, 153n
Fonzo, Erminio 129n
Forenza, Eleonora 118n, 139n
Forni, Cesare 30n
Fovel, Massimo 50n, 177
Francioni, Gianni 10n, 84n, 102n, 108n, 141n, 143n, 185n, 187n, 190n
Frankel, Richard 144n
Fresu, Gianni 17n, 152n
Frosini, Fabio xi, 63n, 88n, 89n, 96n, 108n, 113n, 117n, 129n, 131n, 142n, 152n, 154n, 155n, 156n, 160n, 161, 163n, 165, 171n, 172n, 177n, 186n, 187n, 191n, 193n, 198n, 200n

Gagliardi, Alessio 23n, 152n, 154n, 155n, 170n, 177n, 178n, 179n, 187n
Gajda, Radola 140n
Gallo, Elisabetta 93
Garibaldi, Giuseppe 91
Garzarelli, Benedetta 152n, 154n
Gentile, Emilio 150n, 153n, 194n
Gentile, Giovanni 88n
Gervasoni, Marco 28n, 29n, 136n
Gianni, Emilio 11n
Giasi, Francesco 10n, 11n, 12n, 13n, 20n, 75n, 76n
Giocanti, Stéphane 5n, 34n
Gioda, Mario 29–31, 33
Giolitti, Giovanni 15, 23, 48n, 87, 165
Giuliano, Balbino 39n
Gobetti, Piero 38
Gollwitzer, Heinz x
Green, Marcus 169n
Griepenburg, Rüdiger x, 8n
Griffin, Roger 153n
Groh, Dieter x, 7n, 92
Guizot, François Pierre Guillaume 6n
Gurland, Arkadij (Arcadius Rudolf Lang Gurland) 8

Hájek, Milos 8n
Hamilton, Richard 32n
Hammer, Karl x
Hanisch, Ernst x
Hartmann, Claus x
Hayes, Peter 95n

NAME INDEX

Hegel, Georg Wilhelm Friedrich   37, 62–4, 69, 74, 90, 131n, 172
Hilferding, Rudolf   50n
Howell, David   147n
Hugo, Victor   5, 28, 31, 34, 135

Izzo, Francesca   11n, 28n, 71n, 129n, 202

Jacini, Stefano   190n
Jackson, Robert   31n, 112n, 181n
Jay, Martin   170n
Jessop, Bob   65n

Kahn, Otto   148
Kalyvas, Andreas   170n, 193n
Kerensky, Alexander Fyodorovich   52
Kipling, Rudyard   23, 24n
Kitchen, Martin   x, 8n
Kramer, Alan   16n

La Porta, Lelio   156n, 187n, 193n
Labriola, Antonio   12n, 13n, 134n
Labriola, Arturo   64n, 65n
LaPorte, Norman   37n
Lassalle, Ferdinand   11, 12, 13n
Ledru-Rollin, Alexandre-Auguste   32
Lenin (Vladimir Ilyich Ulyanov)   44n, 47, 48n, 50n, 105, 200
Liguori, Guido   xi, 10n, 28n, 29n, 59n, 62n, 73n, 82n, 83n, 84n, 86n, 87n, 88n, 93n, 105n, 108n, 111n, 113n, 117n, 118n, 123n, 129n, 132n, 134n, 139n, 144n, 149n, 155n, 156n, 164, 170n, 180n, 181n, 182n, 184n, 187n, 191n, 193n, 194n
London, Jack   50n
Lorenzo il Magnifico (Lorenzo de' Medici)   119n
Losurdo, Domenico   49n
Louis Bonaparte, *see* Bonaparte, Charles-Louis-Napoléon
Louis Napoleon, *see* Bonaparte, Charles-Louis-Napoléon
Lucarini, Federico   20n
Lucas, Marie   103n
Lucian   74
Ludendorff, Erich Friedrich Wilhelm   53
Luxemburg, Rosa   82, 113n

Maccabelli, Terenzio   177n

MacDonald, Ramsay   104, 147n, 148–9
Machiavelli, Niccolò   99n, 102n
Mackenbach, Werner   x
Maggi, Michele   153n
Maladrino, Corrado   105n
Malot, Hector-Henri   30
Maltese, Pietro   194n
Manacorda, Mario Alighiero   194n
Mancina, Claudia   111n, 194n
Mangoni, Luisa   x, 7, 73, 128n, 145n, 152n, 155n
Marinetti, Filippo Tommaso   30
Marramao, Giacomo   8n
Martelli, Michele   180n
Martin, James   18n, 134n
Martov, Julius (Yuliy Osipovich Tsederbaum)   81
Masaryk, Thomas   140n
Matard-Bonucci, Marie-Anne   194n
Matteotti, Giacomo   34, 50, 57, 68
Maurras, Charles   103, 113n, 140n
Mazlish, Bruce   74n
McDaniel, Iain   x
McDarmott, Kevin   188n
McDonough, Terrence   48n
McLoughlin, Barry   188n
McMillan, James   120n
McNally, Mark   25n, 36n, 46n, 50n, 57n, 112n
Medici, Rita   105n, 134n
Mehring, Franz   28n
Menotti Serrati, Giacinto   19, 20, 25–7, 47
Michelini, Luca   38n, 49n
Michels, Robert   88n, 105–10, 151, 195–6
Milza, Pierre   2n, 194n
Missiroli, Mario   80
Misuraca, Pasquale   108n
Mitzman, Arthur   106n
Modonesi, Massimo   139n, 140n
Molitor, Jacques   76
Momigliano, Arnaldo   x
Mommsen, Wolfgang   106n
Mongini, Luigi   11
Morera, Esteve   108n
Morgan, Kevin   37n, 147n
Morton, Adam David   111n, 138n
Mosca, Gaetano   88n, 163
Muir, Ramsey   149n
Mumford, Andrew   66n
Musolff, Andreas   66n

Mussolini, Benito 26n, 33–5, 57, 69, 70, 104–5, 107, 110, 150n, 151–2, 177, 179, 189n, 191n, 193, 199–200

Napoleon I, see Bonaparte, Napoléon
Napoleon III, see Bonaparte, Charles-Louis-Napoléon
Natoli, Claudio 8n, 20n, 44n
Nenni, Pietro 8
Newman, John 38n

Odilon Barrot, Camille Hyacinthe 68n
Olsaretti, Alessandro 13n

Paggi, Leonardo 10, 17n, 20n, 21n, 24n, 25, 26n, 30n, 34n, 39n, 45n, 46n, 54n, 55n, 57n, 58n, 59n, 62n, 63n, 64n, 65n, 66n, 71n, 90, 152n
Paladini Musitelli, Marina 28n
Palmerston (Henry John Temple, third Viscount Palmerston) 75n
Panaccione, Andrea 20n
Panichi, Alessio 62n
Panunzio, Sergio 187n
Pasetti, Matteo 178n
Patenaude, Betrand 82n
Patriarca, Silvana 144n
Paxton, Robert 150n
Payne, Stanley 50n, 153n
Petersen, Jens 170n
Pissarello, Giulia 23n
Pons, Silvio 37n, 82n, 83n, 132n, 180n, 184n, 185n, 187n, 188n
Ponson du Terrail, Pierre Alexis 30
Poulantzas, Nicos x
Prawer, Siegbert Salomon 33n, 34n
Prestipino, Giuseppe 123n, 132n
Price, Roger 2n
Proudhon, Pierre-Joseph 2–3, 5, 135
Prutsch, Markus x

Rafalski, Traute 177n
Ragazzini, Dario 127n, 139n, 193n, 194n
Rapone, Leonardo x, 8n, 10n, 16n, 20n, 21n, 24n, 25n, 37n, 38, 39n, 44n, 49n, 152n
Razeto Migliaro, Luis 108n
Rees, Tim 37n
Riall, Lucy 144n
Ricardo, David 131n
Richebourg, Émile 30
Richter, Melvin x
Righi, Maria Luisa 13n
Riosa, Alceo x
Roberts, David 18n, 73n, 152n, 153n, 154n
Rocca, Massimo 30, 31
Rolland, Romain 48
Romieu, Auguste 1, 2
Rosati, Massimo 108n
Rosengarten, Frank 83n
Rossi, Angelo 185n
Rossi, Cesare 189n
Rubel, Maximilien 3n
Rusconi, Gian Enrico 144n
Ryazanov, David (David Borisovich Goldendach) 13n

Saccarelli, Emanuele 187n, 191n
Salamini, Leonardo 105n, 108n
Santangelo, Federico 129n
Santomassimo, Gianpasquale 178n
Santoro, Lorenzo 73n, 105n, 177n
Schecter, Darrow 41n
Schifrin, Alexander (Alexander Michailowitsch Schifrin) 8
Schucht, Tatiana 75n, 76
Schwarzmantel, John 79n
Showstack Sassoon, Anne 111n
Sillanpoa, Wallace 152n
Sismóndi, Jean Charles Léonard Simonde de 4
Smith, Stephen 188n
Smith, W. Rand 18n
Somai, Giovanni 13n
Sorel, Georges 63, 108
Sorgonà, Gregorio 73n
Sotgiu, Girolamo 187n
Spirito, Ugo 177
Spriano, Paolo 18n, 41n
Stalin (Iosif Vissarionovich Dzhugashvili) 185, 186, 187, 188n, 191n
Steffek, Jens 178n
Steinberg, Jonathan 144n
Sue, Eugène 28, 30–1, 105n
Suppa, Silvio 134n
Swain, Geoffrey 82n

Taviani, Ermanno 73n
Telò, Mario 37n

NAME INDEX 227

Thalheimer, August   8, 153n
Thierry, Jacques-Nicolas-Augustin   6n
Thomas, Peter   xi, 44n, 60n, 83n, 89n, 113n, 116n, 119n, 131n, 134n, 138n, 139n, 180n, 186n, 191n, 193n, 195n, 197n, 198n, 199n, 200n
Thorpe, Andrew   37n
Tjaden, Karl Hermann   x, 8n
Togliatti, Palmiro   9, 12n
Tomba, Massimiliano   33n, 74n
Traverso, Enzo   170n
Treves, Claudio   25n
Trotsky, Leon (Lev Davidovich Bronstein)   8, 44n, 79, 81, 82, 83, 84, 85, 153n, 183, 185, 186n, 190, 191n, 192
Tsankov, Aleksander Tsolov   104, 122n
Tsereteli, Irakli   52
Tuccari, Francesco   106n, 108n
Turati, Filippo   20, 25
Twiss, Thomas   82n

Umberto I di Savoia   23

Vacca, Giuseppe   xi, 9n, 11n, 132n, 138n, 169n, 180n, 185n, 191n, 193n
Valera, Paolo   30
Valois, George   140n
Van Der Berg, Axel   65n

Vivanti, Corrado   85n, 144n
Vogt, Karl   75
Volpe, Gioacchino   88n
Volpicelli, Arnaldo   177
Voza, Pasquale   28n, 29n, 59n, 62n, 73n, 82n, 83n, 84n, 86n, 87n, 88n, 93n, 105n, 108n, 111n, 113n, 117n, 118n, 123n, 129n, 132n, 134n, 138n, 139n, 144n, 149, 155n, 156n, 164n, 170n, 180n, 181n, 182n, 184n, 187n, 191n, 193n

Warburg, Paul   148
Weber, Max   88, 90, 106, 107n
Wetherly, Paul   65n
Weydemeyer, Joseph   3n
White, Jonathan   193n
Wilhelm II   92, 145n
Williams, Gwyn   41n
Winkler, Heinrich August   6n
Wippermann, Wolfgang   x, xi, 3n
Wistrich, Robert   8n
Worley, Matthew   37n

Ypi, Lea   193n

Zancarini, Jean-Claude   131n, 136n
Živković, Petar   101, 104, 121, 137
Zunino, Pier Giorgio   23n, 152n

Subject Index

This list does not include the terms 'Caesarism' and 'Bonapartism', since they appear on almost every page of the book. Analogously, I have indexed the terms 'hegemony' and 'modernity' (which also occur very frequently) only in relation to their major conceptual/historical distinctions.

Absolute monarchy   1, 6n, 173n
   See also crown
Abstentionism   113
Aesopic language   180n, 191n
Agitation vs propaganda   85–6
Alliance between workers and peasants   22n, 40–6, 49, 53n, 55n
Americanism   78–9, 155, 178, 183–4, 192
   See also fordism
Anachronism   97–9, 110
Ancient Rome   4, 129–30
   See also Caesar
Animality   78, 183
   See also industrialism
Anti-determinism   13n, 14, 46, 71–2
Arbitration   114, 127, 173–5
   See also balance (or equilibrium) of class forces; crown; totalitarian phenomena
Army / military element   1, 16–8, 69, 79–85, 91–5, 120–2, 125, 145, 162n, 175, 179, 188n, 201
   Military associations   163, 166
   Military hierarchy   17, 54n
   Military-political element   92, 95
   Technical-military element   92, 95
   See also bureaucracy; Cadornism; coup d'État; Napoleonism
Assassination of Giacomo Matteotti   34, 50, 57, 68
Authoritarian attitude   81–5, 183–7
   See also Cadornism; industrialism; Trotsky

Balance (or equilibrium) of class forces   36–7, 51–72, 104, 110–8, 120, 122, 127, 153, 157–8, 193, 201
   Catastrophic   51, 112n, 115–7, 203
   Unstable   58–9, 66, 113, 150, 191
   See also arbitration; catastrophe; crisis
Barometer (metaphor)   190–2
   See also Trotsky; USSR

Bismarckism   137, 145
Bourgeoisie
   Petty   15, 23–4, 32–3, 57–62, 69, 93, 163, 178–9
   Rural   92–6, 163, 178–9, 201
Bureaucracy   61–3, 69, 88–97, 111n, 121, 149n, 162n, 163–6, 169n, 176, 177n, 184–5, 186n, 192–3, 201
   Actual and potential   92
   As caste   163n
   Bureaucratic attitude   18
   Civil and military   90, 104, 162n, 203
   Democratic-bureaucratic character of 20th century regimes   161
   See also army / military element; dark powers; rural bourgeoisie; totalitarian phenomena

Cadornism   18, 69, 79–85, 185, 187–8, 203
   See also authoritarian attitude; Cadorna; Caporetto
Caesarism without a Caesar   110, 128n, 193–200
   See also collective man; modern prince
Caporetto (defeat of)   16n, 17–8, 80, 188n
Catastrophe   37, 197
   As profound and long-lasting crisis   113
   Catastrophic tendency or perspective (*Prison Notebooks*)   115–8, 122–4, 127, 156–7, 191
   Moral   42
   vs crisis   49
   See also balance (or equilibrium) of class forces; crisis; tragedy / dramatic element
Centralisation   45, 157, 161, 169
   See also hegemony
Centralism   114n, 176, 177n
Charismatic leadership   33, 97, 104–11, 140, 150–1, 158, 161–2, 195–6, 199–201, 203
   Michels' conception of   105–10

SUBJECT INDEX 229

See also Boulanger; Hero; Michels; Mussolini
Church   160, 162, 170, 190
Coalition governments   121, 125, 147–50, 194
Coercion / violence   80–1, 161, 164, 171, 175, 179, 181–2, 186, 200
  See also control / surveillance; hegemony
Collective man (*uomo collettivo*)   193–5
Comintern (Communist International)   37–53, 153n, 180n
  See also crisis; dialectic of crisis and revolution
Conception of the world (*concezione del mondo*)   170n
Conformism   194n, 195n
  See also discipline
Constituent (*costituente*)   47n, 191n
Contemporary *vs* modern   132–3
Control / surveillance   160–72
  See also centralisation; coercion / violence; hegemony
Corporatism   155, 177–9, 189, 192
  See also Fascism
Cosmopolitanism   129–30
Council theory / factory councils   40–1, 43–5, 64
Coup d'État (*Putsch*)   1, 68n, 120–1, 122n, 140n
  Cadorna's attempted   16–8, 162
  Louis Napoleon's   2, 3, 14, 16, 67, 69, 75, 120, 135
  See also army / military element; Cadorna; dark powers
Cretinism
  Economic   89n
  Parliamentary   21–5, 27, 46n, 56, 70, 72, 89n
Crisis
  Catastrophic crisis of capitalism (pre-prison writings)   37–54
  Moral   39n, 47
  Of the liberal state   53–64, 71–2
  Organic   53, 102n, 118, 123, 125, 146–7, 153, 155–61, 162, 165, 181, 193, 196, 198, 202–3
  Permanent   79
  See also balance (or equilibrium) of class forces; catastrophe; dialectic of crisis and revolution; hegemony

Critique / self-critique   187–8, 192
  See also USSR
Critique of sociology   108, 128
Crown   23, 172–4
  See also arbitration

Dark powers (*potenze oscure*)   17, 161–3, 175n
  See also bureaucracy; church; police
Demagogue (*demagogo*)   34, 151
  See also charismatic leadership
Determinism   82
Dialectic of crisis and revolution   39–51
  See also Comintern; crisis
Dictatorship
  Of the bourgeoisie   53–6
  Of the proletariat   42–3, 53–6, 64n, 65, 85
Dilemmatic way of reasoning   119n
Direction (*direzione*)   134n, 155n, 161, 164, 165
  Military / political   91
  Political-cultural direction of the state   173
  See also hegemony
Discipline / self-discipline   46, 79, 81, 184
  See also conformism
Dreyfus Affair   115–8, 140–4
  See also latent or marginal forces

Economic-corporative (*economico-corporativo*)   181–2, 203
Economism   79n, 82–3
Effectual reality (*realtà effettuale*)   144–5
Elements of the Philosophy of Right (Hegel)   37, 62–5, 69, 74, 90, 131n

Fascism / fascist ideology   7–8, 16n, 23–4, 29–35, 57–72, 147–8, 150–5, 161, 165–6, 173, 176–181, 187–9, 192–3, 199–200, 204
  See also crisis; hegemony; Mussolini; one-party system; totalitarian phenomena
Five-year plan   185
Fordism   78–9, 155, 178, 183–4
  See also americanism
Foundation of the PCd'I   51, 55–6
  See also Livorno congress of the PSI

France 131–6
  1848 revolution 5–6, 32–3, 135
  France after 1848 2–6, 33–34, 67, 203
  French revolution (1789) 84n, 113n, 132, 134
  July Monarchy 33
  July Revolution 4
  Paris Commune 6, 132
  Second French Empire 2–6, 34, 124n, 132–3, 135–6, 201
  Third French Republic 132–3, 136n
  See also Dreyfus Affair; hegemony; history; Jacobinism; legality / breakdown of legality
Freemasonry 61–2
French serial novels (*Feuilleton*) 28–35, 72, 151n
French and Italian Culture 29–33

General Confederation of Labour (*Confederazione Generale del Lavoro*) 19–20
General strike of July 1919 41n, 51
Germany 144
Grand Council of Fascism (*Gran Consiglio del Fascismo*) 173n
Greece 94

Hegemony
  Bourgeois 131–4
  In the post-war period 160–79
  See also France; crisis; Jacobinism; totalitarian phenomena
Hero / heroic personality 5, 31, 118, 125, 128, 129, 194–6
  See also charismatic leadership
Historical analogies 4, 66–9, 118–9, 203
History
  Conception of 115, 130–5
  Gramsci's theory of historical transitions 142, 156
  Waves (metaphor) 135
Hypocrisy 79, 94n, 184, 188
  See also critique / self-critique; Totalitarian phenomena

Imbalance between theory and practice 81, 89, 184
  See also Trotsky
Independence 6, 96, 162, 174

Individual *vs* collective 193–6
Industrialism 78–9, 82–3, 183–5, 203
  See also animality
Intellectual and moral reform (*riforma intellettuale e morale*) 39, 198–9
Intellectuals 157n, 160, 169n, 178
Interregnum 36, 112, 159
Involvement of the masses in political life 103, 156n, 160, 168, 175, 193
  See also hegemony
Italian elections
  Of May 1921 15, 48–9
  Of November 1919 43, 47, 48n, 51

Jacobinism 121, 134, 138n, 160, 186n, 203
  Substantial 134
  Superficial 134
  See also hegemony

Labour army 82, 185
  See also industrialism; Trotsky
Latent or marginal forces 116, 124, 139, 140–4, 154n, 160, 191, 197, 199
  See also crisis; Dreyfus Affair
Legality / breakdown of legality 18n, 55–6, 67–9, 115, 169, 175–6, 190–192, 201
  See also crisis; Fascism; parliamentarism; USSR
Legal *vs* real 190
Liquidation (*liquidazione*) 190–2
  See also Trotsky; USSR
Livorno congress of the PSI (1921) 18n, 20, 22
Lumpenproletariat 32, 69, 95–6

Marx
  1859 Preface to *A Contribution to a Critique of Political Economy* 14, 41, 116n, 142
  Eighteenth Brumaire of Louis Bonaparte, The 1, 3–6, 11, 13n, 21, 29, 32–7, 59, 62, 66–75, 89–90, 95, 97, 114, 136n, 158, 201
  Holy Family, The 28–35, 70, 74n
  Marx-Gramsci relationship (pre-prison writings) 69–72
  Marx-Gramsci relationship (*Prison Notebooks*) 201–2

SUBJECT INDEX 231

Sources (pre-prison writings)   11–4
Sources (*Prison Notebooks*)   75–6
Marxism
    Heterodoxy   8, 153n
    Orthodoxy   38
Maximalism (Italian Socialist Party)   11, 15, 18–9, 21n, 24, 26, 47, 50–1, 67n
Middle Ages   113n, 132, 157
Modern prince (*moderno principe*)   133, 193–200, 202, 204–5
    See also Caesarism without a Caesar; collective man
Modernity (as historical epoch)   130–3
    vs pre-modernity   120, 132, 195, 196
    See also hegemony; history
Molecular transformation   117–8, 123, 135, 139–40
    See also passive revolution
Monkey People, The   23–5, 32, 61, 70, 152n
    See also Fascism
Morto di fame   163

Napoleonism   84–5, 183–7, 188n, 203
    See also Cadornism; Trotsky
National-popular (*nazionale-popolare*)   29
New Economic Policy (NEP)   185

Occupation of the factories (September 1920)   16n, 48n
One-party system   151, 171, 172–6, 181, 184, 187–192, 199, 204
    See also Fascism; hegemony; totalitarian phenomena; USSR
Organic *vs* conjunctural (or occasional)   123, 158–9

Parliamentarism   18n, 38, 45–6, 55–6, 63, 121, 187–92, 204
    Black (*parlamentarismo nero*)   187–92, 204
    See also crisis; Fascism; legality / breakdown of legality; one-party system; USSR
Parody / farce   5, 28–35, 74, 87
    See also tragedy / dramatic element
Passive revolution   73, 79n, 84n, 88, 89n, 116n, 131, 132n, 135, 138–46, 153, 155, 165, 178–9, 200, 203, 205
    See also to be epoch-making / to last; Fascism; molecular transformation

Permanent revolution   83, 116, 121, 134, 135n, 138n, 186
Police   122, 162n, 163–6, 176, 203
    Economic policing (*polizia economica*)   179n
    See also dark powers
Primitivism   107n, 109–10
    Returning   110, 181
Puritan ideology   79, 183
    See also americanism; fordism

Red Biennium or Two Red Years (*biennio rosso*)   16n, 38, 48n
Reformism (Italian Socialist Party)   11, 15, 20–6, 42–3, 49, 51
Relations of force (*rapporti di forza*)   51, 59–60, 97, 100n, 111, 142
    See also balance (or equilibrium) of class forces
Repression of factory occupations (September 1920)   48
Revolution from above   140
    See also Cadornism
Revolution-reaction (or revolution-restoration)   118, 120, 141, 143–5
Romance / romanticism   28–35, 39n, 70, 151n
    See also Fascism
Risorgimento   85–91, 144, 162n, 163n, 165, 190
    See also bureaucracy; passive revolution; legal *vs* real
Russian revolution (1917)   83–4, 132n, 182

Science   60n
Siege   158, 167–9
    See also hegemony; totalitarian phenomena
Southern Question   93, 94n
Spain   94
Squadrismo   50, 55
State as *veilleur de nuit*   182
    See also statolatry
state-government (*Stato-governo*)   86
Statolatry (*statolatria*)   179–82, 187, 203
    Returning   182n
    See also state as *veilleur de nuit*
Stay in Moscow and Vienna   13, 28, 57, 71
Subaltern groups   169n
Suffrage   45, 68n, 103, 136, 201

Superuomo   200n
　See also Mussolini, French serial novels
Suppression of autonomies   169, 172
　See also centralisation; coercion / violence; control / surveillance

Taylorism   183, 195n
　See also americanism
Theory of the united front   50–1
To be epoch-making (*fare epoca*) / to last (*durare*)   117, 144, 159, 189, 190n
Totalitarian phenomena   79, 150n, 152, 155, 158n, 167–175, 184–5, 186n, 187–94, 199, 202, 204
　Historical materialism as totalitarian phenomenon   170, 171n
　Totalitarian party   172–5, 187–92
　See also crisis; Fascism; hegemony; one-party system; siege; USSR
Tragedy / dramatic element   33–5, 46n, 74, 122, 124, 168, 187
　See also parody / farce
Transformism (*trasformismo*)   87, 165
Translatability (*traducibilità*)   131n

United Kingdom   147
USSR   81–85, 176–7, 179–93, 203

War of movement (or war of manoeuvre)   79, 81–5, 102n, 139, 167, 179
War of position   79n, 81–5, 102n, 139, 153, 159, 161, 167–9, 179, 204
World War I   7, 16n, 37, 42n, 132, 137, 150, 203

www.ingramcontent.com/pod-product-compliance
Lightning Source LLC
Chambersburg PA
CBHW070920030426
42336CB00014BA/2465